Educational Research and Evidence-based Practice

This Reader is part of *Educational Enquiry* (E891), a course belonging to the Open University MA in Education programme.

The Open University MA in Education

The Open University MA in Education is now firmly established as the most popular postgraduate degree for education professionals in Europe, with over 3000 students registered each year. It is designed particularly for those with experience of teaching, the advisory service, educational administration or allied fields. Specialist lines in management, applied linguistics, special needs/ inclusive education and lifelong learning are available within the programme. Successful study on the MA entitles students to apply for entry into the Open University Doctorate in Education programme.

Details of this and other Open University courses can be obtained from the Student Registration and Enquiry Service, The Open University, PO Box 197, Milton Keynes MK7 6BJ, United Kingdom: Telephone +44 (0) 845 300 6090, e-mail general-enquiries@open.ac.uk.

Alternatively, you may wish to visit the Open University website at http://www.open.ac.uk, where you can learn more about the wide range of courses and packs offered at all levels by The Open University.

Educational Research and Evidence-based Practice

Edited by
Martyn Hammersley

Los Angeles | London | New Delhi
Singapore | Washington DC

The Open University
Walton Hall
Milton Keynes
MK7 6AA
United Kingdom
www.open.ac.uk

 SAGE Publications Ltd
1 Oliver's Yard
55 City Road
London EC1Y 1SP

SAGE Publications Inc.
2455 Teller Road
Thousand Oaks, California 91320

SAGE Publications India Pvt Ltd
B 1/I 1 Mohan Cooperative Industrial Area
Mathura Road, New Delhi 110 044

SAGE Publications Asia-Pacific Pte Ltd
33 Pekin Street #02-01
Far East Square
Singapore 048763

Library of Congress Control Number: 2006940354

British Library Cataloguing in Publication data

A catalogue record for this book is available from the British Library

ISBN 978-1-4129-4561-5
ISBN 978-1-4129-4562-2 (pbk)

Typeset by C&M Digitals (P) Ltd., Chennai, India
Printed in Great Britain by the MPG Books Group
Printed on paper from sustainable resources

Contents

Acknowledgements   vii

Introduction   viii

Part 1: Debates about evidence-based practice   **1**

1   Teaching as a research-based profession:
    possibilities and prospects   3
    David H. Hargreaves

2   Educational research and teaching: a response
    to David Hargreaves' TTA Lecture   18
    Martyn Hammersley

3   In defence of research for evidence-based teaching:
    a rejoinder to Martyn Hammersley   43
    David H. Hargreaves

4   A reply to Hargreaves   61
    Martyn Hammersley

5   Making evidence-based practice educational   66
    John Elliott

6   Making evidence-based practice educational:
    a rejoinder to John Elliott   89
    Ann Oakley

7   Evidence-informed policy and practice:
    challenges for social science   91
    Ann Oakley

8   Intellectuals or technicians? The urgent role of theory
    in educational studies   106
    Stephen J. Ball

9   Beyond reflection: contingency, idiosyncrasy and
    reflexivity in initial teacher education   121
    Alex Moore

Part 2: The nature of educational research   **139**

10 On the kinds of research in educational settings   141
    Michael Bassey

11 The paradigm wars and their aftermath: a 'historical'
    sketch of research on teaching since 1989   151
    Nathaniel Gage

12 Action research   167
    Stephen Kemmis

13 Increasing the generalizability of qualitative research 181
    Janet W. Schofield

14 Critical incidents and learning about risks: the case
    of young people and their health   204
    Martyn Denscombe

15 Interrogating the discourse of home–school
    relations: the case of 'parents' evenings'   220
    Maggie MacLure, with Barbara Walker

16 Labouring to learn? Industrial training for
    slow learners   245
    Paul Atkinson, David Shone and Teresa Rees

17 An appraisal of 'Labouring to learn'   263
    Martyn Hammersley

18 The obviousness of social and educational
    research results   276
    Nathaniel Gage

Index   291

Acknowledgements

Edited by Martyn Hammersley
Chapter 1
Taken from: Teacher Training Agency Annual Lecture, London, 1996.
© David H. Hargreaves April 1996
Reproduced by kind permission of the author.

Chapter 2
Taken from: *British Educational Research Journal*, Vol. 23, No. 2, 1997,
pp. 141–61.
© 1997 British Educational Research Association
Reproduced by kind permission of Taylor & Francis Ltd.
http://www.tandf.co.uk/journals

Chapter 3
Taken from: *British Educational Research Journal*, Vol. 23, No. 4, 1997,
pp. 405–20.
© 1997 British Educational Research Association
Reproduced by kind permission of Taylor & Francis Ltd.
http://www.tandf.co.uk/journals

Chapter 4
Submitted in 1997 to *British Educational Research Journal* and then to
Research Intelligence, but previously unpublished.
© Martyn Hammersley 1997

Chapter 5
Taken from: *British Educational Research Journal*, Vol. 27, No. 5, 2001,
pp. 555–74.
© 2001 British Educational Research Association
Reproduced by kind permission of Taylor & Francis Ltd.
http://www.tandf.co.uk/journals

Chapter 6

Taken from: *British Educational Research Journal*, Vol. 27, No. 5, 2001, pp. 575–6.
© 2001 British Educational Research Association
Reproduced by kind permission of Taylor & Francis Ltd.
http://www.tandf.co.uk/journals

Chapter 7

Published by: Manchester Statistical Society, Manchester, UK, 13th February, 2001.
© Manchester Statistical Society 2001
Reproduced by kind permission.

Chapter 8

Taken from: *British Journal of Educational Studies*, Vol. 43, No. 3, 1995, pp. 255–71.
© Blackwell Publishers Ltd. and SCSE 1995
Reproduced by kind permission of Blackwell Publishing.

Chapter 9

Taken from: Hammersley, M. (ed.) *Researching School Experience*, (London: Falmer, 1999), pp. 134–53.
© A. Moore 1999
Reproduced by permission of Taylor & Francis Books UK.

Chapter 10

Extract taken from: Bassey, M., *Creating Education through Research: a global perspective of educational research for the 21st Century*, (Newark: Kirklington Moor Press, in association with the British Educational Research Association, 1995), pp. 32–52.
© Michael Bassey 1995
Reproduced by kind permission of the author.

Chapter 11

Taken from: *Educational Researcher*, Vol. 18, pp. 4–10.
© 1989 by the American Educational Research Association
Reproduced with permission of the publisher.

Chapter 12

Taken from: Keeves, J. P. (ed.) *Educational Research, Methodology and Measurement: An international handbook*, (Oxford: Pergamon, 1988), pp. 177–90.
© S. Kemmis 1988
Reproduced by kind permission of Elsevier.

Chapter 13
Taken from: Elliot W. Eisner & Alan Peshkin (eds.), *Qualitative Inquiry in Education: The Continuing Debate*, (New York: Teachers College Press, 1989).
© 1990 by Teachers College, Columbia University
Reprinted by permission of the Publisher. All rights reserved.

Chapter 14
Taken from: Hammersley, M. (ed.), *Researching School Experience*, (London: Falmer, 1999), pp. 187–203.
© M. Denscombe 1999
Reproduced by permission of Taylor & Francis Books UK.

Chapter 15
Taken from: MacLure, M., *Discourse in Educational and Social Research*, (Buckingham: Open University Press, 2003), pp. 48–69.
© Maggie MacLure 2003
Reproduced by kind permission of the Open University.

Chapter 16
Taken from: Barton, L. & Tomlinson, S. (eds.), *Special Education: Policy and Practices and Social Issues* (London: Paul Chapman Publishing, 1982).
© P. Atkinson, D. Shone & T. Rees 1981
Reproduced by kind permission of the authors.

Chapter 17
Taken from: Gomm, R. & Woods, P. (eds.), *Educational Research: In Action*, (London, Paul Chapman Publishing, 1993), pp. 171–183.
© Martyn Hammersley 1993

Chapter 18
Taken from: *Educational Researcher*, Vol. 20, no. 1, pp. 10–16.
© 1991 by the American Educational Research Association
Reproduced with permission of the publisher.

Introduction

Over the past fifty years, there have been recurrent debates about the role that educational enquiry, and social science generally, should play in relation to policymaking and practice. We can identify contrasting extreme positions here. On the one hand, there is the view that research should be integral to practice, or at least very closely designed to serve it. On the other hand, there is the idea that research should be autonomous, being entirely concerned with pursuing knowledge for its own sake. While this contrast certainly indicates the *range* in orientation to be found amongst researchers, most of them adopt more subtle positions that occupy the space between these poles. Many claim that their work both contributes to human knowledge *and* has practical payoff. Those who focus on trying to resolve particular educational problems often see their work as simultaneously producing knowledge that is of wider value; while those who pursue general knowledge about educational issues frequently insist on the direct relevance of this knowledge to policy and practice. At the same time, there are important differences in emphasis here, and there is significant variation in view about exactly how research can contribute to policymaking and/or practice. There are also some researchers today who question whether research can produce knowledge that is superior to what is available from other sources. They see the role of the researcher either as producing rhetorically effective accounts that serve some legitimate cause or as challenging all claims to expert knowledge, perhaps in order to open out a space for new kinds of educational practice (see, for example, Atkinson, 2000 and 2002; and Ball, this volume).

In recent years, in the UK and elsewhere, the issue of the contribution of educational research to policymaking and practice has become more politically significant than ever before. In large part, this results from increasing demands that educational practice should become 'evidence-based', with research being seen as the key source of evidence. In the UK, this development followed several waves of Government-led reform of the state education system, beginning with the institution of a national curriculum for schools in the late 1980s. An important motive for these reforms was to make various parts of the education system, initially schools but later further education colleges and universities, more accountable, not just to government itself, as their primary source of funds, but also to local stakeholders, such as students, parents, and employers. It was in this context that the notion of 'evidence-based practice' took hold, on the model of the evidence-based medicine movement that had arisen in the 1980s (see Trinder with Reynolds, 2000; Thomas and Pring, 2004).

One important effect of the evidence-based practice movement was to revive the fortunes of some ideas about how educational research ought to be pursued that had been extremely influential around the middle of the twentieth century, but whose influence had declined significantly in the last few decades of that century. These ideas have come to be given the label 'positivism', though this is a term that is so frequently abused that it now carries quite diverse meanings, and sometimes indicates little more than a negative evaluation. Central to its meaning in the early twentieth century was the idea that natural science is the primary methodological model for social and educational research.[1] This did not imply that social and educational researchers should simply imitate the work of natural scientists. Instead, what was taken from natural science was the idea that experimental method is the key to intellectual progress; that it was this that had produced the great gains in scientific knowledge from the seventeenth century onwards. What was seen as important about experiments was that they involve controlling and measuring the effects of causal factors on outcomes by means of explicit, and therefore replicable, procedures. Where experimentation was not possible, positivists argued that statistical methods of controlling variables should be employed. The idea was that by understanding the laws governing human social life, research could facilitate practical control over it for collective benefit, just as natural science enables us to control our physical environment to a considerable extent.

Positivist ideas, in various forms, were influential for much of the twentieth century. However, especially from the 1960s onwards, questions came to be asked about whether the sort of social and educational research it inspired could achieve the kind of knowledge promised. Certainly, this research had not enjoyed the same success as the natural sciences. As a result, the appropriateness of the natural science model came to be questioned. These doubts initially drew on ideas about alternative forms of scientific enquiry that had developed from the nineteenth century onwards among historians and philosophers. Central here was the argument that human beings and their actions differ sharply from the phenomena studied by natural science, that their character is constituted by meanings that can only be captured by a distinctive form of understanding, sometimes labelled with the German word *Verstehen* (see Truzzi, 1974). On some interpretations, this implied empathising, imaginatively, with other people. Other accounts stressed the role of culture, and especially of language, in human affairs, and how understanding people's attitudes and actions requires learning these.

Later, even positivist accounts of *natural* science came to be criticised: the uncertainties involved in experimental work were highlighted, the role of theoretical ideas came to be emphasised, and the difficulties faced by attempts to replicate previous studies were underlined (see Chalmers, 1999). As result of this, there was a growing challenge to the idea that science produces a distinctive and superior form of knowledge, as against the sorts of enquiry to be found in the humanities and arts; or even by comparison with the practical knowledge we all use in everyday life.

This critique opened the floodgates, across the social sciences, to a variety of ideas about how research should be pursued and what its relationship is to policy-making and practice. In thinking about that relationship, one contrast that has sometimes been drawn is between the engineering and enlightenment models. The engineering model corresponds, in many ways, to one version of the positivist idea of science, where research findings play a direct functional role in improving the world: they develop specific techniques that are more effective than traditional ones, and/or show which ones work best. By contrast, the enlightenment model suggests a much more complex and indirect relationship between research, policy and practice. It takes a variety of forms, being used to justify disinterested scholarship, 'critical' enquiry concerned with challenging the socio-political status quo, and forms of action research that treat practice as reflective rather than instrumental in character.

As this brief discussion makes clear, there are conflicting views about what role educational research should play in relation to policymaking and/or to practice; and about the implications of this for the form that such research should take. Furthermore, with the revival in fortunes of positivism and the engineering model in recent years, these differences in perspective have once more begun to generate highly charged debates (see, for instance, Denzin and Giardini 2006).

The contents of this book

The chapters in this volume exemplify the range of views about the proper role of educational research, as well as illustrating some of the different forms it takes today. The first part of the book is concerned with debates over the role of research in facilitating evidence-based, or evidence-informed, educational policymaking and practice. It opens with a key document in this debate in the UK: David Hargreaves' Teacher Training Agency lecture from 1996. In this lecture, Hargreaves argues that it is as a result of the failings of educational research that schoolteaching is not currently a research-based profession. He criticises this research for not cumulating well-established knowledge, and for having little practical relevance. He argues that the public funds spent on educational research in the UK offer poor value for money. In making his case, Hargreaves draws a contrast with the situation in medicine, where (he suggests) clinical research is increasingly playing a vital role in shaping practice. He argues that radical changes are needed to the way that educational research is organised and carried out, if it is to facilitate evidence-based practice. And some of his proposals formed a key part of the UK Government's efforts to reform educational research in the late 1990s.

There were many responses from educational researchers to Hargreaves' critique. One of these is included here as Chapter 2. Hammersley accepts Hargreaves' criticism of educational research as having failed to develop cumulative knowledge, but he argues that the difficulties involved in remedying this are more severe than is acknowledged. Furthermore, he suggests that what Hargreaves proposes is likely to worsen rather than to solve the problem, since this stems in part from the pressure for 'actionable knowledge'. Indeed, Hammersley questions whether research can fulfil the direct role in relation to practice that Hargreaves envisages. He examines the case of evidence-based medicine, suggesting that this is far from being unproblematic in itself, and that Hargreaves does not take proper account of the distinctive character of educational practice. Towards the end, Hammersley raises concerns about the sort of central planning of educational research that seems to be implied by Hargreaves' argument.

The following two chapters consist of Hargreaves' response to this critique, and Hammersley's reply. As with many debates among researchers, further clarification of the two positions is provided, but there is little sign of movement on either side. Subsequent to his TTA lecture, Hargreaves produced a number of papers that developed his ideas, and it is to one of these that John Elliott responds in Chapter 5. Elliott begins by outlining Hargreaves' argument, noting the contrast he draws between the engineering and enlightenment models, and his criticism of the latter for leading educational researchers to believe that their work can only have an indirect and long term effect on practice, discouraging them from making it more directly relevant. Hargreaves argues that while research can have an effect in this way, it is necessary to adopt a more direct approach. And he also complains that the work of some writers has not 'enlightened' practitioners at all, but rather has had a damaging effect on their work, citing the examples of Jean Piaget, B. F. Skinner, and Basil Bernstein. Implicit here is the idea that researchers are responsible for whether and how their work is used, that this must be brought under control. In some significant respects, Elliott shares this perspective, along with the idea that educational practitioners must play a central role in carrying out educational research if its relevance is to be assured. But he differs from Hargreaves in his view of the nature of educational practice, and of how research can influence it. Where Hargreaves treats the relationship as a largely instrumental one, with research providing tools that teachers must use to increase the effectiveness of their work, Elliott sees educational practice as involving an internal relationship with aims that are intrinsic to the very nature of education. Much of his paper is concerned with outlining this concept of education, drawing on the work of the philosopher Richard Peters and the educationist Lawrence Stenhouse.

Another key strand in Elliott's argument is that the kind of research that Hargreaves sees as playing a key role in relation to educational practice is simply incapable of serving that purpose. In the article Elliott is discussing, Hargreaves explicitly identifies randomised controlled trials as a major source of knowledge about 'what works'. In response, drawing on the work of the philosopher Alasdair MacIntyre, Elliott argues that this kind of research is only capable of producing statistical generalisations whose application to any particular case is always uncertain. Instead, following Stenhouse, he recommends 'case study' as the most appropriate mode of educational research for informing practice, following the example of historical investigation. What is involved here is the investigation of unique situations with a view to deciding what can be done to improve them in educational terms. Moreover, given this focus, the person who is in an ideal position to carry out educational research is the educational practitioner. The role of outsiders, such as university academics, can only be as collaborators, providing assistance. At one point, Elliott draws a distinction between research *for* education and research *on* education; though he does not elaborate on the latter. A somewhat similar distinction is adopted by Hargreaves, and also by Michael Bassey in Chapter 10.

In the next chapter, Ann Oakley, one of the leading figures in attempts to reconstruct educational research so as to facilitate evidence-based practice, responds to Elliott's critique. This response is very brief, and indicates the rather different starting points of the two authors: she apparently fails to recognise the implications of the conception of education that Elliott has outlined, being preoccupied with rather different matters. A fuller understanding of Oakley's position can be derived from Chapter 7. She begins from the question of how facts or evidence can be produced so as to serve practice, suggesting that the failure of education and social policy to operate on a secure knowledge base, in the way that medicine does, stems from the lack of systematic, experimental research in these fields. She draws a contrast between controlled experimentation as a method of discovering the facts and both the 'unsystematic research' that she sees as dominating the field of education and 'the enormous amount of uncontrolled experimentation that passes for everyday practice' (p. 93). Her implication is that, if we are going to carry out research on education, or for that matter engage in educational practice, we ought to do this in ways that produce knowledge about the effectiveness of different approaches. Equally important, there is a need to synthesise the information available from relevant studies in a systematic and effective manner. She criticises traditional forms of reviewing research literatures for lack of exhaustiveness and explicitness, arguing instead for 'systematic' reviews. She makes clear that she believes that in the field of educational and social policy it is necessary to include non-experimental studies in these reviews, in order not to exclude potentially relevant material. At the same time, she raises the question of how it is possible to distinguish 'trustworthy' from 'untrustworthy' qualitative studies, and how information from these studies can be combined with that from experimental or other quantitative research. While she recognises the value of qualitative work, she suggests that non-experimental studies often involve bias: by comparison with randomised controlled trial results, they exaggerate the impact of interventions, as regards both positive and negative effects.

In Chapter 8, Stephen Ball presents a very different view from all of the previous writers about the role that educational research should play. He starts from what he sees as the current weakness of the field of educational studies in the UK. What is meant by 'educational studies' here is the set of disciplines in the humanities and social sciences – mainly philosophy, history, sociology and psychology – that formed the core of the academic, as against the practical, component of teacher education in the 1950s and 60s. Ball's particular focus is on one of these disciplines – the sociology of education. In his title, he sets up a contrast between the role of the intellectual and that of the technician, and this more or less corresponds to the dichotomy he draws in one section of his chapter between policy scholarship and policy science. He sees policy science as framed by what he refers to as a form of empiricism, and illustrates this with a discussion of school effectiveness research. This work is concerned with measuring the contribution that schooling makes to pupils' achievement levels, and comparing the effectiveness of different schools, at different times, in this respect: in other words, the aim is to measure the 'value' they add to pupils' learning. Ball regards this kind of policy science as serving current attempts to transform the public sector in accordance with neo-liberal principles. It is in resistance to this that he argues for a 're-envisioning of educational studies via critical reflexivity' (p. 112), drawing on the ideas of those often labelled as post-structuralists or postmodernists, notably Foucault.

In the final chapter of this first part of the book, Alex Moore addresses an issue that has been touched on in many of the previous chapters: the nature of educational *practice*. He outlines some influential discourses that have shaped initial teacher education, notably those focusing on the *competent practitioner* and on the *reflective practitioner*. He provides a critical assessment of these paradigms, suggesting that they share more in common than is often recognised. Following on from this, he argues the case for an additional paradigm, one that celebrates the idiosyncratic, contingent aspects of teaching and learning. This alternative discourse, which re-emphasises the significance of intra- as well as inter-personal relationships in classroom practice, encourages teachers to explore critically their own classroom behaviours and those of their pupils against the background of the wider social context. Needless to say, the conflicting discourses Moore outlines have very important implications for the role that educational research can play in relation to practice.

The second part of the book focuses on the various forms that educational research has taken, and the conflicts over these. In Chapter 10, Michael Bassey begins by briefly reviewing some of the public debate that took place about educational research in the UK at the end of the twentieth century, arguing that this highlights the importance of being clear about its proper character. He distinguishes it from social science research in educational settings, on the grounds that it must be directed towards critically informing educational judgements and decisions 'in order to improve educational action' (p. 148). This is a conception of educational research which is broadly shared by Hargreaves, Elliott, and

Oakley, despite differences in their views about exactly what this involves. However, it is at odds with the positions taken by both Hammersley and Ball, even though these differ significantly in other respects.

In the next chapter, Nathaniel Gage provides a 'future historical' account, written in 1989, of the development of educational research up to 2009. He identifies conflicting 'paradigms' that are at war with one another, focusing on various critiques of the sort of 'scientific' (in the terms defined above, positivist) research that he and others had done, and that had dominated educational research in the United States until the 1980s. He outlines what he labels as the 'anti-naturalist critique', the 'interpretivist critique', and the 'critical theorists' critique'. He examines three quite different scenarios detailing the effects of these critiques. In one version, the critics triumphed, marking the end of 'objectivist-quantitative, or scientific, research on teaching' (p. 155). In the second scenario, he paints a picture of the different paradigms becoming reconciled with one another, and recognising that their work is complementary. The final version of events portrays a continuation of the paradigm wars, in much the same manner as in the 1980s.

Having now entered the twenty-first century, we are in a position to make some judgment about which of Gage's scenarios best captures what has happened since he wrote. However, the picture is mixed. To a large extent, warfare was replaced by uneasy truce in the 1990s, but for the most part this did not mean that Gage's optimistic second scenario had been realised. In many areas there was a decline in the amount of quantitative educational research, but there was also a proliferation of conflicting qualitative approaches, with some disputes emerging among these. As we noted earlier, at the beginning of the twenty-first century there has been something of a revival in the status of quantitative method; and also increasing calls for the combining or 'mixing' of quantitative and qualitative approaches. And, far from leading to widespread rapprochment, this seems to have revived the paradigm wars.

In Chapter 12, Stephen Kemmis provides an outline of action research, one of the most influential kinds of work in the field of education, and in some other areas too (see Reason and Bradbury 2006). He traces its origins, and outlines how more recent versions have diverged from Kurt Lewin's original conception. He examines the purposes, objects and methods of action research, and outlines the criteria by which he believes it should be judged. He concludes by looking at how action research can be facilitated by outsiders, and examines the relationship between it and other kinds of educational research. He specifically highlights what he calls 'emancipatory action research', seeing this as a form of critical social science, and he explains why he believes it to be desirable.

In Chapter 13, Janet Schofield focuses on a key methodological topic, one that has long been an issue of dispute between quantitative and qualitative researchers: generalisability. It is quite common for qualitative enquiry to be criticised for producing findings that cannot be generalised; and, in response, many of its exponents have insisted that this is not part of their aim. Schofield examines several attempts by qualitative researchers to address this issue, and identifies some kinds of generalisation they can legitimately pursue. Particularly useful is her discussion of the strategies that can be used to achieve these forms of generalisation, their advantages and disadvantages. She illustrates her discussion with examples from her own research.

In the following chapter, Martyn Denscombe employs qualitative analysis to explore specific aspects of the personal experience of young people relevant to health issues. He is particularly concerned with critical incidents that might shape their attitudes towards health risks; notably those involved in smoking, the use of alcohol, and other substance abuse. He relies here on open-ended questionnaire and focus-group data from 15–16-year-olds, coming to the conclusion that what is crucial in this process is not the nature of the experiences themselves but rather how the young people interpret these experiences. His study exemplifies the character of a great deal of qualitative work carried out today.

Chapter 15 is an example of a form of qualitative research that became particularly influential in the last decade of the twentieth century in the UK and elsewhere: discourse analysis. This label covers a variety of rather different kinds of work, but in this chapter Maggie MacLure uses an approach loosely modelled on conversation analysis to examine the nature of the talk-in-action characteristic of parents' evenings in schools. She identifies the predominant pattern of the exchanges, the sorts of categorisation work involved, the ways in which parental voice is constrained, and the potential 'double binds' involved for participants in constructing and sustaining identities through this form of talk.

Chapter 16 provides an example of another kind of qualitative research that has been quite influential since the middle of the twentieth century: ethnography. Atkinson, Shone and Rees report a study of a government-funded unit providing industrial training for 'slow learners'. They investigated the nature of the training provided, being concerned in particular with uncovering the hidden assumptions implicit in the training regime, for example those surrounding the notion of the 'model worker'.

In the penultimate chapter, Hammersley provides a methodological assessment of Atkinson et al.'s study. He examines the central claims made by the authors and the evidence they offer in support of them. He argues that while the study is presented as descriptive in character, it also involves some evaluative claims whose value base is not made clear. He concludes that, while most of the descriptive claims are well supported, not all of them are; and insufficient grounds are provided for generalisation from the unit studied to others of a similar type.

The final chapter, a classic article by Gage, addresses a widespread criticism of social and educational research: the charge that its findings are obvious. He examines a number of examples of this criticism, some of which are bound up with the old battle between 'the two cultures': the sciences and the humanities. He discusses research designed to explore people's reactions to contrasting research findings, showing that sometimes what people take to be obvious is at odds with these findings. He argues that frequently research results are not the truisms they are claimed to be by critics. Furthermore, even when they are, the research often provides us with information about when the truism does and does not apply to particular cases. On this basis, Gage argues that educational research is not as vulnerable to criticism on grounds of obviousness as is often supposed.

Conclusion

The chapters in this book highlight some of the complexities surrounding the relationship between educational research, policymaking and practice. They illustrate how these arise from variation in forms of enquiry and in ideas about the proper character of educational research. Equally significant, though, are divergent conceptions of the nature of educational practice. Underlying the complexity and divisions are fundamental differences in view about the nature of the social world, how we can understand it, and the values that should prevail within it.

Note

1 Interestingly, this was not the view of the inventor of the term 'positivism', Auguste Comte: see Heilbron 1991.

References

Atkinson, E. (2000) 'In defence of ideas, or why "what works" is not enough', *British Journal of Sociology of Education*, 21, 3, pp. 317–30.

Atkinson, E. (2002) 'The responsible anarchist: postmodernism and social change', *British Journal of Sociology of Education*, 23, 1, pp. 73–87.

Chalmers, A. F. (1999) *What Is This Thing Called Science?*, Third edition, Maidenhead, Open University Press.

Denzin, N. K. and Giardini, M. (eds.) (2006) *Qualitative Inquiry and the Conservative Challenge*, Walnut Creek CA, Left Coast Press.

Hargreaves, D. H. (1999) 'Revitalizing educational research: lessons from the past and proposals for the future', *Cambridge Journal of Education*, 29, 2, pp. 239–49.

Heilbron, J. (1991) 'Theory of knowledge and theory of science in Auguste Comte', *Review de Synthese*, fourth series, 1, pp. 75–89.

Reason, P. and Bradbury, H. (eds.) (2006) *Handbook of Action Research*, London, Sage.

Thomas, G. and Pring, R. (eds.) (2004) *Evidence-based Practice in Education*, Maidenhead, Open University Press.

Trinder, L. with Reynolds, S. (eds.) (2000) *Evidence-Based Practice: a critical appraisal*, Oxford, Blackwell Science.

Truzzi, M. (1974) *Verstehen: subjective understanding in the social sciences*, Reading MS: Addison-Wesley.

Part One

Debates about evidence-based practice

Chapter 1

Teaching as a research-based profession: possibilities and prospects (The Teacher Training Agency Lecture 1996)

David H. Hargreaves

Introduction

Teaching is not at present a research-based profession. I have no doubt that if it were, teaching would be more effective and more satisfying. The goal of enhancing effectiveness and satisfaction can be achieved only by a combination of several means, of which an adequate research base is just one. It is in my view a singularly important one which deserves to be given priority. However, I shall argue in this lecture that providing that research base will require a radical change both in the kind of research that is done and the way in which it is organised. To make my case I look inside the profession and the research community to examine what we now do; but I shall also look at another profession to detect what lessons can be learned about creating a genuinely research-based profession.

The £50–60 million[1] we spend annually on educational research is poor value for money in terms of improving the quality of education provided in schools. In fundamental respects the teaching profession has, I believe, been inadequately served by us. It need not be so. If the defects in the way educational research is organised were remedied, research would play a more effective role in advancing the professional quality and standing of teachers. Left to ourselves, we educational researchers will not choose the necessary radical reforms. It needs others, including practising teachers, to give the firm push to get researchers on the move.

My lecture is in three parts – educational research in a comparative professional framework; diagnosing what went wrong; and finally, the way forward.

Part One: Educational research in a comparative professional framework

Rarely have teachers looked at other professional fields to examine whether they might learn from their structures and cultures. The comparison I make now is with medicine, and in particular with doctors in hospitals. The medical profession has gained in public prestige concurrently with the growth of its research. The teaching profession has not. We need to investigate why this is so and what can be done to change things.

My own research in schools and hospitals indicates that both education and medicine are profoundly people-centred professions. Neither believes that helping people is merely a matter of a simple technical application but rather a highly skilled process in which a sophisticated judgment matches a professional decision to the unique needs of each client. Yet the two professions see the role of scientific knowledge in informing professional practice in very different ways. The kind of science, and so the kind of research, involved in each profession is very different. The academic infrastructure of medicine is rooted in the natural sciences (anatomy, physiology, pharmacology etc.). No doctor denies that medical competence requires a grasp of this infrastructure[2]. Doctors draw on this knowledge-base for the technical language of the profession.

There is no agreed knowledge-base for teachers, so they largely lack a shared technical language. It was once hoped that the so-called foundation disciplines of education – psychology, sociology, philosophy and history – would provide this knowledge-base[3] and so were given great importance in the curriculum of teacher training, BEd. courses especially. Unfortunately, very few successful practising teachers themselves had this knowledge-base or thought it important for practice. It remains true that teachers are able to be effective in their work in almost total ignorance of this infrastructure. After qualification teachers largely abandon these academic influences and the use of social scientific terms within their professional discourse declines[4]: the disciplines of education are seen to consist of 'theory' which is strongly separated from practice. Trainee teachers soon spot the yawning gap between theory and practice and the low value of research as a guide to the solution of practical problems.

In medicine, as in the natural sciences, research has a broadly cumulative character. Research projects seek explicitly to build on earlier research – by confirming or falsifying it, by extending or refining it, by replacing it with better evidence or theory, and so on.

Much educational research is, by contrast, non-cumulative[5], in part because few researchers seek to create a body of knowledge which is then tested, extended or replaced in some systematic way. A few small-scale investigations of an issue which are never followed up inevitably produce inconclusive and contestable findings of little practical relevance. Replications, which are more necessary in the social than the natural sciences because of the importance of contextual and cultural variations, are astonishingly rare. Moreover educational researchers, like other social scientists, are often engaged in bitter disputes among themselves about the philosophy and methodology of the social sciences. Given the huge amounts of educational research conducted over the last fifty years or more, there are few areas which have yielded a corpus of research evidence regarded as scientifically sound and as a worthwhile resource to guide professional action – and this is true in areas which might be regarded as fundamental[6]. In many educational areas a line of research ends with a change of fashion, sometimes (and often pretentiously) called a 'paradigm shift', not because the problems in it have been solved. Post-modernists argue that it has been an illusion to imagine that the social sciences could ever be cumulative: social science is just another mode of discourse with no legitimate claim to any special or privileged authority. To concede this is, in my view, to undermine the *raison d'être* of most of the research that is currently funded. Nor for a minute do I accept the charge that educational research is *in principle* misguided; my argument is that the profession needs educational research but that it must be a very different kind of research if it is to influence practice.

A yet more striking difference between the professions is the identity of the people who actually *do* the research. In medicine, it is possible to draw on the basic sciences which are not in themselves specifically medical – genetics, biochemistry, neuro-physiology – where developments and discoveries are potentially relevant to medical advance. In the same way, educators can draw on other basic sciences – say, cognitive science – where there is potential for educational application.

But there is a very sharp difference in the way the two professions approach *applied* research. Much medical research is not itself basic research (which is left to the basic sciences or medical scientists drawing on such work) but a type of applied research which gathers evidence about what works in what circumstances. It is a search for more accurate means of diagnosing medical problems; better ways of managing the patient; the determination of more effective treatments. The people best placed to do this work are not basic scientists or a special category of medical researchers, but medical practitioners. A considerable proportion of the articles in popular as well as specialist medical journals comes from practitioners in hospitals and general practice.

A tiny proportion of educational research – that is, funded research, carried out by proper procedures and then made public knowledge through publication – is undertaken by practising teachers: the vast majority of such research is conducted by university-based academics involved in teacher education who do not teach in schools.

In medicine, then, there is little difference between researchers and users: all are practitioners. In education, by contrast, researchers are rarely users and so there are major problems of communication. This shows in the way research is written up and transmitted in the two professions. In medicine there are journals (*The British Medical Journal, The Lancet*) which aim to communicate to the whole profession on general medical issues as well as selected advances within specialties. In education the only regular journal which potentially reaches most teachers is the *Times Educational Supplement* where relatively little space is given to research. There is not a scrap of evidence that teachers complain about their lack of access to the findings of educational research. Educational researchers write mainly for one another in their countless academic journals, which are not to be found in a school staffroom.

It is this gap between researchers and practitioners which betrays the fatal flaw in educational research. For it is the researchers, not the practitioners, who determine the agenda of educational research. If practising doctors, especially those in hospitals, stopped doing research and left it almost entirely to a special breed of people called 'medical researchers' who were mainly university academics without patients, then medical research would go the same way as educational research – a private, esoteric activity, seen as irrelevant by most practitioners. Educational research is caught between two stools, that of the basic social sciences (psychology, sociology) and that of practitioners in schools. Educational researchers have become adept at falling off both stools, achieving neither prestige from the social scientists (e.g. mainstream psychologists) nor gratitude from classroom teachers.

How different it is for doctors! The spread of evidence-based medicine is rooting much medical research firmly in the day-to-day professional practices of doctors. In the past, a surgeon, asked why he was treating a patient by means of a particular operation, or why he was using one operating technique rather than another, would often refer back to his training – 'I do it this way because I trained under Sir Lancelot Spratt at St. Swithin's'. Today doctors are relying less heavily on the clinical practices in which they were trained and more on an evidence-based approach, in which research into the effects of treatment is used, by both trainers and trainees, as the basis and justification for treatment. In short, some of the most important research in medicine, conducted by practitioners, aims to evaluate the effects of one treatment or one technique rather than another. Is lumpectomy as effective as radical mastectomy as a treatment for breast cancer? Because evidence-based medicine, though fallible, has direct and often immediate relevance to the improvement of their practice and patient benefit, there is a huge incentive for doctors to keep up to date.

Far less medical practice is based on evidence than lay people commonly suppose. Medical treatment is not invariably followed by clinical improvement any more than classroom teaching is invariably followed by student learning. Indeed, when doctors concede that

> a large proportion of treatments, not to say investigations and referrals, are no more than a face-saving disguise for medical impotence[7]

one is tempted to shout a deeply sympathetic 'snap' with an equivalent admission that much teaching, specific lessons and acts of individual attention to students, are no more than a face-saving disguise for pedagogic impotence. 'All day and every day,' says another leading medical expert,

> we are forced to make what we hope are adequate decisions on woefully inadequate evidence. We are not altogether comfortable living in a world of uncertainty, but we have grown accustomed to it.[8]

Does not this sound more like a teacher than a doctor?

The significant difference between the professions, however, is that whereas doctors are demanding and getting more evidence-based research, teachers are not even seeing their severe lack of evidence-based research as a problem in urgent need of remedy.

To become an effective doctor, then, means learning both from one's seniors and from research – and the two are tied because one's seniors are researchers and are familiar with more research than the juniors. Doctors learn to respect and call upon research evidence. In hospitals in particular, doctors will introduce references to research and to scholarly journals within their routine conversations about patients and the diagnosis or treatment of their condition.

In education there is simply not enough evidence on the effects and effectiveness of what teachers do in classrooms to provide an evidence-based corpus of knowledge. The failure of educational researchers, with a few exceptions, to create a substantial body of knowledge equivalent to evidence-based medicine means that teaching is not – and never will be – a research-based profession unless there is major change in the kind of research that is done in education. Today teachers still have to discover or adopt most of their own professional practices by personal preference[9], guided by neither the accumulated wisdom of seniors nor by practitioner-relevant research. They see no need to keep abreast of research developments and rightly regard research journals as being directed to fellow academics, not to them. Teachers rely heavily on what they learn from their own experience, private trial and error. For a teacher to cite research in a staffroom conversation about a pupil would almost certainly indicate that he or she was studying for a part-time higher degree in education or rehearsing for an OFSTED visit – and would be regarded by most colleagues as showing off[10].

In hospital medicine, then, the acquisition of expertise means becoming more effective not just in terms of practical skills, but also by familiarity with the practice-relevant research. Promotion in hospitals is slow: one remains a junior doctor, working under the supervision of a consultant who 'owns' the patients, until one's late thirties or so. Promotion to the higher echelons of the profession is closely related to the acquisition of knowledge well beyond that required for initial registration, namely the FRCS and equivalent examinations, which are difficult and have a specified content. Consultants are outstanding practitioners and they have to prove it. A consultant in (say) surgery, and even more so a professor of surgery, would be a practising surgeon of outstanding achievement. Advances in medicine are made by leading practitioners who are for this reason deeply respected by juniors – and trusted by their patients.

In education, by stark contrast, we have de-coupled promotion from both practitioner expertise and knowledge of research. A headteacher or a professor of education, though perhaps formerly an outstanding practitioner, rarely has regular teaching duties in a school[11]. Teachers get transformed by promotion into managers, administrators or academics and lack the deep respect junior doctors show to their seniors[12]. A higher degree in education may be advantageous to a teacher's promotion, but it is not a necessary condition. A Master's degree is nowadays easily gained, is variable in content, and gives little indication of the knowledge or skills thereby acquired.

Now the purpose of this comparison has been not to suggest we slavishly imitate doctors – though in some ways we could with advantage be more like them – but rather to show that in other professions there is a far more productive relationship between research and professional practice and to suggest that solutions to the problems in educational research may require structural and cultural change. In education, to achieve an end result not unlike that of the medics means taking a different research route.

Part Two: Diagnosing what went wrong

Something has indeed gone badly wrong. Research is having little impact on the improvement of practice and teachers I talk to do not think they get value for money from the £50–60 millions we spend annually on educational research. The research community has yet to face up to the problem. It protects itself and the *status quo* by a series of defences.

Educational research used to be dominated by the linear model, which draws a direct line from basic research (say psychological research on learning) to applied research (on school children learning an aspect of the curriculum) to the dissemination of findings (which then lead to an improvement in professional practice everywhere). It was widely believed that this model would transform schools and produce professional practice that would be research-based. We now know that this model is simplistic and does not work in its classic form: indeed, most researchers say that they no longer believe in it. It was concluded that research has an *indirect* influence on 'policy and practice[13], which whilst true, had the unintended side-effect of deflecting investigation into the reasons for this lack of direct impact and of persuading many researchers that it was not worth trying to achieve direct effects on practice. Rationalising failure to improve practice through research became a self-fulfilling prophecy.

In reality, researchers continue to adhere to some aspects of the linear model, for they define one of the main problems of educational research to be the *dissemination* of research findings to practitioners[14]. Some researchers blame themselves for not disseminating their results; others blame their sponsors for not funding dissemination; and yet others – to my astonishment – blame the teachers for ignoring the research findings and failing to act on them[15]. Seeing the main problem as one of dissemination assumes there is something worthwhile to be disseminated. It also assumes that the process of commissioning research and the research itself is in good shape: apparently all would be well if one could simply improve the dissemination of results.

I think these conclusions by researchers are for the most part off-target. There is no vast body of research which, if only it were disseminated and acted upon by teachers, would yield huge benefits in the quality of teaching and learning. One must ask the essential question: just how much research is there which (i) demonstrates conclusively that if teachers change their practice from x to y there will be a significant and enduring improvement in teaching and learning and (ii) has developed an effective method of convincing teachers of the benefits of, and means to, changing from x to y?

We do not have much powerful evidence about effective professional practice, which indicates that the main problem is not with dissemination but at the other end of the research process: how the research is commissioned and set in train. Almost all the money devoted to educational research is allocated on the basis of peer review, that is, researchers themselves decide which research and researchers are worth funding. Even where the body commissioning the research does not itself consist of researchers, the commissioners almost always rely to a considerable degree on peer review.

Now there is much sense in peer review. Those who, on the basis of knowledge and experience, are experts in a field are in many ways most fitted to make judgments on the quality of a research proposal. In a research field that is successful and healthy, peer review works well. But educational research is not in a healthy state; it is not having adequate influence on the improvement of practice; it is not good value for money. In these circumstances peer review serves to perpetuate a very unsatisfactory *status quo*. Researchers continue their work on their own self-validating terms; they are accountable to themselves; so there is absolutely no reason why they should change. Educational research lacks the 'pull' of industry which generates the effective application of engineering research and the 'push' of the Health Service and drug companies which ensures the application of medical research. In education the key fault is the lack of involvement of 'users', that is, practitioners and policy makers, in the peer review or allocation system: it is their exclusion which prevents the re-direction of educational research towards the improvement of practice.

Part Three: The way forward

I offer two ways of introducing the necessary pressures and incentives to change educational research so that it improves the practice of teachers in schools. The first concerns how the educational research agenda is set and the process of research managed; and the second concerns research funding.

Changing the research agenda and research process means adopting as an essential prerequisite of improvement, the involvement of user communities, policy makers and practitioners, in all aspects of the research process, from the creation of strategic research plans, the selection of research priorities and the funding of projects through to the dissemination and implementation of policies and practices arising from or influenced by research findings. It means establishing the machinery for creating **a national strategy for educational research,** including the formulation of short- and long-term priorities, with some mechanism for co-ordinating the work of the various funding agencies to increase knowledge of all parties about what topics are being funded for what reasons and what the outcomes of research are.

A new partnership between researchers and practitioners must be at the heart of any reform. Success here will help to solve so many other problems. Partnerships must (and of course do) exist at the level of the individual research institution and individual research project. All this is to be applauded, as is the pressure the ESRC now puts on researchers to demonstrate consultation with, and involvement of, users as a condition of getting a research grant.

In the field of education much more is needed to change the culture and practices of users or researchers; indeed, there is a danger of researchers playing at user involvement in a rhetorical way because the rules of the 'game' of obtaining funds and doing research have only superficially changed. Practitioners and policy makers must take an active role in shaping the direction of educational research as a whole, not just in influencing projects in which they happen to be involved; and researchers need to know that users are powerful partners whom many aspects of research need to be negotiated and to whom in a .cal sense the research community is in part accountable.

It would be desirable to establish a **National Educational Research Forum,** whose function would be to establish a continuing dialogue between all the stakeholders[16] and to shape the agenda of educational research and its policy implications and applications. The Forum's directors would be formed from a mixture of policy makers (at national and local levels), practitioners (heads, teachers), representatives from funding bodies (research councils, charities and trusts) and relevant lay persons (governors, parents) as well as researchers themselves. The Forum would be the arena in which all stakeholders could talk to one another in that necessarily broad and open conversation about matters of educational interest in which research 'is just *one* element in the complex mix of experience, conventional wisdom and political accommodation that enters into decision making'[17].

Building on these interchanges, the Forum would, say every four to five years, conduct or commission a review of current achievements, omissions and problems in educational research, leading to a research foresight exercise[18], involving researcher, user and lay communities, and the establishment thereafter of a national research strategy. Such a strategy[19] would be in broad outline, based on the Forum's conclusions on the most desirable, practicable and applicable research.

The establishment of the Forum and the involvement of users would, I believe, lead to one significant change in the character of research: there would be a dramatic increase in the need for evidence-based research relating to what teachers do in classrooms. Devoting a substantial proportion of the research budget – £10–20 million? – to providing the evidence on effective practice would rapidly change the nature of educational research. Some of the money would be used to fund teachers as researcher-practitioners rather than the objects of the activities of academic researchers. This is one lesson to be learnt from the medical profession. It has to be accepted that, just as it is appropriate to 'buy out' practising teachers to be mentors in teacher training, hard cash is needed to fund teachers to buy time for research. Teacher trainers were slow to yield on the first of these; sadly they may follow rather than lead in the case of the second.

The way money is routed into educational research must be changed. Research councils, especially the ESRC, should have at least their present share, for they have a fine record of funding high-quality educational research, as do the various charities. This must continue. Curiosity-driven, long-term 'basic' and 'blue skies' research is as vital in education as in any other scientific field[20]. What would come to an end is the frankly second-rate educational research which does not make a serious contribution to fundamental theory or knowledge; which is irrelevant to practice; which is uncoordinated with any preceding or follow-up research; and which clutters up academic journals that virtually nobody reads. It would sharply curtail what Professor Michael Bassey has rightly derided as 'the dilettante tradition' in educational research[21]. From this source a substantial proportion of the research budget can be prised out of the academic community, who currently distribute it to one another as they think fit, and over several years transferred in phases to agencies committed to evidence-based research and to full partnership with teachers in the interests of improving practice.

Some of this research money should be allocated through the Teacher Training Agency. The recent development by the TTA of national standards for teacher 'experts', in subject leadership and in school leadership, as well as qualifications for headteachers, is an exciting development which would make the professional structures and cultures of education and medicine more closely aligned. But there is no virtue in expert teachers and newly qualified heads studying substantial bodies of educational theory and research that is mostly remote from practical application. It is evidence-based research that is particularly relevant here. Expertise *means* not just having relevant experience and knowledge but having *demonstrable* competence and clear *evidence* to justify doing things in one way rather than another. If the expertise claimed by those given the title is to be authoritative, it must be closely related to knowledge of the evidence about practice, otherwise it is no more than a plea for deference to seniority.

Caroline Cox has pointed to four grounds teachers use to justify their practices:

- **tradition** (how it has always been done);
- **prejudice** (how I like it done);
- **dogma** (this is the 'right' way to do it); and
- **ideology** (as required by the current orthodoxy).

Doctors have used similar justificatory grounds:

- **tradition** ('we continue to base our clinical decisions on increasingly out of date primary training'[22])
- **prejudice** ('most doctors have a very narrow perspective, limiting themselves to their own experience and those of a relatively few colleagues'[23])
- **dogma** ('some operations will continue to be done because they are the fashion'[24])
- **ideology** ('in law, if enough doctors do it, then it is right'[25])

– quotations taken from commentaries on the advantages of evidence-based medicine.

Both professions have the humility to acknowledge that some of their time-honoured practices prove to be worthless or even harmful; teachers must join doctors in seeking to put professional decision-making to evidential test. When educational leaders have evidence for their practices, they may even command the respect of politicians, who advocate their pet ideas in the secure knowledge that the profession lacks convincing evidence to the contrary[26]. The TTA, as its work on expertise develops, must be able to commission evidence-based research to support and justify its endeavours.

And should not OFSTED be allocated some research funding? Without question OFSTED has the most comprehensive data-base on what teachers do and how it relates to their effectiveness. Would the profession benefit if OFSTED had a research division to analyse the evidence inspectors collect? Would the process of inspection improve if inspectors were better trained in garnering harder evidence about effective practice? Should schools and teachers defined as good by inspectors be funded to investigate further the evidential basis for their success? After all, OFSTED believes in inspection for improvement, but school improvement is currently a largely research-free zone.

Evidence-based medicine is gaining support because the number of variables affecting the selection of the right treatment are so great that no individual doctor can expect to be a constant master of this complexity. It is much the same complexity of variables influencing student attitudes and behaviour that bewilders teachers. In education we too need evidence about what works with whom under what conditions and with what effects. 'The practice of evidence-based medicine,' says the journal of that title,

> is a process of life-long, problem-based learning in which caring for our patients creates the need for evidence about diagnosis, prognosis, therapy and other clinical and health-care issues. In the evidence-based medicine process we
>
> - convert these information needs into answerable questions
> - track down with maximum efficiency the best evidence with which to answer them ...
> - critically appraise that evidence for its validity ... and usefulness ...
> - apply the results of this appraisal to our clinical practice, and
> - evaluate our performance[27].

Can any of you say that a parallel approach in teaching, compatible as it is with the notion of the teacher as reflective practitioner, would not be powerfully beneficial?

Educational researchers may not be enthusiastic about these suggestions, which are perhaps too radical for them[28]. Most academics fear any loss of their autonomy and control over the research process; and they claim practitioner interests are short-termist. There would indeed be some loss of autonomy, and there would be a danger of short-termism that a National Forum would need to take into account. But the end result would be far more research that is closely related to policy and practice, that is carried out by and with users, and that leads to results which are more likely to be applied in practice. There is much to gain and little to lose in moving as soon as possible to an evidence-based teaching profession. The TTA will, I hope, work with the profession and researchers to make the prospects match the exciting possibilities.

Notes

1 Until recently it has been virtually impossible to make even a reasonable estimate of annual expenditure on educational research. There is now greater transparency in relation to the 'QR' or research money allocated to universities and the Research Assessment Exercise permits a calculation of the research income of Departments and Schools of Education in universities. QR amounts to some £27M a year and research income from other sources (research

councils, charities, local and central government, industry and business etc.) around £20M a year. To this has to be added the costs of educational research done in social science rather than education faculties, which includes the ESRC's research centres dedicated to educational research. There is also the cost of the research element of higher degree students in education (at least £5M a year). I estimate therefore that £50M is almost certainly an underestimate and the true figure may well be in excess of £60M. But it is important to remember how difficult these calculations are. Cf K Bick and Gregg B Jackson, 'Research and Education Reform: a study of the federal role in United States' education research and development,' in *Education Research and Reform: an international perspective,* O.E.C.D./U.S. Department of Education, 1994: 'One of the most difficult tasks we faced was trying to figure out how much is spent in this country on education research and development by all parties, how that compares with prior levels and expenditures, and how it compares with research and development expenditures in other fields.'

2 The success of the occasional impostor suggests this requirement might be exaggerated.

3 A particularly elegant and incisive overview of this and related matters is provided by Paul H Hirst, 'The theory-practice relationship in teacher training', in M Booth, J Furlong and M Wilkins (eds.) *Partnership in Initial Teacher Training,* Cassell, 1990, pp. 74–86.

4 'One of the most notable features of teacher talk is the absence of a technical vocabulary. Unlike professional encounters between doctors, lawyers, garage mechanics and astrophysicists, when teachers talk together almost any reasonably intelligent adult can listen in and comprehend what is being said ... [This] absence of technical terms is related to another characteristic of teacher talk: its conceptual simplicity. Not only do teachers avoid elaborate words, they also seem to shun elaborate ideas ... This is the tendency to approach educational affairs intuitively rather than rationally. When called upon to justify their professional decisions, for example, my informants often declared that their classroom behaviour was based more on impulse and feeling than on reflection and thought.' (Jackson P W. *Life in Classrooms,* Holt, Rinehart and Winston, 1968)

'Teachers' doubts about possessing a common technical culture affects their collective status in two ways: they make them less ready to assert authority on educational matters and less able to respond to the demands of society.' (Lortie, D C, *Schoolteacher,* University of Chicago Press 1975)

5 Some writers seem unduly dogmatic and pessimistic in denying any cumulative character to social science, rather than acknowledging it as a greater problem in the social sciences than in the natural sciences. Take for instance the following: 'Knowledge about policy questions is not cumulative in a scientific sense, partly because the problems are intractable and also because the environment changes so that old solutions do not fit the new circumstances.' Martin Rein, *Social science and public policy,* Penguin Books, 1976, p. 23.

6 'Individual [teachers] must resolve recurrent problems largely unaided by systematic, relevant knowledge.' (Lortie, 1975)

7 William G Pickering, 'Does medical treatment mean patient benefit?' *Lancet,* 347, 1996, 379–80.

8 A G Bearn, 'The growth of scientific medicine' in G. McLachlan (ed.) *Medical Education and Medical Care,* Oxford University Press, 1977. Bearn is Professor of Medicine at Cornell.

9 'Teaching has not been subjected to the sustained, empirical and practice-oriented inquiry into problems and alternatives which we find in university-based professions. It has been permitted to remain evanescent; there is no equivalent to the recording found in surgical cases, law cases and physical models of engineering and architectural achievement. Such records, coupled with commentaries and critiques of highly trained professors, allow new generations to pick up where earlier ones finished. ... [T]o an astonishing degree the beginner in teaching must start afresh, uninformed about prior solutions and alternative approaches to recurring practical problems. What student [teachers] learn about teaching, then, is intuitive and imitative rather than explicit and analytical; it is based on individual personalities rather than

pedagogical principles ... One's personal predispositions are not only relevant but, in fact, stand at the core of becoming a teacher.' (Lortie, 1975)

10 Cf. William Taylor, 'Knowledge and research' in W. Taylor (ed.) (1973) *Research Perspectives in Education,* Routledge & Kegan Paul, p. 195. 'The serving teacher who is widely read in the psychology and sociology of education, and who substitutes judgements from these spheres for the traditional recipe knowledge of the staffroom, may find himself regarded as an outsider, already half-way to becoming a college of education lecturer or local authority organizer.'

11 'This is, of course, particularly so in the case of secondary headteachers, but in recent years it has become much more common for primary heads to have few or no teaching responsibilities.

12 'A teacher today can be considered outstanding by those who are familiar with his work without being thought to have made a single contribution to knowledge of teaching in general; the ablest people in the occupation are not expected to add to the shared knowledge of the group. There is, in short, no tradition honoring the contributions to the craft ...' (Lortie, 1975)

13 The classic and highly influential statement of this position is that by Nisbet J & Broadfoot P, *The impact of research on policy and practice in education,* Aberdeen University Press, 1980, which concludes that their historical and comparative review, 'demonstrates the complexity of the variables affecting impact and the degree to which impact is bound to be problematic. Some of these variables are bound up with the essential nature of educational research and with the scope and scale of the enterprise in practice, while others are concerned with the characteristics and predilections of the receiving individuals and groups ... Thus although the available literature is weak in dealing with specific instances of impact, the theoretical insights it provides should help to identify the future contribution of educational research even if the task of actually improving impact turns out to be a more intractable problem.' Many leading researchers have attempted to preserve an optimistic outlook. For example, William Taylor writes that educational research 'exerts its influence by helping to determine the agenda of problems and difficulties, and in providing some of the elements that shape individual and group orientations towards particular issues ... Although the influence of research in education on staffroom conversation and school committee decision is more tenuous and indirect ... it is none the less real and is growing. All this points to the need to be aware of simplistic assumptions regarding the actual and likely pay-offs from research. Some of these are readily traceable, but most make their way into thinking and practice less directly – through the literature on education ... [and] through courses, conferences and lectures ... The fact that ... most discussions about education, except among researchers themselves and some of the professionals in universities and colleges, contain few explicit references to research, is no real guide to its influence and certainly no basis on which to calculate its usefulness in cost/benefit terms.' (William Taylor, 'Knowledge and research' in W. Taylor (ed.) (1973) *Research Perspectives in Education,* Routledge & Kegan Paul, p. 200.) For a similar view see Maurice Kogan in Husen T & Kogan M (eds.) (1984) *Educational Research & Policy,* Pergamon Press, p. 48.

14 This was amply demonstrated in an unpublished survey of educational researchers conducted by Professor M Beveridge and myself and funded by the Leverhulme Trust.

15 This is even stated in print. A recent example is Thomas K Glennan, 'In search of new structures and procedures for organizing government funded education research and development,' in *Education Research and Reform: an international perspective,* O.E.C.D./U.S. Department of Education, 1994: '... increased research quality and quantity will have little impact on the quality of education policy and practice if there is little demand by the education community for the products of that research. In my view the demand is weak for three key reasons: (a) low levels of incentives for improvement of educational practice, (b) the absence of resources to improve school performance, and (c) a practitioner culture that does not value research-based knowledge.'

16 'Each stakeholder group is entitled to state its wants and to assert them to the needs to which society should pay attention. ... tensions and conflicts are inevitable and even necessary ingredients of development ... We can look forward ... to strengthening through negotiation the shared interests of the many groups in the improvement of education.' Centre for Educational Research and Innovation, Educational research and development trends, issues and challenges, OECD, 1995, ch. 6.

17 T Husen in Husen T & Kogan M (eds.) (1984) *Educational Research & Policy*, Pergamon Press, p. 31.

18 In developing my view on the role of research foresight in educational research I have been strongly influenced by the report *Technology Foresight: a review of recent international experiences*, written by Ben R Martin (of the ESRC Centre for Science, Technology, Energy and Environment Policy in the Science Policy Research Unit, University of Sussex) for the Office of Science and Technology, Cabinet Office.

19 An outline strategic plan should be shared with all the community involved in educational research, the individual bodies of which, whether a major funder like a Research Council or Charitable Trust or a minor player like an individual researcher, would make their own decisions in the light of, but without being bound by, the national strategy. The Forum would play a major role in keeping major players informed of what other players were doing, and would in due course publish the emergent match between research activity and the guiding national strategy. Such feedback loops between a national strategy and the constant decision making by funders and researchers are essential to better communication, co-ordination and coherence in educational research. In this way the Forum would have a duty to keep the research and user communities informed as to progress within the national strategy; to keep a register of current and recent research; and to encourage and support the various forms of networking that are essential to good quality and sustained communication, co-ordination and collaboration both among researchers and between researchers and other stakeholders. In the absence of such improved co-ordination, there is little hope that there will be the cumulative development of research in the field on which successful application rests. The national strategy and its associated processes would be evaluated as part of the lead in to the next research foresight exercise.

20 Michael Bassey has usefully distinguished between educational research and psychological or sociological research in education. It is the latter which must be carefully protected by research councils and the charities.

21 Michael Bassey, *op. cit.* p. 130.

22 William Rosenberg &. Anna Donald, 'Evidence based medicine: an approach to clinical problem-solving,' *British Medical Journal*, 310, 29 April 1995, pp. 1122–5.

23 Quoted from David Grahame-Smith, 'Evidence based medicine: Socratic dissent,' *British Medical Journal, 310, 29* April 1995, pp. 1126–8.

24 William G Pickering, 'Does medical treatment mean patient benefit?' *Lancet*, 347, 1996, 379–80.

25 *ibid.*

26 There has been a particular problem in this regard with sociologists of education in recent years, for they have favoured writing 'critiques' of government policy, which sometimes have been little more than dressed-up criticism from a different political perspective. As a result, (conservative) politicians have come to distrust sociologists even further and see any research they do as biased – perhaps not unreasonably, since the sociologists have been among the first to reject the notion of value-free research.

27 D L Sackett and R B Haynes, 'Notebook', *Evidence-based Medicine,* 1 (1), 1995, p. 5.

28 In an interesting piece under the exciting title 'Near the Chalk Face: new approaches to research for education renovation', in *Education Research and Reform: an international perspective*, O.E.C.D./U.S. Department of Education, 1994, Bob W Connell, who has a distinguished record in educational research in Australia and the USA, gives indications of

understanding just how deep the problems are in educational research, but reaches conclusions that are far too weak to provide adequate solutions because he will not challenge the research community – The statement 'I do not wish to open the door to academic-bashing any more than to teacher bashing; there are good reasons why academic work should have a consider-able degree of autonomy' precedes the under-developed suggestions that 'research funding structures that encourage links between particular groups of academics and particular groups of schools' and 'a designated part of research budgets should be invested in dissemination' and 'I would certainly favor opening up academic journals to the work of teachers.'

Chapter 2

Educational research and teaching: a response to David Hargreaves' TTA Lecture

Martyn Hammersley

Educational research in Britain is currently under threat. There are several causes. External changes and pressures are among the most important factors, especially continuing cuts in resources for both education and academic research, along with the disruption created by multiple government-sponsored reforms at all levels of the education system. But there are also internal problems, for example the effects of what has been termed the 'crisis of representation', which increasingly afflicts the whole of the humanities and social sciences. This throws doubt on the capacity of research to produce knowledge, in the commonly understood sense of that term (see, for example, Clifford & Marcus, 1986; Lather, 1991; Denzin & Lincoln, 1995). One consequence of both external and internal crises has been an increased insistence that research should have a significant impact on professional or political practice. There is by no means universal agreement about exactly what this involves, but commitment to the idea is widespead. Among researchers themselves it is to be found in diverse forms, for example in greater preoccupation with policy issues, in growing advocacy of action research, and in moves towards open partisanship. Similarly,

Taken from: *British Educational Research Journal*, Vol. 23, No. 2, 1997, pp. 141–61.

funding agencies insist more and more on policy relevance, on negotiation by researchers with prospective 'users', on explicit plans for dissemination designed to maximise impact, and sometimes on contracts which give funders control over publication[1]. Moreover, it seems likely that the emergence of the Teacher Training Agency (TTA) as a funder of educational research will reinforce many of these trends.

Against this background, David Hargreaves' recent and controversial lecture on 'Teaching as a Reseach-based Profession', sponsored by the TTA, has considerable significance (Hargreaves, 1996 [Chapter 1 of this volume]; see also *Research Intelligence* 57 & 58, *Times Educational Supplement*, 28 June, plus letters in subsequent issues). Hargreaves claims that the effectiveness of teaching in schools would be substantially improved if it were a research-based profession; and he lays the blame for the fact that it is not research-based on researchers rather than on teachers. He argues that current educational research is neither sufficiently cumulative nor sufficiently relevant to practical concerns for it to make the contribution required of it. To support his argument, Hargreaves draws a contrast between the role of research in relation to education and its contribution to the practice of medicine. He uses as a model the recent development of evidence-based medicine, in which clinical decision-making is to be founded on, and justified in terms of, research findings about the relative effectiveness of different medical treatments. On the basis of his critique of educational research, Hargreaves argues that radical changes are required in the way that it is organised and carried out. In particular, 'practitioners and policy makers must take an active role in shaping the direction of educational research ...' [p. 10 of this volume]. He proposes the establishment of a National Educational Research Forum to facilitate dialogue amongst the various stakeholders. This would sponsor research foresight exercises to provide the basis for a national strategy, specifying short- and long-term priorities, and he recommends the reallocation to the TTA and the Office for Standards in Education (OFSTED) of some of the money currently given to universities for educational research. Above all, he argues that more educational research should be carried out by practising teachers, since this would enhance its practical relevance.

In this paper I want to assess Hargreaves' criticisms of educational research and the remedies he proposes. First, though, I need to spell out his critique in a little more detail.

The ills of educational research

Towards the end of his lecture, Hargreaves summarises his criticisms as follows:

> what would come to an end is the frankly second-rate educational research which does not make a serious contribution to fundamental theory or knowledge; which is irrelevant to practice; which is uncoordinated with any preceding or follow-up research; and which clutters up academic journals that virtually nobody reads, (p. 11)

Two main charges seem to be involved here. The first is that much educational research is non-cumulative, in the sense that it does not explicitly 'build on earlier research – by confirming or falsifying it, by extending or refining it, by replacing it with better evidence or theory, and so on'. The problem is that 'a few small-scale investigations of an issue which are never followed up inevitably produce inconclusive and contestable findings of little practical relevance'. Moreover, replications, 'which are more necessary in the social than the natural sciences because of the importance of contextual and cultural variations, are astonishingly rare'. This situation is worsened by the fact that 'educational researchers, like other social scientists, are often engaged in bitter disputes among themselves about the philosophy and methodology of the social sciences'. This means that lines of research are abandoned when there is a change in fashion, rather than because problems have been solved. As a result, despite considerable work, 'there are few areas which have yielded a corpus of research evidence regarded as scientifically sound and as a worthwhile resource to guide professional action' [p. 5].

As can be seen, this first argument leads straight into the second: that research is not found useful by teachers. Hargreaves claims that 'few successful practising teachers' use the knowledge provided by the foundation disciplines (psychology, sociology, philosophy and history) or think it important for their practice. Indeed, 'teachers are able to be effective in their work in almost total ignorance of this infrastructure'. As a result:

> the disciplines of education are seen to consist of 'theory' which is strongly separated from practice. Trainee teachers soon spot the yawning gap between theory and practice and the low value of research as a guide to the solution of practical problems. [p. 4]

The fundamental defect is that there is no substantial body of research 'which, if only it were disseminated and acted on by teachers, would yield huge benefits in the quality of teaching and learning'. Thus, Hargreaves asks:

> just how much research is there which (i) demonstrates conclusively that if teachers change their practice from x to y there will be a significant and enduring improvement in teaching and learning and (ii) has developed an effective method of convincing teachers of the benefits of, and means to, changing from x to y?

On this basis, Hargreaves argues that the money allocated to educational research is not well spent:

> Something has indeed gone badly wrong. Research is having little impact on the improvement of practice, and teachers I talk to do not think they get value for money from the £50–60 millions we spend annually on educational research. [p. 8]

Educational research as non-cumulative

Criticism of the non-cumulative character of research on education has been a persistent theme in Hargreaves' writings. As long ago as 1981 he took the sociology of education to task for its failure to develop a cumulative body of knowledge:

> As time goes by, theories do not become better, by which I mean broader in scope and more economical in content, either as a result of careful testing or as a result of subsuming earlier theories. Theories simply 'lie around' in the field, relatively vague and relatively untested. Empirical research fares no better. Very few studies actively seek to build on the work of earlier researchers, confirming or disconfirming earlier findings to put our knowledge on a sounder basis. Too often research evidence is inconsistent or incompatible. It is thus that many of the introductory text books to the sociology of education inevitably end up as *catalogues* of theory and research, for there is no way that a reviewer can integrate the field into a coherent whole. There are very few areas in our discipline where we can confidently say that either theory or research is much better established than it was several years ago. (1981, p. 10)

I have considerable sympathy with Hargreaves's argument here. Commitment to one-off studies is an important defect of much educational research, and indeed of social research generally. It reduces the extent to which findings from particular investigations are tested across different situations and minimises the division of labour, thereby undermining the cumulation of knowledge. There is little doubt that we need to move to a situation where new research builds more effectively on earlier work, and where greater attention is given to testing competing interpretations of data, whether descriptive or explanatory. And this may require replications, even though the form these take cannot be the same in naturalistic as in experimental research. In addition, as might be inferred from the above, I believe that Hargreaves is right to assume the appropriateness of a scientific approach to the study of education, despite the strong trend in the opposite direction in recent times.

Nevertheless, I think that there are also some serious problems with Hargreaves' critique. One is that he is not as clear as he might have been about what criteria he is using to assess educational research. In the early parts of his lecture he stresses its failure to accumulate knowledge by building on earlier work, but the concept of cumulation is not a simple one: there are different forms it can take (see Freese, 1980, pp. 40–49). Moreover, many educational researchers *do* claim that their work has produced theoretical development (see, for example, Woods, 1985, 1987). Hargreaves does not make clear why he would deny these claims[2]. Later in his lecture, this first criticism turns into the charge that educational research is not, or that not enough of it is, 'evidence-based'. Again, clarification is required. What is and is not being accepted as evidence here, and what counts as basing claims on evidence? Some of the language that Hargreaves uses implies commitment to a methodological perspective that many educational researchers will dismiss as positivist. That dismissal would be a mistake, in my view; but some specification and justification of the model of research he is employing is necessary. Reference to examples of evidence-based and non-evidence-based educational research might also have been illuminating.

A second problem is that Hargreaves seems to present the failings of current educational research as if they stemmed solely from a lack of commitment on the part of researchers to rigorous and cumulative inquiry. There is no doubt that this commitment has become attenuated. But, to some extent, this is a response to genuine problems. It should be pointed out that the move away from the scientific model, and from a concern with testing the effectiveness of different pedagogic techniques, is relatively recent. Much educational research in the first two-thirds of the twentieth century was devoted to scientific investigation of effective teaching; and one of the reasons for the changes in educational research over the past 20 years is precisely the failure of this work to produce conclusive, cumulative findings (Dunkin & Biddle, 1974; Chambers, 1991, 1992; Glass, 1994; though see also Gage, 1985 and 1994)[3].

As Hargreaves knows, since he was a leading figure in it, the shift to qualitative method in the 1970s was prompted by powerful criticisms identifying unresolved problems in 'positivist' research. Some of these related to the difficulties of *measuring* what is of educational significance (Delamont & Hamilton, 1984; Barrow, 1984; ch. 6). Others concerned the peculiar complexities of 'social causation', including interaction effects (Cronbach, 1975). The most radical versions of these arguments drew on philosophical writings to the effect that human social life is quite different in character from the physical world studied by natural scientists (and, we might add, from that investigated by most medical researchers) (see, for example, Winch, 1958; Schütz 1967). From this it was often concluded that the kind of knowledge produced by natural scientists is not available to social and educational researchers.

In my judgement, the arguments for the distinctiveness of the social world have been overplayed; and are associated with too homogeneous a view of the phenomena studied, and of the methods used, by natural scientists. Nevertheless, there can be no denying the serious problems involved in producing conclusive knowledge about causal patterns in social phenomena. This is one reason why educational researchers, like social scientists generally, have become embroiled in philosophical and methodological disputes. Hargreaves treats these disputes as if they were merely a matter of fashion. It is true that some of the discussion is self-indulgent, but the underlying problems are real enough. At the core of them is precisely the question of the extent to which one can have a science of human behaviour of a kind that models itself, even remotely, on the natural sciences. By failing to mention these problems, Hargreaves implies that the sort of cumulative, well-founded knowledge he wants can be created simply by researchers pulling themselves together and getting back to work (under the direction of teachers). The situation is not so simple; and not so easily remedied.

I can only sketch the problems briefly here. As already noted, they centre on two areas: the measurement of social phenomena and the validation of causal relationships amongst those phenomena. As regards the former, there are problems involved in identifying distinct and standardised 'treatments' in education; witness the difficulties faced by researchers seeking to distinguish teaching styles (see Bennett, 1976, 1985; Wragg, 1976; Galton *et al.,* 1980). Indeed, there are unresolved measurement problems even in relation to the most specific and concrete aspects of teaching, for example types of questions asked (Scarth & Hammersley, 1986a, 1986b). The problems are also formidable at the other end of the causal chain, in operationalising the concept of learning. There is room for considerable disagreement about what students *should* learn, and what they *actually* learn, in any particular situation: in terms of different knowledge, skills, and/or values; different areas of content; depth versus surface learning; degrees of transferability etc. More than this, very often what are regarded as the most important kinds of learning – relating to high-level, transferable cognitive skills or personal understanding – are extraordinarily difficult to measure with any degree of validity and reliability; and there are doubts about whether replicable measurement of them is possible, even in principle. In short, in both areas, there are questions about whether it is possible to move beyond sensitising concepts to the definitive concepts that seem to be required for scientific analysis of the kind proposed by Hargreaves[4].

The problems relating to the establishment of causal patterns are equally severe. Since we are interested in what goes on in real schools and colleges, and because strict experimentation is often ruled out for practical or ethical reasons, this task becomes extremely difficult. How are we to control competing factors in such a way as to assess the relative contribution of each one in what is usually a complex web of relationships? More than this, can we assume that causation in this field involves fixed, universal relationships, rather than local, context-sensitive patterns in which interpretation and decision on the part of teachers and students play an important role? Unlike in most areas of medicine, in education the 'treatments' consist of symbolic interaction, with all the scope for multiple interpretations and responses which that implies. What kind of causal relations are involved here, if they are causal at all? And what kind of knowledge can we have of them?

These are, then, some of the fundamental problems facing educational researchers attempting to produce the kind of knowledge that Hargreaves demands. I do not want to suggest that such knowledge is impossible. Indeed, I have claimed elsewhere that Hargreaves' earliest work forms part of one of the few cumulative programmes of research that develops and tests theory to be found in sociology and education. However, problems remain with that programme, and there are questions about whether it can provide a model for work in other areas (Hargreaves, 1967; Hammersley, 1985).

There is another point too. In my view, one important cause of the unsatisfactory nature of much educational research is that it is too preoccupied with producing information that will shape *current* policy or practice. This seems likely to be one source of the lack of testing and cumulation of knowledge that Hargreaves complains about. He touches on this when he notes that educational researchers have fallen between two stools: 'achieving neither prestige from the social scientists ... nor gratitude from classroom teachers' [p. 6 of this volume]. The problem, in part, is that while working under the authority of academic disciplines concerned with contributing to theory, researchers have also sought to address the changing political agendas that define pressing educational problems. This is partly a product of sharp competition for funding. But it has also been encouraged by conceptions of research which imply that it is possible simultaneously to contribute to scientific theory and to provide solutions to practical or political problems. This view is characteristic of some forms of positivism and also of Marxism, both of which have been influential in the field; and there are signs that Hargreaves is committed to a version of it, though these are more evident in his 1981 article than in his 1996 lecture. However, it seems to me that this view is fallacious, since the production of information of high practical relevance usually depends on a great deal of knowledge that does not have such relevance. In other words, for science to be able to contribute knowledge that is relevant to practice, a division of labour is required: a great deal of coordinated work is necessary tackling smaller, more manageable problems that do not have immediate pay-off. Moreover, this requires sustained work over a long period, not short bursts of activity geared to political and practical priorities. In other words, the wrong time schedule has been in control: that of educational policy-making and practice rather than that appropriate to scientific research.

In my view, then, the commitment of educational researchers to addressing the 'big questions' and to producing answers to them in the short rather than the long term, along with parallel expectations on the part of funders, has been a major contributing factor to the weaknesses that Hargreaves identifies. And his call for educational research to be more practically effective will only worsen this problem. He insists that 'curiosity-driven, long-term. "basic" and "blue skies" research is as vital in education as in any other scientific field' [p. 11]. But he neglects the extent to which the funding for this has already been eroded. For example, the main source which he mentions, the Economic and Social Research Council (ESRC), has increasingly moved towards non-responsive funding of strategic and even applied research. This is despite the fact that its predecessor, the Social Sciences Research Council (SSRC), was specifically established to fund basic research – government departments and other sources were expected to finance applied work. Moreover, Hargreaves applauds 'the pressure the ESRC now puts on researchers to demonstrate consultation with, and involvement of, users as a condition of getting a research grant' [p. 10]. Yet it is a feature of basic research that who the users will be and what use they might make of it are largely unknown.

Contributing to practice

Let me turn now to the second complaint in Hargreaves' lecture, to what is indeed its central theme: that educational research has not produced sufficient practically relevant knowledge[5]. I certainly agree that an important ultimate aim (but, for reasons already explained, not an immediate one) of all research should be to produce knowledge which has relevance. But there is room for much disagreement about what such relevance amounts to, and about what kinds of knowledge are possible and of value. In his lecture, Hargreaves adopts a narrowly instrumental view of practical relevance: that research should be able to tell practitioners which is the best technique for dealing with a particular kind of problem. In this respect, though his analogy is with medicine, he seems to be committed to what has been referred to as the 'engineering model' of the relationship between research and practice (Janowitz, 1972; Bulmer, 1982; Finch, 1986). This portrays research as directed towards finding or evaluating solutions to technical problems[6].

The question of whether educational research can supply the sort of knowledge assumed by the engineering model has already been dealt with in the previous section, but there is also the issue of whether the problems that teachers face are of a kind that is open to solution by research; in other words, whether they are technical in character. Early on in his lecture, Hargreaves seems to recognise that they may not be. He comments:

> both education and medicine are profoundly people-centred professions. Neither believes that helping people is merely a matter of a simple and technical application but rather a highly skilled process in which a sophisticated judgment matches a professional decision to the unique needs of each client. [p. 4 of this volume]

However, his subsequent discussion of the contribution which he would like to see research making to educational practice seems to contradict this; for example, his reference to research needing to 'demonstrate conclusively' that a particular pedagogical approach will produce 'a significant and enduring improvement' [p. 9].

At one time it was widely assumed that educational practice could, and should, be based on scientific theory, with teachers using techniques whose appropriateness had been determined by the results of scientific investigation (O'Connor, 1957; Dunkin & Biddle, 1974). However, much recent work on the nature of teaching by philosophers, psychologists and sociologists has emphasised the extent to which it is practical rather than technical in character; in brief, that it is a matter of making judgements rather than following rules (Schwab, 1969; Hirst, 1983; Carr, 1987; Olson, 1992). In an earlier article, Hargreaves himself contributed to this line of thinking, referring to the 'enormous complex whole which we call the teacher's common sense knowledge of life in classrooms'.

He emphasised its largely tacit nature, and the fact that it must have this nature if it is to enable the teacher to do his or her work: 'Decisions are made partly on the basis of social skills and partly on the basis of certain value commitments: both are encapsulated and rapidly processed in every routine classroom decision' (Hargreaves, 1979, p. 79). This line of argument throws doubt on the idea that teaching can be *based* on research knowledge. It implies that it necessarily depends on experience, wisdom, local knowledge, and judgement. And, I suggest, it is precisely the practical character of teaching, as much as any failing on the part of researchers, which is the main source of the 'yawning gap' between theory and practice; witness the fact that complaints about such gaps are a commonplace of professional education in all fields[7].

One of the features of much practical activity, and particularly of teaching, is that goals are multiple, and their meaning is open to debate and difficult to operationalise. In this context, Hargreaves' focus on the 'effectiveness' of pedagogy obscures some of the most important issues. Put into practice, an exclusive focus on effectiveness leads to an overemphasis on those outcomes which can be measured (at the expense of other educational goals), or results in a displacement of goals on to the maximisation of measured output. We see this problem in the currently influential research on 'school effectiveness'. While researchers in this field are usually careful to note that the outcome measures they use do not exhaust or measure all the goals of schooling, their work is sometimes presented and often interpreted as measuring school effectiveness *as such*[8].

Now, of course, we need to take care not to adopt too sharp a distinction between technical and practical activities[9]. What is involved is more of a continuum, and it seems likely that educational practice is not homogenous in this respect: there may be some educational problems that are open to technical solution, even though many are not. Nevertheless, all teaching beyond that concerned with very elementary skills, seems likely, in general terms, to come close to the practical end of the dimension. And the practical character of most teachers' work is increased by the fact that they deal with batches of pupils, rather than with single clients, one by one, as in the case of medicine[10]. It is this which makes the classroom situation a particularly demanding one in terms of the need for reliance on contextual judgement (Jackson, 1968; Doyle, 1977).

All this is not to suggest that research can make no contribution to teaching. But it may mean that the contribution cannot take the form of indicating what is the appropriate technique to use in a particular situation, or even what are the chances of success of a technique in a particular type of situation. The nature of the contribution may be closer to the enlightenment model, involving the provision of information that corrects assumptions or alters the context in which teachers view some aspect of their situation, for example by highlighting possible causal relations to which they may not routinely give attention. Equally important is the capacity that research has for illuminating aspects of teachers' practices that are below the normal level of their consciousness. A good example of this is research on teachers' typifications of children. Documentation of how these are built up, how they affect the ways in which teachers deal with pupils, and the consequences of this, is surely of considerable value (see, for example, Hargreaves *et al.*, 1975). For the most part, such contributions are not dramatic in their consequences. But it is just as much a mistake to try to judge the value of research in terms of its immediate and identifiable practical impact as it is to judge the quality of a school solely by its examination results.

In earlier publications Hargreaves seems to adopt a position closer to the enlightenment than the engineering model. In the preface to his book *Interpersonal Relations and Education* he argued that the most important task in applying the human sciences to education is to 'shed light on the old problems as well as throwing up new problems, or at least problems that are not adequately acknowledged, formulated or discussed' (Hargreaves, 1972, p. 2)[11]. This seems to me to be a more realistic expectation than the instrumental function he assumes in his recent lecture, and it parallels conclusions that have been reached in studies of the relationship between research and policy-making (Weiss, 1980). In his lecture, Hargreaves quotes Nisbet & Broadfoot (1980) and Taylor (1973) arguing for the enlightenment view, but he does not explain why he rejects their conclusions. Instead, he simply asserts that this view is a self-fulfilling prophecy.

All this raises questions about Hargreaves' judgement that educational research does not offer value for money. This phrase has become a popular one, but it involves a judgement that is a good deal more complex and uncertain than its use generally suggests. Thus, Hargreaves gives no indication of how he thinks the cost–benefit analysis involved could be carried out. Even measuring the real cost of a particular piece of research would be a formidable task, and measuring the value of its 'impact' would be virtually impossible and always open to debate. Nor does he acknowledge the problems with the whole cost–benefit approach. These have long been recognised within economics, if not always given the weight they deserve[12]. Because of their reliance on values, all judgements about cost-effectiveness are likely to be subject to considerable instability across time, circumstances and judges. So the question arises of who is to judge, when, and how? Hargreaves relies on the judgements of teachers he has talked to [p. 9]. Even apart from the sampling and reactivity problems involved here, we can ask whether teachers are the best judges, given that according to him they have little knowledge of the findings of educational research. Furthermore, teachers are not the only proper audience for such research. Its main function, it seems to me, is to inform public debates about educational issues: to provide information for use by anyone concerned with those issues, not only teachers but also parents, governors, administrators, pressure groups, politicians, and citizens generally. How well it does this is an important question, and some assessment of its cost-effectiveness in this respect may be unavoidable; but this can be no more than a speculative and contestable estimate.

Hargreaves' lecture is effectively an evaluation of educational research, and as with all evelutions the conclusions are very sensitive to the standard of evaluation employed. One's attitude to the practical value of current educational research will depend a great deal on one's expectations about the contribution to practice that it *could* make. In my view (Hammersley, 1995, ch. 7), researchers have promised – and funders, policymakers and practitioners have expected – too much; assuming that, in itself, research can provide solutions to practical problems. Disappointment, recriminations and a negative attitude towards research have been the result. Hargreaves' lecture is more of the same in this respect, and as a result it is likely to worsen rather than to improve the situation. By reinforcing the idea that research can provide a scientific foundation for practice, he exaggerates the contribution that it can make, *even in principle.* And the risk is that when it fails in this task, as it almost certainly will, it will be dismissed by even more potential users as worthless.

The parallel with medicine

In his critique of the practical failure of educational research, Hargreaves relies heavily on the analogy with medicine. I have no doubt at all that this comparison can be illuminating, but it ought to be pointed out that implicit in its use is a conception of professionalism which emphasises reliance on an established body of scientific knowledge. And this conception ought not to be taken for granted. We should remember that this has never been a feature of the other occupation whose status as a profession has always been beyond question: the law. Furthermore, as with all analogies, it is important to recognise that there may be significant differences, as well as similarities, between what is being compared. Also, analogies are sometimes based on misconceptions about that which is being used as a comparative standard. We must be very cautious, then, about using medicine as a basis for evaluating educational research and practice. Its appropriateness has to be argued for, not assumed.

In the previous two sections I have discussed aspects of education which mark it off from medicine, in ways that challenge Hargreaves's negative judgements about the relative success of educational research. Certainly, it seems likely that much medical research avoids many of the problems that face educational researchers, in particular those deriving from the peculiarities of the social world. Where it does not, I suggest, we find the same lack of cumulative evidence that Hargreaves bemoans in education. Similarly, medical practice may generally be closer to the technical rather than to the practical end of the spectrum, so that research is able to play a role there which is much closer to that envisaged by the engineering model than is possible in education.

At the same time, it is easy to exaggerate the differences between the two cases. Thus, I think it is misleading to claim that in the case of medicine 'there is little difference between researchers and users; all are practitioners', whereas in educational contexts, 'by contrast, researchers are rarely users' [p. 6]. As

Hargreaves recognises, much medical research is laboratory-based rather than clinic-based; and is not carried out by practising clinicians[13]. Equally, most educational researchers are also educational practitioners, even though they are often not practitioners in the same type of context as that in which they do research. Moreover, in their role as academics, they use their own and others' research for teaching purposes, much in the manner that secondary schoolteachers use subject knowledge in theirs[14]. It is also worth noting that most educational researchers are ex-schoolteachers whose research relates to schools of the same general type to that in which they previously taught. (Hargreaves is himself an example.) I do not want to deny that there are important differences in the organisation of research and practice in the fields of education and medicine, but the differences are less sharp and more complex than Hargreaves implies.

There are also respects in which the assumptions Hargreaves makes about medical research, and about the way it contributes to medical practice, are open to doubt. One concerns the contrast in quality that he draws between medical and educational research. It is of note that rather similar criticisms to those made by him of educational research have been directed at medical research carried out by doctors. In an article entitled 'The scandal of poor medical research', Altman comments:

> When I tell friends outside medicine that many papers published in medical journals are misleading because of methodological weaknesses they are rightly shocked. Huge sums of money are spent annually on research that is seriously flawed through use of inappropriate designs, unrepresentative samples, small samples, incorrect methods of analysis, and faulty interpretation. (Altman, 1994, p. 283)[15]

It is worth emphasising the reasons that Altman puts forward for the poor quality of much medical research, since these relate directly to what Hargreaves claims to be its great strength: the fact that it is carried out by practising doctors. Altman lays the blame on the fact that doctors are expected to engage in research, but are often inadequately prepared for or committed to it. What we may conclude from this is that while there is undoubtedly a great deal more cumulation of well-founded knowledge in medicine than in education, it is not at all clear that this results primarily from the participation of clinicians. And we might reasonably fear that increasing the proportion of educational research that is carried out by practising teachers would not provide a remedy for the methodological ills that Hargreaves has identified.

There are also questions about the assumptions which Hargreaves makes about medical *practice*. Sociological research investigating this has highlighted the role of clinical judgement, and pointed to the emphasis that clinicians themselves place on it (Becker *et al.*, 1961, pp. 231–238; Freidson, 1970, ch. 8). Thus, Becker *et al.* argue that clinical experience 'can be used to legitimate a choice of procedures for a patient's treatment and can even be used to rule out use of some procedures that have been scientifically established' (Becker *et al.*

1961, p. 231). Similarly, Atkinson describes the clinician as 'essentially a pragmatist, relying on results rather than theory, and trusting in personal, first-hand knowledge rather than on abstract principles or "book knowledge" (Atkinson, 1981, p. 5). And, in a more recent study of haematologists, he shows how personal, traditional and scientific knowledge interpenetrate in clinical discourse away from the bedside (Atkinson, 1995, p. 48 and *passim*).

There are two closely related aspects of the picture of clinical practice presented by this research that are relevant here. First, clinical decision-making is not based solely, or even primarily, on knowledge drawn directly from research publications. Second, it often does not conform to what we might call the rational model of medical procedure. According to this (rather economistic) model, practice takes the following form: the relevant problem is clearly identified at the start; the full range of possible strategies for dealing with it are assessed in terms of their costs and benefits, on the basis of the best available evidence; and, finally, that strategy is selected and implemented which promises to be the most effective. As has been pointed out in many fields, including economics, for a variety of reasons practical activity deviates substantially from this rationalistic model: goals are not always clearly formulated and undergo change over the course of the activity; only a limited range of strategies may be considered, with little search for information about alternative strategies, stock assumptions being relied on; and the aim may not be to maximise pay-off but only to achieve a satisfactory solution, with scope for disagreement about what this amounts to[16].

In one way, Hargreaves recognises these features of medical practice. Referring to some comments from Caroline Cox about teachers, he points out how medical practitioners also often rely on 'tradition, prejudice, dogma, and ideology' [p. 12]. In adopting this loaded characterisation, he aligns himself with the proponents of evidence-based medicine, who argue that research must play an increased role in clinical practice if the latter's effectiveness is to reach acceptable levels. It is argued that there are reasons to doubt the effectiveness of a substantial proportion of medical treatments currently used by clinicians. Advocates of evidence-based medicine put forward two main explanations for this. First, they claim that the quality of clinical practice deteriorates over the course of the careers of practitioners. This is because they are dependent on the state of research knowledge when they trained, which becomes progressively outdated. The second argument is that the huge number of medical research reports now produced is too great for clinicians to access directly. What is required, therefore, is the use of bibliographical strategies and technology for summarising and making available the information produced by research, and the training of clinicians in the use of these.

What does not come through in Hargreaves' lecture is that evidence-based medicine is by no means an uncontroversial matter (see *The Lancet*, 1995; Grahame-Smith, 1995; Court, 1996; and the letters in *The Lancet*, 1995, 346, pp. 837–840 and pp. 1171–1172; and *British Medical Journal*, 1995, 311, pp. 257–259, and 1996, 313, pp. 114–115 and pp. 169–171)[17]. Critics have argued that it places too much emphasis on the role of research findings in clinical decision-making; in fact, that it is a misnomer, since all medicine is evidence-based, even when it does not make the kind of systematic use of the research literature that advocates of evidence-based medicine recommend. One critic points out that it would be better referred to as 'literature-based medicine' (Horwitz, cited in Shuchman, 1996, p. 1396). Another suggests that the presumption built into the term is that the practice of medicine 'was previously based on a direct communication with God or the tossing of a coin' (Fowler, 1995, p. 838). What is at issue is not the use of evidence as against reliance on something else ('tradition, prejudice, dogma, and ideology'), but the relative importance of different kinds of evidence. And we should, perhaps, also note that the appropriate balance amongst these will not just vary across medical specialities but also at different stages of treatment. In diagnosis, for example, particular emphasis is likely to be given to evidence from medical histories, physical examinations and/or test results.

Critics also point out some problems in the use of research evidence to inform clinical decision-making. One is that the literature is very variable in quality, and that there is much more research in some areas than others. A consequence of this is that there are significant gaps in knowledge which render the practice of evidence-based medicine problematic in many fields. More significantly, the fact that there may be evidence about some treatments and not others, or better evidence about them, could lead to misleading conclusions being drawn about their relative efficacy. A second point is that there may be biases in the research literature, for example resulting from the tendency of journals to be less interested in publishing negative than positive findings. A third problem is that the process of summarising the findings and methods of research may itself introduce distortions. Certainly, it makes the critical appraisal of evidence, which advocates of evidence-based medicine emphasise, more difficult and subject to increased threats to validity.

There are also problems surrounding the application of information about aggregates to particular patients. The authors of a key text in clinical epidemiology, one of the foundations of evidence-based medicine, report a senior doctor as opining that it is immoral to combine epidemiology with clinical practice (Sackett *et al.*, 1985, p. ix). It is not clear from the context what the reasoning was behind this criticism, but two problems seem relevant. One is that there may be circumstances where the requirements of research conflict with those of treating a particular patient. An illustration is provided by Jadad (1996), in an article entitled 'Are you playing evidence-based medicine games with our daughter?'. He seems to have fed his 3½-year-old daughter shrimp in order to test a consultant's diagnosis of allergy, which he believed was not based on sound research evidence. Whatever the rights and wrongs of this particular case, it is not difficult to see that conflicting motivations can be involved where clinicians (or parents!) are also engaged in research (see also Dearlove *et al.*, 1995, p. 258).

Another issue relates to the problem of treating a patient as an instance of a category for which one has research data. Clinicians are directly responsible for the treatment of individual patients, not primarily concerned with what works in general. Patients always have multiple characteristics, some of which may be such as to render the treatment indicated by the research literature inappropriate; and these characteristics can include patients' preferences (see Thornton, 1992; Charlton, 1995, p. 257; Jones & Sagar, 1995, p. 258)[18].

Even putting aside the problem of applying aggregate data to individual cases, it is not necessarily in a patient's best interests for a clinician to use what is reported in the literature as the most effective treatment. Treatments can demand considerable skills, which a particular practitioner may not have, most obviously (but not exclusively) in the case of surgery. Thus, a formally less effective treatment of which the doctor already has experience may be more advantageous than a less than fully successful attempt at something more ambitious (see Burkett & Knafl, 1974, pp. 94–95). Literature-based knowledge can only provide a guide; it is no substitute for first-hand experience or for that of immediate colleagues, who can be questioned further in the event of unforeseen complications. Thus, a particular technique may be used because it seems to have been effective in the past, and also because much is known about what to expect from it: one knows what normally happens as well as the routine deviance associated with it. Using new drugs or surgical techniques can increase the level of uncertainty, and the danger of running into situations that one does not know how to deal with.

It seems unlikely that any clinician would deny the value of research evidence. What is at issue is the degree and nature of its use. The advocates of evidence-based medicine vary in what they recommend. Sometimes, they simply point to the capacity for searching the research literature that is now provided by information management strategies and technology; emphasising that this cannot substitute for experience and clinical judgement. On other occasions, however, more radical proposals seem to be implied, where systematic literature searches are treated as obligatory and as providing benefit/risk ratios which can form the basis not just for clinical decision-making but also for accountability. In this, advocates of evidence-based medicine follow Cochrane's dismissal of clinical *opinion,* and his argument that there is little or no evidence about the effectiveness of many routinely used techniques, where 'evidence' is interpreted as the outcome of randomised controlled trials or as 'immediate and obvious' effects (Cochrane, 1972, p. 30). What is at issue here, then, is not just what is, and is not, to count as adequate evidence, but also the approach to be adopted in clinical decision-making, how it is to be assessed, and by whom.

Sociologists have often noted the role that an emphasis on clinical judgement and uncertainty has played in the power that the medical profession exercises. Evidence-based medicine threatens this, in that there is a close association between it and demands for greater accountability on the part of doctors, in terms not just of efficacy but also of cost-effectiveness. It is this that has led to much of the reaction against evidence-based medicine[19]. However, only if there were good reasons to be confident that research evidence could replace clinical judgement, and that the rational model could be applied, would it be justifiable to dismiss the resistance of doctors as ingrained conservatism or self-interested concern with preserving professional power. And it seems to me that there are no grounds for such confidence, even though moves towards clearer guidelines for clinicians and increased use of the medical literature may well be desirable.

As in the National Health Service (NHS) so also in the education system there has been growing emphasis on professional accountability, and attempts to set up quasi-markets which maximise efficiency. Moreover, Hargreaves clearly has accountability very much in mind when he argues that: 'expertise *means* not just having relevant experience and knowledge but having *demonstrable* competence and clear *evidence* to justify doing things in one way rather than another' [p. 12]. From this point of view, a research-based teaching profession is one that accounts for itself in terms of the details of its practice to those outside by appeal to the following of explicitly formulated procedures backed by research evidence. As Hargreaves comments, though with questionable predictive validity: 'when educational leaders have evidence for their practices, they may even command the respect of politicians' [p. 12].

However, this move towards evidence-based accountability does not seem likely to enhance the professionalism of teachers, quite the reverse. Just as evidence-based medicine threatens to assist attacks on the professionalism of doctors by managers in the NHS, so Hargreaves' arguments may be used by those who seek to render teachers more accountable. In both areas there are grave doubts about whether this will improve quality of service. It seems more likely further to demoralise and undermine the professional judgement of practitioners, in occupations that have already been seriously damaged in these respects.

Conclusion

Hargreaves' lecture raises very important issues, and some of his criticisms of educational research are sound. It does seem to me that researchers need to be more focused about what their goals are, about the degree of success they have had in achieving them, and about the problems they face. Furthermore, we need to try to make our research both build more effectively on earlier work and provide a better foundation for subsequent investigations. We also ought to take more care in disseminating the results of research, and to think more clearly about how it is used. Hargreaves' arguments could play a productive role in stimulating developments in these areas. Moreover, the parallel with medicine is surely worth exploring. Indeed, I think we could learn much from examining the role of research in relation to a range of occupations and organisations.

At the same time, I have argued that there are some fundamental problems at the core of Hargreaves' analysis. One is that he is not very explicit about the form he believes educational research should take, in terms of which he evaluates current work negatively. Another is his neglect of the severe methodological problems that educational researchers face. His failure to address these problems is exemplified by his comment that *'without question* OFSTED has the most comprehensive data-base on what teachers do and how it relates to their effectiveness' ([p. 12], my emphasis). While he refers only to comprehensiveness not to validity, the fact that he recommends the transfer of money to OFSTED from universities to fund analysis of these data implies that he thinks they could provide a sound basis for reaching scientific conclusions about the relative effectiveness of different pedagogical techniques. What evidence is there to support this assumption? Hargreaves does not provide or refer to any; nor is the claim plausible. This is partly because of the problems I discussed earlier relating to measurement and causal analysis. On top of this, though, the quality of the data collected by OFSTED is likely to be poor, given the pressures under which the inspectors work, the range of different aspects of schools they have to cover, and the nature of the Framework within which they operate[20]. Hargreaves seems to see the task of developing cumulative knowledge about the effectiveness of different pedagogical techniques as much more straightforward than it is.

Here, as elsewhere, his reliance on the medical analogy is potentially misleading. Much medical research, while by no means easy or unproblematic, does not involve the distinctive problems associated with studying social phenomena. We might also note that while he stresses the amount of money spent on educational research, this is only a tiny fraction of that allocated to medical research (for which he provides no estimate). Like is not being compared with like here, in either respect.

Another problem concerns the nature of the relationship that is possible between research and practice in the field of education. In my view, Hargreaves uses a standard to judge current educational research which assumes too direct and instrumental a form of that relationship. Even in the field of medicine it is not clear that this model can be closely approximated. And the thoroughly practical character of teaching – the diverse and difficult-to-operationalise goals, the multiple variables and complex relationships involved – may mean that research can rarely provide sound information about the relative effectiveness of different techniques which is directly applicable. The history of research on 'effective teaching' points strongly in this direction. Furthermore, in my view there is a tension between seeking to improve the rigour of educational inquiry so as to contribute to the cumulation of knowledge, on the one hand, and trying to make its findings of more practical relevance, on the other. There are, of course, those who see no tension here at all; but Hargreaves does not make a case for this, and I do not believe that a convincing one is possible. In the past, he has quoted Lewin's dictum that 'there is nothing so practical as a good theory'

(Hargreaves *et al.,* 1975, p. ix). Yet, the history of action research, in education and elsewhere, provides compelling evidence for the tension between these two orientations[21].

While I disagree with Hargreaves's diagnosis, I do not reject his prescriptions entirely. I have no doubt that practical research carried out by teachers and educational managers in order to further their work can be useful; so long as it is recognised that not every problem needs research to find a solution, and that not every question can be answered by research. However, there are dangers, I think, in this kind of work being required to be scientific. It is designed to serve a different purpose, so that, while there will be some overlap in techniques and relevant considerations, the orientation should be different[22]. Such inquiries are no substitute for academic research, just as the latter is no substitute for them.

I also accept that the establishment of a forum for discussing educational research and its relationship to educational policy-making and practice could be worthwhile. However, I do not believe that giving such a forum a role in planning educational research would be at all helpful. In my view, the currently fashionable view that research can be centrally planned is based on fallacious assumptions about the nature of research and how it can best be coordinated and pursued. The arguments against this were well put by Michael Polanyi in the context of natural science many years ago, and they do not need to be repeated here (Polanyi, 1962); the problems and dangers involved in previous attempts to plan educational research are also instructive (Nisbet & Broadfoot, 1980, pp. 14–17). Moreover, down the road that Hargreaves recommends, and not very far down it at all, lies the extension to the whole of educational research of the contract model recommended by Rothschild for applied research funded by government departments (Rothschild, 1971). That is a destination from which there is probably no return, and not one that is likely to lead to the flourishing of educational research; instead, the latter may become little more than one more public relations tool.

I recognise that the current state of educational research is not healthy, then; but I do not believe that what Hargreaves proposes will remedy it. The diagnosis is mistaken and, taken as a whole, the prescription is likely to be lethal. He emphasises several times the radical nature of what he is proposing, chiding educational researchers for shying at such radicalism. Personally, I have no problem in refusing this fence: radical change is not *necessarily* a good thing (it will often be for the worse rather than for the better); it ought to be adopted only as a last resort, when there is little to be lost (since, at best, it is much more likely to result in unforeseen consequences or unacceptable side effects than less radical change). And I do not accept Hargreaves' judgement that educational research suffers from a *'fatal* flaw' ([p. 6], my emphasis) or that *'there is* [...] *little to lose* in moving as soon as possible to an evidence-based teaching profession' ([p. 13], my emphasis). What could be lost is the substantial researcher and teacher expertise that we currently have.

It is also of significance, though he does not emphasise it, that the evidence-based education which Hargreaves recommends involves a transformation of teaching as well as of research[23]. In particular, it involves extending the accountability of teachers beyond examination league tables and national tests to justifying the details of classroom practice in terms of research evidence. In my view the consequences of his proposals are likely to be as disastrous in this area as they are for educational research.

I would not deny that there is much wrong with the quality of teaching in schools, nor do I believe that research is incapable of providing knowledge that is of practical relevance to improving it. But is seems to me that educational research can only play a fairly limited role in resolving the problems. It can highlight and analyse them, and attempt to provide some understanding. But remedying the failings of schools is a practical business that necessarily depends on professional expertise of a kind that is not reducible to publicly available evidence, even that provided by research. Moreover, in part, the problems stem from the same external factors that have affected research in recent years.

There is one further aspect of Hargreaves' lecture that deserves attention. This is to do with its rhetorical form rather than its content. It is not simply a contribution to debate among researchers about how their work should be organised and carried out. The audience for his lecture was wider. There is nothing wrong with this, of course; but what is unfortunate is that he engages in pre-emptive dismissal of the arguments of fellow researchers who disagree with him, implying that these are rationalisations:

> The research community has yet to face up to the problem. It protects itself and the status quo by a series of defences. [p. 8]

> Rationalising failure to improve practice through research became a self-fulfilling prophecy. [p. 9]

Along with this, Hargreaves dismisses those who are committed to a more conventional approach as simply unwilling to put their house in order:

> Left to ourselves, we educational researchers will not choose the necessary radical reforms. [p. 4]

> Researchers continue their work on their own self-validating terms; they are accountable to themselves; so there is absolutely no reason why they should change. [p. 9]

In effect, he addresses what he has to say over the heads of researchers to those who have the power to intervene: he is inviting in the state troopers! In this sense, his lecture is a political intervention, not just a contribution to scholarly debate; and it will be responded to as such.

For me research, like teaching, is a profession. This does not mean that researchers should have total control over their own affairs, but it does mean that they must have considerable autonomy. Hargreaves portrays us as having more than enough of this. And he is quite open that what he is proposing would involve 'some loss of autonomy' [p. 13]. He argues that this is justified because educational research is not in a healthy state. But where is the evidence to show that his proposed treatment is the most effective means of curing the illness, and that its side effects will fall within acceptable limits? If we are to have evidence-based practice, surely we should have evidence-based policy-making too?[24]

Advocates of evidence-based medicine have often been challenged because they are not able to support their proposals with the kind of evidence that they demand of medical practitioners (see, for example, Norman, 1995). Hargreaves is particulary vulnerable to this challenge, given the admittedly radical character of surgery proposed. He certainly does not provide evidence that 'demonstrates conclusively that if (researchers) change their practice from x to y there will be a significant and enduring improvement in teaching and learning'. Nor has he 'developed an effective method of convincing [researchers] of the benefits of, and means to, changing from x to y'. The fact that he declares researchers unwilling to change is an admission of failure on his part in this latter respect. Instead of accepting responsibility for this, however, which seems to be what he expects researchers to do if they fail to convince teachers, he blames researchers. Moreover, his view of researchers is in danger of being self-fulfilling. The rhetorical strategy he employs – which is not dissimilar to the anti-professional mode of speech found in many government communications directed at teachers, for example in the report of the 'three wise men' (see Hammersley & Scarth, 1993) – is likely to lead to political opposition and counter-argument, rather than to reflection and considered discussion. Researchers are not a powerful constituency, of course. However, to the extent that the aim is to improve educational research rather than to save money by eliminating it (and the motives of those who listen to Hargreaves may well differ from his own), little progress can be made without their support. In these terms, his lecture seems likely to inflame the illness rather than to cure it.

Acknowledgements

My thanks to Roger Gomm for discussion of the ideas in this paper and for drawing my attention to material in the *Health Service Journal*; also to Paul Atkinson, Richard Edwards and Donald Mackinnon for comments on an earlier version of the paper.

Notes

1 On the last of these, see Pettigrew (1994) and Morris (1995).

2 Though I think he is right to deny them, see Hammersley (1987a,1987b).

3 On the recurrent scepticism that has been displayed about the practical contribution of educational research, see Nisbet & Broadfoot (1980, ch. 2).

4 On the contrast between sensitising and definitive concepts, see Blumer (1969). For a review of the distinction, see Hammersley (1989).

5 Hargreaves begins his lecture by stressing the need for cumulative and well-founded research knowledge, as well as for greater applicability. By the end, the emphasis is largely on the latter. In the final paragraph he claims that the changes he is recommending would produce 'far more research that is closely related to policy and practice, that is carried out by and with users, and that leads to results which are more likely to be applied in practice' [p. 13]. By this point, the issue of the quality of the research seems, at best, to have become absorbed into applicability.

6 Hirst (1990) has pointed out that this model may not be an accurate picture of the relationship between theory and practice even in science and technology.

7 See Schön (1983 and 1987) for an influential response to this problem.

8 For a highly critical assessment of school effectiveness research along these lines, see Elliott (1996).

9 In an influential article, Jamous & Peloille seek to operationalise the distinction between professional and non-professional occupations in terms of a ratio between 'technicality' and 'indetermination' (see Jamous & Peloille, 1970, pp. 112–113).

10 For an underused account of 'the structure of formally organized socialization settings' that highlights this dimension, see Wheeler (1966, especially pp. 60–66).

11 Also relevant here is his identification of appreciative, designatory, reflective, immunological and corrective capacities of symbolic interactionist research (Hargreaves, 1978, pp. 19–21).

12 For an early critique, see Little (1950).

13 Indeed, there is evidence to suggest that in some areas at least it is non-clinical research that has led to the major advances (see Strong, 1984, pp. 342–343).

14 It is my view that one of the problems with social science research generally is that this use has come to dominate all others.

15 For a substantial discussion of methodological failings in medical research, see Anderson (1990); see also Feussner (1996).

16 On deviation from the rational model see, for example, Simon (1955) and March (1988). In a recent book explicating the assumptions involved in his research in the health field, and elsewhere, Anselm Strauss argues that these empirical features of action are central to the model of action adopted by symbolic interactionists. See Strauss (1993, ch. 1).

17 Evidence-based medicine could be seen as part of what Strong has referred to as statistical imperialism, as also could the critiques of medical research quoted earlier. See Strong (1984, pp. 344–345 and 350–351).

18 As a common saying has it: 'no patient is ever like a textbook' (cited in Burkett & Knafl, 1974, p. 89). For an illuminating discussion of this issue which provides grounds for caution about reliance on clinical judgement, see Meehl (1957).

19 For some evidence that what is feared is no mirage, see Culyer (1986), Jennett (1988), Brahams (1991), Deighan & Hitch (1995), Clancy (1996), Roberts et al. (1996) and Watson (1996). The person who is widely cited as laying the basis for evidence-based medicine, A. L. Cochrane, had no doubt that efficiency as well as effectiveness is important. His aim was the application of cost–benefit analysis throughout the NHS (see Cochrane, 1972). For a recent

discussion of some of the dilemmas and how they should be resolved, which involves medical practitioners being free to override guidelines in particular cases, see Sackett (1996).

20 Hargreaves' recommendation of better training is unlikely to resolve these problems.

21 For a discussion of the dilemma and ways of handling it in the context of the work of the
Tavistock Institute, see Rapoport (1970, pp. 505–507). It is puzzling that Hargreaves gives no attention to the history of educational action research, in the USA and in Britain. It is surely close to the
kind of development he wants to see, and there is much to be learned from it; not all positive.

22 Indeed, at one point, Hargreaves seems to recognise that what may be most useful in
developing the professional culture of teachers is not so much scientific research as 'accumulated wisdom' in the form of case records, with commentaries and critiques [pp. 7 and 13].

23 This comes out more clearly in Hargreaves (1994).

24 On the latter, see Ham *et al.* (1995) and the letters in the *British Medical Journal* (1995)
310, p. 1141.

References

Altman, D. G. (1994) The scandal of poor medical research, *British Medical Journal*, 308,
  pp. 283–284.
Anderson, B. (1990) *Methodological Errors in Medical Research* (Oxford, Blackwell).
Atkinson, P. A. (1981) *The Clinical Experience* (Farnborough, Gower).
Atkinson, P. A. (1995) *Medical Talk and Medical Work* (London, Sage).
Barrow, R. (1984) *Giving Teaching Back to Teachers* (Brighton, Wheatsheaf).
Becker, H. S., Geer, B., Hughes, E. C. and Strauss, A. (1961) *Boys in White: student culture
  in medical school* (Chicago, University of Chicago Press).
Bennett, N. (1976) *Teaching Styles and Pupil Progress* (London, Open Books).
Bennett, N. (1985) Recent research on teaching–learning processes in classroom settings,
  mimeo.
Blumer, H. (1969) *Symbolic Interactionism* (Englewood Cliffs, NJ, Prentice Hall).
Brahams, D. (1991) Effectiveness research and health gain, *The Lancet*, 338, p. 1386.
Bulmer, M. (1982) *The Uses of Social Research* (London, Allen & Unwin).
Burkett, G. and Knafl, K. (1974) Judgment and decision making in a medical speciality,
  Sociology of Work and Occupations, 1, pp. 82–109.
Carr, W. (1987) What is an educational practice?, *Journal of the Philosophy of Education*, 21,
  pp.163–175.
Chambers, J. H. (1991) The difference between the abstract concepts of science and the general
  concepts of empirical educational research, *Journal of Educational Thought*, 25, pp. 41–49.
Chambers, J. H. (1992) *Empiricist Research on Teaching: a philosophical and practical
  critique of its scientific pretensions* (Boston, MA, Kluwer).
Charlton, B. (1995) Megatrials are subordinate to medical science, *British Medical Journal*,
  311, p. 257.
Clancy, C. (1996) Evidence-based medicine meets cost-effectiveness analysis (editorial),
  Journal of the American Medical Association, 276, pp. 329–330.
Clifford, J. and Marcus, G. (eds) (1986) *Writing Culture: the poetics and politics of
  ethnography* (Berkeley, CA, University of California Press).
Cochrane, A. L. (1972) *Effectiveness and Efficiency* (London, Nuffield Provincial Hospitals
  Trust).
Court, C. (1996) NHS Handbook criticises evidence based medicine, *British Medical Journal*,
  312, pp. 1439–1440.

Cronbach, L. (1975) Beyond the two disciplines of scientific psychology, *American Psychologist*, 30, pp. 116–127.

Culyer, A. J. (1986) Health Service ills: the wrong economic medicine (a critique of David Green's *Which Doctor*), Discussion Paper 16, Centre for Health Economics, University of York.

Dearlove, O., Sharples, A., O'Brien, K. and Dunkley, C. (1995) Many questions cannot be answered by evidence based medicine, *British Medical Journal*, 311, pp. 257–258.

Deighan, M. and Hitch, S. (eds) (1995) *Clinical Effectiveness from Guidelines to Cost-effective Practice* (Health Services Management Unit, University of Manchester, Earlybrave Publications).

Delamont, S. and Hamilton, D. (1984) Revisiting classroom research: a continuing cautionary tale, in: S. Delamont (ed.) *Readings on Interaction in the Classroom* (London, Methuen).

Denzin, N. K. and Lincoln, Y. (eds) (1995) *Handbook of Qualitative Research* (Thousand Oaks, CA, Sage).

Doyle, W. (1977) Learning the classroom environment, *Journal of Teacher Education*, 28, pp. 51–55.

Dunkin, M. J. and Biddle, B. J. (1974) *The Study of Teaching* (New York, Holt, Rinehart and Winston).

Elliott, J. (1996) School effectiveness research and its critics: alternative visions of schooling, *Cambridge Journal of Education*, 26, pp. 199–224.

Feussner, J. (1996) Evidence-based medicine: new priority for an old paradigm, *Journal of Bone and Mineral Research*, 11, pp. 877–882.

Finch, J. (1986) *Research and Policy: the uses of qualitative methods in social and educational research* (Lewes, Falmer Press).

Fowler, P. B. S. (1995) Letter, *The Lancet*, 346, p. 838.

Freese, L. (1980) The problem of cumulative knowledge, in: L. Freese (ed.) *Theoretical Methods in Sociology* (Pittsburgh, PA, University of Pittsburgh Press).

Freidson, E. (1970) *Profession of Medicine: a study of the sociology of applied knowledge* (New York, Dodd, Mead and Co.).

Gage, N. L. (1985) *Hard Gains in the Soft Sciences: the case of pedagogy* (Bloomington, IN, Phi Delta Kappa).

Gage, N. L. (1994) The scientific status of the behavioral sciences: the case of research on teaching, *Teaching and Teacher Education*, 10, pp. 565–577.

Galton, M., Simon, B. and Croll, P. (1980) *Inside the Primary Classroom* (London, Routledge and Kegan Paul).

Glass, G. V. (1994) Review of Chambers, John, H., 1992, *Empiricist Research on Teaching*, *Journal of Educational Thought*, 28, pp. 127–130.

Grahame-Smith, D. (1995) Evidence based medicine: Socratic dissent. *British Medical Journal*, 310, pp. 1126–1127.

Ham, C., Hunter, C. J. and Robinson, R. (1995) Evidence based policymaking, *British Medical Journal*, 310, pp. 71–72.

Hammersley, M. (1985) From ethnography to theory, *Sociology*, 19, pp. 244–259.

Hammersley, M. (1987a) Ethnography and cumulative development of theory: a discussion of Woods's proposal for "phase two" research, *British Educational Research Journal*, 13, pp. 283–296.

Hammersley, M. (1987b) Ethnography for survival? A reply to Woods, *British Educational Research Journal*, 13, pp. 309–317.

Hammersley, M. (1989) The problem of the concept: Herbert Blumer on the relationship between concepts and data, *Journal of Contemporary Ethnography*, 18, pp. 133–159.

Hammersley, M. and Scarth, J. (1993) Beware of wise men bearing gifts: a case study in the misuse of educational research, in: R. Gomm and P. Woods (eds) *Educational Research in Action* (London, Paul Chapman).

Hargreaves, D. H. (1967) *Social Relations in a Secondary School* (London, Routledge and Kegan Paul).

Hargreaves, D. H. (1972) *Interpersonal Relations and Education* (London, Routledge and Kegan Paul).

Hargreaves, D. H. (1978) Whatever happened to symbolic interactionism? in: L. Barton and R. Meighan (eds) *Sociological Interpretations of Schooling and Classrooms* (Driffield, Nafferton Books).

Hargreaves, D. H (1979) A phenomenological approach to classroom decision-making, in: J. Eggleston (ed.) *Teacher Decision Making in the Classroom* (London, Routledge and Kegan Paul).

Hargreaves, D. H. (1981) Schooling for delinquency, in: L. Barton and S. Walker (eds) *Schools Teachers and Teaching* (Lewes, Falmer Press).

Hargreaves, D. H. (1994) *The Mosaic of Learning: schools and teachers for the next century* (London, Demos).

Hargreaves, D. H. (1996) Teaching as a research-based profession: possibilities and prospects, Teacher Training Agency Annual Lecture 1996 (London, Teacher Training Agency). [Chapter 1 of this volume].

Hargreaves, D. H., Hester, S. and Mellor, F. (1975) *Deviance in Classrooms* (London, Routledge and Kegan Paul).

Hirst, P. H. (1983) Educational theory, in: P. H. Hirst (ed.) *Educational Theory and its Foundation Disciplines* (London, Routledge and Kegan Paul).

Hirst, P. H., (1990) The theory–practice relationship in teacher training, in: M. B. Booth, V. J. Furlong and M. Wilkin (eds) *Partnership in Initial Teacher Training* (London, Cassell).

Jackson, P. (1968) *Life in Classrooms* (New York, Holt, Rinehart and Winston).

Jadad, A. R. (1996) 'Are you playing evidence-based medicine games with our daughter?' *British Medical Journal,* 347, p. 247.

Jamous, H. and Pelloile, B. (1970) Professions or self-perpetuating system: changes in the French university-hospital system in: J. A. Jackson (ed.) *Professions and Professionalisation* (Cambridge, Cambridge University Press).

Janowitz, M. (1972) *Sociological Models and Social Policy* (Morristown, NJ. General Learning Systems).

Jennett, B. (1988) Medical ethics and economics in clinical decision-making, in: G. Mooney and A. Mcguire (eds) *Medical Ethics and Economics in Health Care* (Oxford, Oxford University Press).

Jones, G. and Sagar, S. (1995) No guidance is provided for situations for which evidence is lacking, *British Medical Journal,* 311, p. 258.

The Lancet (1995) Editorial, 346, p. 785.

Lather, P. (1991) *Getting Smart: feminist research and pedagogy with/in the postmodern* (New York, Routledge).

Little, I. M. D. (1950) *A Critique of Welfare Economics* (Oxford, Oxford University Press).

March, J. G. (ed.) (1988) *Decisions and Organisations* (Oxford, Blackwell).

Meehl, P. (1957) When shall we use our heads instead of the formula? *Journal of Counselling Psychology,* 4, pp. 268–273

Nisbet, J. and Broadfoot, P. (1980) *The Impact of Research on Policy and Practice in Education* (Aberdeen, Aberdeen University Press).

Norman, G. R. (1995) Letter, *The Lancet,* 346, p. 839.

Norris, N. (1995) Contracts, control and evaluation, *Journal of Education Policy,* 10, pp. 271–285.

O'Connor, D. J. (1957) *An Introduction to the Philosophy of Education* (London, Routledge and Kegan Paul).

Olson, J. (1992) *Understanding Teaching* (Milton Keynes, Open University Press).

Pettigrew, M. (1994) Coming to terms with research: the contract business, in: D. Halpin and B. Troyna (eds) *Researching Education Policy* (London, Falmer Press).

Polanyi, M. (1962) The republic of science, *Minerva*, 1, pp. 54–73.

Rapoport, R. (1970) Three dilemmas in action research, *Human Relations*, 23, pp. 499–513.

Roberts, C., Lewis, P., Crosby, D., Dunn, R. and Grundy, P. (1996) Prove it, *Health Service Journal*, 7 March, l06, 5493, pp. 32–33.

Rothschild, Lord (1971) The organisation and management of government R and D, Cmnd 4184 (London, HMSO).

Sackett, D. L. (1996) *The Doctor's (Ethical and Economic) Dilemma, Office of Health Economics Annual Lecture* (London, Office of Health Economics).

Sackett, D. L., Haynes, R. B. and Tugwell, P. (1985) *Clinical Epidemiology: a basic science for clinical medicine* (Boston, MA, Little, Brown).

Scarth, J and Hammersley, M. (1986a) Some problems in assessing closedness of tasks, in: M. Hammersley (Ed.) *Case Studies in Classroom Research* (Milton Keynes, Open University Press).

Scarth, J. and Hammersley, M. (1986b) Questioning ORACLE'S analysis of teachers' questions, *Educational Research*, 28, pp. 174–184.

Schön D. (1983) *The Reflective Practitioner* (London, Temple Smith).

Schön, D. (1987) *Educating the Reflective Practitioner* (San Francisco, CA, Jossey-Bass).

Schütz, A. (1967) *The Phenomenology of the Social World* (Evanston, IL, Northwestern University Press).

Schwab, J. J. (1969) The practical: a language for curriculum, *School Review*, 78, pp. 1–24.

Shuchman, M. (1996) Evidence-based medicine debated, *The Lancet*, 347, p. 1396.

Simon, H. (1955) A behavioral model of rational choice *Quaterly Journal of Economics*, 69, pp. 99–118.

Strauss, A. L. (1993) *Continual Permutations of Action* (New York, Aldine de Gruyter).

Strong, P. (1984) Viewpoint: the academic encirclement of medicine? *Sociology of Health and Illness*, 6, pp. 341–358.

Taylor, W. (1973) Knowledge and research, in: W. Taylor (ed.) *Research Perspectives in Education* (London, Routledge and Kegan Paul).

Thornton, H. M. (1992) Breast cancer trials: a patient's viewpoint, *The Lancet*, 339, pp. 44–45.

Watson, P. (1996) Knowing the score, *Health Service Journal*, 14 March, 106, 5494, pp. 28–31.

Weiss, C. (1980) *Social Science Research and Decision Making* (New York, Columbia University Press).

Wheeler, S. (1966) The structure of formally organized socialization settings, in: O. G. Brim and S. Wheeler, *Socialization after Childhood: two essays* (New York, Wiley).

Winch, P. (1958) *The Idea of a Social Science and its Relationship to Philosophy* (London, Routledge and Kegan Paul).

Woods, P. (1985) Ethnography and theory construction in educational research, in: R. G. Burgess (ed.) *Field Methods in the Study of Education* (Lewes, Falmer Press).

Woods, P. (1987) Ethnography at the crossroads: a reply to Hammersley, *British Educational Research Journal*, 13, pp. 297–307.

Wragg, E. C. (1976) The Lancaster Study: its implications for teacher training, *British Journal of Teacher Education,* 2, pp. 281–290.

Chapter 3

In defence of research for evidence-based teaching: a rejoinder to Martyn Hammersley

David H. Hargreaves

Introduction

I warmly welcome Martyn Hammersley's critique of my lecture on *'Teaching as a research-based profession: prospects and possibilities'* [Chapter 2 of this volume]. This rejoinder is offered in the same spirit: a concern with quality in both educational research and the professional practice of teachers. In a critique that is twice the length of my original lecture there are, perhaps inevitably, many points with which I take issue. The more minor ones I ignore in this rejoinder, for Hammersley's canvas is wide and it is important not to lose sight of the great issues.

The core of my original argument is simply stated. It is that educational research should and could have much more relevance for, and impact on, the professional practice of teachers than it now has. In the same way, the core of Hammersley's critique is reducible to the view that educational research cannot have the relevance and impact that I claim.

Taken from: *British Educational Research Journal*, Vol. 23, No. 4, 1997, pp. 405–20.

© 1997 British Educational Research Association

Reproduced by kind permission of Taylor & Francis Ltd.

http://www.tandf.co.uk/journals

Elements of both arguments have been made before. The novelty in the present debate is that my argument was strongly coloured by a comparison between education and medicine, with special reference to the way research relates to professional practice. (My argument could have been made without the comparison, as could much of Hammersley's critique.) The essence of the comparison is to highlight similarities and differences between two professions and then draw out some implications. Some differences between the two are essential; it would otherwise be hard to see what one profession could possibly learn from the other. Substantial similarities are also necessary to a useful comparison; the two must be close enough to make transfer of 'good practice' between them a plausible idea.

Hammersley does not reject the value of comparing doctors and teachers. He has 'no doubt at all that this comparison can be illuminating', though he does not disclose in what ways. His critique, like my original argument, focuses on similarities and differences between:

   (i) teachers and doctors;
  (ii) the nature of research in the two professions; and
 (iii) the relation of research to professional practice in both.

Let us examine in turn each of the three sets of similarities and differences.

Doctors and teachers – similarities and differences

At the beginning of my lecture, in the opening section on the comparison, I allude to what I take to be the key similarity, namely that:

> both education and medicine are profoundly people-centred professions. Neither believes that helping people is a matter of simple technical application but rather a highly skilled process in which a sophisticated judgment matches a professional decision to the unique needs of each client.

Now my argument is this. Practising doctors and teachers are applied professionals, practical people making interventions in the lives of their clients in order to promote worthwhile ends – health or learning. Doctors and teachers are *similar* in that they make decisions involving complex judgements. Many doctors draw upon research about the effects of their practice to inform and improve their decisions; most teachers do not, and this is a *difference*. Educational research could and should generate a better equivalent for teachers; reducing the difference would enhance the quality of teachers' decision-making.

In his critique, Hammersley also takes the view that teaching is not a technical activity but one which involves judgement. Teaching, he asserts, is 'practical rather than technical in character ... a matter of making judgements rather than following rules'. In short, he agrees with me in full on this matter. Why, then, in his critique does he make the point at such length, including reference to my own earlier writings? Because he wants to argue that (i) this is incompatible with my view that there can and should be some hard evidence, on 'what works' to enhance teachers' professional practices, and (ii) that such evidence cannot be achieved in the field of education, even in principle.

The precise extent to which Hammersley shares my view that doctors and teachers are very similar with regard to the importance of judgement in decision-making is never made explicit. His emphasis is on the salience of 'practical' (judgement-rich) rather than 'technical' (just rule-following) decisions among teachers. Sensibly he does not deny that there is some rule-following among teachers. In many of their routine classroom decisions teachers learn to follow the kinds of 'recipes' described by Alfred Schütz (1964) – the typical means for bringing about typical ends in typical situations – that are used for:

> interpreting the social world and for handling things and men in order to obtain the best results in every situation with a minimum of effort by avoiding undesirable consequences. (p. 28)

Within many professions, similar rules form a tacit professional common-sense knowledge. In daily practice, every competent practitioner, says Donald Schön (1983):

> makes innumerable judgements of quality for which he cannot state adequate criteria, and he displays skills for which he cannot state the rules and procedures ... On the other hand, both ordinary people and professional practitioners often think about what they are doing, sometimes even while doing it ... It is this entire process of reflection-in-action which is central to the 'art' by which practitioners sometimes deal with situations of uncertainty, instability, uniqueness and value conflict. (p. 50)

Schön's 1983 book has been profoundly influential in teacher education and it is through his attack on 'technical rationality' that this concept is best known to teacher educators. It was statements such as the one above that I had in mind when pointing out that judgement was inherent in the decision-making of both doctors and teachers.

Hammersley portrays the distinction between 'technical' and 'practical' as a continuum, and locates teachers generally at the 'practical' end where decision-making depends on 'experience, wisdom, local knowledge and judgement'. He suggests that doctors are towards the 'technical' end of the spectrum[1]. I know of no research which quantifies such decisions in medicine and education, and Hammersley cites none. I am not even persuaded that this distinction involves a continuum. In my experience both doctors and teachers sometimes engage in rule-following and sometimes make decisions on the basis of explicitly considered judgement. Novices in both have to be taught the recipes and their limits.

To cite that great physician, Oliver Wendell Holmes (1871), 'The young man knows the rules, but the old man knows the exceptions', a maxim as applicable in education as in medicine. When junior doctors thoughtlessly apply a rule-based recipe, learnt from textbooks, they are rebuked by the supervising consultant for treating the X-ray or the disease *rather than the patient.* They are, in other words, failing to take account of the distinctive features of the patient-in-context which make the application of the recipe inappropriate. Doctors learn to read the patient-in-context in order to be expert clinicians, just as teachers learn to read pupils-in-context, but both, as Schön says, continue to use recipes sometimes.

Hammersley realises that he cannot make too much of this purported difference between teachers and doctors, for he rightly points to the importance of clinical judgement in medical decision-making. He refers to the work of sociologists. (Howard Becker, Eliot Freidson, Paul Atkinson) on whose authority[2] he announces that 'Clinical decision-making is not based *solely,* or even primarily, on knowledge drawn *directly* from research publications' (italics added). Of course it isn't, nor did I argue that it is or should be. Nor do doctors themselves so contend. Indeed, the cited sociologists are not making a grand discovery, but merely reporting what doctors themselves say about their diagnostic and therapeutic decisions.

> The preliminary assessment of the diagnostic possibilities stems from the unique qualities of the human mind which is able to take in a very large number of data, to sift their relative significance in an incredibly short time, and to recognize therefrom a pattern … It is skill more closely allied to the skill of a connoisseur examining a picture or an old violin than it is to what we normally think of as science. (Lord Platt, physician, 1972, p. 26)

> Any man who is not positively ham-fisted to begin with can in the end achieve the dexterity to perform safe, sound surgery … The decision to operate, when to operate and what operation to do, is in nearly every circumstance more important for the patient's welfare then precisely how the operation is done. (Sir Hedley Atkins, surgeon, 1977, p. 60)[3]

In short, Hammersley acknowledges the significance of judgement in clinical decision-making, and so concedes my core similarity between doctors and teachers. He seeks to weaken this similarity by claiming a key difference, that doctors' decisions are mainly 'technical' whereas teachers' are mostly 'practical', but he does not substantiate the claim.

The nature of research in the two professions – similarities and differences

Hammersley sees a vast difference in the nature of research in the two professions. He is right, but only partly so. That he is also partly wrong vitiates much of his argument. The thrust of his case is that (i) medical research is 'positivist', concerned with 'fixed, universal relationships rather than local context-sensitive patterns in which interpretation and decision … play an important role' ; and that (ii) the kind of research I advocate for evidence-based teaching as a parallel to evidence-based medicine is mistaken because teaching is not open to such research[4]. He is wrong on both counts, as I shall show.

The practice of medicine has a complex knowledge-base, which is by no means some homogeneous 'science'. One must distinguish at least three levels to the knowledge-base that underpins clinical practices:

- at the root are the natural, and especially the biological, sciences;
- on these are then built the specifically medical and clinical sciences;
- and finally come the studies of 'what works' in clinical practices.

All are in some sense scientific, but not in the same sense. It is not a simple linear structure: medical decisions and practices are far from being a direct application of universal laws characteristic of the underlying natural sciences. To undercut the parallel between medical and educational practice, Hammersley has to condense these three levels into one, as when he asserts that medicine 'is a conception of professionalism which emphasises reliance on an established body of scientific knowledge[5]. This condensation confuses and oversimplifies the nature of medical research and its relationship to the complexities of medical practice.

In line with the importance of judgement in clinical decision-making, some aspects of medicine have been described by 'insiders' as more like the arts than the sciences.

[S]cience by its very essence is concerned with the general, the repeatable elements in nature including human nature; but medicine, using science, is concerned with the particularity, the uniqueness of individual patients. In its concern with the particular and the unique, medicine resembles the arts. … [I]n its concentration on the repeatable patterns and laws of nature science must of necessity be impersonal; it records the meaningless processes which would continue whether we were there or not to participate. Medicine, on the other hand, must be concerned with what illness and disease mean for a given patient. This is not to say that disease has a meaning (diseases are impersonal like any other processes which can be understood by science), but it is to say that diseases have meanings for patients. One and the same disease might have quite a different meaning for two patients and therefore different treatments might be appropriate. The arts are vehicles through which human beings articulate the meanings of their lives … (Downie, 1994, p. xvii)

This perspective has a long history within medicine. Oliver Wendell Holmes (1871) expressed it memorably: 'Medicine is the most difficult of sciences and the most laborious of arts'. In other words, in making a clinical decision a doctor strikes a balance between what is known from natural science (basic laws and causes), from medical sciences (e.g. the effects of a drug on organs), from tradition (inherited within the specialty), from what one was taught (early professional socialisation) and from personal experience (what therapeutic action one has learnt works with what kind of patient in what situation). Whilst recognising all these elements in their decisions, doctors may nevertheless use scientific investigation into the effects of decisions to contribute to improving the quality of the final judgement. What I draw from evidence-based medicine is that research into practice becomes an explicit but *additional* component in clinical judgement to enhance, not displace, the sophisticated skills involved. The same notion, I urged in the lecture, could be usefully developed to improve teachers' practices and decision-making.

Hammersley's error is to treat the research underlying medical practice as essentially homogeneous and as positivistic, working on physical phenomena in the interests of discovering universal laws and patterns of physical causation. Doubtless this applies to the root natural sciences and to some degree to the medical and clinical sciences. But with research into practice, the kind of research at the heart of evidence-based medicine, we are in the world of human beings making complex decisions. Hammersley's claims that 'much medical research ... does not involve the distinctive problems associated with studying social phenomena' or that 'much medical research avoids many of the problems that face educational researchers, in particular those deriving from the peculiarities of the social world' are contextually untenable when applied to the medical research with which my lecture was concerned (and to the kind of research I am advocating in education). My thesis is not concerned with basic medical research, but with the research that uses scientific methods to assess the effects of clinical decisions on patients. When Hammersley writes, 'human social life is quite different in character from the physical world studied by natural scientists (and we might add, from that investigated by most medical researchers)', his point may apply to the natural sciences at the root of medicine, but is off-beam when applied to research into the effects of doctors' clinical decisions about patients. His depiction of the knowledge-base of medical practice is, in short, crude oversimplification.

The relation of research to practice in medicine and education – similarities and differences

Isaiah Berlin (1996) speaks of 'practical wisdom' as:

> a sense of what will 'work' and what will not. It is a capacity, in the first place, for synthesis rather than analysis, for knowledge in the sense in which trainers

know their animals, or parents their children, or conductors their orchestras, as opposed to that in which chemists know the contents of their test tubes or mathematicians know the rules that their symbols obey ... Above all it is an acute sense of what fits with what, what springs from what, what leads to what; how things seem to vary to different observers, what the effects of such experience upon them may be; what the result is likely to be in a concrete situation of the interplay of human beings and impersonal forces – geographical or biological or psychological ... (pp. 46–47)

Such 'practical wisdom' pervades expert medical and educational practice. There is some hard science deep in the knowledge-base of doctors, but the closer a doctor gets to an individual patient, the stronger the elements of judgement or of 'practical wisdom' that also enter into the decision. Teachers acquire 'practical wisdom' too; but, in comparison with doctors, they have little accepted scientific knowledge to insert into their decision-making.

The knowledge-base of teachers is less rich than that of doctors – a key difference. Two elements are weaker. First, there is a poor infrastructure to the knowledge-base of teachers comparable to the natural sciences and biology for doctors. It was once thought that this could be created through psychological and sociological theory and research, from which general laws on learning and organisations might be applied to educational phenomena. The outcome so far has been disappointing, though it may be that cognitive psychologists and neuroscientists will soon produce something finer. The argument of my lecture was plainly not suggesting how to generate this deep scientific infrastructure for education, though I urge protection of 'blue skies' and basic research that might. Secondly, for teachers there is relatively little hard evidence of 'what works'; and what exists is often not readily available in a form on which teachers can draw as a resource to guide their practices. My lecture sought to stimulate this different, but complementary, research around professional practice. To forge the right relationship between research and practice in education, both elements need to be strengthened. Take the case of literacy. We need basic research on how children learn to read and write, and from this draw possible implications for teachers' practices. One can also start with evidence on which teacher practices are most effective in the teaching of literacy and work backwards, so to speak, to implications for how basic studies on pupil learning might proceed. Each feeds the other. Progress does not always have to wait for advances at the basic level. Some educational research contributes to neither; it is much of that which falls between the two that I rejected as second rate.

Teachers and doctors are pragmatic professionals. They are primarily interested in *what works in what circumstances* and only secondarily in *why* it works. There are immense difficulties in disentangling what works from what does not, and even more in giving a satisfactory explanation in some scientific sense. Doctors can produce a scientific explanation for what they do in far more areas of their professional activities than teachers can. At the same time, in the lecture I cited several doctors to show that there is a much weaker scientific base to medical practice than is commonly assumed – and for obvious reasons doctors do not strive to undermine this public confidence in their knowledge-base. Much medical decision-making proceeds on the basis of experience of what works rather than knowledge of precisely how and why it works. Indeed, some medical specialties, such as anaesthetics, would be severely retarded if practice were disallowed in the absence of scientific explanation. Many clinical practices have developed on the basis of trial and error – a very old friend to human learning. As biologist George C. Williams (1996) puts it:

> The evolution of fishhooks has undoubtedly been much influenced by a selection process. Those variants found to catch more fish were more likely to be made (or ordered) than those that caught fewer – a process that takes place *with or without understanding*. If a hook with a 20 mm shank was more reliable than one with a 25 mm shank, it would be favourably selected. There was no heed to *understand* why 20 was better than 25. (pp. 12–13, italics added)

Much, possibly most, of what teachers do in classrooms cannot at present be given a firm explanatory grounding in social science, but they do not remain inactive until one is found. They 'tinker', engaging in trial and error learning, just as doctors (or fishermen) often do:

> Essentially teachers are artisans working primarily alone, with a variety of new and cobbled-together materials, in a personally designed work environment. They gradually develop a repertoire of instructional skills and strategies ... through a somewhat haphazard process of trial and error, usually when one or other segment of the repertoire does not work repeatedly. Somewhere in that cycle they may reach out to peers or even to professional trainers, but they will typically transform those inputs into a more private, personally congenial form ... [This] makes technical communication between teachers a very difficult exercise because the repertoire under discussion is a wholly personal invention and because so much of it has been automatized. The information is unique and, in important ways, inarticulate ... One finds, of course, the same phenomenon among superior artists, athletes, craftspeople, mechanics and even surgeons ... (Huberman, 1993, p. 136)

It is here that the significance of evidence-based medicine lies. Much clinical work depends on 'best practice' (i.e. what works) derived from tradition and personal experience. Both are potentially deeply flawed, so must be subject to scientific test. When evidence is produced on whether one therapy rather than another makes for a more effective or speedier benefit to patients in certain categories or circumstances, it becomes a valuable component in the matrix of factors considered by a doctor in making a clinical decision. Research transforms individual tinkering into public knowledge that has greater validity and can be shared among the profession as the evidential base for better clinical practice.

Teachers' lack of a deep, scientific knowledge-base for their professional practice is no bar against using scientific procedures to assess the effects of pedagogic practices and decisions. Such research can proceed even if the likelihood (or, as Hammersley might think, the very possibility) of discovering the scientific laws and the deep causal structures affecting classroom life is denied. Such research already exists in education; my argument is that we need more of it of a higher quality. In the lecture I did not identify what I judge to be good (or bad) research; naming names invariably upsets people and distracts from the argument. Hammersley cites two names – Neville Bennett and Maurice Galton – to exemplify the difficulties inherent in the pursuit of classroom research. To me they also exemplify worthwhile research in education of the type that evidence-based teaching requires[6]. Bennett's 1976 research on teaching styles and pupil progress did indeed reveal some of the complexities both of teaching and of researching it. No simple patterns or universal laws were uncovered or causative structures disclosed. Judged from the angle of positivistic science, Bennett's work scores badly. Judged from a very different scientific angle, on whether it contributes to an understanding of what works in what circumstances, the study makes a useful, if necessarily tentative, advance. The book became entangled in two disputes. The first was a political dispute on the study's (oversimplified) policy implications. The second was a methodological dispute among social scientists. The effect was to scare off other educational researchers from further advances in the field. That a decade later Galton and his colleagues on the ORACLE project made significant progress within this broad field is a credit to their growing sophistication at both policy and methodological levels. Here is work I admire: it does not aspire to be 'basic' social science; it is cumulative, for it contributed to later work by, for example, Peter Mortimore and Robin Alexander; and it contributes usefully to decisions on policy and practice.

Hammersley notes that in the lecture I ignored 'action research' in education and its potential here, and I should rectify the omission. The father of action research is Kurt Lewin, who is also regarded as the father of experimental social psychology. I frequently quote Lewin's dictum that 'there is nothing so practical as a good theory' precisely because Lewin believed that research has a double function – *both* to produce high-quality social science *and* to generate applications for human betterment. This is no mean task, especially within a single project rather than a research programme. Although some action researchers in education, notably those associated with the name of the late Lawrence Stenhouse, in the UK and Australia especially, acknowledge Lewin's influence, they seem largely to have abandoned the first element in his double function of research, perhaps in part because they have turned to Habermas and Schön as inspirational sources. Whilst this school has championed the 'teacher as researcher', and doubtless teachers have profited as individual 'reflective practitioners' from their studies, I have no evidence that, taken as a whole, teachers-as-researchers and their supervisors have generated the cumulative body of knowledge of the kind that Lewin envisaged[7] or that the outcomes have been widely disseminated. Educational research inspired by evidence-based medicine would probably be closer to Lewin and Galton, and the teacher-led research done under the Teacher Training Agency's Research Grants Scheme, than to some versions of action research.

I am, however, a pluralist, believing that a diversity of research approaches is most likely to produce high-quality applications *and* a scientific infrastructure. The research needed to support evidence-based teaching is characterised in terms of its motive and purpose – the wish to throw light on professional practice in an 'actionable' form[8] not a specific methodology. Ethnography – the sphere of Hammersley's expertise – may not be in the vanguard here, but I do not rule out any approach in principle. Evidence-based teaching is likely to promote much more experimental work than has been undertaken in education in recent years, but I accept that such a trend might not gladden the hearts of interactionists.

Is evidence-based medicine worth emulating?

Hammersley accepts that there are many similarities between doctors and teachers. He cannot deny that there is research on clinical practices and that some doctors use this as part of their clinical decision-making. He can deny that such research is possible with education, even in principle. But he knows that many educational researchers, from traditions other than his own, will not accept such a principled rejection of the possibility of an educational equivalent. To save his case he must throw doubt on the very notion of evidence-based medicine, the idea that research on clinical practice can be practically useful to doctors in their clinical decision-making. If he can succeed in so doing, he undermines my suggestion that we should change educational research to produce an equivalent for teachers.

Now Hammersley is right that evidence-based medicine is by no means uncontroversial among doctors. He correctly records features of the dispute, including views that too much emphasis may be placed on the salience of research findings in clinical decision-making, or that advocates of evidence-based medicine vary in their recommendations, or that the quality of the evidence is not always strong enough to warrant the conclusions drawn. Clearly, in both medicine and education, the more robust the research evidence, the more trustworthy it is likely to be as an element in shaping professional practice. For example, if a number of well-designed studies all confirm that treatment X is more effective than Y in the vast majority of cases of Z condition, then the argument for accepting an influence on professional practice is very strong. In medicine it is not always easy to reach a high standard in this regard, which is why there seems to be more self-criticism in medical than in educational research. The evidence is often imperfect. The outcomes of research into the impact of treatment X versus Y is a probability – the 'exceptions' form the focus of further research[9]. If the effects are demonstrated on a significant number of subjects against controls, and are replicated, the research can be treated as conclusive, i.e. relied upon.

In an important paper, Wynn Harlen (1997) draws attention to the guidelines being used by doctors in Scotland to judge the quality of the evidence. At the highest level (of six) stands evidence obtained from meta-analysis of several randomised controlled trials; at the lowest level is evidence obtained from expert committee reports or opinions and/or clinical experience of respected authorities. Harlen then creatively explores an equivalent scale for educational researchers. In educational research we have little at the highest level. In noting that the best evidence rests on randomised controlled trials that have been replicated, doctors are setting rigorous standards: they know the dangers of relying on a poorly designed single study or on expert opinion. Over the last two years I have witnessed how many young consultants and their juniors are very dubious about research where the evidence falls short of the top two categories. As Dunn & Everitt (1995) advise medical students: 'In all situations we should be demanding to see the evidence that a particular claim is merited so that we can assess its validity for ourselves' (p. 2).

Thus, in my lecture I set a high standard: research should provide decisive and conclusive evidence that if teachers do X rather than Y in their professional practice, there will be a significant and enduring improvement in outcome.

> If 60 per cent of observed cases have produced the given result, then we conclude that, on the evidence, there is a 60 per cent probability of the next case doing so as well. (Scruton, 1997, p. 16).

Without high probabilities of an improved outcome, and demonstration of enduring effects, supported by confirming replications, the outcome is probably trivial or merely Hawthorne effect and cannot reasonably be used as decisive grounds for urging a teacher to change from X to Y. It is as vital in education as in medicine to make evidence trustworthy before expecting practitioners to use it to inform their practice[10]. Doctors are raising standards over what should count as a usable research finding, as Hammersley confirms[11]. We in education should follow suit. In the absence of decisive evidence, changing from X to Y is, and should remain, a matter of shifting fashion, current ideology or personal preference.

This is one of the lessons to be learnt from Bennett's research: it is not that it was mistaken in principle, but that the reanalysis of the findings led to different conclusions and implications and exposed the danger of over-hasty application of unreplicated findings. In both professions evidence at a lower level is worthwhile[12], if recognised as flawed and/or provisional and so treated with caution. Hammersley dismissively claims that in education 'strict experimentation is often ruled out for practical or ethical reasons' without pausing to examine the severe ethical and practical difficulties that doctors have overcome to pursue randomised controlled trials[13] or the significance of natural experiments in the social sciences that are relevant to education (e.g. Sherif, 1966; cf. Hargreaves, 1994).

Hammersley's account culminates in the argument that evidence-based medicine may become a means of challenging the autonomy of the clinician and an instrument of increasing the accountability and efficiency of doctors. He is right that evidence can be used in a drive for greater efficiency and accountability from doctors. Indisputable evidence that there is no detectable advantage to patients in using an expensive drug rather than a cheap alternative might be used to limit the freedom of doctors to prescribe the expensive drug. Indeed, it is arguable that the value of such evidence is that it allows the service to be more effective and efficient without diminishing the treatment of the patients but at the cost of limiting one element of professional discretion. This may sometimes be justifiable and socially beneficial, but is not a line Hammersley allows. He leaps instead from one premature conclusion that 'evidence-based medicine threatens to assist attacks on the professionalism of doctors by managers in the NHS' to another populist speculation that 'this move towards evidence-based accountability does not seem likely to enhance the professionalism of teachers, quite the reverse. It seems more likely further to demoralise and undermine the professional judgement of practitioners'. Policy-makers or politicians could indeed use evidence about teaching as a means of making teachers more accountable or of increasing efficiency in the system – it already happens in the matter of class size and its relation to student achievement. But it seems bizarre to conclude from this that we should avoid creating evidence about what does and does not work in classrooms, for fear it might be distorted and used against the profession by outsiders. The logical consequence would be to do no more research at all on 'what works', reducing the matter to a contest between a professional opinion and a political one. It may be that sometimes the profession will find that research fails to substantiate its preferences or gets distorted. Professionalism means facing up to that possibility, not disengaging from research for fear of its consequences.

There are risks in striving towards a more evidence-based teaching but I believe teachers would welcome more evidence (in the words of my lecture) on 'what works with whom under what conditions and with what effects' as a means of improving the quality of what they do in classrooms. Hammersley implies that debate among doctors about the power and value of evidence-based medicine somehow throws doubt on the whole enterprise. Some doctors do indeed believe that the claims for evidence-based medicine have been exaggerated by the enthusiasts, but the considered judgement of *The Lancet's* editorial[14] leaves no doubt about the acceptance of the underlying principles. 'Advocates of evidence-based medicine', it sagely advises, 'can now afford to lower their profile to ensure that their evolving ideas find a secure place in medical practice'. This does not support Hammersley's implied case against trying something similar in education. The promotion of evidence-based teaching would stimulate a heated debate among teachers and researchers about the quality of research evidence and its place in shaping the decisions and judgements of teachers, a debate which would in my view be healthy for the professionalism of both. Hammersley's appeal to teachers' fears is geared to kill the very idea of evidence-based teaching in its infancy. Evidence-based clinical decision-making, say Haynes *et al*, (1997), has three components: clinical expertise; patient preferences; evidence from research. Three steps are essential: getting the evidence straight; developing clinical policy from evidence; applying the policy in the right place and time. Pursuing a parallel to these three components and three steps, in a new partnership between researchers and practitioners, in order to improve the quality of teacher decision-making is still an option.

Hammersley's conclusions: some comments

That 'educational research can only play a fairly limited role in resolving the problems' of teachers' practices; that 'remedying the failings of schools ... depends on professional expertise of a kind that is not reducible to publicly available evidence, even that provided by research'; and that educational research's 'main function ... is to inform public debates about educational issues' are among Hammersley's presuppositions which shape his critique, not conclusions from it. The Conclusion section of Hammersley's critique is not a summary of, or a series of implications derived from, the preceding argument, but a tailpiece with some different and curiously emotive arguments.

Hammersley thinks I 'exaggerate the contribution [educational research] can make, *even in principle*' (original italics). I will accept that, to interactionists or phenomenologists, much of my argument may be flawed or rejected in principle. If, however, this sceptical position were to be generally adopted by educational researchers, many current research lines would come to an abrupt end. This is the unstated conclusion to be drawn from his argument. Most educational researchers are not interactionists, however, and may be more open-minded to the idea that research can guide professional practice, and so continue, as I do, to adhere to the British Educational Research Association's early mission, namely that the:

> broad aim of the Association is to encourage the pursuit of educational research and its application for both *the improvement of educational practice* and for the general benefit of the community. (italics added)

If Hammersley's conviction that researchers have promised, and users have expected, too much from research is sound, one is bound to question whether it is worth spending some £70 million[15] each year, for I doubt whether funders would supply this level of funding (let alone the increase being sought) if educational research is limited to the 'enlightenment' model[16]. Hammersley is clearly unhappy that I should raise the value for money question[17]. My conclusion on this matter was not, of course, based only on what a few teachers say (an unworthy suggestion), but if the improvement of educational practice is an aim of educational research, then practising teachers should be key judges of the quality and value of research outputs. Hammersley doubts whether teachers are the best judges. They may lack the skills to pronounce on the technical quality of research, but as judges of the relevance of research to, and usefulness for, professional practice, teachers are indispensable. By implication, for Hammersley the best judges are researchers themselves, for he says they are a profession that must enjoy considerable autonomy. Not surprisingly, Hammersley is unhappy at my proposal of a National Educational Research Forum in which teachers and policy-makers play a role alongside researchers in constructing an agenda for research priorities, which he represents as meaning that research would be 'centrally planned' or done 'under the direction of teachers', which are distortions to support his opposition to an idea which has wide support among researchers[18].

Hammersley takes exception to the 'rhetorical form' of the lecture. It was a public lecture, lasting 45 minutes, not a journal article, and I was addressing a wide audience. It was a call for change and there is nothing reprehensible in that. As in Socrates's questions[19]:

> To give a general definition, is not the art of rhetoric a method of influencing men's minds by means of words, whether the words are spoken in a court of law or before some other public body or in private conversation? ... [and] ... if a speech is to be classed as excellent, does not that presuppose knowledge of the truth about the subject of the speech in the Mind of the speaker? (pp. 71–73)

By this definition, both of us engage in rhetoric – and both of us seek to ground our persuasion in a true understanding of research and practice in medicine and education. The lecture was not 'a pre-emptive dismissal of arguments of fellow researchers who disagree': my reputation is one of provoking debate, not stifling it. Hammersley admits that what distressed him is that I talk to people outside the circle of educational researchers. In a revealing sentence he complains that:

> [i]n effect, he addresses what he has to say *over the heads of researchers* to those who have power to intervene: he is inviting in the *state troopers!* In this sense, his lecture is a *political* intervention, not just a contribution to scholarly debate: and it will be responded to as such. (italics added)

What Hammersley means by 'political intervention' is unclear, though his disapproving tone is unmistakable. If by politics is meant, in Oakeshott's (1951) famous definition, 'the activity of attending to the general arrangements of a set of people whom chance or choice have brought together' (p. 136), then I plead guilty. We researchers survive largely on public money and the social arrangements which structure our relationships with one another and our various partners could and should be something we constantly monitor and at times question. Indeed, on the very day I gave the Teacher Training Agency lecture (16 April 1996) the newspapers ran the story that a report of the National Academies Policy Advisory Group, formed by the British Academy, the Medical Royal Colleges, the Royal Academy of Engineering and the Royal Society – state troopers? – recommended that £50 million should be taken away from research in subject areas such as art and design, business studies *and education* and redirected to fund the training of university teachers. If *we* do not question the quality and value of educational research, and take whatever action flows from that analysis, then others will. In the light of such developments, Hammersley's implication that we just get on with making our contributions to scholarly debate is dangerously myopic.

Hammersley does not reject my prescriptions entirely – though what he commends rarely goes beyond vague generalities – but concludes that 'taken as a whole, the prescription is likely to be lethal'. A similar pessimism is sometimes found in medicine: major advances are often greeted with scepticism or opposition among gerontocrats. Hammersley's complacency with the *status quo,* his narrowing conception of what is legitimate or feasible research, and his advocated reduction in the aspirations of researchers, all these are more likely in time to damage educational research than what I now propose. Without question it will take time, ingenuity and massive determination to give teaching a stronger, variegated, scientific knowledge-base to complement professional judgement. It is on such qualities that most scientific advance ultimately rests; success will not come to us overnight, any more than it did in medicine.

> There was no convincing evidence, in the early part of the [nineteenth] century, that the physician trained in science had better results that the older physicians who were not thus trained ... [I]t was not at all obvious that the knowledge of, say, chemistry, enabled a nineteenth century physician to provide better health care ... Medical science had not as yet become translated into convincing practical results. There was no good evidence that long and expensive training in the medical sciences was the sole means of making effective doctors. (King, 1982, p. 297)

The rapid development of cognitive science (for example) in recent times gives me rising confidence that in the next decade we might achieve something comparable for teachers to the significance of chemistry in the knowledge-base of doctors. In the interim, an equivalent for teachers to evidence-based medicine is an intermediate goal. I unashamedly identify with George Eliot's (1871) doctor, Tertius Lydgate, with his:

> conviction that the medical profession as it might be was the finest in the world: presenting the most perfect interchange between science and art; offering the most direct alliance between intellectual conquest and the social good.

I feel much the same about teaching and educational research.

Notes

1 My hospital fieldwork makes me uneasy with this generalisation, for there are differences between medical specialities. Orthopaedic surgery, and operations such as hip or knee replacement, have more 'technical' elements associated with 'the engineering model' than, say, psychiatry. Similarly, there are big differences for teachers within classrooms. Dealing with a persistent miscreant is likely to be less 'technical' than telling a pupil that a proffered answer to a question is correct.

2 Hammersley takes a narrow view of the literature, which is too extensive to detail here. Readings edited by Arkes & Hammond (1986), Dowie & Elstein (1988) and Llewelyn & Hopkins (1993) provide useful introductions. I will supply any interested reader with a fuller bibliography. Some of my own work relevant to this is reported in two books in press – see note 3 below.

3 Both quotations are used in the chapters devoted to clinical judgement in Hargreaves *et al.* (1997) *On-the-job Training for Surgeons: a practical guide,* and Hargreaves *et al.* (1997) *On-the-job Training for Physicians: a practical guide.*

4 My position appears to Hammersley to be one 'that many educational researchers will dismiss as positivist'. He does not label me a positivist; we both know that to be described as a 'positivist' – and a 'narrowly instrumental' one at that – is to be dismissed by many educational researchers: the term is now one of disparagement, not useful description.

5 This lies uneasily alongside such claims as that by Vice-Chancellor Henry Miller: 'The fact is that medicine consists of a few well-lit islands of scientific certitude surrounded by a boundless ocean of uncertainty and ignorance' (Lock & Windle, 1977). But which of my three levels is Hammersley referring to?

6 One research study which exemplifies many of the points I make in the original article and here is Adey & Shayer's project on cognitive acceleration (1994), because it designs an intervention, relates it to basic research and theory, and then evaluates its impact over an extensive sample and time period with control groups. See also note 9 below.

7 Action research could nevertheless be restored to its earlier commitments:

'We consider Lewin himself to be an action scientist, but since his time there has been a tendency to divorce his contributions to science from those to practice. Research in social psychology has relied on experimental methods for testing hypothesized relationships between a small number of variables, and it has become distant from practice. Practitioners in the applied behavioural sciences, with some exceptions, have focused on helping clients and have given little attention to testing scientific generalizations … Lewin was committed to the kind of science that would improve social practice ... The Lewinian tradition of action science … is that of scholar practioners in group dynamics and organization science who have sought to integrate science and practice … Members of the tradition have emphasized continuities between the activities of science and the activities of learning in the action context, the mutually reinforcing values of science, democracy and education, and the benefits of combining science and social practice ... In action science we create communities of inquiry in communities of practice … Action science builds on the preferences of practitioners for valid information and consistency, by creating conditions for public testing and disconfirmation of knowledge claims' (Argyris *et al.,* 1985)

8 'There is a profound gap ... between applicable and actionable knowledge. The former tells you what is relevant; the latter tells you how to implement it in the world of everyday practice' (Argyris & Schön, 1974).

9 Leo & Galloway (1996) have ingeniously provided a range of possible explanations for the lack of effect of the intervention on some of Adey & Shayer's students – see note 6

above – which should lead both to better explanation of findings and to adjusted intervention with even more powerful outcomes,

10 I also set a second criterion that researchers should have developed a method of convincing teachers of the benefits and a means of implementing them in their practice. This, too, is a very tough criterion; but is there much point in developing the possibility of better practice if the problems of actually getting it into practice are ignored?

11 Ironically, he makes my case for me in that this does not invalidate evidence-based medicine or evidence-based teaching, but reinforces the need for stringent criteria for educational research used to influence professional practice.

12 Note that I do not claim, as Hammersley implies, a 'contrast in quality' (p. 15) between medical and educational research. I am simply not competent to begin to judge the quality of medical research any more than Hammersley is, and for that reason cannot say – could anyone? – whether one is better than the other. I have no interest in judging 'relative success' except in the sense of saying that in medicine, research is used to inform practice more often than in education (which is indisputable) because of the ways researchers behave (which Hammersley disputes).

13 A recent example of the determination to overcome these problems is Russell (1995).

14 Editorial of *The Lancet,* 346, 23 September, 1995, p. 785. It is worth noting that the 29 April 1995 Editorial of the *British Medical Journal* stated that the issue was 'a celebration of evidence-based medicine'. Editorials are probably a better gauge of medical opinion than the letters on which Hammersley relies; letters to these journals are probably as typical of their population as are, say, letters to *The Times* of British attitudes as a whole.

15 Michael Bassey's revised estimate of £66 million *(Research Intelligence, 59,* 1997) excludes some elements of my own earlier estimate of £50–60 million, such as the £5 million annual cost of higher-degree students undertaking research of various kinds.

16 Hammersley suggests that I reject the enlightenment model. I cannot see how he reaches this conclusion since I say quite clearly that it is true that educational research has an indirect influence on policy and practice. My concern is the implications that arise if there is *only* indirect influence and a complete absence of something more usable. This appears to be Hammersley's version of enlightenment: if so, it is indeed one I reject.

17 Of course there are problems with a cost-benefit approach, but this does not mean we can ignore the need to make judgements about value for money. Funders, whether they be government departments, agencies or charities, do it all the time. So should we. If we did it more frequently, we might get better at it. Here, as elsewhere in his critique, Hammersley seems to be arguing that inaction is the prudent course when there are difficulties.

18 It is curious that Hammersley slides into such language, since his early summary of my lecture accurately states my position that the Forum is (in his words) 'to facilitate dialogue among the stakeholders'. The Forum would have no funds and funding bodies would retain their freedom to allocate money as they thought fit, taking account of my agenda to emerge from the Forum's discussion. William Kay's representation of the Forum as a 'Stalinist central planning model' *(Research Intelligence, 59,* 1997, p. 20) is a risible example of the paranoid defence deployed by some researchers to preserve their rights to decide what research they should do. Such a Forum could do much to ensure a more cumulative approach to research, on the need for which Hammersley agrees. The idea of a Forum has been floated by the group of professors of education, chaired by John Gray, to the Economic and Social Research Council in 1992; the Review Panel of the Australian Research Council, chaired by Barry McGaw also in 1992; and by the Organisation for Economic Cooperation and Development report *Educational Research and Development* (1995).

19 Plato, *Phaedrus,* translated by Walter Hamilton (1973).

References

Adey, P. & Shaver, M. (1994) *Really Raising Standards* (London, Routledge).

Argyris, C. & Schön, D. A. (1974) *Theory in Practice* (San Francisco, CA and London, Jossey-Bass).

Argyris, C., Putnam, R. & Smith, D. M. (1985) *Action Science* (San Francisco, CA and London, Jossey-Bass).

Arkes, H. R. & Hammond, K. R. (eds) (1986) *Judgment and Decision Making: an interdisciplinary reader* (Cambridge, Cambridge University Press).

Atkins, H. (1977) *Memoirs of a Surgeon* (London, Springwood).

Berlin, I. (1996) *The Sense of Reality* (London, Chatto & Windus).

Dowie, J. & Elstein, A. (eds) (1988) *Professional Judgment: a reader in clinical decision making* (Cambridge, Cambridge University Press).

Downie, R. S. (1994) *The Healing Arts* (Oxford, Oxford University Press).

Dunn, G. & Everitt, B. (1995) *Clinical Biostatistics: an introduction to evidence-based medicine* (London, Edward Arnold).

Eliot, George (1871) *Middlemarch,* 1965 edn (London, Penguin).

Hargreaves, D. H. (1994) *The Mosaic of Learning* (London, DEMOS).

Hargreaves, D. H., Bowditch, M, G. & Griffin, O. R. (1997) *On-the-job Training for Surgeons: a practical guide* (London, Royal Society of Medicine Press).

Hargreaves, D. H., Southworth, G., Stanley, P. & Ward, S. (1997) *On-the-job Training for Physicians: a practical guide* (London, Royal Society of Medicine Press).

Harlen, W. (1997) Educational research and educational reform, in: S. Hegarty (ed.) *The Role of Research in Mature Educational Systems,* (Windsor, National Foundation for Educational Research).

Haynes, R. B., Sackett, D. L., Muir Gray, J. A., Cook, D. L. & Gyatt, G. H. (1977) Transferring evidence from research into practice, *Evidence-based Medicine,* 2, pp. 4–6.

Holmes, Oliver Wendell (1871) *Medical Essays* (New York, Houghton Mifflin).

Huberman, M. (1992) Teacher development and instructional mastery, in: A. Hargreaves & M. Fullan (eds) *Understanding Teacher Development* (London/New York, Cassell/Teachers' College Press).

Huberman, M. (1993) The model of the independent artisan in teachers' professional relations, in: J. W. Little & M. W. McLaughlin (eds) *Teachers' Work* (New York, Teachers' College Press).

King, L. S. (1982) *Medical Thinking: a historical perspective* (Princeton, NJ, Princeton University Press).

Leo, E. L. & Galloway, D. (1996) Conceptual links between cognitive acceleration through science education and motivational style: a critique of Adey and Shayer, *International Journal of Science Education,* 18, pp. 35–49.

Llewelyn, H. & Hopkins, A. (eds) (1993) *Analyzing How We Reach Clinical Decisions* (London, Royal College of Physicians).

Lock, S. & Windle, H. (1977) *Remembering Henry* (London, British Medical Association).

Oakeshott, M. (1951) Political education, in: T. Fuller (ed.) (1989) *Michael Oakeshott on Education* (New Haven, CT and London, Yale University Press).

Plato *Phaedrus,* T. W. Hamilton, 1973 (London, Penguin Books).

Platt, Lord (1972) *Private and Controversial* (London, Cassell).

Russell, I. (199) Evaluating new surgical procedures, *British Medical Journal,* 311, p. 1243.

Schön, D. (1983) *The Reflective Practitioner* (New York, Basic Books).

Schütz, A. (1964) The stranger: an essay in social psychology, reprinted in: B. R. Cosin, R. Dale, G. M. Esland, D. Mackinnon & D. F. Swift (eds) (1971) *School and Society* (London, Routledge & Kegan Paul).

Sherif, M. (1966) *Group Conflict and Co-operation* (London, Routledge & Kegan Paul).

Scruton, R. (1997) *An Intelligent Person's Guide to Philosophy* (London, Duckworth).

Williams, G. C. (1996) *Plan and Purpose in Nature* (London, Weidenfeld & Nicolson).

Chapter 4

A reply to Hargreaves*

Martyn Hammersley

In [Chapter 3] David Hargreaves responded to my critique of his 1996 TTA lecture (Hargreaves, 1997). As he says, while there is disagreement about some fundamental matters, he and his critics share a commitment to quality in both educational research and teaching. The issues that his lecture raises are important and timely ones, and his views deserve attention. However, I still do not find them convincing, and there are a number of points I want to make in reply.

First of all, there remain questions about whether research can supply what he demands. His welcome provision of examples of the kind of work that he believes to be necessary reinforces points that I made in my article about the problems facing educational enquiry. What he is recommending is not new, it has been tried before, and the evidence for its success is not very encouraging. While I would certainly not want to dismiss the value of Bennett's research or that of the ORACLE team, I do not believe that either produced sound *instrumental* knowledge of the kind that Hargreaves argues should be the goal of educational research. As he acknowledges, both studies have been subjected to considerable and effective criticism, and some of that criticism throws doubt on whether this kind of knowledge is possible (see, for example, Barrow, 1984).

It is also worth noting that the form of action research he recommends in his rejoinder is not new either. He dismisses the relevance of recent British and Australian work of this kind on the basis that it abandoned the goal of

---

producing high-quality social science, suggesting that this may have resulted in part from the influence of Habermas and Schön. But similar problems arose with the educational action research movement in the United States during the 1950s, which was free from these influences (Corman 1957; Hodgkinson 1957). Hargreaves does not mention the fate of this movement, even though what was attempted was very close to what he recommends. In this and other respects it seems to me that the evidence base for his proposals is weak.

A second point relates to the internal consistency of Hargreaves' position. We clearly agree that teaching is a practical more than a technical activity, placing on one side the admittedly problematic character of that distinction. While this point was mentioned it was not given a central place in Hargreaves' lecture, but it *is* emphasised in his rejoinder. Interestingly, we also agree that medicine is practical. While I suggested that education may lie further towards the practical end of the spectrum, I stressed the role of judgment in medical work; that was the basis for the questions I raised about some of the views put forward by advocates of evidence-based medicine.[1] Thus, I certainly did not deny that medicine deals with particular cases, indeed I emphasised this point. Medical *research*, however, even the clinical research that is Hargreaves' model, *is* generally concerned with aggregate results. As he notes, the touchstone for evidence-based medicine is the randomised controlled trial. This kind of investigation follows the logic of experimental method, and it is positivistic in that sense. This is not a defect, and I have no doubt at all about the value of the results of such research for medical practitioners.[2] What is important to note, though, is that the findings of this or any other research must be subjected to considerable interpretation by practitioners if they are to use them well. This is something that Hargreaves accepts, just as do the proponents of evidence-based medicine, under criticism. But it raises the question of how research can be *actionable* rather than simply *relevant to action*. If education is a practical activity, in the sense outlined by Hargreaves, how can research 'demonstrate conclusively that if teachers change their practice from x to y there will be a significant and enduring improvement in teaching and learning' (Hargreaves, 1996 [Chapter 1: p. 9 of this volume]) or tell us *how to implement* its findings (Hargreaves, 1997 [Chapter 3: note 8, p. 58 of this volume])?

Hargreaves still seems to me to assume a strong form of instrumental knowledge that is at odds with the practical character of teaching: there is a mismatch between the two halves of his argument. And, given that educational research is more focused on social interaction than is most medical research, both the production and the use of generalisations about 'what works' are particularly problematic in the educational field. What works for one teacher in one context may well not work for other teachers in other circumstances. Furthermore, as I noted in my article, 'what works', or what is 'effective', is an evaluative matter. As such, it is not open to determination by research alone; even if research can tell us what could be the consequences of particular kinds of pedagogy under given conditions. In medicine the evaluative considerations are often (but not always or entirely) consensual. In education, however, there is much more disagreement even about what would count as a good education, as well as about what would be educational for whom and in what circumstances.

Early on in his rejoinder, Hargreaves argues that many doctors draw on the results of research but that most teachers do not, and claims that reducing this difference 'would enhance the quality of teachers' decision making' [p. 44 of this volume]. While I accept that it is desirable for teachers to familiarise themselves with and critically assess the educational research literature, I doubt that the relationship between this activity and improvement in their practice can be as close as Hargreaves implies. This is partly because good practice depends on too many other factors, but also because I do not assume that increased knowledge always leads to better action (Hammersley, 1995: ch. 7). Hargreaves quotes Oakeshott's definition of politics at one point [p. 56], but it seems to me that what underpins his lecture is precisely the kind of rationalism that Oakeshott criticised: a belief in the possibility of reducing experience to explicit formulae and a commitment to restructuring practice on that basis (Oakeshott, 1962). Similarly, while Hargreaves dismisses Kay's reference to 'Stalinist central planning' as laughable, there is a serious point underlying it. Attempts to centrally plan scientific research are increasing today, and those who criticised earlier efforts did so precisely because these rested on anti-liberal economic and political assumptions (see Polanyi, 1962 and 1964). It is one of the ironies of recent history that governments which claimed to be committed to neo-liberalism sought to establish economic regimes in public sector institutions that repeat the mistake of central economic planning in Eastern Europe by assuming that there can be standardised 'performance indicators' (Nove, 1969). Hargreaves' lecture seems to imply the use of research to deepen the application of this sort of approach to education, and perhaps even to extend it to the organisation of research itself. While he may not intend the Forum he proposes to be directly involved in the allocation of funds and the monitoring of research 'impact', it is difficult to see how that body could hope to achieve the radical change he wants without it effectively doing so.

Contrary to what Hargreaves implies, I did *not* argue that there should be a ban on research designed to produce the kind of knowledge that he calls for. I too am a pluralist, and am certainly not interested in simply defending the status quo; indeed, I can hardly be accused of being uncritical of the present state of social and educational research (see, for instance, Foster et al., 1996). Rather, I disagree with a major part of Hargreaves' diagnosis of the problems, and with the remedy he proposes. But those who believe that educational research can produce actionable knowledge should continue to pursue it, and the rest of us might learn a great deal from their work, perhaps even that our scepticism was ill-founded. What they must *not* do, though, is to exaggerate the prospects of success at the expense of other kinds of research. What I rejected in my article was Hargreaves' criticism of educational researchers for not having achieved instrumental knowledge, his implication that they were culpable for this, and his appeal to outside agencies to remedy the situation.

At one point Hargreaves expresses doubt about whether funders would supply the current level of funding 'if research is limited to the "enlightenment" model' [p. 56]. However, he still ignores the fact that a very great deal more is spent on medical than on educational research. And the undervaluing of research that serves other functions than telling practitioners what it is best to do is a product of the instrumental view of knowledge that is currently widespread, and which Hargreaves' lecture itself promotes (despite his own expressed commitment to the continued funding of 'blue-skies' social science research). In my opinion, this is precisely the shortsighted orientation that has done and continues to do very serious damage not only to social science but also to research in the humanities and the natural sciences in Britain and elsewhere.[3]

Finally, I did *not* criticise Hargreaves for addressing other audiences than researchers (an unworthy suggestion!). What I objected to was the way in which some of his comments effectively disqualified researchers from participating in the debate by implying that any resistance to his arguments on their part arose from a concern with protecting their own interests. As I noted, this is the way that the views of education professionals were dismissed in much public debate in the 1980s and early 1990s; and there is ample evidence that it does not aid the productive discussion of important issues or facilitate sound policy and practice. Hargreaves' rejoinder to my article is entirely free of this kind of rhetoric, and is clearly designed to encourage constructive debate; which, as he says, was his original intention. I very much hope that discussion of these matters will continue. Indeed, I believe that it is essential that the kind of arguments and proposals which Hargreaves presented in his lecture do not become the basis for policy before the problems they involve have been properly addressed and dealt with.

Notes

1 Incidentally, I cited sociological work in support of this point to show that this sometimes disparaged form of knowledge could assist us in the debate. The fact that there are distinguished medical practitioners who have also emphasised the role of judgment does not undercut the value of this research; indeed, it provides further supporting evidence. The research was based on observation of medical practice as well as on the accounts of practitioners. And it conflicts with the picture of medicine as *based on* scientific method, or as involving the *implementation* of scientific results, which is still quite influential, not least in some advocacy of evidence-based medicine.

2 At the same time, I do not accept that in education we can set up the kind of hierarchy of sources of evidence, with experimental research at the top, which Hargreaves mentions – for me different research methods have contrasting strengths and weaknesses. This does not mean, however, that I 'dismiss' the value of experimental research.

3 This is evaluative language, and emotive too in the sense that it reflects strong feelings on my part; but it is not emotive in the sense of being designed to appeal solely to the emotions of readers. I would also note that David Hargreaves is no exponent of passionless prose!

References

Barrow, R. (1984) *Giving Teaching Back to Teachers* (Brighton, Wheatsheaf).

Corman, B. (1957) Action research: a teaching or a research method?, *Review of Educational Research*, 27, pp. 544–47.

Foster, P., Gomm, R. and Hammersley, M. (1996) *Constructing Educational Inequality* (London, Falmer).

Hammersley, M. (1995) *The Politics of Social Research* (London, Sage).

Hargreaves, D. H. (1996) Teaching as a research-based profession: possibilities and prospects, Teacher Training Agency Annual Lecture 1996 (London, Teacher Training Agency). [Chapter 1 of this volume].

Hargreaves, D. H. (1997) In defence of research for evidence-based teaching: a rejoinder to Martyn Hammersley, *British Edticational Research Journal*, 23, 3, pp. 405–19. [Chapter 3 of this volume].

Hodgkinson, H. L. (1957) Action research: a critique, *Journal of Educational Sociology,* 31, 4, pp. 137–53.

Nove, A. (1969) *The Soviet Economy*, Third edition (London, Allen and Unwin).

Oakeshott, M. (1962) *Rationalism in Politics* (London, Methuen).

Polanyi, M. (1962) The republic of science, *Minerva*, I, pp. 54–73.

Polanyi, M. (1964) *Science, Faith and Society*, Second edition (Chicago, University of Chicago Press).

Chapter 5

Making evidence-based practice educational

John Elliott

Redirecting educational research in the service of outcomes-based education

There is a great deal of current debate about the future direction of educational research. According to some current commentators, like David Hargreaves, it has lost its way. Educational research needs to be redirected towards the systematic development of a body of knowledge that is capable of informing the practical judgments of teachers. The idea of 'evidence-based practice' is central to this redirection. It orients research towards the goal of maximising the utility of its findings for teachers. In this context, Hargreaves (1997 [Chapter 3 of this volume]) argues that:

> research should provide decisive and conclusive evidence that if teachers do X rather than Y in their professional practice, there will be a significant and enduring improvement in outcome. [p. 53]

More recently, Hargreaves (1999) has displayed an increasing sensitivity to accusations of 'positivism' (see Hammersley, 1997 [Chapter 2 of this volume]).

Taken from: *British Educational Research Journal*, Vol. 27, No. 5, 2001, pp. 555–74.
© 2001 British Educational Research Association
Reproduced by kind permission of Taylor & Francis Ltd.
http://www.tandf.co.uk/journals

He qualifies the idea of 'evidence-based practice' by suggesting that 'evidence-informed practice' is a less ambivalent expression. It more clearly indicates that relevant research *informs* rather than *displaces* the judgement of teachers. He also appears to qualify the injunction that research evidence should be *decisive and conclusive* for practice.

Such evidence does not presume the existence of universal causal laws as a basis for generating means–ends rules that are beyond doubt and the need for any further speculation.

Hargreaves sees the future of educational research to require more experimental studies and randomised controlled trials, in search of *what works* in practice to produce improvements in outcome. These studies investigate 'some "reasonably stable relationships"' (1999, p. 247) but are open to revision in the light of exceptions and changing circumstances. Their generalisable findings deal in statistical probabilities only.

Moreover, in discussing the relationship between research and policy-making, Hargreaves acknowledges that practical decisions are context-bound. He argues that they need to be based on a wider range of considerations than 'relevant research'. Knowledge derived from research 'serves as a supplement to, not a substitute for, the policy-maker's existing knowledge' (1999, p. 246).

By attempting to uncouple educational experiments into *what works* from positivistic assumptions, Hargreaves (1999) aims to strengthen the case for an 'engineering model' of educational research, as opposed to an 'enlightenment model'. The former, he contends, aims to exert a direct influence on educational action in the areas of policy and practice, by generating evidence of *what works*. The latter, in contrast, aims only to shape the way people think about situations and the problems they raise. The influence of such research on their concrete decisions and actions is at best indirect. Hargreaves acknowledges that 'enlightenment research' can in the longer term indirectly impact on policy and practice by permeating the prevailing climate of opinion. However, this 'uncontentious fact', he argues, is no excuse for a *hermit stance,* 'in which the researcher withdraws from the messy world of short-term, practical problems into intellectual obscurities masquerading as profundities whilst dreaming of ultimate recognition' (1999, p. 243). Indeed, Hargreaves claims that the transmission of theories and ideas alone to 'enlighten' professional practitioners is a dangerous enterprise. By way of example, he points to the intellectual monopoly social scientists in education have, 'until recently', exercised over the initial training of teachers. In the process, they have purveyed the ideas of researchers like Piaget, Skinner and Bernstein (1999, p. 244) in distorted forms. Arguably, he contends, this has done 'untold damage' to teachers' professional practices.

Hargreaves portrays the 'enlightenment model' as an oppositional stance to an 'engineering model' framed by naive positivistic assumptions. By uncoupling the 'engineering model' from such assumptions, he aspires to disarm the opposition in the academy, and to reinstate it at the core of social science research generally and educational research in particular. In this way, the future of social and educational research can be redirected to generating *actionable knowledge* for both policy-makers and practitioners.

Has Hargreaves succeeded, in his latest writing, at finally uncoupling his endorsement of an 'engineering model' of social and educational research from the charge that it presumes a crude and naive positivism? Has he thereby exposed, as mere rationalisation, the grounds for opposing such a model with one that dissociates knowledge from any direct link with social action, and in doing so restricts its aim to influencing the 'climate of opinion'? I would argue that Hargreaves has only partially succeeded. From the standpoint of social philosophy, his arguments are not exactly novel ones. They echo in some respects those developed by Alasdair MacIntyre (1981) in chapter 8 of his seminal text entitled *After Virtue.*

Discussing *The Character of Generalizations in Social Science and their Lack of Predictive Power,* MacIntyre identifies the discovery of statistical regularities as an important source of predictability in human behaviour. He argues that generalisations of this kind, couched in terms of probabilities rather than strict causal laws, do not entail explicability in terms of such laws. This point is echoed by Hargreaves [Chapter 3] in his rejoinder to Martyn Hammersley's [Chapter 2] contention that many educational researchers would perceive his account of 'evidence-based practice' as positivistic. MacIntyre also argues that knowledge of statistical regularities plays an important role in informing human choices between alternatives, in terms of their chances of success and failure. They constitute what Hargreaves calls *actionable knowledge.* However, unlike Hargreaves, MacIntyre does not view the existence of exceptions to constitute a platform for improving the predictability of research findings and therefore their utility as *actionable knowledge.*

According to Hargreaves (1999), educational research evidence about *what works* in classrooms should be cumulative and based on a process of continuously investigating exceptions (pp. 247–248). He appears to assume that such exceptions constitute counter-examples in the sense that they expose deficiencies in the original generalisations which need to be improved upon by further research. However, MacIntyre argues that the probabilistic generalisations of social science are different in kind from those which obtain in natural science fields like statistical mechanics. Unlike the former, probabilistic generalisations in such natural science fields do not merely consist of a list of instances to which there are exceptions. Rather, they 'entail well-defined counter-factual conditionals and they are refuted by counter-examples in precisely the same way and to the same degree as other law-like generalizations are' (1981, p. 91).

Given this difference, Hargreaves's assumption that exceptions to social science generalisations can function as counter-examples, and thereby constitute a basis for cumulative research which improves the actionability of its findings, is an erroneous one. MacIntyre emphasises Machiavelli's point, that in human life people may act 'on the best available stock of generalizations' and yet, when faced with unpredicted exceptions, see no way to improve them or reason to abandon them (p. 93). Relatively speaking, such generalisations are predictively weak. Hargreaves's belief that they can be improved upon, rather than simply added to or changed, in a way which leads to a progressive diminution of unpredictability in human affairs, suggests that he has not entirely shed the assumptions of positivism.

However much Hargreaves has modified his position on evidence-based practice in response to accusations of 'positivism', there is a consistent theme running through his writing since the Teacher Training Agency (TTA) lecture he delivered in 1996. It is that the major task of educational research is to improve the *performativity* of teachers with respect to the outcomes of their teaching. At first sight, this view of the aim of educational research appears to be a matter of common sense and not open to question. Teaching is an intentional activity directed towards bringing about learning outcomes for pupils. What is more open to dispute (see Stenhouse, 1970a, 1975) is a thread of ideas which originally stemmed from Bloom's *Taxonomy of Educational Objectives* (1956) and Bloom's research into *Mastery Learning* (1971). In the 1980s, these ideas were further developed under the name of *outcomes-based education* (OBE). Within the thread of ideas that make up OBE are the injunctions that learning outcomes should be the same for all students, operationally defined as *exit behaviours,* and progress towards them measured against *benchmarks.* The terminology employed tends to shift over time and context, but its meaning remains constant. Hence, within the UK National Curriculum framework, specifications of *outcomes for all students* are referred to as 'standards', *exit behaviours* as 'targets', and *benchmarks* as 'attainment levels'.

One of the attractions of OBE is that it appears to provide a framework of practical rules for designing teaching interventions and measuring teaching effectiveness. In applying these rules to instructional design, the outcomes of teaching are conceived as measurable *outputs.* As such, they are specified in a form which renders them predictable and amenable to technical control by the teacher. Within the OBE framework, 'evidence-based teaching' can be characterised as a means of improving teaching as a form of technical control over the production of learning outcomes, thereby rendering them increasingly predictable. In spite of various adjustments Hargreaves has made to his accounts of 'evidence-based practice', and the role of educational research in relation to it, they continue to embrace and endorse the control ideology of OBE. In this respect, they remain open to the charge of positivism.

In what follows, the phrase 'outcomes-based education' will be used to refer to the particular strand of ideas sketched above. In so doing, I will in no way wish to deny the truism that teaching involves the intention to bring about worthwhile learning outcomes for students. What I would deny is that teaching, to become effective, has to take on the particular ideological baggage of OBE. The truism referred to does not necessarily entail that the teacher should have the same outcomes in mind for all students, or that he or she should specify outcomes in the form of exit behaviours or outputs, or assess the effectiveness of his or her teaching by measuring students' progress in learning against benchmarks. Hargreaves's account of the role of educational research can be interpreted as an attempt to reposition it as the handmaiden of OBE and the educational policies which are increasingly shaped by the ideology which underpins it.

I will return to the question of what constitutes *actionable knowledge* in the context of social practices like education shortly. First, I want to explore Hargreaves's view of the role of *educational research* in the prevailing policy context. I shall do so in the light of MacIntyre's account of the use of social science generalisations in the management of society.

The policy context of educational research

Hargreaves endorses political interventions to shape pedagogical practices in school classrooms so long as they are informed by research evidence rather than ideology. He writes (1999):

> In England and Wales policy makers were formerly limited, or limited themselves, mainly to decisions about the structure of the education service; the internal activities of what teachers did in classrooms, even the curriculum itself, was largely left to the discretion of teachers enjoying a high level of professional autonomy. Today a new link is being forged between what hitherto have been mainly distinct areas [of policy and practice] and marks the end to the convention by which ministers remain distant from classroom practice.
>
> Policy makers' interventions in classroom activities will, I suspect, increase, especially if the national literacy and numerary strategies succeed in raising levels of students' measured achievement. Ministers now recognize that standards of teaching and learning are unlikely to be raised by policy action that never penetrates classrooms. This is less dangerous than it initially appears, as long as ministers retain some distance by a pragmatic attention to 'what works' and by an acknowledgement that the discovery of 'what works' is more a matter of evidence, not just ideology or of political preference. (p. 246)

From MacIntyre's point of view, Hargreaves's optimism about the uses of educational research in the policy context, as depicted above, would appear to be ill-founded. [MacIntyre] argues (pp. 106–108) that the claims of politicians and bureaucrats to expertise in the 'social engineering' of society is a masquerade for a histrionic imitation of scientifically managed social control. Such claims, he argues, arise from 'the dominance of the manipulative mode in our culture', but which 'cannot be accompanied by very much actual success in manipulation' for 'our social order is in a very literal sense out of, and indeed anyone's, control'. MacIntyre concludes that it is 'histrionic success which gives power and authority in our culture' and not scientific evidence about how to manipulate/engineer the social order to achieve certain purposes. In doing so, he anticipates a likely response from social managers and bureaucrats that, interestingly, echoes Hargreaves's account of the role of educational research:

> We make no large claims [to expertise] ... We are as keenly aware of the limitations of social science generalizations as you are. We perform a modest function with a modest and unpretentious competence. But we do have specialized knowledge, we are entitled in our own limited fields to be called experts. (p. 107)

MacIntyre argues that these modest claims do little to legitimate the possession and uses of power 'in anything like the way or on anything like the scale on which that power is wielded' in bureaucratic systems. He sees them as an excuse for continuing 'to participate in the charades which are consequently enacted'. His account of how political and managerial power is generated in our culture seems credible, in which case Hargreaves's account of the significant, if modest, contribution of educational research to the production of *actionable knowledge* in the current policy context is based on a fiction about the capacity of such research to inform and shape policy interventions. It is a fiction which, nevertheless, provides an excuse for an unprecedented extension of the operation of political and bureaucratic power to regulate the pedagogical activities teachers engage their students in within classrooms. Hargreaves, it appears, from this point of view, has cast educational researchers for a role in the histrionic production of the power and authority of the state and its officials over the processes of education.

MacIntyre 'reminds' educational researchers that they also will need to be good actors when he writes:

> The histrionic talents of the player with small walking-on parts are as necessary to the bureaucratic drama as the contributions of the great managerial character actors. (p. 108)

I would contend that in giving the 'engineering model' of educational research a central role for the future, Hargreaves takes for granted a set of prevailing assumptions about the nature of social practices, like 'education', and their relationship to desirable social outcomes. These assumptions are embedded in a climate of opinion which currently surrounds the formation of social policy in the post-industrial nations and the systems of quality assurance associated with the process. In the field of education, such assumptions are embedded in the notion of *outcomes-based education* outlined earlier. They can be summarised as follows:

1. That social practices are activities which need to be justified as *effective* and *efficient* means of producing desirable outputs.
2. That means and ends are contingently related. What constitutes an appropriate means for bringing about the ends-in-view needs to be determined on the basis of empirical evidence.

3. That the determination of means requires a clear and precise pre-specification
    of ends as tangible and measurable outputs or targets, which constitute
    the *quality standards* against which the performance of social practition-
    ers is to be judged.

The prevailing policy context in education, as in other areas of social policy,
tends to reflect these assumptions, inasmuch as it prioritises *target-setting* and
forms of evaluation and quality assurance which measure the *performativity*
(efficiency) of practices against *indicators* of success in achieving the targets. In
other words, it is a context in which practices are treated as manipulative devices
(technologies) for engineering desired levels of output.

Hargreaves's vision of the future of educational research neatly fits this policy context and he apparently sees no problem with it. He clearly assumes that
restrictions on the autonomy of teachers by the interventions of policy-makers
to shape classroom practice are justified, so long as they are informed and dis-
ciplined by empirical evidence of *what works* to produce a given level of output.
What he fails to consider is MacIntyre's point that such evidence can never provide 'the managers of society' with the amount of predictive power that is com-
mensurate with the concept of *managerial effectiveness.* Such a concept, for
MacIntyre, is a moral fiction (pp. 106–107). If we accept his line of argument,
then, in a policy context characterised by 'managerialism', empirical evidence
about statistical regularities is only *histrionically useful* as a masquerade for
arbitrary preferences. In which case, Hargreaves's vision of government ministers distancing themselves from their ideological preferences and pragmatically
attending to evidence of *what works* is somewhat fanciful and no basis on which
to sanction restrictions on teacher autonomy. Indeed, the fact, evidenced by the
limited forms of empirical generalisations produced by the social sciences, that
human life is accompanied by a high degree of unpredictability as a permanent
condition, is a good reason for giving teachers a measure of autonomy from
political and bureaucratic control. Trusting in their capacities to exercise wisdom
and judgement in the unpredictable circumstances they regularly encounter in
the course of their activities is the wise policy.

We need a third vision of educational research to either the 'enlightenment' or
'engineering' models; one which places the judgment of teachers at the centre of
the research process. It is the articulation of this third vision that the rest of this
article is devoted to.

Hargreaves's vision of the future of educational research ignores a tradition of
philosophical thinking about social practices, like education, which goes back to
Aristotle and is exemplified in contemporary thought by MacIntrye's *After Virtue.*
According to MacIntyre, this philosophical tradition defines a social practice as:

> any coherent and complex form of socially established cooperative human
> activity through which goods internal to that form of activity are realized
> in the course of trying to achieve those standards of excellence which are

appropriate to, and partially definitive of, that form of activity, with the result that human powers to achieve excellence, and human conceptions of the ends and goods involved, are systematically extended. (1981, p. 187)

From this *ethical perspective,* goods internal to a practice are distinguished from external goods because one cannot specify them independently of the activities and processes the practice itself consists of. They are norms and values which define what are to count as the worthwhile activities and processes which make up the practice, and not some extrinsic goods which may result from participating in it. Moreover, unlike the latter, goods internal to a practice can only be identified and recognised 'by the experience of participating in the practice in question' (see MacIntyre, 1981, p. 189).

The concept of education and the role of educational research

In the field of education, such a perspective constituted in the 1960s and early 1970s a major resource for two highly influential and interlinked bodies of work. I am referring to Richard Peters's work in establishing the Philosophy of Education as a major discipline in education (see *Ethics and Education* [1966] and 'Aims of education – a conceptual inquiry' [1973]) and Lawrence Stenhouse's use of Peters's work in developing research-based teaching as a coherent and integrated form of educational practice (see Stenhouse, 1971, 1975, 1979a, 1979b). In fact, the linkage between Peters's educational theory and Stenhouse's work in placing the idea of 'research-based teaching' at the core of the curriculum development process in schools, as exemplified by his Humanities Project (1970b), is not sufficiently acknowledged by either philosophers of education or educational researchers. Yet, it provides a significant exception to Hargreaves's contention (1999, p. 244) that the transmission of theories of education have not been accompanied in the past by a sound body of empirical evidence related to teachers' routine practices (see, for example, Stenhouse, 1971, 1977, 1979b; Elliott & MacDonald, 1975; Elliott, J., 1976–7; Stenhouse et al., 1979; Ebbutt & Elliott, 1985; Elliott, 1991).

Peters was a member of the Humanities Project's Steering Committee, and Stenhouse viewed this project as an example of curriculum development grounded in a well-articulated philosophy of education. Consistently with this, Stenhouse sent a member of his team (me) to study the philosophy of education under Peters, on a part-time basis, at the London Institute of Education.

In this section, I will revisit Peters's work on the aims of education and their relationship to educational processes, and argue that its implications for educational research and evidence-based practice are very different from Hargreaves's position. In the final section, I will sketch out Stenhouse's vision of the relationship between educational research and teaching and indicate its congruence with the educational theory of Peters.

For Peters, *educational aims* do not refer to ends which 'education might lead up to or bring about' (1973). From his point of view, economic ends like 'providing students with jobs' and 'increasing the productivity of the community' are goods extrinsic to education. *Education,* Peters argues (1966), is not 'a neutral process that is instrumental to something that is worthwhile which is extrinsic to it' (p. 27). Such extrinsic ends are more appropriately referred to as *purposes* rather than *aims of education.* The latter refer to norms and values which define what it means for a person to become *educated,* and what is to count procedurally as a worthwhile *educational* process for realising such a state. They define 'goods' that are intrinsic to *education* as a process. A process which is solely directed towards *extrinsic* ends such as economic ones, Peters (1966) argues, is best described in terms of *training* rather than *education.* However, people can be taught a body of knowledge, such as science, or a practical skill, like carpentry, for both 'their own intrinsic value and because of the contribution which they make to extrinsic ends' (Peters, 1966, p. 29). *Education* and *training* are not necessarily discrete processes.

According to Peters, the norms and values which define the intrinsic goods of education fall into two closely connected clusters (1973, pp. 18–24). First, there are those which provide general criteria of education when it is viewed as an achievement. Peters claims that success at becoming an educated person involves:

- coming to care about an activity for 'what there is in it as distinct from what it may lead onto', e.g. 'the pursuit of truth' or 'making something of a fitting form' (p. 18);
- possessing 'depth of understanding' by grasping the principles which underpin an activity;
- not being narrowly specialised but able to see the connection between an activity one cares about and understands and a 'coherent pattern of life'. Peters calls this ability, to make connections between specific human activities (e.g. science, history, or engineering) and a wider pattern of meaning in life, *cognitive perspective.*
- having one's way of looking at things in life generally, one's *cognitive perspective,* transformed by what one has learned in pursuing specific worthwhile activities.

The implication of this analysis, of what it means to be *educated,* is that becoming such a person involves a process that is qualitatively different from one which involves merely learning bodies of knowledge and skills that are valued solely in terms of their relationship to extrinsic economic and social purposes. *Education,* for Peters, involves the transformation of a person's way of seeing the world in relation to him or herself. It is a holistic process. He argues that a person is never *educated* 'in relation to any specific end, function, or mode of thought' (1966, p. 34). The acquisition of specific competencies in these respects is more appropriately described in terms of *training*. Nor do people become *educated* additively, by virtue of the sheer amount of knowledge and skills they acquire. Knowledgeable or omnicompetent individuals are not necessarily *educated*. From this we might conclude that our Government's current project of 'driving up standards' in schools has little to do with improving the quality of *education* within them, since the acquisition of specific competencies are not in themselves *educational achievements*. The latter refer to the *manner* in which people learn and involve qualitative transformations in their general outlook on life, the conditions of which can be specified by the kinds of general criteria Peters has drawn our attention to. His purpose, in attempting to clarify aims which are intrinsic to the process of becoming educated, is 'to clarify the minds of educators about their priorities' (1973, p. 21). The need for such clarification is perhaps greater now at a time when the educational policy context is being driven by economic imperatives in an age of globalisation, and teachers at all levels of the education system are being held to account in terms of standardised learning outputs which are believed to posses *commodity value* for the labour market.

The second cluster of aims cited by Peters refers to procedural values and principles rather than the achievement aspect of education. Some of these aims, he argues, are linked to the claims of the individual in the process of education, and draw attention 'to a class of *procedures* of education rather than prescribe any particular content or direction to it' (1973, p. 22). Aims like 'self-realization' and 'the growth of the individual' imply principles of procedure such as 'learning by discovery', 'inquiry learning', 'autonomous learning', 'learning by experience'. Other procedural aims refer to the rules or standards that are built into *educationally* worthwhile activities, such as respect for reasons and evidence (1973, p. 25). Procedural aims and principles are emphasised, Peters argues, 'when the educational system is either geared towards the demands of the state ... or when individuals are being moulded relentlessly in accordance with some dull and doctrinaire pattern' (1973, p. 23). Under these conditions, there is a point in stressing the need, for example, to respect the individuality of learners by allowing them a measure of self-direction and control within any *educationally* worthwhile process. There may also be a point in emphasising the intrinsic value of procedural standards built into an activity, such as 'respect for evidence', in contexts where the activity is in danger of being valued only for its instrumentality as a vehicle for producing goods which are extrinsic to *education*.

If, for Peters, general aims function to remind educators of their priorities with respect to what they should be trying to achieve in *educating* students as opposed to merely training them, then procedural values and principles function to remind them that their methods should be consistent with both the standards that define and discipline *educationally* worthwhile activities, and the moral claims of individuals as learners. Procedural principles based on the latter remind educators of the ethical limits *education* as a task places on the peda-gogical methods they employ to structure students' learning.

According to Peters, procedural values and principles cannot be characterised independently of his characterisation of education as an achievement. Although they specify criteria which characterise those processes 'by means of which people gradually become educated' (1973, p. 15), they do not, Peters argues, specify 'efficient means for producing a desirable end' (1973, p. 15).

The connection between *educational* processes and becoming an *educated* person is a conceptual rather than a contingent one. Why, he asks, are values and principles embedded in *educational* procedures treated as *aims* of education? The answer, he argues:

> is connected with the impossibility of conceiving of educational processes in accor-dance with a means–ends model and of making any absolute separation between content and procedure, matter and manner, in the case of education. (1973, p. 24)

Peters here is not denying that considerations of instrumental effectiveness, in achieving specific educational outcomes, are pedagogically relevant. What he is denying is their relevance to judging the *educational quality* of pedagogical meth-ods. This is because, for him, both the achievement and procedural criteria of edu-cation characterise different aspects of the same process of *initiating* people 'into a public world picked out by the language and concepts of a people and structured by rules governing their purposes and interactions with each other' (1973, p. 26). The achievement criteria characterise *educational outcomes* in a form that renders them inseparable from the process of *becoming educated.* They characterise *qual-ities of being* which are manifested *in* a process of *becoming educated* and cannot be described independently of it. Such a process, Peters argues, is inconsistent with both the view of teachers as operators who shape minds 'according to some spec-ification or "top them up" with knowledge' and the view that their function is sim-ply to 'encourage the child to "grow"' as if s(he) were an 'organism unfolding some private form of life' (1973, p. 26). The function of procedural criteria, according to Peters, is to act as a guide to teachers in helping learners, viewed as active and developing centres of consciousness, 'to explore and *share* a public world whose contours have been marked out by generations which have preceded both of them' (1973, p. 26). The central pedagogical problem for teachers as edu-cators, Peters claims, is the procedural one of how to get students to enter into this public world and enjoy their public heritage. Procedural values and principles articulated as *aims of education* remind them that this can only be achieved by methods that acknowledge both the internal standards which govern the activities that people are being initiated into, and the moral standards appropriate to their sta-tus as 'developing centres of consciousness'.

Since there are multiple criteria for judging both what it means to become *educated* and what are to count as *educational* methods or procedures, it is obvi-ous, Peters argues, that some will be emphasised more than others at particular times, 'according to the defects and needs of the contemporary situation' (1973, p. 20). The demand for aims in education serves to focus attention on a neglected priority. The existence of multiple criteria, for Peters, means that educators can be pulled in different directions by conflicting educational priorities, and that such dilemmas cannot be resolved by the formulation of a single overall aim of education which everyone could agree about. Which aim(s) should be emphasised in any particular circumstance must be left to the discretion and practical wisdom of the teacher(s) concerned (1973, pp. 27–29).

Let us now briefly explore the implications of Peters's theory of education for a future direction of educational research that is very different to the one enunciated by Hargreaves.

Hargreaves's account of the sort of research evidence which can be used to inform pedagogical development confines itself to evidence of 'instrumental effectiveness'. However, from Peters's account of the procedural aims and principles implicit in the concept of education alone, one might argue that educational research, if it is to inform *educational* practice, should prioritise the gathering of empirical evidence which can inform teachers' judgements about the ethical consistency of the teaching and learning process with the procedural values and principles that define what is to count as a worthwhile process of *education* (see Elliott, 1989). The primary role of *educational* research, when understood as research directed towards the improvement of *educational* practice, is not to discover contingent connections between a set of classroom activities and pre-standardised learning outputs, but to investigate the conditions for realising a coherent *educational* process in particular practical contexts.

Both the indeterminate nature of educational values and principles, and the context-dependent nature of judgements about which concrete methods and procedures are consistent with them, suggest that *educational* research takes the form of case studies rather than randomised controlled trials. The latter, via a process of statistical aggregation, abstract practices and their outcomes from the contexts in which they are situated. Case studies entail close collaboration between external researchers and teachers on 'the inside' of an educational practice. As Alasdair MacIntyre points out, the identification and recognition of goods which are internal to a practice depend on the experience 'of participating in the practice in question' (1981, p. 189). In the context of research directed towards the improvement of *educational* practice, teachers need to be involved in prioritising their *educational* aims in a given situation, in defining what is to count as relevant evidence of the extent to which they are being realised and interpreting its practical significance for them. In other words *educational* research, as opposed to simply research *on* education, will involve teachers in its construction and execution and not simply in *applying its findings*. Teachers *engage* in *educational* research and not simply with it.

The implications outlined above, of Peters's educational theory for educational research, are highly consistent with Stenhouse's *process model* of curriculum development and the central role of *research-based teaching* within it.

Stenhouse on research-based teaching

Stenhouse drew on Peters's work in *Ethics and Education* (1966) to develop his *process model* of curriculum and pedagogy in opposition to the emerging 'objectives model', which forged the basis of what has now become widely known as 'outcomes-based education'. In demonstrating the process model in practice through the *Humanities Curriculum Project,* Stenhouse saw himself to be addressing the issue:

> can curriculum and pedagogy be organised satisfactorily by a logic other than the means–ends model? (pp. 84–85)

He derived this alternative logic substantially from the arguments Peters sketched out in *Ethics and Education.*

> Peters (1966) argues cogently for the intrinsic justification of content. He starts from the position that education 'implies the transmission of what is worthwhile to those who become committed to it' and that it 'must involve knowledge and understanding and some kind of cognitive perspective, which are not inert'. (p. 45) Believing that education involves taking part in worthwhile activities, Peters argues that such activities have their own in-built standards of excellence, and thus 'can be appraised because of the standards immanent in them rather than because of what they lead on to'. They can be argued to be worthwhile in themselves rather than as means towards objectives. (Stenhouse, 1975, p. 84)

Stenhouse was emphatic that the intrinsic 'standards of excellence', which Peters links to the development of 'knowledge and understanding', could not be specified as 'objectives'. The term 'process objectives', used by some curriculum theorists, to refer to standards intrinsic to the learning process, was also misleading (1975, p. 39). In selecting content to exemplify 'the most important procedures, the key concepts and criteria and the areas and situations in which the criteria hold' (p. 85), one does not designate objectives to be learned by the students.

> For the key procedures, concepts and criteria in any subject – *cause, form, experiment, tragedy* – are, and are important precisely because they are, problematic within the subject. They are the focus of speculation, not the object of mastery. ... Educationally they are also important because they invite understanding at a variety of levels. ... It is the building of curriculum on such structures as procedures, concepts and criteria, which cannot adequately be translated into the performance levels of objectives, that makes possible Burner's 'courteous translation' of knowledge and allows of learning which challenges all abilities and interests in a diverse group. ... The translation of the deep structures of knowledge into behavioral objectives is one of the principal causes of the distortion of knowledge in schools. (Stenhouse, 1975, pp. 85–86)

For Stenhouse, the dynamic nature of the procedural standards and principles that structure intrinsically worthwhile activities implies that they constitute *resources for thinking* about experience, and leave space for students' *individuality, creativity and imagination.* They structure thinking in ways which open rather than close the mind to new ways of interpreting the world. Stenhouse claims that 'the principles which obtain for knowledge within a field are problematic within that field' and therefore pedagogically should always be treated as 'provisional and open to debate'. This echoes Peters's view that procedural principles refer to both standards internal to an activity and the claims of individuals as learners participating in it.

I have argued elsewhere (Elliott, 1988, p. 51 and 1998, ch. 2) that the translation of the structures of knowledge into objectives through the English National Curriculum was a considerable error, and has denied students in schools that 'courteous translation of knowledge' that is a condition of giving them equality of access to our cultural heritage. I predicted that it would result in widespread disaffection from schooling, and this now appears to be manifest, even to policy-makers. The Secretary of State's proposals for revising the National Curriculum acknowledged that it 'was failing to engage a significant minority of 14–16 year olds, who were as a consequence becoming disaffected from learning' (see Elliott, 2000).

Stenhouse did not discount the appropriateness of an objectives model of curriculum design in particular contexts. He argues (1975, p. 80) that education in a broad sense is comprised of at least four different processes: *training, instruction, initiation,* and *induction.* Training is concerned with the acquisition of specific skills, such as speaking a foreign language or handling laboratory apparatus. The use of an objectives model in this context is quite appropriate, Stenhouse argues. Instruction is concerned with the retention of information, e.g. learning the table of chemical elements, dates in history, the names of countries, German irregular verbs, and cooking recipes. In this context too, the objectives model is appropriate. Contrary to Peters, Stenhouse views Initiation as 'familiarization with social values and norms' leading to a capacity 'to interpret the social environment'. As a process, it appropriately takes place as a by-product of living in a community and operates in schools as the 'hidden curriculum'. Induction, according to Stenhouse, appropriately describes the introduction of people to the thought systems of the culture and is concerned with developing their 'understanding'. This is 'evidenced by the capacity to grasp and to make for oneself relationships and judgments'. For Stenhouse, induction is at the core of any *educational process.* Within such a process, both training and instruction have important but subsidiary functions, for 'skills and information are often learned in the context of knowledge, which is, in one of its aspects, an organization of skills and information'. It follows that in designing an educationally worthwhile curriculum, there is a place for specifying objectives in terms of the information and skills to be learned. The danger, for Stenhouse, lies in extending its scope to include the most important aspect of education; namely, the process of inducting students into the thought systems of our culture. Its scope, he argues, should be confined to designing subordinate units within the curriculum that play a service role to the induction process.

One pedagogical implication of Stenhouse's account of the relationship between 'process' and 'objectives' models of curriculum design is that technical means–ends reasoning about the most *effective* and *efficient* training and instructional methods has a place, albeit a subsidiary one, in teachers' decisions about how to improve teaching and learning in an *educational* situation. His account does not deny the value of a form of research aimed at discovering statistical correlations between teaching and learning processes and the acquisition of specific skills and information. Such studies might play a subordinate role in informing the judgements of educators. I will explore Stenhouse's views on this point a little later. For the moment, I want to examine his central arguments for research-based teaching.

Stenhouse's idea of 'research-based teaching' is linked to a 'process model' of curriculum design. This, in turn, rests on the belief that the structures of knowledge into which students are to be inducted are intrinsically problematic and contestable, and therefore objects of speculation. This implies that teachers ought to cast themselves in the role of learners alongside their students. Stenhouse argues (1975, p. 91) that:

> Either the teacher must be an expert or he must be a learner along with his students. In most cases the teacher cannot in the nature of the case be the expert. It follows that he must cast himself in the role of a learner. Pedagogically this may in fact be a preferable role to that of the expert. It implies teaching by discovery or inquiry methods.

For Stenhouse, the teacher who casts him or herself in the role of a learner alongside his or her students must have 'some hold on, and a continual refinement of, a philosophical understanding of the subject he is teaching and learning, of its deep structures and rationale' (1975, p. 91). It is this depth of understanding in relation to the subject matter that makes the teacher into a learner with something to offer to students; namely, a research stance towards the content they teach. From such a stance, they model how to treat knowledge as an object of inquiry. Stenhouse argues that a teacher who casts him or herself in the role of expert, representing knowledge as *authoritative* and therefore beyond doubt and speculation, is misrepresenting and distorting that knowledge. His major objection to the use of the 'objectives model' to map learning in the fields of knowledge is that it reinforces authoritative teaching, and in the process compounds error. This argument was most developed in his *Inaugural Lecture* at the University of East Anglia entitled *'Research as a basis for teaching'* (1979), and subsequently published in a posthumous collection of his essays (1983). In it, he argued that:

> No teacher of normal endowments can teach authoritatively without lending his authority to errors of fact or of judgment. But my case goes deeper than

that. Were the teacher able to avoid this, he would, in teaching knowledge as authoritative, be teaching an unacceptable proposition about the nature of knowledge: that its warrant is to be found in the appeal to the expertise of persons rather than in the appeal to rational justification in the light of evidence. I believe that most teaching in schools and a good deal in universities promotes that error. The schooled reveal themselves as uneducated when they look towards knowledge for the reassurance of authoritative certainty rather than for the adventure of speculative understanding. (1979, p. 6, mimeo)

For Stenhouse, *research-based teaching* is an implication of a theory of education that places induction into knowledge structures at its centre, and then characterises them as *objects for speculative thought*. This theory of education implies a logical framework for a teaching and learning process. At the centre of this framework is a pedagogical aim that he characterises in the following terms:

> to develop an understanding of the problem of the nature of knowledge through an exploration of the provenance and warrant of the particular knowledge we encounter in our field of study. (1979, p. 7)

As an aim for all learners, Stenhouse was aware that some would doubt its realism. However, anything less would consign many children to a permanent condition of educational disadvantage, for 'we are talking about the insight which raises mere competence and possession of information to intellectual power of a kind which can emancipate'. Such an aim, for Stenhouse, implied certain procedural values and principles governing methods of teaching and learning, e.g. 'inquiry' or 'discovery' learning, and 'teaching through discussion'. 'Research-based teaching' can also be regarded as a procedural principle implied by the aim, inasmuch as it characterises the personal stance to knowledge the teacher must adopt in support of the other principles of procedure.

As I indicated earlier, Stenhouse did not view his methodology of induction to be incompatible with instruction. He argues that in order to cover the curriculum, we need instruction and 'text-books too'. The key to the relationship between, say, 'discovery' or 'discussion' methods and instruction, he argues, lies in the pedagogical aim.

> The crucial difference is between an educated and an uneducated use of instruction. The educated use of instruction is skeptical, provisional, speculative in temper. The uneducated use mistakes information for knowledge. Information is not knowledge until the factor of error, limitation or crudity in it is appropriately estimated, and it is assimilated to structures of thinking ... which give us the means of understanding. (1979, p. 8)

Stenhouse was concerned to transform teaching in the state educational system from a system in which the great majority of children experienced their teacher as *an authority* on the content of education to one in which the teacher was *in authority* with respect to the process of *education* and the maintenance of procedures that are consistent with his or her pedagogical aim as an educator. This involved inquiry in particular contexts into how to effect such a transformation in practice.

He cast the problem in a form that turned it into an agenda for *educational* research:

> The problem is how to design a practicable pattern of teaching which main-tains authority, leadership and the responsibility of the teacher, but does not carry the message that such authority is the warrant of knowledge. (1979, p. 7)

The major task of educational research is to show how teaching and learning can be made more *educational*. For Stenhouse, such research produced *actionable evidence* as a basis for teaching, but included evidence of a rather different kind to that envisaged by Hargreaves. It is evidence that is relevant to the problem of how to make the concrete activities of teaching and learning more *ethically con-sistent* with the criteria that define what it means to become educated (e.g. those cited by Peters). Evidence that is relevant to simply making teaching and learn-ing a more effective and efficient process for the production of specific learning outputs is not sufficient as a basis for inducting students into the deep structures of knowledge. Indeed, the ethical requirements of the latter may impose limits on the strategies the teacher employs to secure specific instructional or training outputs.

Educational research of the kind Stenhouse envisages, as a basis for teaching, implies a similar stance from the teacher to the one he describes in relation to his or her subject matter:

> Just as research in history or literature or chemistry can provide a basis for teach-ing those subjects, so educational research can provide a basis for teaching and learning about teaching. Professional skill and understanding can be the subject of doubt, that is of knowledge, and hence of research. (1979, p. 18)

Stenhouse's view of educational research implies *doing* research as an integral part of the role of the teacher, just as a teacher who *uses* research into their sub-ject as a basis for teaching implies that s(he) *does* research into the subject *through* their teaching. In this respect, both dimensions of research-based teach-ing are similarly conceptualised in terms of their relationship to educational practice. Neither implies that research, whether it be in history or education, can only be carried out by 'insiders' who are actively engaged in educational prac-tice. However, for Stenhouse *educational* research does imply that 'outsiders' engaged in such research need to collaborate with educational practitioners. His reasons for this are clearly stated. *Educational* research is a form of *action research,* and this means that:

> real classrooms have to be our laboratories, and they are in the command of teachers, not of researchers ... the research act must conform to the obligations of the professional context. This is what we mean by action research. It is a

pattern of research in which experimental or research acts cannot be exempted from the demand for justification by professional as well as by research criteria. The teacher cannot learn by inquiry without undertaking that the pupils learn too; the physician cannot experiment without attempting to heal. ... Such a view of educational research declares that the theory or insights created in collaboration by professional researchers and professional teachers, is always provisional, always to be taught in a spirit of inquiry, and always to be tested and modified by professional practice. (1979, p. 20)

Stenhouse would agree with Hargreaves about the limitations of an 'enlightenment model' of educational research. He argues (1979, p. 18) against 'the received doctrine' that 'has been at the core of education for teaching' since the 1950s; namely, that it should be based 'in the findings of research in the "contributory disciplines" of philosophy, psychology and sociology'. Stenhouse proposes an alternative to the constituent disciplines approach, which was 'to treat education itself – teaching, learning, running schools and educational systems – as the subject of research' (see also Elliott, 1978). In this respect, Hargreaves appears to echo Stenhouse in a common aspiration for educational research to directly inform the concrete activities of education rather than studying them for the contribution they can make to the development of theory within a particular discipline. However, as I have indicated, their ideas about what constitutes *actionable evidence* from research are somewhat different.

Stenhouse claims that his alternative proposal does not imply a neglect of the disciplines, because research in education draws eclectically upon them, particularly with respect to 'methods of inquiry and analysis together with such concepts as have utility for a theory of education'. In relation to the very last point, I have attempted to show how Stenhouse's idea of 'research-based teaching' is informed by Peters's theory of education as a process. What distinguishes his idea from Hargreaves's idea of 'evidence-based teaching' is that 'what counts as evidence' is not simply evidence about the instrumental effectiveness of the strategies employed to secure certain learning outcomes, but evidence about the extent to which teaching strategies are ethically consistent with *educational* ends. What characterises Stenhouse's view of educational research is its focus on the problems of realising a form of teaching in particular contexts of professional practice. He writes:

The problems selected for inquiry are selected because of their importance as educational problems; that is, for their significance in the context of professional practice. Research and development guided by such problems will contribute primarily to the understanding of educational action through the construction of theory of education or a tradition of understanding. Only secondarily will research in this mode contribute to philosophy, psychology or sociology. (1979, p. 19)

Here Stenhouse is alluding to the inseparability of developing a theoretical understanding of educational action and doing educational research into the practical problems of education. If educational research focuses on the problems which arise in trying to realise a form of *educational* practice, then it will pose questions both about which actions in the context are constitutive of such a practice and about the educational criteria employed in deciding this. Educational research, on Stenhouse's account, is a process which involves the joint development of educational practice and theory in interaction.

In another paper entitled *'Using research means doing research'* (1979b), Stenhouse explicitly examines the usefulness to teachers of the kind of evidence that Hargreaves advocates as a basis for teaching; namely probabilistic generalisations. He does so in the context of his own research into teaching about race relations in schools, which compared the effects of two teaching strategies on student attitudes. The research was undertaken in the wake of the publicity surrounding Stenhouse's Humanities Project. In this project, some teachers were asked to adopt a 'procedurally neutral' role in handling race relations as a controversial issue within the school curriculum. Some members of the public objected to an open-ended pedagogy in this area, on the grounds that it was the role of the teachers to inculcate 'positive attitudes' in students towards the members of other races by adopting an anti-racist stance in the classroom. They persisted in doing so in spite of evaluation evidence which showed that procedurally neutral teaching did not harden racist attitudes in students, and indeed appeared to shift those of girls in the direction of greater tolerance of racial differences in society. In this context, Stenhouse felt that the effects of an open-minded teaching strategy aimed at 'understanding issues' needed to be compared with one that was explicitly aimed at combating racism. If the latter proved to be more effective in this respect, then the former would be inappropriate, however defensible it might appear to be on purely *educational* grounds. Hence, the follow-up research Stenhouse carried out in the form of an experimental trial.

Having gathered and analysed the evidence statistically, he tried to imagine how it might inform a teacher's decision about which strategy to adopt. His imaginary teacher had been adopting a 'procedurally neutral' stance (strategy A) within the research project. Others had been experimenting with a strategy that was explicitly anti-racist (strategy B).

In the scenario Stenhouse depicts, the statistically significant discriminations 'when presented through means and standard deviations' suggests that 'strategy B does not look markedly superior from strategy A'. The imaginary teacher concludes that 'I don't seem to need to change my teaching style'. However, s(he) then examines another page of the research report, which presents the same data in a different form 'to show the situation in individual schools'. This complicates the issue for the teacher. The analysis of variance for both strategies shows that in a number of schools, the results of each strategy are either doubtful or alarming. Also, when the pupil data is examined in detail, it looks as if 'the same teaching style and the same subject matter make some people worse as they make other people better'. The teacher concludes that:

what I have to find out now is whether teaching about race relations by
Strategy A is good for *my* pupils in *my* school. (1979b, p. 6)

What Stenhouse does, through this scenario, is to show that psycho-statistical
research is no substitute for teachers undertaking *case studies* of their own teaching. However, it can inform teaching as a source of *hypotheses* for teachers to
test through systematically conducted experiments in case study form.
Stenhouse would not deny Hargreaves's contention that probabilistic evidence
of statistical regularities can inform teachers' decisions and constitute actionable
knowledge. What he does is to describe the conditions under which teachers can
make the best use of such evidence to inform their decisions. This involves the
adoption of a research stance towards their teaching and gathering case study
evidence about its effects. Stenhouse's *Teaching about Race Relations* research
combined both statistically based experimental trials and case studies, in which
teachers collaborated with professional researchers.

In *'Using research means doing research'*, Stenhouse appears to be providing
us with an account of research-based teaching that is not simply concerned with
the extent to which teaching strategies are ethically consistent with *educational
aims*. In a context where teachers are expected to produce specific outcomes for
the benefit of society, they are presented with the problem of whether they can
teach in ways that are both ethically consistent with their *educational* aims and
instrumentally effective. Such a problem can be defined as an *educational* one,
since educational values and principles are put at stake by the demand that teaching and learning serve purposes that are extrinsic to education. This introduces
a third dimension to *research-based teaching*. Whether, and how, socially man-
dated learning outcomes can be brought about through an educationally worthwhile process of teaching and learning is a problem for research-based teaching
to address. In making a wise and intelligent response to the problem, teachers
need to base their teaching on evidence about both its *instrumental effectiveness*
and its *ethical consistency* with educational aims and procedures.

Although Stenhouse excludes *educational* considerations from his imaginary
scenario of a teacher exploring the findings of an experimental trial, it is clear
from his paper that the research design was informed by educational values
which the public reaction to the 'neutral teacher', as a strategy for teaching about
race relations, had put at stake.

In his imaginary scenario about the usefulness of probabilistic evidence to a
teacher, Stenhouse (see 1979b, p. 11) argues that a condition of a teacher making good use of such evidence is that s(he) engages in case study research that
requires a qualitative analysis of meaningful actions and interactions in particular situations. Hence, *using* research means *doing* research. The latter will be
largely qualitative because it involves the study of *meaningful actions,* i.e.
actions which cannot be defined simply on the basis of observed behaviour
'without interpretation of the meanings ascribed in the situation by participants'.
Although, Stenhouse argues, such situational analysis can draw on probabilistic

generalisations, in addition to intuitive organisations of experience and theory, they cannot provide the sole evidential basis for teaching. Teachers themselves, Stenhouse believed, had a critical role to play in constructing an evidence base for informing professional judgements. He writes:

> Given that by participating in educational settings, he is in a position to inter-
> pret meanings in action, he is not able to fulfill his professional role on the
> basis of probabilistic generalizations but on the contrary is expected to exer-
> cise his judgment in situational analysis. (1979b, p. 11)

Taking Stenhouse's work on 'research-based teaching' as a whole, it is clear that the situational analysis he refers to can involve a teacher in an examination of both learning outcomes and the *educational* quality of classroom processes in contexts of meaningful action. Such an analysis will be based on evidence about the complex transactions between the teacher and his or her students, and between both, and 'contextual actors' (parents, principals, other teachers, etc.). Such evidence will include evidence of both the observable behaviour of partic-ipants and the meanings they ascribe to their own and others' behaviour in the situation (see Stenhouse, 1979b, p. 11).

From Hargreaves's writing, the extent to which he would go along with Stenhouse's view that *using* research means *doing* research is not entirely clear. He acknowledges the limits of probabilistic generalisations as evidence on which to base practice. Hence, the notion of 'evidence-informed practice'. He also acknowledges the significance of *reflection* about the practical situation as a link between evidence and judgement. However, for Hargreaves, 'reflective practice' does not satisfy the conditions for it to be called 'research'. He tends to redefine Stenhouse's teacher-researchers as reflective practitioners. Perhaps the major difference between them is one of perspective. Whereas Hargreaves is pri-marily concerned with *defining research as a 'basis' for practice,* Stenhouse is primarily concerned with *defining practice as a basis for research.*

Concluding remarks

In this article, David Hargreaves's ideas, about the nature of 'evidence-based practice' and the future direction for educational research, have been explored in the light of the linked work of Richard Peters, on the aims of education, and of Lawrence Stenhouse, on curriculum design and 'research-based teaching'. This has involved revisiting a body of once influential thinking about the nature of education and educational research respectively. If the tone of this article, with respect to this work, has been expository rather than critical, it can be justified in terms of the need to produce a largely descriptive account of a neglected system of thought. It then becomes accessible to further critique and development. Educational theory should be dynamic rather than static.

Central to both Peters's and Stenhouse's work is a view about the relationship between educational aims and processes, which is neglected in Hargreaves's account of the role of educational research in informing educational practice. The explanation appears to lie in Hargreaves's unquestioning commitment to an outcomes-based view of education. I have tried to show how Stenhouse drew on Peters's educational theory to construct a comprehensive view of *educational* research as 'research-based teaching'.

Although I have set my exposition of Peters and Stenhouse against Hargreaves's vision of the relationship between educational research and practice, I have, hopefully, avoided oppositional thinking. In comparing Hargreaves's thinking with that of Stenhouse in particular, I have indicated how elements of it are consistent with Stenhouse's account of 'research-based teaching' as it evolved.

What is lacking in the contemporary discourse about the future direction and practical utility of educational research is any consideration of the contribution of educational and curriculum theory to conceptualising its aims and processes. The current discourse is uninformed by any theory about the nature of *educational* practice, and therefore excludes any consideration of the implications of such a theory for educational research. In rectifying this situation, we could make a beginning by revisiting the work of Richard Peters and Lawrence Stenhouse. This article is a contribution to that 'beginning'. In drawing attention to work that shaped 'a new direction' for both teaching and learning *and* educational research in the recent past, I have tried to demonstrate that its potential, as a resource to draw on in conceptualising links for the future, has not yet been exhausted.

References

Bloom, B. S. (ed.) (1956) *Taxonomy of Educational Objectives I. Cognitive Domain* (London, Longmans).

Bloom, B. S. (1971) Mastery learning, in: J. H. Block (ed.) *Mastery Learning; theory and practice* (New York, Holt, Rinehart & Winston).

Ebbutt, D. & Elliott, J. (eds) (1985) *Issues in Teaching for Understanding* (London, Longmans/Schools Curriculum Development Committee [SCDC]).

Elliott, J. (1976–7) 'Developing Hypotheses about classrooms from teachers' practical constructs: an account of the work of the Ford Teaching Project', *Interchange*, 7(2) (Toronto, OISE).

Elliott, J. (1978) Classroom Research: science or commonsense, in: R. McAleese & D. Hamilton (eds) *Understanding Classroom Life* (Slough, National Foundation for Educational Research).

Elliott, J. (1988) The state v education: the challenge for teachers, in: H. Simons (ed.) *The National Curriculum*, pp. 46–62 (London, British Educational Research Association).

Elliott, J. (1989) Teacher evaluation and teaching as a moral science, in: M. L. Holly & C. S. McLoughlin (Eds) *Perspectives on Teacher Professional Development* (London, Falmer Press).

Elliott, J. (1991) *Action Research for Educational Change* (Buckingham, Open University Press).

Elliott, J. (1998) *The Curriculum Experiment: meeting the challenge of social change* (Buckingham, Open University Press).

Elliott, J. (2000) Revising the National Curriculum: a comment on the Secretary of State's proposals, *Journal of Education Policy*, 15, p. 248.

Elliott, J. & MacDonald, B. (Eds) (1975) *People in Classrooms,* CARE Occasional Publications no. 2 (Norwich, University of East Anglia).

Ford Teaching Project (1974) *Implementing the Principles of Inquiry/Discovery Teaching* (Norwich, Ford Teaching Project Publications, University of East Anglia).

Hammersley, M. (1997) Educational research and teaching: a response to David Hargreaves's TTA Lecture, *British Educational Research Journal*, 23, pp. 141–161. [Chapter 2 of this volume].

Hargreaves, D. (1996) Teaching as a research-based profession: possibilities and prospects, Teacher Training Agency Annual Lecture (London, Teacher Training Agency). [Chapter 1 of this volume].

Hargreaves, D. (1997) In defence of research for evidence-based teaching: a rejoinder to Martyn Hammersley, *British Educational Research Journal*, 23, pp. 405–419. [Chapter 3 of this volume].

Hargreaves, D. (1999) Revitalizing educational research: lessons from the past and proposals for the future, *Cambridge Journal of Education*, 29, pp. 239–249.

MacIntyre, A. (1981) *After Virtue: a study in moral theory,* 2nd edn 1985, pp. 88–108 (London, Duckworth).

Peters, R. S. (1966) *Ethics and Education*, pp. 23–45 (London, Allen & Unwin).

Peters, R. S. (1973) Aims of education – a conceptual inquiry, in: R. S. Peters (Ed.) *The Philosophy of Education,* Oxford Readings in Philosophy, pp. 11–57 (Oxford, Oxford University Press).

Stenhouse, L. (1970a) Some limitations of the use of objectives in curriculum research and planning, *Paedagogica Europaea*, 6, pp. 73–83.

Stenhouse, L. (1971) The Humanities Curriculum Project: the rationale. *Theory into Practice,* 10, pp. 154–162.

Stenhouse, L. (1975) *An Introduction to Curriculum Research and Development* (London, Heinemann).

Stenhouse, L. (1977) *Problems and Effects of Teaching about Race Relations,* a report to the Social Science Research Council on Project HR 2001/1 (Lodged in the British Library).

Stenhouse, L. (1979a) 'Research as a Basis for Teaching', Inaugural Lecture at the University of East Anglia, Norwich. Subsequently published in L. Stenhouse (1983) *Authority, Education and Emancipation* (London, Heinemann).

Stenhouse, L. (1979b) Using research means doing research (mimeo version); published version in: H. Dahl, A. Lysne & P. Rand (Eds) *Spotlight on Educational Problems*, pp. 71–82 (Oslo, University of Oslo Press).

Stenhouse, L., Verma, G., Wild, R. & Nixon, J. (1979) *Problems and Effects of Teaching about Race Relations* (London, Ward Lock).

Chapter 6

Making evidence-based practice educational: a rejoinder to John Elliott

Ann Oakley

In the current climate of debate about the status of educational research in relation to notions of evidence-informed policy and practice, debates of the kind
engaged in in this article are signs of disciplinary health. There is much that
needs discussing, and a great deal of work to be done on all levels – theoretical,
methodological, epistemological and so forth.

My major criticism of the article is that it does not really advance this debate
much, if at all. Much of it is taken up with representations of the views of three
philosophers of social science/educationalists – MacIntyre, Peters and Stenhouse –
which are then juxtaposed to those of Hargreaves as a front-line advocate of the
need for educational researchers to get their methodological house in order.
These three theorists are argued to present more attractive alternatives to
Hargreaves's 'engineering' 'outcomes-based' model. The utility of discussing
these 'neglected' thinkers is regarded as self-evident (p. 86).

It is clear that Elliott dislikes the Hargreaves approach, regards positivism and
randomised controlled trials (RCTs) as terrible enemies, and wishes to defend
the terrain of educational theory from any invasion of 'scientifically managed'
control. But at the end of the article, I am no clearer why he thinks this than I
was at the beginning. He has not, contrary to his stated hope (p. 86), avoided

Taken from: *British Educational Research Journal*, Vol. 27, No. 5, 2001, pp. 575–6.
© 2001 British Educational Research Association
Reproduced by kind permission of Taylor & Francis Ltd.
http://www.tandf.co.uk/journals

'oppositional thinking' – merely rehearsed some of the most well-known strategies for engaging in it.

One problem is his lack of specificity about his targets for attack: what *is* positivism, for example; why is 'the charge of positivism' (p. 69) so self-evidently a bad thing; what is inherently wrong with 'statistical aggregation' (p. 77), why are RCTs antithetical to case studies (what about N of 1 trials, for example, or the numerous examples of RCTs with case studies and process evaluations embedded in them)? In short, he should familiarise himself with the *real* literature and the actual methodological positions of the side he attacks, rather than simply inviting others to join with him in the pointless activity of setting up a straw man and then knocking him down.

There are genuine problems with experimental research in any field, which I had hoped would be discussed in this article: the question of generalisability, for example, or that of user involvement in design and implementation. The latter may be an issue signalled in Elliott's preference for a third model of educational research – one which centres on teachers' *judgements* (p. 72). The problem here is that all professionals are interested stakeholders, and stakeholding is a well-known source of bias. This is one reason why systematic research synthesis offers an engagingly democratic alternative (cf. the challenges that have accrued to professional 'knowledge' in the field of medicine).

From this point of view, I found it disappointing that Elliott does not engage with the perspectives of other key players – students and parents, for example – who may well have more to gain from explicit, open, even outcomes-based accounts of educational practices than from an outdated reliance on 'expert opinion' models of how knowledge is best constituted.

Chapter 7

Evidence-informed policy and practice: challenges for social science

Ann Oakley

Introduction: the problem of social facts

My topic is a set of challenges that have represented an endemic problem for the social sciences throughout their history [...]. I am referring to the difficult issue of 'social facts'; what are they, how do we find them, how do we know when we have got them, and what (and whom) are they for? As these are somewhat global questions, I shall focus on a specific subset of issues about social facts – those concerning the term 'evidence' and contemporary interpretations of this and its relationship to public policy.

These days we are increasingly hearing about the importance of this thing called 'evidence'. From a variety of motives, including, I suspect, establishing their credibility, people are freely using terms such as 'evidence-informed' and 'evidence-based'; but rather fewer probably give any serious thought to what these terms mean, and even fewer ponder the implications of this new emphasis on evidence for methodological practices in social science as the domain which has historically been preoccupied with the task of assembling reliable knowledge about society.

Published by: *Manchester Statistical Society*, Manchester, UK, 13th February, 2001.
© Manchester Statistical Society 2001
Reproduced by kind permission.

One way to illustrate what I want to talk about is a story that appeared in the *Sydney Morning Herald* in 1999.[1] Diane Ravitch, a Research Professor in Education, flew back to New York from a trip to California and the following day developed pains in her left leg together with a strange shortness of breath. Her neighbour, a radiologist, recognised the signs of pulmonary embolism, and directed her to the hospital. While in hospital, listening to the doctors discussing her condition, Ravitch began to fantasise about what would happen if the doctors gathered round her bed discussing her treatment were to be replaced with education experts. She decided that the first thing that would happen would be the disappearance of the doctors' certainty that she had a problem. The education experts would argue about whether anything *was* actually wrong with her at all – after all, illness is a socially constructed experience. Some would point out that attributing problems to people is simply to blame the victim, and it is wrong to stigmatise people just because they have a sore leg and find it difficult to breathe – one may have these problems and still be normal and happy.

In Ravitch's fantasy (or nightmare) the hospital administrator walks in at this point and announces that the hospital has just received a large grant to treat people like her. Immediately the experts, who all want a share of the money, decide that her symptoms *are* real after all. But now they are unable to agree on what to do. Each has their favourite cure, and each cites different sets of research 'findings' to support their case. One recommends exercise, another disagrees, one recommends drug X, one drug Y: there is apparently no database of research evidence constructed according to consensual standards of scientific validity which can arbitrate between the different approaches. Ravitch, who does get better, because there *is* an established and effective treatment for her complaint, is left wondering why medicine and education should behave so differently.

It may seem obvious to many people that medicine, on the one hand, and education and other social fields, on the other, *should* behave differently, although neither history nor logic really support this case. The origins of social science are strongly associated with what today we would deem a scientific concern for policy-relevance.[2] In the first half of the nineteenth century, extending the scientific method of systematic observation to the social field was seen by European thinkers such as Comte[3] and Quételet[4] as rescuing society from moral chaos, and enabling social reformers to base their actions on strategies for social improvement that were likely to work, precisely because they were based on a sound understanding of social relations. [...] The collection of facts about how people lived was a necessary precursor to designing effective and appropriate policies to improve living conditions. Collecting facts demanded methods for so doing. The early enquiries in the 1830s and 1840s were, as one would suspect, methodologically unselfconscious, although they did include both an early example of systematic sampling in a survey of working class families, and a study of the effects of education which in rather modern tradition relied for its evidence on qualitative data gathered in a somewhat random manner (using that word in its pejorative sense) from people who thought they had something useful to say.[5]

Uncontrolled experimentation and unsystematic research

The early social scientific thinkers disagreed about the relevance to social enquiry of one particular scientific method – that of the experiment. J.S. Mill's *A System of Logic*[6], regarded by many as the foundational text for social science methodology, dismissed experimental methods as artificial and impossible; Comte said they had a place, though an inferior one. There were those, including, later on, Beatrice and Sidney Webb, who well grasped the point made much later in health care, that the controlled experiments conducted by researchers are insignificant in relation to the enormous amount of uncontrolled experimentation that passes for everyday practice. In their *Methods of Social Study* the Webbs argued that there was far more experimenting going on in 'the world sociological laboratory in which we all live', than anywhere else, including in all the laboratories of science. Every finance minister, they said, experiments when he imposes a new tax, as do legislators who draft laws affecting employment, the water supply, or the regulation of food and drugs. In such cases there are theories about the right things to do, things are done, and the effects observed. It is important to recognise that, 'These experiments on human behaviour … are none the less, experiments, because they are … put into operation … by persons in authority as entrepreneurs, legislators, or ministers, often having no consciousness of the experimental nature of their work and no scientific interest in the results.' Such experiments are not, of course, designed according to the specifications of the scientific investigator: 'Those made in the course of capitalist business enterprise are nearly always wrapped in secrecy and accordingly yield nothing to science. Those carried out by public authorities are seldom described with precision, and the publication of their outcome is in many ways imperfect. In the results, as far as made known, no allowance is or can be made with any pretence at accuracy, for plurality of causes and intermixture of effects. No inference can be drawn with any certainty as to what would have happened under other conditions, in other places, at other times, or among people of other races, other religions or other traditions'.[7]

These remarks of the Webbs contain many points which are being made with a new vigour today. The comments about secrecy, publication bias, about simplistic interpretations of causal relationships, and about policy-makers' lack of interest in reliable evidence of effectiveness, could, differently phrased, have come straight out of the mouths of some of those politicians, academics and practitioners who are currently waking up to the realisation that social policy science has a long way to go in catching up with health policy science as regards this extremely key enterprise of being rooted in a body of systematically gathered and critically evaluated knowledge.

'It should be self-evident that decisions on Government policy *ought* to be informed by sound evidence,' said the Secretary of State for Education, David

Blunkett, in 2000: 'Social science research *ought* to be contributing a major part of that evidence base. It should be playing a key role in helping us to decide our overall strategies. Too often in the past policy has not been informed by good research: a former Permanent Secretary once ruefully described the old Department of Education and Science as a "knowledge-free zone"'.[8] David Hargreaves, Professor of Education at Cambridge, gave a lecture to the Teacher Training Agency in 1996[9] which began with the inflammatory words 'Teaching is not at present a research-based profession' and went on to argue that the £50–60 million spent annually in this country on educational research is poor value for money in improving the quality of education because most of it is not spent on providing a sound research base. Hargreaves compares educational research unfavourably with medical research on a number of grounds. First, it is at best confused about, and at worse dismissive of, the role of scientific knowledge in improving professional practice; second, it is non-cumulative, repetitive and unsystematic in its approach to improving knowledge; and third, most educational research is carried out by people other than practitioners, a stark contrast with medicine where doctors, nurses and others are highly involved in attempts to improve the research base of their discipline. Hargreaves' allegations about the quality of educational research, which have provoked much fierce debate, were subsequently supported by government sponsored reports, including one to the ESRC's Teaching and Learning Programme,[10] and another by the Institute of Employment Studies[11] which expressed dismay at the low level of impact most educational research has on policy, reiterated concerns about its non-cumulative nature, and complained about its tendency to spawn large numbers of small-scale qualitative projects which are inherently incapable of yielding reliable and generalisable findings.

These rather damning observations were extended to social science and policy research more generally – including such fields as criminology and social welfare – by Adrian Smith, a Professor of Statistics, in an address to the Royal Statistical Society of London in 1996. Smith argued that, 'We are, through the media, as ordinary citizens, confronted daily with controversy and debate across a whole spectrum of public policy issues. But typically, we have no access to any form of a systematic 'evidence base' – and therefore no means of participating in the debate in a mature and informed manner.[12]

The example of daycare

One of the largest socio-economic changes of the twentieth century has been the increasing combination of paid employment and motherhood; surveys of employed mothers show that finding good quality childcare is a huge problem, and the demand for this normally substantially outstrips supply. When it comes to reliable information about the effects of daycare on children – a common concern in the social policy field and for individual parents – the messages emanating from the enormous quantity of research literature are very mixed indeed. While some research suggests that daycare has adverse effects on children's health and well-being,[13] other studies come to very much the opposite conclusion, identifying it as an intervention with long-lasting effects on a wide range of health, education and welfare outcomes of social policy interest. These include beneficial effects on children's measured IQ, less need for special education, more employment among mothers in the short run, and less criminal behaviour, unemployment and unintended pregnancy among young people in the longer run.[14] The salient methodological point here is that the findings derived from well-designed experimental studies of daycare are in noted contrast to those of observational studies, which generally founder on the rock of being unable to disentangle the effects of daycare as an educational and social intervention from those of poor socio-economic background, a characteristic of many children attending daycare in countries such as the UK and the USA.

The conclusions about the experimental evidence on daycare come from a systematic review which is part of the Cochrane Library, an electronic library of systematic reviews produced as part of the work of the Cochrane Collaboration.[15] The Cochrane Collaboration is an international network of health care researchers named after Archie Cochrane, a doctor and epidemiologist much given to astute and entertaining reflections on health care. There are currently some 50 different review groups in the Cochrane Collaboration, and they have to date produced 923 completed reviews, with another 827 in protocol stage.

The major emphasis of the Cochrane Library is on well-designed experimental studies – randomised controlled trials – of the effectiveness of health care treatments. But there is also a concern with prevention, and especially with the health-promoting potential of social interventions. Social interventions have been subjected to much more controlled experimental evaluation than the redoubtable Webbs imagined. A database called SPECTR – a Social, Psychological, Educational and Criminological Trials Register – assembled initially by a Cochrane Collaboration group had no difficulty in finding some 10,500 controlled trials of interventions in these fields.[16] Much of this research has been carried out in the USA where, for a variety of reasons, there has been a much stronger tradition of experimental social science.[17] The USA is the home for the Campbell Collaboration [named] after the methodologist Donald Campbell, which [provides] the infrastructure for systematic research synthesis in social science and policy fields.

Critical challenges

So what are the central challenges for social science arising from this move towards what some have (rather dismissively) called 'evidence-based everything'? These are four of the most important, as I see them:

1. Establishing the methods and importance of systematic research synthesis.
2. Developing methods for critically appraising different study designs.
3. Reducing bias in evaluations of policy and practice.
4. Abolishing methodological divides between disciplines.

Systematic research synthesis

The first pre-requisite of a sound evidence base for anything is a system for locating, critically assessing and synthesising the results of research that has already been done, and holding the results of this effort in a form that is transparent and easily updated. Social science has traditionally operated with the very different notion of 'literature reviews'. Most literature reviews in social science are selective, opinionated and discursive rampages through literature which the reviewer happens to know about or can easily lay his or her hands on. This is a million miles away from the notion of research synthesis as an activity governed by principles of clearly defined inclusion and exclusion criteria, systematic searching, and specified methods for appraising the quality of different studies.[18]

Table 7.1   Health focus of effectiveness reviews in health promotion[19]

Total	401
Substance abuse (drugs/alcohol/tobacco)	156
Sexual health	71
Accidents/injury	31
Healthy eating	31
Obesity	27
Cardiovascular disease	26
Mental health	24
Physical activity	19
Cancer	14
Other	65

Table 7.1 is taken from a piece of work carried out for the Department of Health by a team of researchers in the Social Science Research Unit in London. The aim of the work was to find and critically assess existing reviews of health promotion effectiveness, a subject of keen interest to health promotion practitioners. The first finding was *how many* such reviews there are – all claiming to be definitive reviews of effectiveness in a particular area. We found 401 completed reviews, including 156 focussing on substance abuse and 72 on sexual health promotion.

The quality of these reviews was extremely variable. For example, while most of the reviews stated their aims, only a third said anything about how studies had been found, less than half specified their inclusion criteria, and only a quarter their validity criteria. Most of the studies went no further than a narrative synthesis.

Table 7.2   Six reviews of older people and accident prevention[20]

Total studies included	137
Common to at least two reviews	33
Common to all six reviews	2
Treated consistently in all reviews	1

One result is the different numbers of studies included in reviews carried out at the same time and supposedly drawing on the same literature. Table 7.2 gives some figures for reviews of older people and accident prevention. In six reviews there were a total of 137 studies, only 33 of which were common to at least two reviews, and only two of which were common to all six reviews. Only one study was treated consistently in all six reviews. Table 7.3 shows another example from studies of anti-smoking education for young people: two so-called systematic reviews carried out at the same time, 27 studies included in both reviews, only three common to both. The last figure here, 70, is the number of studies we knew from our systematically keyworded bibliographic database were available to be included in these reviews at the time they were done.

Table 7.3   Two reviews of smoking prevention programmes for young people[21]

Total studies included	27
Common to both reviews	3
Available for review at the time	70

The consequence of this chaos is, of course, that reviewers reach very different conclusions about what the social facts represented by research actually are. This is no help to the policy-maker or practitioner who wants to know what the evidence is for different policy and practice decisions that might be made in any particular case.

A second problem is that the comprehensiveness of the universe of studies included in systematic reviews reflects the search strategies used to find them, and this is an area where social science databases have a long way to go. Table 7.4 shows the percentages of the same group of studies found on five electronic databases: the figures go from 65% for Medline to 9% for ERIC (Educational Resources Information Center). Different databases use different methods for finding and keywording studies; for example, study design is indexed differently on Medline and EMBASE (a database of medical journal articles produced by Elsevier Science),

Table 7.4   'Known' outcome evaluations [N = 46] on different electronic databases[22]

EMBASE	46%
ERIC	9%
Medline	65%
PsycLit	46%
Social Science Citation Index	59%

and ERIC and PsycLit (a database of psychology literatureproduced by the American Psychological Association) do not index for study type at all.

Critically appraising different study designs

We all know life is full of trials, and, while the ones which are the focus of this paper are perhaps the least of our worries, the move towards evidence-based everything always sooner or later raises the issue of whether life, in a methodological sense, is about trials or whether it is also about other study designs as well. My own answer to this is unequivocally that research synthesis needs to be about more than trials. One reason is that, in social science and policy fields, restricting included studies to trials will result in excluding large volumes of potentially relevant literature.

Table 7.5   A review of mental health and young people[23]

Total citations	11,638
Met inclusion criteria	948
RCTs	68

Data from another project we are involved in, a review of barriers and facilitators relating to young people's mental health, are shown in Table 7.5. Our search strategies found over 11,000 citations, of which only 68 or 0.6% were randomised controlled trials (RCTs). Sifting through the total universe of over 11,000 studies and attempting some assessment of the 880 studies included in the review which were not RCTs involves an enormous amount of effort. It also immediately raises the problem of how to quality assess the full range of research designs. Trials are relatively easy; we can, for example, specify that there should have been concealed random allocation to experimental and control groups, that baseline and post intervention data should be provided for all study participants, and so forth. But how on earth do we sort out trustworthy from untrustworthy qualitative studies?

There are various suggestions in the literature as to how this might be done. In one exercise, we looked at the criteria for assessing qualitative studies suggested by eight research groups. The first four groups[24] [25] [26] [27] proposed 'quantitative' criteria; altogether, 46 criteria were suggested, of which 28 occurred in only one of the lists, ten in two, and six in three, with only two being common to all four lists – a clear description of the sample and how it was recruited, and an adequate description of how the findings were derived from the data. The second four research groups[28] [29] [30] [31] suggested 'qualitative' criteria for assessing the trustworthiness of qualitative studies. There were 28 different criteria in these four lists; thirteen of the criteria appeared once and 11 twice; one – the collection of 'thick' data appeared in three lists, but none were common to all four. Next, we went on to use the seven most commonly cited criteria proposed by these groups in a review of peer-led health promotion studies for young people. The seven criteria for assessing the quality of qualitative research were: a clear statement of aims and objectives; a clear description of the context of the research; including enough original data to mediate between evidence and interpretation; an explicit theoretical framework and/or

Table 7.6   Qualitative studies displaying different methodological quality criteria (N = 15)[32]

Aims and objectives clearly stated	73%
A clear description of context	67%
Inclusion of sufficient original data to mediate between evidence and interpretation	67%
Explicit theoretical framework and/or literature review	47%
A clear description of sample	47%
A clear description of methodology and systematic data collection	47%
Analysis by more than one researcher	20%

literature review; a clear description of the sample used; a clear description of the methods used and systematic data collection; and data analysis by more than one researcher. We looked in detail at 15 studies; Table 7.6 gives the results. The proportion of studies failing to meet the criteria went from around a quarter for stating aims and objectives to 80% for data analysis by more than one researcher.

There is also the awkward question of how to integrate the results of reviews of qualitative research with those of experimental and other quantitative research. In an ongoing review of barriers to, and facilitators of, young people's mental health, we included all types of study design – an ambitious exercise – and ended up with two very different sets of findings: on the one hand, there were the conclusions of high-quality evaluations of interventions aimed at promoting young people's mental health; and, on the other, there were the results of surveys reporting young people's views on what they regarded as the most useful and important strategies. It was impossible to combine these sets of findings in any straightforward way. Instead we constructed a matrix laying out the key themes from the studies of young people's views alongside descriptions of the intervention studies and existing systematic reviews. This enabled us to say something about the matches and mismatches between the two sets of data. For example, physical and material problems with schooling such as work overload, or, conversely, 'having nothing to do', appeared in the young people's reports, but were not any kind of focus for the intervention studies. The young people reported fear of violence and bullying as a big problem, but this was not addressed in the interventions. A rather fundamental problem not picked up in the intervention studies was that young people failed to relate to the term 'mental health' – they did not see it as having anything to do with their own experiences of feeling bad or feeling good. What this means is a big gap between the usefulness of qualitative research – its ability to tell us about people's views and experiences – on the one hand, and policy and practice attempts to change things for the better, on the other. This is not a route to evidence-based anything.

Reducing bias

One difficulty with this methodological work is its apparently highly technical nature. On the surface it has little to do either with scholarship (a venture that perhaps still hides somewhere in universities these days) or with the burning policy and practice questions that affect people on the ground. So this gives us another critical challenge for social science in the move towards taking the notion of evidence seriously: the need to lay our methodological and ideological posturing on one side and get down to the really important business. However much we adopt sophisticated methodological postures for professional reasons, in our personal lives we *do* behave as though facts exist. We *do* operate with commonsense notions of truth – for example, the truth about the relationship between long-distance flying in cramped seats and deep vein thrombosis, or the truth about the effects on little children of being looked after on a regular basis by people other than their parents, or the truth about levels of police patrols and the incidence of street crime, or the truth about effective social work intervention for supporting families under stress.

A central issue is bias. How can we best ensure that what we *say* we know about the effects of policies and practices is likely to be valid and reliable knowledge? According to what has been called 'the iron law of evaluation studies', almost any comparison of experimental studies using random assignment, on the one hand, with other kinds of studies, on the other, shows that the better an evaluation is technically, the less likely it is to show positive results.[33] A particularly interesting finding, which has been unearthed by Bob Boruch and colleagues in the USA in the field of training and employment programmes for socially excluded youth, is that non-randomised studies may show damaging effects which disappear when the evaluation design is that of an RCT.[34] More commonly the use of randomisation to create control groups reduces the likelihood of an intervention being shown to be effective. Table 7.7 shows the relationship between research design and 'successful' versus 'unsuccessful' interventions in two reviews of crime prevention research; Table 7.8 gives a more recent example from our health promotion work. In the crime prevention area, experimental evaluations using random or matched control groups were considerably less likely to demonstrate effectiveness (Table 7.7); studies of attempts to reduce cholesterol which include qualitative data gave the highest estimates of effectiveness, and well-designed trials the lowest (Table 7.8).

Disciplinary divides and stakeholders

The fourth challenge on my list is that of disciplinary divides. As I noted earlier, the custom of claiming an inevitable methodological divide between the social and natural sciences is deep-seated. Academics are used to trading in arguments about ownership of different research methods; this is part of their professional claims to expertise. But the time has come for considering the point of such debates. Like many other academic activities these days, disciplinary posturing and arguments about methods produce publications which look good on our CVs; they may also get us to nice meetings in interesting places, and help to earn our institutions money which we may, or may not, get our own hands on, depending on the unsystematic views our institutions take of the research

Table 7.7   Crime prevention research: research design and effectiveness claimed

	'Successful' Intervention	'Unsuccessful' Intervention
Logan 1972[35] [N = 100 studies]		
Random control groups	27%	73%
Non-random control groups	50%	50%
No control groups	69%	31%
Wright and Dixon 1977[36] [N = 96]		
Random/matched control groups	25%	75%
Other control groups	51%	49%

Table 7.8   Workplace health promotion interventions aimed at reducing cholesterol level[37] (N = 52)

	Effective according to authors
Studies including qualitative data	87%
All studies	81%
All trials	70%
Well-designed trials*	58%

*Comparable intervention and comparison groups, pre- and post-intervention data, reporting on all outcomes

assessment and higher education funding exercise. But the danger is that we become slaves to technique: 'Much that purports to be theory of evaluation is scholastic: evaluations are endlessly categorized, and chapels are dedicated to the glorification of particular styles. Latter-day theologians discuss how best to reify such chimeras as "goals" and "benefits". The technicians debate over numerological derivations from artificial models – "How many angels ...?". All too rarely does discussion descend to earthy questions such as, "Is worthwhile information being collected?"'[38]

Like controlled experiments, research synthesis has a strong but buried history in social science. This history illustrates another key aspect of evidence-based endeavours in social science or anywhere else – the immense difficulty of conducting them without offending the numerous stakeholders involved. The term meta-analysis, used to describe the statistical side of systematic reviewing, was coined by the educational psychologist Gene Glass in 1976.[39] Glass had been undergoing psychotherapy for many years, and was also married to a therapist, Mary Lee Smith, so he had a double motivation for wanting to know whether therapy worked or not. The various famous criticisms of the benefits of psychotherapy around at the time[40] were based on unsystematic reviews, so Glass decided to see if he could do any better. He and his wife computed 833 effect sizes derived from 375 studies obtained from over 1000 citations, coding through breakfast, lunch and dinner for many years, which must have made them rather difficult to live with, and may even have contributed to the ultimate failure of their marriage. Using a simple and subsequently much criticized procedure of comparing group means, and taking the difference divided by the standard deviation of control groups, Glass and Smith eventually concluded there is evidence that psychotherapy *does* work.[41]

This conclusion made the psychotherapists happier than their colleagues in the social work field, who around the same time had to deal with a discouraging review about casework,[42] which suggested that troubled clients left to their own devices did no worse and sometimes distinctly better than those who were 'helped' by social workers. In the aftermath of this conclusion, 'bruised and angry'[43] social workers complained that the methodology of systematic reviews is far too blunt an instrument to discover the truth. As a matter of fact, a re-analysis[44] of some of the studies in the original Smith and Glass review of psychotherapy, focussing only on studies using placebo groups, came to the opposite conclusion from Glass's original one, thereby instituting an equality between the psychotherapists and the social workers by making them equally unhappy.

The view that systematic reviews are too blunt an instrument to unearth the truth remains a highly popular opinion in some circles today. My colleagues and I at the Social Science Research Unit have spent [several] years encountering it in our health promotion work, and [...] we have now started to engage with much the same set of arguments in the education field.

This Centre, the Evidence for Policy and Practice Information and Co-ordinating Centre or EPPI-Centre for short, has been funded [...] to provide the infrastructure for a kind of mini-Cochrane Collaboration in the field of education. [...] Our EPPI-Centre work is based on the following principles: that different user groups need access to high-quality review of research; that collaborative developments are needed in systematic review methodology; and that such moves towards a firmer evidence base for social science and policy will get nowhere unless they follow principles of openness and equal participation of all stakeholders. [...].

Conclusion

So, to conclude, we live in exciting times, full of trials and all sorts of other animals which challenge us intellectually, methodologically and politically. Social science may be in a process of transition, which could alternatively be regarded, depending on the disciplinary camp you belong to, as its final coming of age or a sad deviation down the dead end of positivism. There will be lots and lots of arguments; some people will foster the move towards evidence-informed policy and practice, and others will resist; there are likely, I think, to be considerable changes of position, probably both ways. The relationship between social science and government, never simple, will continue to perplex us all.

As the founding father of meta-analysis, Gene Glass, said some years ago: 'One can imagine a future for research ... in which questions are so sharply put and techniques so well-standardized that studies would hardly need to be integrated by merit of their consistent findings. But that future seems unlikely. Research will probably continue to be an unorganized, decentralized, non-standardized activity pursued simultaneously in dozens of places without thought to how it will all fit together in the end.'

Glass and colleagues go on to say, and I agree, that 'The approach ... [of systematic reviews] seems to be too plainly reasonable to be false in any simple sense. Whether it will be useful is a different matter.'[45]

Notes

1 Ravitch, D. (1999) Physicians leave education researchers for dead. *Sydney Morning Herald,* 22 February.

2 Abrams, P. (1968) *The Origins of British Sociology.* Chicago: University of Chicago Press.

3 Comte, A. (1877) *Cours de philosophie positive.* Paris: Bailiière,

4 Quételet, A. (1837) *Correspondance mathèmatique et physique.* Paris: Bachelier.

5 Kent, R. A. (1981) *A History of British Empirical Sociology.* Hants.: Gower, pp. 199–201.

6 Mill, J. S. (1973–4, originally published 1843) *A System of Logic.* ed. Robson J. M. Toronto: University of Toronto Press.

7 Webb, S., Webb, B. (1932) *Methods of Social Study.* London: Longmans, Green and Co., pp. 224–6.

8 ESRC/DfEE (2000) *Influence or Irrelevance: can social science improve Government?* Secretary of State's ESRC Lecture Speech, 2 February.

9 Hargreaves, D. H. (1996) *Teaching as a Research-based Profession: possibilities and prospects.* Teacher Training Agency Annual Lecture.

10 McIntyre, D., McIntyre, A. (1999) *Capacity for Research into Teaching and Learning.* Confidential report to the ESRC Teaching and Learning Programme, Cambridge: University of Cambridge School of Education.

11 Hillage, J., Pearson, R., Anderson, A., Tamkin, P. (1998) *Excellence in Research on Schools.* Sudbury, Suffolk: DfEE Publications.

12 Smith, A. F. M. (1996) Mad cows and ecstasy: change and choice in an evidence-based society. *Journal of the Royal Statistical Society.* 159(3): 367–83.

13 Clarke-Stewart, A. (1991) A home is not a school: The effects of child care on children's development. *Journal of Social Issues.* 47: 105–124.

14 Zoritch, B., Roberts, I., Oakley, A., Day care for pre-school children (Cochrane Review). In: *The Cochrane Library,* Issue 2, 2000. Oxford: Update Software.

15 Chalmers, I., Sackett, D., Silagy, C. (1997) The Cochrane Collaboration. In: (eds) Maynard, A., Chalmers, I. *Non-random Reflections on Health Services Research.* London: BMJ Publishing Group.

16 Petrosino, A. J. et al. (1999) A Social, Psychological, Educational and Criminal Trials Register (SPECTR) to facilitate the Preparation and Maintenance of Systematic Reviews of Social and Educational Interventions. Report prepared for Planning Meeting on Research Synthesis and Public Policy, University College, London.

17 See Oakley, A. (1998) Public policy experimentation: lessons from America. *Policy Studies.* 19(2): 93–114.

18 Chalmers, I., Altman, D. (1995) *Systematic Reviews.* London: BMJ Publishing Group.

19 Peersman, G., Harden, A., Oliver, S., Oakley, A. (1999) *Effectiveness Reviews in Health Promotion*. London: EPPI-Centre, Institute of Education, University of London, p. 28.

20 Oliver, S., Peersman, G., Harden, A., Oakley, A. (1999) Discrepancies in findings from effectiveness reviews: the case of health promotion for older people in accident and injury prevention. *Health Education Journal*. 58: 66–77.

21 Oakley, A., Fullerton, D. (1995) *A Systematic Review of Smoking Prevention Programmes for Young People*. London: EPPI-Centre, Institute of Education, University of London.

22 Peersman et al. (1999), p. 48.

23 Harden, A., Rees, R., Shepherd, J., Brunton G., Oliver, A., Oakley, A. (2000) *Young People and Mental Health: a systematic review of research on barriers and facilitators*. London: EPPI-Centre, Institute of Education, University of London.

24 Boulton, M., Kitzpatrick, R., Swinburn, C. (1996) Qualitative research in health care II: a structured review and evaluation of studies. *Journal of Evaluation in Clinical Practice*. 2(3): 171–179.

25 Cobb, A. K., Hagemaster, J. N. (1987) Ten criteria for evaluating qualitative research proposals. *Journal of Nursing Education*. 26(4): 138–143.

26 Mays, N., Pope, C. (1995) Rigour and qualitative research. *British Medical Journal*. 311: 109–112.

27 Medical Sociology Group (1996) Criteria for the evaluation of qualitative research papers. *Medical Sociology News*. 22(1): 69–71.

28 Harden, A., Weston, R., Oakley, A. (1999) *A Review of the Effectiveness and Appropriateness of Peer-delivered Health Promotion Interventions for Young People*. London: EPPI-Centre, Institute of Education, University of London, p. 79.

29 Leininger, M. (1994) Evaluation criteria and critique of qualitative research studies. In: (ed.) Morse, J. M. *Critical Issues in Qualitative Research Methods*. Thousand Oaks, Cal.: Sage Publications.

30 Lincoln, Y. S., Cuba, E. G. (1985) *Naturalistic Inquiry*. Beverly Hills, Cal.: Sage Publications.

31 Muecke, M. A. (1994) On the evaluation of ethnographies. In: Morse op.cit. 14

32 Popay, J., Rogers, A., Williams, G. (1998) Rationale and standards for the systematic review of qualitative literature in health services research. *Qualitative Health Research*. 8(3): 341–51.

33 Rossi, P. H. (1987) The iron law of evaluation and other metallic rules. In: (eds) Miller, J. L., Lewis, M. *Research in Social Problems and Public Policy*. Greenwich, Conn.: JAI Press.

34 LaLonde, R. J. (1986) Evaluating the econometric evaluations of training programs with experimental data. *American Economic Review*. 76(4): 504–619.

35 Logan, C. H. (1972) Evaluation research in crime and delinquency: a reappraisal. *Journal of Criminal Law, Criminology and Police Science*. 63(3): 378–87.

36 Wright, W. E, Dixon, M. C. (1977) Community prevention and treatment of juvenile delinquency. *Journal of Research in Crime and Delinquency*. 35: 67.

37 Peersman, G., Harden, A., Oliver, S. (1998) *Effectiveness of Health Promotion Interventions in the Workplace: a review*. London: Health Education Authority.

38 Cronbach, L. J. (1981) Our ninety-five theses. In Freeman, H.E., Solomon, H.A. (eds) *Evaluation Studies Review Annual* Vol. 6. Beverly Hills: Sage, pp. 27–8.

39 Glass, G. (1976) Primary, secondary and meta-analysis of research. *Educational Researcher*. 5: 3–8.

40 For example Eysenck, H. J. (1952) The effects of psychotherapy: an evaluation. *Journal of Consulting Psychology*. 16: 319–324.

41 Smith, M. L., Glass, G. V. (1977) Meta-analysis of psychotherapy outcome studies. *American Psychologist*. 32: 752–760.

42 Fischer, J. (1973) Is casework effective? A review. *Social Work*. January: 5–20.

43 Macdonald, G., Sheldon, B. (1992) Contemporary studies of the effectiveness of social work. *British Journal of Social Work.* 22(6): 615–643, p. 616.

44 Prioleau, L., Murdock, M, Brody, N. (1983) An analysis of psychotherapy versus placebo studies. *The Behavioral and Brain Sciences.* 6: 275–310.

45 Glass, G. V., McGaw, B., Smith, M. L. (1981) *Meta-analysis in Social Research.* Beverly Hills: Sage, pp. 230–231.

Chapter 8

Intellectuals or technicians? The urgent role of theory in educational studies[1]

Stephen J. Ball

Game opening

In this paper I reflect upon my practice as an educational researcher and theorist and, in more general terms, consider the current state of educational studies. In doing so, I allow myself to be playful and, perhaps, at times outrageous. I am not attempting to be definitive. What I offer here is coming close to an approximation of something I might hope to say more clearly in the future. The spirit of what I am attempting, and some of the substance I wish to argue, are conveyed rather effectively in the following quotation from Michel Foucault:

> I wouldn't want what I may have said or written to be seen as laying any claims to totality. I don't try to universalize what I say; conversely what I don't say isn't meant to be thereby disqualified as being of no importance. My work takes place between unfinished abutments and anticipatory strings of dots. I like to open out a space of research, try it out, then if it doesn't work try again somewhere else. On many points ... I am still working and don't yet know whether I am going to get anywhere. What I say ought to be taken as 'propositions', 'game openings' where

Taken from: *British Journal of Educational Studies*, Vol. 43, No. 3, 1995, pp. 255–71.
© Blackwell Publishers Ltd. and SCSE 1995
Reproduced by kind permission of Blackwell Publishing.

those who may be interested are invited to join in; they are not meant as dogmatic assertions that have to be taken or left en bloc ... (Foucault, 1991, pp. 90–91)

My 'proposition', then, my 'game opening' here, is that educational studies is in a sorry state and in danger of becoming sorrier. That is to say, the weak grammars of educational studies, those concepts, relations and procedures upon which it rests, are becoming weaker. The serial segmented structures, those differentiating rituals which distinguish us from each other and from other fields of knowledge, are becoming more detached and insulated from one another. As Basil Bernstein might put it, the invisible light that shines wanly within the knowledge structures of educational studies is in danger of being snuffed out entirely.

It is hardly novel to suggest that the discourses and knowledge structures of educational studies are shifting in response to the political and ideological repositioning of the academy and of scholarship in the United Kingdom. It is important to make it clear that the state of affairs I am addressing here is, at least in part, symptomatic of a more wholesale reworking of the relationship between higher education and research and the state. However, the resultant changes in the practices of scholarship seem particularly marked and particularly paradoxical in the field of educational studies. More specifically, what I have called the sorry state of educational studies seems to me to stem in part from both the wholesale appropriation of other 'unreflexive' and utilitarian languages and an internal lack of dynamism, exacerbated by intellectual isolationism as educational studies pointedly ignores significant theoretical developments in cognate fields. The problem with educational studies, I am arguing, is that they are both too open to other discourses and not open enough.

This state of affairs is my topic. I want to spend some time exploring the problems with educational studies as I see them. I shall then consider the role of theory in reconstituting a new present for educational studies and conclude with some brief thoughts about the nature of theorising and the problem with theory. While bearing in mind the initial disclaimer quoted above, I will have, necessarily, to indulge in some generalisations. I must also acknowledge from the start that I will leave my argument only partially developed as well as embedded with contradictions. At times I will be likely to appear self-destructive and perhaps intellectually schizophrenic. I shall leave the reader to judge. I must also acknowledge that what I say may have somewhat less relevance to some disciplines within educational studies than it does to others.

British sociology of education as a case in point

To begin I want to take as my particular case in point my own discipline – the sociology of education – but, as I say, I intend my thesis to be more generalised.

I shall rehearse a kind of vulgar history of the discipline in order to establish what I call the reincorporation of educational studies.

British sociology of education had its beginnings in and was primarily disseminated from the London School of Economics. The methods and politics of the subject were, from the late 1930s to the late 1960s, driven by the methods and politics of that institution. This placed education as part of both the post-war social reconstruction of Britain and the establishment of a modern welfare state. The concerns of researchers were focussed initially upon the problems of mass participation in the education system and the debilitating effects, for some children, of economic and material deprivation. The sometimes unarticulated assumption of the handful of education researchers at work at this time appeared to be that if these extrinsic sources of inequality could be removed or ameliorated then the repeatedly evident and apparently tight bond between educational attainment and social class could be broken. Crucially, the particular focus upon social class differences served to establish social class as the major, almost the only, dependent variable in sociological research for the next forty years. During this period, the sociology of education aspired to, and occasionally achieved, a positive and influential relationship with policy-making. Particular policy solutions, based upon the outcomes of empirical research, were pursued, particularly in relation to Labour Party policy-making. Both the discipline and its politics and its relationships to policy were set within the grooves of an unproblematic progressive, utopian modernism. This was the enlightenment project writ small. Research linked to ameliorative state policies focussed upon the achievement of equality and prosperity – the better educated we are the better off we are, individually and collectively. The discourse of this policy optimism was founded upon notions like the 'wasted pool of talent' and 'compensatory education'.

As we know this dual optimism (that attached to the welfare state and that embedded in the practices and discourses of the discipline itself) did not last. In the 1970s the academic discourse of programmatic optimism was to be dramatically and decisively replaced by one of radical pessimism. The interpretations of the causes and solutions of inequality were scattered to the winds. Policy became an irrelevance as the reproduction of unequal social relations was discovered to be lurking stubbornly in every classroom nook and cranny and every staffroom conversation; while at the same time it was rooted in the abstract needs of the state and the inevitable and inescapable requirements and workings of the economy. The teacher as cultural dope was now the subject of derision from all sides for failing to deliver either fairness or prosperity. A relationship between research and policy (at least at national level) was now not just pointless but also politically incorrect. Educational researchers found themselves grounded between negativity and complicity. With the collapse of the relationship between educational research and policy and the beginnings of a growing suspicion of liberal expertise within educational politics, the vacuum in the arena of educational policy-making was skilfully filled by the organic intellectuals of the new right.

In the 1980s things became more complicated as class analysis was displaced as the primary variable with race, gender and, later, disability and sexual orientation coming to the fore both in analytical perspectives and in a new but tentative liaison between theory and practice. But race and gender studies were only two parts of a more thorough-going fragmentation of the sociology of education as some researchers began to attach themselves to the industry of educational reform. While some one-time and would-be sociologists and other educational researchers now reinvented themselves as feminists or anti-racists, and indeed brought to educational studies a much needed infusion of invigorating new theory, others began to take on new identities as 'school effectiveness researchers' and 'management theorists'. Around this latter kind of work, a new relationship to policy, or rather inside policy, was forged. Issues related to system design, analysis of provision and social justice were replaced by implementation studies focussed on issues like 'quality', 'evaluation', 'leadership' and 'accountability'.

Policy science and policy scholarship

In the 1990s whole areas of the sociology of education, specifically, and educational studies generally, have been thoroughly reincorporated into the political project and discourse of policy and of educational reform. In some respects the discipline has come full circle. It is tempting here to consider this reincorporation by rehearsing Brian Fay's (1975) distinction between policy science and policy scholarship. It is a temptation I shall not resist. Fay defines policy science as 'that set of procedures which enables one to determine the technically best course of action to adopt in order to implement a decision or achieve a goal. Here the policy scientist doesn't merely clarify the possible outcomes of certain courses of action, he (sic) actually chooses the most efficient course of action in terms of the available scientific information' (p. 14). This, Fay suggests, is a type of 'policy engineering': the 'policy engineer ... is one who seeks the most technically correct answer to political problems in terms of available social scientific knowledge' (p. 14). Here policy is both de-politicised and thoroughly technicised. The purview of the policy scientist is limited to, and by, the agenda of social and political problems defined elsewhere and by solutions already embedded in scientific practice. Fay calls this 'the sublimation of politics' (p. 27).

It also produces, I suggest, another effect. Through a combination of financial restructuring and Faustian deal-making, the academy is tamed. As a result, research perspectives and research funding are increasingly tightly tied to the policy agendas of government. Moreover, the already weak autonomy of higher education is redefined as part of the cause of the nation's economic problems. Further, this problem-solving technicism rests upon an uncritical acceptance of moral and political consensus and operates within the hegemony of instrumental rationalism or, as Fay puts it, 'man (sic) must plan, and the function of the social sciences is to provide the theoretical foundation that makes this planning possible' (p. 27). In this scientific and technical project for research, the debates and conflicts which link policies to values and morals are displaced by bland rationalist empiricism, and the best we can aspire to is to be 'integrated critics' (Eco, 1994).

But, again, other effects are produced here. Firstly, this instrumental, rational empiricism is implicated and interested in the social construction of those subjects about which it speaks. It produces what Donzelot (1979) calls the 'landscape of the social' within which it then acts (I return to this later). Furthermore, in this 'will to knowledge' and the complex interplay between knowledge and the objects of its concern, the very nature of 'the social' is captured and constrained by social science's classifications and nosologies and by the drive to achieve parsimonious and totalising conceptions of social structures and processes. The epistemic assumptions of order, structure, function, cause and effect are variously mobilised to represent 'the social' and, in doing so, work to exclude many of the mobile, complex, ad hoc, messy and fleeting qualities of lived experience. We become locked into the simple but powerful and very productive assumption that 'the social' is susceptible to parsimonious and orderly totalising conceptions. Or, to use a slightly different lexicon, drawing again from Foucault, we can say that:

> In appearance, or rather, according to the mask it bears, historical consciousness is neutral, devoid of passions and committed solely to truth. But, if it examines itself and if, more generally, it interrogates the various forms of scientific consciousness in its history it finds that all these forms and transformations are aspects of the will to knowledge: instinct, passion, the inquisitor's devotion, cruel subtlety and malice ... (Foucault, 1977, p. 162)

Management theory and school effectiveness research

Perhaps it would be helpful at this point if I were to develop an example of policy science at work in a way which begins to illustrate some of the variety of points I have adumbrated above. 'Management theory' offers one example on which I have written previously (Ball, 1990 and 1994). So, let me move away from that slightly by considering the relationship between management theory and school effectiveness research. Again, my style of analysis draws on Foucault, in particular I shall employ his 'master trope' – reversal. I will thus be seeking the negative activity of discourse.

Management theories, as modes of objectification, define human beings as subjects to be managed. This is a 'discourse of right' which legitimates the exercise of authority. Its primary instrument is a hierarchy of continuous and functional surveillance. Effectiveness research can be seen to have played a crucial role in laying the groundwork for the reconceptualisation of the school within which management discourse operates and has played its part in providing a technology of organisational measurement and surveillance. By technology here I refer to 'coherent or contradictory forms of managing and activating a population' which, like Bentham's panopticon, lend themselves to three particular polyvalent tactical applications.

First, effectiveness studies and school-difference studies re-centred the school as the focus of causation in explanations of student performance and variations in levels of achievement; displacing or rendering silent other explanations related to the embeddedness of education in social and economic contexts. And, in so far as the gaze of 'effectiveness' provided a scientific basis for the possibility of 'blaming' the school, it fitted perfectly (in terms of theoretical unity) into the discourses of derision which targeted schools as 'causes' of general social and economic problems within society at large. In addition, the focus on measurable outcomes also articulated directly with the political process of the commodification of education involved in the creation of an education market.

Second, this research provided a scientific concomitant to the political re-emphasis on excellence, diversity and selection and the attempt to develop methods of appraisal which can be used to identify (and punish) 'weak' and 'inadequate' teachers, a process that feeds into systems of incentive and performance-related pay. Third, the effectiveness studies developed a technology of control which enables the monitoring and 'steering' of schools by applying 'neutral' indicators; they also continually 'tap' and measure more of that which is schooling, including 'the "deep structure" of pupil attitudes and perceptions' (Reynolds, 1990, p. 21). Thus, significant discursive and disciplinary work is done by effectiveness research, which is even further reaching in its implications when linked to notions of accountability, school review and school development planning. Here we may see the play and effects of power and domination at work in the direct relationships and immediate structures of school organisation. These are 'the panopticisms of every day' which are constructed and enacted 'below the level of emergence of the great apparatuses and the great political struggles' (Foucault, 1979, p. 223).

In effect, through such schemes, teachers are entrapped into taking responsibility for their own 'disciplining'. Indeed teachers are urged to believe that their commitment to such processes will make them more 'professional'. Moreover, effectiveness is a technology of normalisation. Such research both constructs a normative model of the effective school and abnormalises the ineffective or 'sick' school. In relation to the concepts of 'review', 'development' and 'self-evaluation', it then draws upon the 'confessional technique' (an admission of transgressions and a ritual of atonement) as a means of submission and transformation. The secular confession is founded on the notion of normal as against abnormal transposed from the religious opposition of sin and piety. Such a transposition is most clearly evident in the methods of 'appraisal'.

The normalising effects of 'effectiveness' are noted by Laurie Angus. In a recent review of school effectiveness literature, he comments that 'predictability and efficiency are valued to the extent that schools would surely become dramatically more boring places than they are already' (Angus, 1993, p. 343). He goes on to suggest that 'not only is there a lack of engagement with sociological (or other theory), but also effectiveness work is largely trapped in a logic of common sense which allows it, by and large, to be appropriated into the Right's hegemonic project ... it advocates an isolationist, apolitical approach to education in which it is assumed that educational problems can be fixed by technical means and inequality can be managed within the walls of schools and classrooms provided that teachers and pupils follow 'correct' effective school procedures' (p. 343). By such means 'normalising judgements' are turned upon the whole school and each school is set in a field of comparison – which again articulates with other current aspects of educational policy. An 'artificial' order is laid down, 'an order defined by natural and observable processes' (Foucault, 1979, p. 179). The definitions of behaviour and performance embedded in the order and the norm are arrived at 'on the basis of two opposed values of good and evil' (p. 180). The good school and the bad school, effective and ineffective practice. Through 'value-giving' measures the constraint of a conformity that must be achieved is introduced.

If self-examination fails, the expert, the consultant, the moral disciplinarian is at hand to intervene with their models of 'effective practice'. In this role the scientific and the moral are tightly intertwined. In effect, given the logic of management, ineffectiveness is seen as a disorder of reason and as such susceptible to cure by the use of appropriate techniques of organisation.

Re-envisioning educational studies via critical reflexivity

I could go on, but my point here is to begin to explore an aspect of educational study and educational research by employing a different theoretical language and theoretical perspective, to focus upon unintended and overlooked consequences, so as to render our practice critically problematic. I am also seeking to demonstrate some of the ways in which our research and 'scientific' conceptualisations can be tied back into broader political projects and social processes and to the functions of managing and neutralising social problems. A facade of objectivity obscures this process and further empowers the research enterprise with the capacity to categorise, professionalise and contain a specified social problem.

By employing this kind of critical reflexivity we can re-envision educational studies as a whole as a disciplinary technology, part of the exercise of disciplinary

power. Management, effectiveness and appraisal, for example, as I have suggested, work together to locate individuals in space, in a hierarchical and effi-
ciently visible organisation. In and through our research the school and the
teacher are captured within a perfect diagram of power; and the classroom is
increasingly one of those 'small theatres', in which 'each actor is alone, perfectly individualized and constantly visible' (Foucault, 1979, p. 200). It is thus
that *governmentality* is achieved through the minute mechanisms of everyday
life and the application of 'progressive' and efficient technical solutions to designated problems. Governmentality is 'the ensemble formed by the institutions,
procedures, analyses and reflections, the calculations and tactics, that allow the
exercise of this very specific albeit complex form of power, which has as its target population' (Foucault, 1979, p. 20).

It is in this way that epistemological development within the human sciences,
like education, functions politically and is intimately imbricated in the practical
management of social and political problems. The scientific vocabulary may distance the researcher (and the manager) from the subjects of their action but, at
the same time, it also constructs a gaze that renders the 'landscape of the social'
ever more visible. Through methodical observation the 'objects of concern'
identified in this landscape are inserted into a network of ameliorative or therapeutic practices. The point is that the idea that human sciences like educational
studies stand outside or above the political agenda of the management of the
population, or somehow have a neutral status embodied in a free-floating progressive rationalism, are dangerous and debilitating conceits.

But now I have run ahead of myself and I want to return to Fay's work to consider the alternatives to policy science more closely. Fay (1975) offers two alternatives to policy science; one is interpretive social science, and the other is
critical social science. Both are familiar enough I think not to require extensive
discussion here, except to say this: Fay argues that 'an interpretative social science promises to reveal to the social actors what they and others are doing,
thereby restoring communication by correcting the ideas that they have about
each other and themselves' (p. 90).[2] Now that may be an over-simplification, but
I shall let that go at present and note Fay's comment that interpretative social science is deeply conservative in that 'it leads to reconciling people to their social
order' (p. 91). That may be equally contestable, but again I shall leave that argument for another time. Fay's second alternative, critical social science, rests on
the proposition that 'social theory does not simply offer a picture of the way that
a social order works. Instead, a social theory is itself a catalytic agent of change
within the complex of social life which it analyses' (p. 110). Now this is an
attractive and popular intellectual position for policy scholars. It is a position I
find, at least some of the time, personally comfortable and conducive. But is it a
real alternative to the failings that Fay finds in policy science? Only partially I
think. We need to think carefully here about the use and meaning of terms, especially those in Fay's final phrase, 'a catalytic agent of change within the complex of social life which it analyses'. I have three nagging and related problems
with this formulation. First, social science, here, is set over and against the social,

social life, which it acts upon and analyses but is not part of. The critical social scientist is not seen as part of the struggle for 'truth' but is placed above and outside it with clean hands and clean conscience, representing the 'conscience of society as a whole'. Social scientists are not seen to have interests, careers or identities at stake here; they are free moral agents, unencumbered by everyday ideological limitations and personal ambitions.

The second worry is that 'the critical' in critical social science is too limited and does not extend to a reflexive consideration of the ways in which social science constitutes 'the social' and its own ethical subjects; in this case the 'falsely conscious' and those of 'raised consciousness'. This spartan and familiar duality, upon which the critical social scientist then works, does significant injustice to the 'complex of social life' to which Fay himself refers and trades on a rather simplistic notion of unified and stable social subjects.

Third, in the educative, revelationary role which Fay attributes to the critical social scientist, an uncritical rationalism and progressive humanism are smuggled back into the social scientist's practice in the form of 'consciousness raising'. This is achieved by offering to social actors 'an alternative conception ... of what they are' a simple essentialism, in other words. I am not arguing that Fay's model of critical social science is irredeemably flawed, but its epistemological emphases are in danger of collapsing it back into that which it seeks to distinguish itself from. Cohen (1993) makes the point more dramatically:

> I propose to withdraw the automatic 'cognitive advantage' of university critical writing, on the grounds that no such advantage is warranted: our writings are outfitted for the grooves of 'reason', 'society', 'need' – each of which is a cosmos of mythology unto itself. In making this withdrawal, I am more or less expressing 'no confidence' in the essential activities of the modern university. (p. x)

Towards a post-structural alternative

So can I discern still another position in all this? Is there another, a fourth way? In the way things like this are supposed to work it is probably incumbent upon me to attempt to do so. But I will make my attempt in a rather elliptical fashion I am afraid. Before doing so I shall return once more to Fay's distinctions.

In contemplating my recent visits to British Educational Research Association conferences I want to extend Fay's nosology. Alongside policy scholarship, policy engineering and policy science we also need to recognise the role in educational studies of *policy entrepreneurship*. I intend the term to carry a variety of meanings. It seems clear to me that there are areas of activity which attach themselves to educational studies which have bases in institutions of higher education, which lead to the giving of papers at academic conferences, which display little or no pretence of scholarship or science. The point of policy entrepreneurship is not to research practices, but to change them into an image of policy. It rests on the proselytising and, in some cases, the sale of 'technically correct answers'. The entrepreneur's interests, in terms of identity and career, are bound up directly and immediately, rather than once removed, as in the case of policy science and critical social science, with the success of their dissemination.

We might pick out 'the self-managing school' as an example of one such focus of dissemination, 'enterprise in higher education' is another, 'teacher appraisal' another, 'mentoring' and 'partnership' in initial teacher education are others. The policy entrepreneur is committed to the application of certain technical solutions or organisations and contexts which are taken *a priori* to be in need of structural and/or cultural change. Here inquiry is replaced by belief; questioning by subjects becomes resistance; research is replaced by experience and common sense; data are displaced by anecdotes. I cannot help but be reminded of C. Wright Mills' comment in *The Sociological Imagination* that:

> There is no necessity for working social scientists to allow the political meaning of their work to be shaped by the 'accidents of its setting', or its use to be determined by the purposes of other men (sic). It is quite within their powers to discuss its meanings and decide upon its uses as matters of their own policy. (Wright Mills, 1959, p. 198).

But is it possible again to situate such developments in a broader context? In the era of late modernity the urge to represent is verging on the obsessional and forms of certainty have become valuable commodities as we seek both to know the world a little better than those with whom we compete and assert greater and more detailed control over our environment. Unmediated knowledgability has its attractions and its price in many fields of the human sciences (Beck, 1992).

It is not difficult to anticipate the direction in which I am now moving – towards a post-structural, post-epistemological alternative. I wish to argue that the absence of theory leaves the researcher prey to unexamined, unreflexive preconceptions and dangerously naive ontological and epistemological *a prioris*. I shall wail and curse at the absence of theory and argue for theory as a way of saving educational studies from itself.

As a further aside, it is important to note that the collapse or abandonment of theory within educational studies has its parallels elsewhere in the field of education, like, for example, in the removal of theory work from teacher education courses and the concomitant reduction of teacher development to a matter of skills and competences and on the job training. Teaching like educational studies is thus reconstituted and depoliticised. It is changed from being an intellectual endeavour to being a technical process. Indeed this coincidence of change is in no way surprising for these technologies are all part of the same contemporary *dispositif* – the unity of a discourse through a period of time, 'a limited space of communication'.

Manifestations of this dispositif seem to be increasingly common in my post. Two recent examples come to mind. First, a notice announcing the founding of the UK Evaluation Society which is intended, in part, 'to represent … the views and interests of the evaluation profession'.[3] Second, an invitation to subscribe to a new journal, *Quality Assurance in Education*. Journals and societies are key sites within the academy from which a discursive lexicon may be articulated and disseminated.

The role of theory

But how can theory help? What is the point of theory? The point is that theory can separate us from 'the contingency that has made us what we are, the possibilities of no longer seeing, doing or thinking what we are, do or think' (Mahon, 1992, p. 122). Theory is a vehicle for 'thinking otherwise'; it is a platform for 'outrageous hypotheses' and for 'unleashing criticism'. Theory is destructive, disruptive and violent. It offers a language for challenge, and modes of thought, other than those articulated for us by dominant others. It provides a language of rigour and irony rather than contingency. The purpose of such theory is to de-familiarise present practices and categories, to make them seem less self-evident and necessary, and to open up spaces for the invention of new forms of experience.

Now such a register, I realise, grates upon the Anglo-Saxon, positivist, utilitarian ear. We prefer our intellectualism expressed in the more sober tones and nuances of semantic deliberation and rational planning. Within the British tradition, intellectualism, science or scholarship often only seem to be regarded as valid and useful when weighed and measured by concrete outcomes. Chris Shilling (1993) made just this point in a review of a collection of papers drawn from recent work in the sociology of education. He took it as sign of the times that the editors 'should have to justify the sociology of education and, by implication their own collection, by a highly reflexive positioning of it within an essentially utilitarian tradition of research based upon measuring the social outcomes of educational policies' (p. 103). He goes on to describe the sociology of education as 'a discipline which has been in decline in Britain for far too long' (p. 103). In effect, the sociology of education and educational studies are in a state of 'intellectual stagnation'. Most particularly, we are experiencing what Randall Collins refers to as the 'loss of cultural capital', that is the neglect of significant ideas, concepts and theories. Or, as Shilling puts it in his review: 'Quite simply, the contributors to this volume have paid insufficient attention not only to previous traditions in the sociology of education, but to the most important current developments in sociology. Contemporary sociological theories in such areas as modernity, postmodernism, structuration, self-identity, the civilising process, consumption, and the body have much to offer the study of education' (p. 111). All of this relates back to my initial point about the dangers of isolation. It also illustrates the basic transition, both cultural and structural, which is underway in educational studies – the transition from intellectual intelligence to technical rationalism.

But to return to the role of theory. The point about theory is not that it is simply critical. In order to go beyond the accidents and contingencies which enfold us, it is necessary to start from another position and begin from what is normally excluded. Theory provides this possibility, the possibility of disidentification – the effect of working 'on and against' prevailing practices of ideological subjection. The point of theory and of intellectual endeavour in the social sciences should be, in Foucault's words, 'to sap power', to engage in struggle, to reveal and undermine what is most invisible and insidious in prevailing practices. Theories offer another language, a language of distance, of irony, of imagination. And a part of this, as Sheridan puts it, is 'a love of hypothesis, of invention' which is also unashamedly 'a love of the beautiful' (Sheridan, 1980, p. 223) – as against the bland, technical and desolate languages of policy science and policy entrepreneurship. However, in taking such a stance intellectuals cannot simply seek to reinhabit the old redemptive assumptions based upon an unproblematic role for themselves in a perpetual process of progressive, orderly growth or development achieved through scientific and technological 'mastery' or control over events or by the assertive re-cycling of old dogmas and tired utopias. 'The regime of "truth" gave the intellectual, whose business truth was, a certain "universal" status' (Sheridan, 1980, p. 222). This is no longer available or desirable. The process of disidentification also involves a transformation of intellectuals and their relationship to the 'business of truth'. The post-epistemological theorist will eshew the scientific claim to originality, discovery and the improvement of the human condition.

What I am groping towards here is a model of the educational theorist as a cultural critic offering perspective rather than truth; engaged in what Eco calls 'semiotic guerrilla warfare' (Eco, 1994). Or to put it another way:

> Criticism is a matter of flushing out that thought (which animates everyday behaviour) and trying to change it: to show that things are not as self-evident as one believed, to see that what is accepted as self-evident will no longer be accepted as such ... As soon as one can no longer think things as one formerly thought them, transformation becomes both very urgent, very difficult and quite possible. (Foucault, 1988, p. 154)

For Foucault, freedom lies in our ability to transform our relationship to the past, to tradition and much less in being able to control the form and direction that the future will take; in the mad scramble of late modernist life we seem to need to latch on to elusive images of who we are and what our existence means. But, in the place of such rigid and anterior norms and discourses, we must, as Richard Rorty suggests, locate a playing field on which ideas are toyed with and radical ironies explored. In Rorty's post-epistemological view, edifying conversations, rather than truth-generating epistemological efforts must be the staple of a post-structural social science (Rorty, 1979). To quote Foucault again: 'I think that there are more secrets, more possible freedoms, and more inventions in our future than we can imagine in humanism as it is dogmatically represented on every side of the political rainbow' (Foucault, 1988, p. 15)

But will any theory do? I think not! We must consider *how* as well as *why* we employ theory. Theory can also work to provide comforting and apparently stable identities for beleaguered academics in an increasingly slippery world. Theory can also serve to conjure up anterior norms and lay its dead hand upon the creativity of the mind. Too often in educational studies theory becomes no more than a mantric reaffirmation of belief rather than a tool for exploration and for thinking otherwise. Such mantric uses of theory typically involve little more than a naming of spaces. This is what Dale (1992) calls 'theory by numbers'. The map simply needs to be coloured in rather than researched. We all too easily become stuck in what Althusser (1975) calls a 'descriptive theory', a transitional phase in theory development, based upon a 'special kind of obviousness' (p. 133). 'Every descriptive theory', he argues, 'thus runs the risk of "blocking" the development of the theory . ...' The paradox of critical social science is that our rational, humane utopias are always formed within the discourses, dispositifs and epistemes from which we seek to escape. It is the past that is the problem here, not the future.

There is another sense in which we need to think about how we theorise. It relates to the ambition of our enterprise and the style and scope of our endeavours. On the one hand, there is a kind of theorising that is parsimonius, certain and closed. This is also typically a hard-edged, essentially male form of knowledge. More often than not, critical social science takes this form and is as a result both too sure of itself and overambitious. On the other hand, there is a kind of theorising that rests upon complexity, uncertainty and doubt and upon a reflexivity about its own production and its claims to knowledge about the social. What I am trying to convey here is beautifully expressed by Teresa de Lauretis who describes feminist theory as requiring:

> leaving or giving up a place that is safe, that is 'home' – physically, emotionally, linguistically, epistemologically – for another place that is unknown and risky, that is not only emotionally but conceptually other; a place of discourse from which speaking and thinking are at best tentative, uncertain, unguaranteed. (Lauretis, 1990, p. 138)

Disidentification as a practice for educational studies will almost certainly involve a loss of identity, of universal status. It will threaten our certainty and our sense of usefulness. But, maybe, those things have been swept away anyway. The question is do we reiterate our tired, anterior, mantric theories; do we do whatever we have to do to make ourselves useful as technicians of social management, or do we re-invent ourselves as intellectuals and cultural critics?[4]

I realise in all this that I am teetering between fatalism and scepticism (Sawicki, 1991). Perhaps I am occupying what De Lauretis calls the 'eccentric' perspective. Nonetheless, I take some heart from a comment by Andre Gorz who wrote: 'The beginning of wisdom is the discovery that there exist contradictions of permanent tension with which it is necessary to live and that it is above all not necessary to seek to resolve'.[5]

Notes

1 A version of this paper was given as the Annual Address to the Standing Conference for Studies of Education, Royal Society of Arts, London, November, 1994.

2 Rorty (1989, p. xvi), for example, defines ethnography rather differently.

3 In the light of some of my earlier discussion, it is fascinating to note that the literature advertising the UK Evaluation Society is disseminated by the Social Science Forum whose motto is 'Understanding Today, Shaping Tomorrow'.

4 One of the most common responses to the original version of this text was to ask whether I am leaving myself and educational studies open to the criticism that the point of philosophy is not simply to describe the world, but to help to change it. My text may be read as deficient in those terms, but I intend to convey very much the opposite message. I would see a specific and situated politics, a politics of the immediate, of the everyday, of the personal as the logical concomitant of my arguments. Furthermore, I am counselling both boldness and modesty. Boldness in relation to the specifics of power, both in our own backyards and in our research sites. Modesty in our normative claims and in our general political ambitions. But this is a dangerous politics very different from the safe, fictive revolutionism that remains à la mode in some parts of the academy.

5 I am grateful to Jo Boaler, Alan Cribb, David Halpin, Iram Siraj-Blatchford, Maria Tamboukou and Jack Whitehead for their comments on earlier versions of the text. Some of which I have acted upon, others of which remain as food for thought, for further writing and further conversations.

References

Althusser, L. (1975) _Lenin and Philosophy and Other Essays._ (London, Verso).

Angus, L. (1993) The Sociology of School Effectiveness, _British Journal of Sociology of Education,_ 14(3), 333–345.

Ball, S. J. (1990) Management as moral technology: a luddite analysis. In Ball, S. J. (ed) _Foucault and Education: Disciplines and Knowledge._ (London, Routledge).

Ball, S. J. (1994) _Education Reform: A Critical and Post-Structural Approach._ (Buckingham, Open University Press).

Beck, U. (1992) _Risk Society: Towards a New Modernity._ (Newbury Park, CA., Sage).

Cohen, S. (1993) _Academia and the Luster of Capita._ (Minnesota, Minnesota University Press).

Dale, R. (1992) Recovering from a Pyrrhic Victory? Quality, Relevance and Impact in the Sociology of Education. In Arnot, M. and Barton, L. (eds) _Voicing Concerns._ (Wallingford, Triangle).

Donzelot, J. (1979) *The Policing of Families.* (London, Hutchinson).

Eco, U. (1994) *Apocalypse Postponed,* Lumley, R. (ed) (London, BFI Publishing and Indiana University Press).

Fay, B. (1975) *Social Theory and Political Practice.* (London, Allen and Unwin).

Foucault, M. (1977) *Language, Counter-Memory, Practice: Selected Essays and Interviews.* (Ithaca, NY, Cornell University Press).

Foucault, M. (1979) *Discipline and Punish.* (Harmondsworth, Penguin).

Foucault, M. (1979) On Governmentality, *Ideology and Consciousness,* 6(1), 5–22.

Foucault, M. (1988) *Michael Foucault: Politics, Philosophy and Culture – Interviews and Other Writings 1977–1984.* (New York, Routledge).

Foucault, M. (1988) Truth, Power, Self: An Interview with Michel Foucault. *Technologies of the Self.* (Amherst, The University of Massachusetts Press).

Foucault, M. (1991) Questions of Method. *The Foucault Effect: Studies in Governmentality.* (Brighton, Harvester/ Wheatsheaf).

Lauretis, D. (1990) Eccentric Subjects: Feminist Theory and Historical Consciousness, *Feminist Studies,* 16(1), 133–146.

Reynolds, D. (1990) Research on School/Organizational Effectiveness: The End of the Beginning. In Saran, R. and Trafford, V. (eds) *Management and Policy: Retrospect and Prospect,* (London, Falmer).

Rorty, R. (1979) *Philosophy and the Mirror of Nature,* (Oxford, Basil Blackwell).

Sawicki, J. (1991) *Disciplining Foucault: Feminism, Power and the Body.* (New York, Routledge).

Sheridan, A. (1980) *Michel Foucault: The Will to Truth.* (London, Tavistock).

Shilling, C. (1993) The Demise of the Sociology of Education in Britain, *British Journal of Sociology of Education,* 14(1), 105–121.

Wright Mills, C. (1959) *The Sociological Imagination.* (Harmondsworth, Penguin).

Chapter 9

Beyond reflection: contingency, idiosyncrasy and reflexivity in initial teacher education

Alex Moore

Fortunately, good teaching does not require us to internalize an endless list of instructional techniques. Much more fundamental is the recognition that human relationships are central to effective instruction.

(Cummins, 1996, p. 73)

Teaching, in many of its aspects as practised today, is expressive and emergent, intuitive and flexible, spontaneous and emotional.

(Woods, 1996, p. 6)

Dominant discourses

The last quarter of the twentieth century has seen a plethora of publications about how to teach and how to teach teaching. While many of these publications have concentrated on the organization and broad content of courses of teacher education (Alexander, Craft and Lynch, 1984; Department of Education and Science,

Taken from: Hammersley, M. (ed.) *Researching School Experience*, (London: Falmer, 1999), pp. 134–53.

1981; National Union of Teachers, 1976), others have fallen into the category of the teaching *guide*: that is to say, compilations of the wisdom of experienced educators that offer tips and advice to inexperienced teachers on such matters as managing pupils' learning and behaviour, marking and assessing pupils' work, and long- and short-term lesson planning (Cohen and Manion, 1977; Marland, 1975; Stephens and Crawley, 1994). Such publications may be said to both prefigure and support a 'competence-based' model of initial and continuing teacher education: one that prioritizes the notion of the teacher as trained craftsperson (Council for the Accreditation of Teacher Education, 1992; Department for Education and Employment, 1997a and 1997b; Teacher Training Agency, 1998).

Other publications have moved beyond what might be called the skills-based approach to teaching to offer advice about underlying perceptions, procedures and approaches, in what is recognized as a highly complex set of activities. Such publications, eschewing the notion that teaching is reducible to discrete and finite lists of skills and practices, have focused on the importance of informed *reflection* on what one does in the classroom. The notion of 'reflective practice', though already current under different names in the early 1970s (see, for instance, Combs, 1972 and Wragg, 1974), came to the fore in the 1980s and early 1990s through the work of such writers as Schön (1983, 1987), Valli (1992) and Elliott (1993). This notion places as much emphasis on teachers' own *evaluations* of their practice as on the planning and management skills into which such evaluations feed. One of the central techniques recommended in the reflective practitioner discourse is the keeping of diaries or journals by teachers and student-teachers, in which they reflect systematically on their experiences as they perceive them, keeping a record that can be returned to and reinterrogated in the light of subsequent experiences and providing scope for the self-setting of targets and goals. The reflective practitioner discourse continues to show its popular appeal through bookshop shelves (Loughran, 1996; Loughran and Russell, 1997; Mitchell and Weber, 1996), even as it becomes increasingly marginalized by government-sponsored publications favouring the 'competent craftsperson' approach (DfEE, 1997a, 1997b; Office for Standards in Education and Teacher Training Agency, 1996).

It is the suggestion of this chapter that the two discourses of the competent teacher and the reflective practitioner remain the dominant ones in teacher education and, furthermore, that they are equally responsible for marginalizing alternative teacher-education discourses, including discourses that seek to prioritize the idiosyncratic, contingent aspects of teaching and learning (Maguire, 1995; Moore, 1996). I shall argue that both dominant discourses, though often in apparent opposition to one another, are similarly characterized by and rooted in psychological notions of the ideal, unified 'self' (Lacan, 1977, 1979; Walkerdine, 1982, 1990), and in a pseudo-scientific view of teaching and learning that is circumscribed by a notion of closure and of the naming of parts (Hamilton, 1993; Reid, 1993). Both discourses are essentially *symptomatic* in perspective, in that they seek out and identify what is 'wrong' in classroom interactions through explicit reference both to what has 'happened' and to some normalizing notion of what 'ought to have happened'. Both, as a consequence, lend themselves to the danger of pathologizing the individual teacher or pupil in relation to communicative breakdowns or learning difficulties, rather than seeking their causes in the wider, deeper structures and inter-relations of society, or indeed in the very complex interrelations between teachers and their pupils. While few people would deny that the competent teacher and the reflective practitioner discourses may offer some help and support to teachers and student-teachers in improving classroom relations and practice, experience suggests that they are just as likely to cause concern, confusion and misguided behaviour through their over-personalization of teaching activity (Mitchell and Weber, 1996).

The 'alternative' discourses that I want to promote in this chapter suggest a revision, though not a wholesale rejection, both of lists of skills and of practice-based journals and diaries. Such alternatives involve revisiting such discourses as pupil- and student-centred education, and imply the relevance of teachers re-contextualizing teaching experience within the broader interpersonal experiences of lives lived 'outside' of or prior to the school classroom (Moore, 1997; Quicke, 1988; Schön, 1988; Thomas, 1995): that is to say, teachers perceiving themselves, as well as their classrooms, as constructed and readable 'texts' (Moore and Atkinson, 1998). Unlike the dominant discourses of the competent teacher and the reflective practitioner, these alternative discourses recognize the fragmented, material, multifac-eted nature of the self, and offer constructive strategies for *de*-pathologizing classroom dysfunction – often, in the process, offering more helpful escape routes for teachers locked into apparent impasses with their pupils.

The competent teacher

The recent domination of the competent teacher discourse in initial and continuing teacher development in the UK can be traced to 1992. The discourse was powerful before then, and had already received the full stamp of government approval in the USA (Henry, 1989). However, 1992 marks something of a turning point in the UK, in that the discourse at this point had legitimization bestowed upon it with the full force of the law. The key document in this process was a circular dispatched by the Council for the Accreditation of Teacher Education (CATE) in September of that year to all Higher Education Institutions (HEIs) in the UK providing initial teacher education courses. This circular laid out the basic requirements for all such courses clearly and unambiguously in the terms of the competences discourse:

> The main objective of all courses of initial training is to enable students to become competent teachers who can establish effective working relationships with pupils. To do so, they will need to be knowledgeable in their subjects, to understand how pupils learn, and to acquire teaching skills. ... It is recognised that ... the acquisition of competences is not the totality of training [and] each competence is not a discrete unit but one of many whose sum makes for a con-fident start in teaching.
>
> (CATE, 1992, p. 9)

Emphasis in this circular was placed on key areas of competence that were to become the key 'sub-discourses' of the next six years: 'subject knowledge', 'class management' and 'assessment and recording of pupils' progress'. Since the publication of *Circular 9/92*, the Council for the Accreditation of Teacher Education in the UK has been replaced by the Teacher Training Agency. This change, however, as the new title suggests, has represented not a break from the latter-day discourse of CATE, but rather a natural progression and development of it, in which the identification of 'discrete', universal skills increasingly marginalizes those complex interpersonal relationships and skills that often defy such itemizations in practice (DfEE, 1997a). Such a shift of emphasis, away from the notion of education traditionally favoured by universities and teachers (Alexander et al., 1984; Institute of Education, 1972; National Union of Teachers, 1976; Popkewitz, 1987) towards that of 'training' – always more popular in the official documentation (Allen, 1994; DES, 1981) – also, importantly, marks a shift of emphasis away from debates about the content and structure of pre-service courses, towards issues of assessment and 'quality' *within contents and structures that are 'given'*.

It is not the intention of this chapter to dismiss the competences discourse *in toto*. Much of what is contained within it does, indeed, make relatively uncontentious good sense. Of course teachers do need to have sufficient subject knowledge to teach their pupils effectively; of course they need to be effective planners and classroom managers; of course there was – and still is – some bad teaching in urgent need of having something done about it. The discourse also provides important opposition to another dominant discourse with more immediate popular appeal: that of the 'charismatic subject' (Moore and Atkinson, 1998). The charismatic subject discourse (not to be confused with the reflexive practitioner discourse to which I shall turn later) suggests that good teachers are 'born' rather than 'made', emphasizing mysterious, barely definable 'personal qualities' as the central contributors to success. Within this discourse – arguably responsible for a great deal of poor practice in the past – the effective teacher is often pictured as rejecting what is normally thought of as good practice, succeeding solely through the force of their own unconventional personality. Such a vision of teaching, which remains popular in cinematic representations of schools and classrooms, not uncommonly accompanies student teachers on to their qualifying courses (Moore and Atkinson, 1998; Wragg, 1974), often making life very difficult for them when, in the classroom situation, they discover that they cannot emulate, or be instantly respected in the manner of, the only truly effective teacher they can remember from their own school days.[1]

The power of the competences discourse to 'demystify' teaching processes (Woods, 1996, p. 19), providing for more confident and often more effective teachers, is not to be underestimated. For all its potential, however, the discourse remains problematic. To begin with, there is an obvious difficulty in the way in which it almost inevitably lends itself to misinterpretation. *Circular 9/92* very specifically stated that 'the acquisition of competences is not the totality of training. The criteria do not provide the entire syllabus of initial professional training', and that 'each competence is not a discrete unit but one of many whose sum makes for a confident start in teaching' (CATE, 1992, p. 9). However, the list-like nature of this document has given both teachers and teacher educators a very clear impression that they do, indeed, provide 'the entire syllabus', that the skills listed are indeed 'discrete', and that the lists are intended as finite representations of essential truths (Moore, 1996). This impression, which has been reinforced by subsequent documentation (for example DfEE, 1997a, 1997b), sustains a view – consistently rejected by many teachers and teacher educators – that the ingredients of 'good teaching' can be itemized and that, subject to their being appropriately acquired, anyone can make an effective teacher. The problem with this, of course, is that many student-teachers do appear – to themselves and to others – to acquire, in a satisfactory manner and to a satisfactory degree, the various competences but still have huge difficulties in the classroom and cannot begin to understand why this should be so (Moore, 1996). Similarly, the creators of lists of competences often seem unprepared to accept that language itself defies this kind of inventorizing, so that however many hours go into their construction, such lists will never, finally, be able to answer the question they set themselves: 'What makes an effective teacher?'

A further problem with the competences discourse relates to the very notion of 'competence' itself. Basil Bernstein has addressed this issue through tracing the history of the concept in a variety of fields in the social sciences, including linguistics, sociology and anthropology (Bernstein, 1996, pp. 55–6). Seeking out common ground is the essential difference between various kinds of competence (for example Chomsky's 'linguistic competence' or Saussure's *'langue'*) and various kinds of performance (Chomsky's 'linguistic performance', say, or Saussure's *'parole'*). Bernstein describes competence as 'intrinsically creative and tacitly acquired in informal interactions' *(ibid.,* p. 55). Historically, competence is defined in terms of 'practical accomplishments', constituted by procedures that are essentially 'social'. The universality of competence renders it 'culture free'. Part of its social logic is that 'the subject is active and creative in the construction of a valid world of meanings and practice' and that the development or 'expansion' of this subject is 'not advanced by formal instruction' or 'subject to public regulation' *(ibid.,* p. 56). Competence theories thus have 'an emancipatory flavour', being founded on 'a critical, sceptical view of hierarchical relations'.

This notion of competence – as socially, actively, creatively and yet unconsciously acquired skills, understandings and practices – is critically different from the notion of competences (often conflated with 'competencies') embedded in the competences discourse of CATE and the TTA. Indeed, the term may be said to have been appropriated (Jones and Moore, 1995) to describe something much more closely akin to competence's traditional 'other half': that is to say, 'performance'. The competences (or competencies) discourse as it exists in the areas of teacher education, and – increasingly – in education generally, certainly maintains a somewhat limited notion of the universality and 'culture-freeness' of the old competence discourse, inasmuch as what constitutes effective teaching in one time or place is deemed to constitute it in any other. However, it introduces two important new elements that change its character critically, rendering it anything but 'creative'. These elements are (a) the necessity for competences to be actively, *consciously* taught and learned; and (b) the presentation of *selected lists* of competences whose focus is on the acquisition of 'skills' rather than on understandings or strategies. We might say that through the conflation of competence with performance *combined with* the notion of limited universality, the discourse includes an effective denial of the contingent and idiosyncratic elements that others (Cummins, 1996; Maguire, 1995; Woods, 1996) have placed at the heart of good teaching.

The discourse does more than that, however, as Bernstein has gone on to argue, in that it entails precisely the shift away from 'education' towards 'training' that is implied in the official language of the discourse (in, for example, the shift of terminology from 'the Council for the Accreditation of Teacher *Education*' to 'the Teacher *Training* Agency'). Furthermore, this is a highly problematic notion of training, inevitably implying a corresponding notion of 'trainability'. With reference to school pupils – although the same argument holds good for student-teachers – Bernstein argues that:

> The concept of trainability places the emphasis upon 'something' the actor must possess in order for that actor to be appropriately formed and re-formed according to technological, organizational and market contingencies.
>
> (Bernstein, 1996, p. 73)

This reifying quality of trainability and competences leaves 'an emptiness in the concept [of trainability] … which makes [it] self-referential and thus excluding'. The nature of that emptiness is that the concept ignores the social world from which it was constructed and in which it resides. In particular, it ignores the concept of identity formation, the context of the 'social *order*', and the particular ways in which identities arise 'through relations which the identity enters into with other identities of reciprocal recognition, support, mutual legitimization and finally through a negotiated collective purpose' *(ibid.,* p. 73). The full significance of the appropriation of the competence concept within the competences discourse immediately becomes clear. On the one hand, the discourse devalues the importance of those interpersonal relationships, perceptual matches and mismatches, notions of self and desire, which are so central a part of effective classroom interaction and which are also at the root of many pupils', teachers' and student-teachers' classroom difficulties. In doing this, it simultaneously encourages individuals to seek reasons for success and failure, and answers to questions and difficulties, within their own 'competence', while discouraging them from seeking such reasons and answers in a 'real world' whose authenticity they come to doubt. On the other hand, the discourse deflects broader debates about ineffectiveness in education away from the 'social context' and therefore, by implication, onto the individual protagonist. The power and importance of this aspect of the discourse from the point of view of the central governments that promote it is plain to see: it is far easier, not to mention more economical, to treat perceived social difficulties symptomatically – for example, to concentrate blame on schools and teachers for educational failures – than it is to take a causal approach that might imply a drastic readjustment in the social distribution of power and wealth. This personalization of the difficulty – implicit in the competences discourse but disguised by its 'abstracted', universalized appearance – has the added impact of effectively disguising broader social problems (Moore, 1996) – what Bernstein refers to as a pointing 'away from the macro blot on the micro context' (ibid., p. 56).

The reflective practitioner

Working in parallel with the competences discourse – sometimes in apparent opposition, sometimes in a more complementary way – has been the discourse of the reflective practitioner. This discourse, unlike the competences discourse, emphasizes not discrete skills and areas of knowledge but, rather, the particular skills needed to reflect constructively upon ongoing experience as a way of improving the quality and effectiveness of one's work. Such reflection involves, of course, drawing on the range of strategies and techniques one has at one's disposal, or developing new ones; but it does so selectively, flexibly and strategically – taking full account of the particular circumstances relating to any given problem at any given time. In particular, the discourse encourages teachers and student teachers to take into account the whole picture – analysing the effectiveness of a lesson or series of lessons not simply by measurable outputs such as test scores, but through an attempt to evaluate what was learned, by whom, and how more effective learning might take place in the future. As such, it involves careful evaluation by teachers of their own classroom performance, planning, assessment and so on, in addition to and in conjunction with evaluations of pupils' behaviour and achievement. It also implies a sound understanding on the teacher's part of relevant educational theory and research – including theories of cognitive, linguistic and affective development – in order to address issues not restricted to the 'what' and the 'when' of education but embracing, also, questions of 'how' and even 'why'.

The reflective practitioner discourse is not well favoured within current official discourses of teacher education: the competence category of 'evaluation of one's own teaching', for example, is not included in the Teacher Training Agency's documentation, being relegated in terms of position to the end of another broad area – 'Teaching and Class Management' – and in terms of wordage to '[students must demonstrate that they can] evaluate their own teaching critically and use this to improve effectiveness' (DfEE, 1997a, p. 10; TTA, 1998, p. 8). Such a marginalization only reinforces the notion that the competences discourse is anti-intellectual and anti-theoretical, and that it promotes a view of teachers as, essentially, 'clerks and technicians' (Giroux and McLaren, 1992, p. xiii) rather than thinkers and creators. The reflective practitioner discourse has, however, received much popular support in higher education institutions in Britain offering courses in initial and continuing teacher education, and continues to produce some of the most interesting and insightful practice.

If the competences discourse emphasizes the teacher as technician and 'deliverer', whose 'internalized' skills can be easily monitored through measurable outcomes, the reflective practitioner discourse has always taken a subtler approach to teaching, recognizing the centrality of much-harder-to-identify, codify and quantify skills (concerning communication, presentation, analysis, evaluation and interaction), often promoting, for example, counselling skills on the part of teacher educators and emphasizing the *strategic* aspects of teaching above the acquisition of less flexible methodological approaches (Handal and Lauvas, 1987). Such a difference clearly has implications not only for the way in which teacher education is conducted, but also for research in this domain. The competences discourse, for example, because of its 'self referential' nature *(ibid.)*, suggests an evaluative response, sited within a world of skills and capabilities that, as it were, already exists outside of the individual (prompting such questions as 'Which system of competences works best?', 'Which HEIs implement the discourse most effectively?' and so on). The reflective practitioner discourse, on the other hand, suggests a qualitative, research-based response along the lines, say, of ethnography or action research. Such approaches will focus not on measuring success by outcome ('How many students successfully completed this or that course?', 'What gradings were courses given by Ofsted inspectorates?' and so on) but on exploring the *nature* of the teaching and learning processes that are taking place, through an emphasis on 'the processes of meaning-assignation and situation-defining' and on 'how the social world is constructed by people, how they are continually striving to make sense of the world' (Woods, 1979, p. 2).

Competence, reflection and the pathologization of the individual

'Is teaching a science or an art?' asks Woods (1996, p. 14), subsequently concluding: 'it is both a science and an art – and more besides' *(ibid., p. 31)*.

The differing research implications of the two dominant discourses in teacher education represent, of course, no less than a summary of the two contradictory views of human behaviour that underpin those discourses. To use the terms of Peter Woods's question, the competences discourse may be said to represent a quasi-scientific perception of teaching and learning, firmly sited within a paradigm of educational thinking sometimes critiqued under the term 'modernism'

(Moore, 1998a). Such a paradigm assumes 'the possibility of completeness' (Standish, 1995, p. 133) through viewing the world as 'an ordered place' and the 'elements of the world of knowledge as topologically invariant' (Hamilton, 1993 p. 55). What is knowable – or what 'needs to be known' – is ultimately definable and susceptible to inventorization and tidy assessment: it is underpinned by a tacit assumption that there is, under passing acknowledgment of the possibility of local variations, only one right way or set of ways of doing things. The discourse of reflection, on the other hand, recognizes what Goodson and Walker have called 'the messy complexity of the classroom' and its only 'partially apprehendable practice' (Goodson and Walker, 1991, p. xii). It is a discourse that gives full recognition to 'the central role that people play in the educational process and educational systems' *(ibid.,* p. 1), that legitimizes a range of approaches and behaviours, and that understands that 'much of the most expert practice in schools is based on intuitive judgment' (McIntyre, Hagger and Burn, 1994, p. 57). Such a discourse is often associated, in the philosophy of education, with the use of the term 'post-modernism' as denoting a 'commitment to notions of process, experience and pleasure' (Green, 1995, p. 402; see also Hargreaves, 1993; Hebdidge, 1986; Levin, 1987; Standish, 1995). As such, it views teaching more as art than as science, lending itself to corresponding modes of research. (The charismatic subject discourse, of course, also views teaching as an art, but as a mysterious art, akin to magic.)

Though clearly separated from one another, the two dominant discourses are not 'oppositional': certainly, they are not mutually exclusive, and most student-teachers these days will find themselves being encouraged and helped to be both 'competent' and 'reflective'. Indeed, in some of its cruder manifestations – in which 'checklists, rankings, peer evaluations, etc.' are prioritized while 'student teachers are seldom given an opportunity to have a concrete understanding of their personalities [and therefore] find it difficult to understand why they react to people, situations, or circumstances as they do' (Johnson, 1989, p. 340) – the reflective practitioner discourse overlaps the competences discourse to such an extent that the two may often appear, to the student, to merge into one. Such convergences suggest that, philosophically, the two discourses may be closer to one another than at first appears. In particular, we might suggest that each of these discourses has its roots in an Enlightenment view of social development, founded on the primacy of private and collective 'reason', and of the notion of the unitary, ideal 'self'. Thus, although the competences discourse may be seen as focusing on universals and the reflective practitioner discourse on the contingent and idiosyncratic, both seem to overemphasize a particular form of agency (that which focuses on 'self-improvement' rather than that which looks 'outward' towards reforming society) through implying the existence of 'detached', 'independent', unified identities. Just as success rests on the student's responsibility, with the aid of tutors, to become 'competent' in the competences discourse, so it is incumbent on individual students to use their own reflective, rational powers in the reflective practitioner discourse. In this way, within either discourse it becomes an easy task to pathologize the individual pupil, teacher or student-teacher for any breakdowns that occur in social interaction (Walkerdine, 1982, 1990). Such pathologizing does two things. First, as has already been suggested, it shifts debate away from issues related to broader socio-economic and cultural relations. Second, through its appeal to ideal, universal 'reason', it promotes the discourse (already very familiar to teachers and pupils) of individual blame. The first difficulty, of course, can be addressed initially by ensuring locally that such issues are given adequate coverage as curriculum inputs on courses. The second is rather more difficult to address, since it involves a radical departure for students not only in how they perceive their classrooms but in how they perceive and understand 'themselves'.

Beyond reflection: contingency, idiosyncrasy and reflexivity

'In the postmodern world', argues Hargreaves, 'multiple rather than singular forms of intelligence are coming to be recognized … multiple rather than singular forms of representation of students' work are being advocated and accepted … Many ways of knowing, thinking and being moral, not just rational, "logical" ones, are coming to be seen as legitimate' (Hargreaves, 1993, p. 22). Elsewhere, Anthony Giddens has talked of the 'reflexive project of the self, which consists in the sustaining of coherent, yet continuously revised, biographical narratives' (Giddens, 1991, p. 5), while Cole and Knowles (1995, p. 131) have described teaching practice in terms of its 'multiple roles and contexts'.

The notion of multiple identities, the need for flexible responses to meet the demands of changing situations, an emphasis on accommodation (rather than assimilation) and on navigation (rather than control), are concepts that have variously been included under the banners of post-modernism and high modernism.[2] Unlike the notion of self implied in the competences discourse and, to a lesser extent, the reflective practitioner discourse, these notions of self prioritize individual and collective flexibility and collaboration, along with informed understandings of the multiple contexts within which one operates. In doing this, they introduce – in place of the notion of the unified, ideal, 'Cartesian' self – the material, constructed self: that is, the self as 'text' that is formed (partly *by itself*) at the intersections of various discursive practices and that can be 'read' both by others and 'by the self itself'.

These alternative notions of the self, and of the manner in which it is constructed, have given rise to new modes of practice in initial teacher education as well as to new forms of theoretical enquiry, in which teachers and student-teachers are encouraged to interrogate and critically reflect not only on their pupils' behaviour or upon what happened (in terms of failure and success) in the classroom, but also on their own behaviours – on the ways in which they responded to situations, interacted with other people, experienced emotional responses and so forth. Such practice can be described in terms of a further discourse: that of the *reflexive* practitioner. This discourse, which re-emphasizes the significance of intra- as well as interpersonal relationships in classroom practice, starts from the premise that teachers are, indeed, 'made', though not just in the sense inscribed within the competences discourse. When they come to teaching, for example, teachers already bring with them a history and a culture through which they have negotiated and – however impermanently – 'fixed' meanings, orientations and understandings about such things as how learning works, what schools and education are for and how teachers should conduct themselves, which are immediately subject to revisitations once the practice of teaching begins. (Bourdieu's work on 'habitus' and 'field' provides a useful framework for the exploration of this process: see, for instance, Bourdieu, 1990 and Moore, 1997). Teachers also bring, whether they want to or not, emotional, historical 'baggage' which, in the highly charged atmosphere of the school classroom, can intrude on their practice both positively and negatively (when, for example, the classroom becomes the social space for the playing out or repetition of family-related repressions, irresolutions and role anxieties).

The reflexive discourse encourages teachers, appropriately supported by their tutors (Combs, 1972; Wragg, 1974), not only to reflect critically on ongoing experiences *in themselves*, but to contextualize these experiences within previous experiences as a way of developing more effective teaching strategies (Cole and Knowles, 1995; Quicke, 1988; Schön, 1988; Thomas, 1995). Part of that activity, aimed at helping practitioners to understand more clearly 'the way in which a personal life can be penetrated by the social and the practical' (Thomas, 1995, p. 5) and to make sense of 'prior and current life experiences in the context of the personal as it influences the professional' (Cole and Knowles, 1995, p. 130), involves encouraging individual teachers to critique difficulties they may be experiencing in the here and now within the context of previous roles and experiences they have encountered 'outside' the classroom situation in, for example, their family life or their own schooling. Inevitably, this also introduces issues of *desire* (Hargreaves, 1994; McLaren, 1996) into understandings of practice: 'What do I want from these interactions?' 'What do others want of me?' 'What am I afraid of?' 'What do I want to *do* about the things I don't like here?' With reference to Peter Woods's question we might say that this kind of teaching and research about teaching moves us away from the art/science dichotomy into his area of the 'more besides' (Woods, 1996, p. 31).

There are, of course, obvious dangers in an approach that invites teachers to interrogate their own behaviours textually. Chief among these are (a) that practitioners and their tutors may engage in ill-informed 'amateur psycho-analysis' that ends up benefiting nobody or even worsening an already difficult situation; (b) that the discourse may slip into the very pathologizations implied by the other discourses we have considered, and provide another way of obscuring the 'macro blot' (Bernstein, 1996, p. 56). Such potential dangers call for care and common sense, however, rather than a dismissal of the discourse. We must never forget that the other discourses are also replete with dangers, not least in their refusal (not always the case with the reflective practitioner discourse) fully to acknowledge, in their obeisance to rationality, either the emotive, autobiographical aspects of classroom interactions or the socio-historical contexts within which classroom practice occurs – omissions which often cut off central avenues of explanation for perplexed teachers when things go wrong. Experience, furthermore, suggests that the incorporation of this third discourse (the 'reflexive' discourse) *along with* those of the competent teacher and the reflective practitioner can, if properly handled,[3] have very beneficial effects – not least for student-teachers experiencing classroom difficulties and for those who, in terms of seeking and responding to advice, seem to have reached an impasse of the kind 'I have tried everything, and everything has failed'. As has already been indicated, this is not a question of *replacing* the competences and reflective practitioner discourses with the reflexive discourse, but rather of adding it *to* those discourses in a way that makes it easier and more profitable for students to 'enter', to understand and to negotiate those discourses; that is to say, it serves as a contextualization function that helps replace morbid, unconstructive 'self' criticism ('Something *in me* is wrong') with constructive, reasoned, 'action' criticism ('Something *that's being done* is wrong').

By way of illustration of how effective such an addition can be in terms of both practice and research, the following brief extracts are drawn from a series of reflexive essays written by students on a one-year course of initial teacher education. (For fuller accounts, see Moore, 1997; Moore, 1998b; Moore and Atkinson, 1998.) These extracts are indicative of the altered 'positioning' of the teacher in the reflexive discourse: that is to say, the way in which teachers simultaneously consider past, present and future actions while looking 'inward' to their own histories and perceived character traits and 'outward' to the behaviours of their pupils and to the social conditions within which they and their pupils operate.

Student A

I was getting angry, and was told that this was exacerbating my problems [with this particular class]. I'd tried to sort this out in my lesson evaluations. I felt I was getting angry because the kids were misbehaving and just refusing to do what I was asking of them. I'd tried being patient, but that hadn't got me anywhere either. With two particular kids, I was rapidly developing a 'relationship' that I would describe as dysfunctional. Not only would they refuse to do anything I told them, but they also continually interfered with other children in the class – but the worst thing was that they started ignoring my presence. In the end, I had them removed from the class, but that just seemed to cause resentment among the rest of the class. I must say that the only thing that really helped, in the end, was when I took the advice to focus on my own anger and ask 'Why am I getting so cross here?' After all, this was only two children not working – and I knew my anger was not out of frustration at them not getting on, or anything like that. It was personal. Thinking about other situations that made me angry like this or had done in the past, and just going through with someone some of the feelings of power and powerlessness I had experienced myself as a child in a working-class home meant that when I went home in the evening I was able to think more clearly, get things in perspective and focus on strategies. It also helped me to stop hating these two and to remember that they were probably behaving the way they did because of the lives they had. I won't say my anger has gone away entirely, but I'm definitely getting better at controlling it and I do have the kids back in the class now and generally enjoy a much better relationship with the class as a whole. In a strange way, it's also helped me to appreciate the politics of the situation. I feel much more clued up now about the way society itself can operate against the interests of some kids, and against teachers who try to do something about it.

Student B

The trouble was, I was taking everything personally, and just taking it home with me. I know we were always told not to do that, but it's easier said than done. Instead of, after a lousy lesson or a rotten day, going away and carefully, rationally thinking what I would do next time to make things work better, I was just wallowing in feelings of inadequacy and dreading the next day – so much so that I went in expecting more trouble, and obviously the kids sensed it and obliged me. The reflexive writing we were asked to do did help, though I was very dubious about it at the start and I don't know how useful it would have been if I'd been forced to show it to anyone rather than volunteering it like this. Just talking through things 'with myself' did help me to appreciate that the kids' behaviour, although I experienced it as being directed against me, was really about something much bigger, and instead of acting confrontationally I had to be sympathetic in my heart and firm and sensible in my manner. Part of what I realised was that I'd had this feeling of kind of being watched all the time – as if there was some expectation of classroom performance that I was constantly not living up to. Another bit, related to that, was that I actually wanted the kids to be 'more personal' to me, if that makes any sense. I think I needed to be liked and respected, and, strange as it seems now, I'd never actually understood that myself – how my need was contributing to the overall problem.

The above examples illustrate the potential helpfulness of the reflexive discourse to student-teachers experiencing classroom impasses when the discourse is appropriately introduced: that is to say, when it is introduced in a way that helps students shift their explanations for and related tactics for dealing with classroom difficulties away from the pathologization of either themselves or their pupils, towards a better understanding of their own and their pupils' behaviours and of the interrelations between these behaviours and the wider social conditions – including social inequalities – in which those behaviours are sited (see also McLaren, 1996, pp. 73–4). When student-teachers are encouraged and allowed to develop reflexivity in this particular way, not only are the dangers of pathologization avoided, but the students are enabled to take a more positive view both of themselves and of the possibilities that are available to them. Indeed, the prioritization of this kind of agency – directed politically outward rather than clinically inward – puts them in a far better position not just to deal sensibly with classroom difficulties but to engage, as 'transformative intellectuals' (Giroux 1988), in wider projects aimed both at 'changing the conditions of their own work … and struggling towards a larger vision and realization of human freedom' (Giroux and McLaren, 1992, p. xiii). We should not be surprised if such a struggle, in which teacher education is implicated as a 'progressive force' aimed at 'reaffirming a commitment to justice, equality, and non-exploitive social relations' (Beyer and Zeichner, 1987, p. 298), includes a radical critique of the competences discourse itself as, in essence and in isolation, a tool for social control and cultural reproduction.

Classroom behaviours: latent and manifest meanings

In addition to indicating the potential helpfulness of the reflexivity discourse to the teacher as practitioner, the examples I have quoted also suggest a *theoretical* paradigm within which to locate research in the field of teaching studies, which is implied in Woods' question 'Is teaching an art or a science?' What Woods' question does, in effect, is to point the way forward very clearly and precisely to where qualitative research in education, no less than education itself, needs to be moving as we enter the twenty-first century: that is to say, towards a post-Enlightenment kind of theorizing, supporting and describing a post-Enlightenment kind of practice, in which questions, perspectives and approaches tied to rationality and reason are no longer allowed to dominate at the expense of questions, perspectives and approaches that prioritize human sensibilities in both the intra-personal and inter-personal contexts. Such a paradigm suggests the adoption of, among other things, a revised notion of the workings of hegemony and of the interrelationships between 'dominant' and 'dominated' cultures in the classroom situation. Rejecting a mechanistic view of the operations of hegemony, for example, this theorizing would focus rather on its dialectical characteristics, exploring ways in which people (pupils, teachers and student-teachers) from marginalized cultures do not simply internalize or reject dominant ideologies, but draw on other voices within their own memories and cultural histories to make sense of what they are shown and told and what they experience (Gramsci, 1985; Martin-Barbero, 1993). With reference to related research practice, this might include explorations of the ways in which the teacher and pupils within a given class may, in different ways, respond to similar hegemonic forces, and the often unnecessary conflicts to which these alternative negotiations can give rise.

Treading just this path between ideological determinism and the emancipatory powers of individual and collective agency, Valerie Walkerdine (1990, pp. 173–204) has adapted concepts from Freud's dream theory to argue for a development of *ethnographic* research that enables researchers, through processes of inter-textualization, to look beyond the 'manifest content' of what they observe and hear, to its 'latent content'; that is to say, both the underlying attitudes, fears and aspirations of the observed actors *and* the power relations in the larger society, for which heard and observed practices and dialogues often act *substitutively.*

Although Walkerdine's work is in the area of audience ethnography, there is clearly much potential value in her work for qualitative research in general and for qualitative educational research in particular. To refer back to the two pieces of student writing quoted above, for example, we might say that the competences and reflective practitioner discourses, in their different ways, revealed to the student-teachers the *manifest* meanings of classroom interaction. The reflexive discourse, which introduced aspects of idiosyncrasy and contingency, suggested *latent* meanings which then enabled a more effective reading of – and, ultimately, response to – the manifest meanings, in both cases facilitating the more effective use of available strategies as a way of helping the students through their impasses. In each case the competences and reflective practitioner discourses were useful – but it was the reflexive discourse that fully 'activated' that usefulness, that made it accessible to the student and that opened the way to a more critical engagement with the interface between personally experienced difficulties and systemic failings.

The notion of an educational theory that recognizes and homes in on the complexity of classroom interrelations, seeking to overcome traditional dichotomies between subjectivity and objectivity, agency and determinism, uniqueness and conformity is, of course, nothing new (e.g. Blumer, 1969; Woods, 1979). In the area of teacher education, however – where, arguably, it has the most to offer and the most to learn (Moore, 1997) – it is in danger of becoming an increasingly overlooked, underdeveloped paradigm with reference both to the education of teachers and to research about the education of teachers. At its centre is the need for teachers to understand their own historical positionings and developments as much as they are able, in addition to trying to understand how their pupils 'tick', and for researchers to explore not only social interactions but also the discourses and contexts within which those interactions take place. From the perspective of manifest and latent content and meaning, classrooms – like cinemas or sitting-rooms – are viewed not just as places of ideological and cultural reproduction and coercion, but also as forums, in which actors with divergent interests, histories, interests and perceptions actively negotiate new meanings and new futures.

Notes

1 The charismatic subject discourse is not to be confused with the notion that teaching is often 'expressive and emergent, intuitive and flexible, spontaneous and emotional' (Woods, 1996, p. 6). The charismatic subject discourse is characterized by an over-reliance on 'personality' and an under-reliance on technique, often involving restrictive efforts to mimic the words and behaviours of teachers remembered from one's own school days. What Woods is suggesting is that teaching is not reducible to learnable competences – although these may be helpful – and that we ignore the specific (and variable) *contexts* of teaching at our peril.

2 I am aware that the terms 'modernism' and 'postmodernism' remain problematic and open to interpretation. 'Modernism' and 'postmodernism' as they are applied to educational settings often have, for example, very different meanings than when they are applied to, say, more directly political situations (Moore, 1998a). As long as we accept and are appropriately wary of this ambiguity, the terms can, however, provide a helpful taxonomy for distinguishing between radically different approaches to education in ways that are potentially more encompassing than those offered in the past by such expressions as 'progressive' and 'traditional' or 'transmissive' and 'pupil-centred'.

3 Related activity must, for instance, have a clear *voluntary* basis and not be subject to formal assessment.

References

Alexander, R. J., Craft, M. and Lynch, J. (eds) (1984) *Change in Teacher Education*, New York: Praeger.

Allen, G. (1994) *Teacher Training: The Education Bill 1993/4: Research Paper 94/58*, London: House of Commons Library.

Bernstein, B. (1996) *Pedagogy, Symbolic Control and Identity*, London: Taylor & Francis.

Beyer, L. E. and Zeichner, K. (1987) 'Teacher education in cultural context: beyond reproduction', in Popkewitz, T. S. (ed.) *Critical Studies in Teacher Education: Its Folklore, Theory and Practice*, London: Falmer Press, pp. 298–334.

Blumer, H. (1969) *Symbolic Interactionism*, Englewood Cliffs: Prentice Hall.

Bourdieu, P. (1990) *In Other Words*, Cambridge: Polity Press.

Cohen, L. and Manion, L. (1977) *A Guide to Teaching Practice*, London: Methuen.

Cole, A.L. and Knowles, J. G. (1995) 'Methods and issues in a life history approach to self-study', in Russell, T. and Korthagen, F. (eds) *Teachers Who Teach Teachers*, London: Falmer Press, pp. 130–54.

Combs, A. W. (1972) 'Some basic concepts for teacher education', *Journal of Teacher Education*, 23 (Fall), pp. 286–90.

Council for the Accreditation of Teacher Education (CATE) (1992) *Circular 9192*, London: CATE.

Cummins, J. (1996) *Negotiating Identities: Education for Empowerment in a Diverse Society*, California: CABE.

Department for Education and Employment (DfEE) (1997a) *Teaching; High Status, High Standards*, London: DfEE.

Department for Education and Employment (DfEE) (1997b) *Annex A to Teacher Training Circular 1197: Standards for the Award of Qualified Teacher Status*, London: DfEE.

Department of Education and Science (1981) *Teacher Training and the Secondary School*, London: DES.

Elliott, J. (1993) 'The relationship between "understanding" and "developing" teachers' thinking', in Elliott, J. (ed.) *Reconstructing Teacher Education*, London: Falmer Press.

Giddens, A. (1991) *Modernity and Self-Identity: Self and Society in the Late Modem Age*, Cambridge: Polity Press.

Giroux, H. (1988) 'Critical theory and the politics of culture and voice: rethinking the discourse of educational research', in Sherman, R. and Webb, R. (eds) *Qualitative Research in Education: Focus and Methods*, London: Falmer Press, pp. 190–210.

Giroux, H. A. and McKaren, P. L. (1992) 'Introduction' to Stanley, W. B., *Curriculum For Utopia: Social Reconstruction and Critical Pedagogy in the Postmodern Era*, Albany: State University of New York Press.

Goodson, I. F. and Walker, R. (1991) *Biography, Identity and Schooling*, London; Falmer Press.

Gramsci, A. (1985) *Selections from Cultural Writings*, London: Lawrence and Wishart.

Green, B. (1995) 'English teaching, cultural politics, and the postmodern turn', *Journal of Curriculum Studies*, 27, 4, pp. 391–409.

Hamilton, D. (1993) Texts, literacy and schooling' in Green, B. (ed.) *The Insistence of the Letter*, London: Falmer Press, pp. 46–57.

Handal, G. and Lauvas, P. (1987) *Promoting Reflective Teaching: Supervision in Action*, Milton Keynes and Philadelphia: Society for Research into Higher Education and Open University Press.

Hargreaves, A. (1993) 'Professional development and the politics of desire', in Vasquez, A. and Martinez, I. (eds*) New Paradigms and Practices in Professional Development*, New York: Teachers College Press.

Hargreaves, A. (1994) *Changing Teachers, Changing Times: Teachers' Work and Culture in the Postmodern Age*, London: Cassell.

Hebdidge, D. (1986) 'Postmodernism and "The Other Side"', *Journal of Communication Inquiry*, 10, 2, pp. 78–98.

Henry, M. A. (1989) 'Change in teacher education: focus on field experiences', in Braun, J. A. Jr (ed.) (1989) *Reforming Teacher Education: Issues and New Directions*, London and New York: Garland Publishing Inc.

Institute of Education (1912) *Education and the Training of Teachers: Statement on the James Report*, London: Institute of Education.

Johnson, B. (1989) 'Developing preservice teachers' self-awareness: an examination of the professional dynametric program', in Braun, J. A. Jr (ed.) (1989) *Reforming Teacher Education: Issues and New Directions*, New York and London: Garland Publishing Inc.

Jones, L. and Moore, R. (1995) Appropriating competence: the competency movement, the New Right and the "culture change" project', *British Journal of Education and Work*, 8, 2, pp. 78–92.

Lacan, J. (1977) *Ecrits*, London: Tavistock.

Lacan, J. (1979) *The Four Fundamental Concepts of Psycho-Analysis*, London: Penguin.

Levin, D. M. (1987) *Pathologies of the Modern Self: Postmodern Studies in Narcissism, Schizophrenia and Depression*, New York: New York University Press.

Loughran, J. (1996) *Developing Reflective Practice: Learning about Teaching and Learning through Modelling*, London: Falmer.

Loughran, J. and Russell, J. (eds) (1997) *Teaching about Teaching: Purpose, Passion and Pedagogy in Teacher Education*, London: Falmer.

Maguire, M. (1995) *Dilemmas in Teaching Teachers: The Tutor's Perspective, Teachers and Teaching*, 1, 1, pp. 119–31.

Marland, M. (1975) *The Craft of the Classroom*, Oxford: Heinemann Educational.

Martin-Barbero, J. (1993) *Communication, Culture and Hegemony: From the Media to Mediations*, London: Sage.

McIntyre, D., Hagger, H. and Burn, K. (1994) *The Management of Student Teachers' Learning*, London and Philadelphia: Kogan Page.

McLaren, P. (1996) *Critical Pedagogy and Predatory Culture,* New York: State University of New York Press.

Mitchell, C. and Weber, S. (1996) *Reinventing Ourselves as Teachers: Private and Social Acts of Memory and Imagination,* London: Falmer Press.

Moore, A. (1996) '"Masking the fissure"; some thoughts on competences, reflection and closure in initial teacher education', *British Journal of Educational Studies,* 44, 2, pp. 200–211.

Moore, A. (1997) 'Unmixing messages: a Bourdieuean approach to tensions and helping-strategies in initial teacher education', unpublished conference paper, International Conference on Bourdieu, Language and Education, University of Southampton.

Moore, A. (1998a) 'English, fetishism and the demand for change: towards a postmodern agenda for the school curriculum', in Edwards, G. and Kelly, A. V. (eds) *Experience and Education,* London: Paul Chapman, pp. 103–25.

Moore, A. (1998b) *Forcing the Issue: An Evaluation of Personal Writing Initiatives with Student Teachers* (updated with new material), University of London, Goldsmiths College.

Moore, A. and Atkinson, D. (1998) 'Charisma, competence and teacher education', *Discourse,* 19, 2, pp. 171–81.

'National Union of Teachers (1976) *Teacher Education: The Way Ahead,* London: National Union of Teachers.

Office for Standards in Education (Ofsted) and Teacher Training Agency (TTA) (1996) *Framework for the Assessment of Quality and Standards in Initial Teacher Training 1996/97,* London: Ofsted.

Popkewitz, T. S. (ed.) (1987) *Critical Studies in Teacher Education: Its Folklore, Theory and Practice,* London: Falmer Press.

Quicke, J. (1988) 'Using structured life histories to teach the sociology and social psychology of education', in Woods, P. and Pollard, A. (eds) *Sociology and Teaching,* London: Croom Helm.

Reid, W. A. (1993) 'Literacy, orality and the functions of curriculum', in Green, B. (ed.) *The Insistence of the Letter,* London: Farmer Press, pp. 13–26.

Schön, D. A. (1983) *The Reflective Practitioner,* New York: Basic Books.

Schön, D. A. (1987) *Educating the Reflective Practitioner,* San Francisco: Jossey-Bass.

Schön, D. A. (1988) 'Coaching reflective teaching', in Grimmett, P. P. and Erickson, G. L. (eds) *Reflection in Teacher Education,* British Columbia: Pacific Educational Press.

Standish, P. (1995) 'Post-modernism and the education of the whole person', *Journal of Philosophy of Education,* 29, 1, pp. 121–36.

Stephens, P. and Crawley, T. (1994) *Becoming an Effective Teacher,* Cheltenham: Stanley Thornes Ltd.

Teacher Training Agency (TTA) (1998) *National Standards for Qualified Teacher Status,* London: Teacher Training Agency.

Thomas, D. (1995) 'Treasonable or trustworthy text: reflections on teacher narrative studies', in Thomas, D. (ed.) *Teachers' Stories,* Buckingham: Open University Press.

Valli, L. (ed.) (1992) *Reflective Teacher Education,* New York: State University of New York Press.

Walkerdine, V. (1982) 'A psycho-semiotic approach to abstract thought', in Beverid¿ (ed.) *Children Thinking Through Language,* London: Arnold.

Walkerdine, V. (1990) *Schoolgirl Fictions,* London: Verso.

Woods, P. (1979) *The Divided School,* London: Routledge and Kegan Paul.

Woods, P. (1996) *Researching the Art of Teaching: Ethnography for Educational Use,* London: Routledge.

Wragg, E.G. (1974) *Teaching Teaching,* Newton Abbot: David & Charles.

Part Two

The nature of educational research

Chapter 10

On the kinds of research in educational settings

Michael Bassey

[...] For too long there has been something rather uncertain about educational research, which leaves it wide open to ill-informed criticism and academic snideness. A significant weakness is that there is no generally accepted definition of what it is. Some see it as research that focuses on educational processes; some as research that seeks to improve educational practice; others as any research carried out in educational settings. In this chapter I explore these uncertainties and then suggest that there are several forms of research in educational settings, which merit clear delineation and mutual respect.

Uncertainties about research in educational settings

Educational research rarely attracts public interest, but in December 1993 it was the subject of debate in the UK House of Lords because of the Government's intention, through the 1993 Education Bill, to make the proposed Teacher

Extract taken from: Bassey, M., *Creating Education through Research: a global perspective of educational research for the 21st Century*, (Newark: Kirklington Moor Press, in association with the British Educational Research Association, 1995), pp. 32–52.

Training Agency responsible for the funding of some (or all?) educational research instead of the Higher Education Funding Councils. Speaking in the debate Lord Skidelsky said:

> It is alleged by many noble Lords that the Bill will stifle objective research into education, destroy a healthy research community, or destroy a sound research base, as though all those things already exist and something healthy is being cut down by the Government. Where have noble Lords been living over the past few years? Much of that is simply fantasy. I have had occasion to study professionally much of the research that has taken place and I have also had experience in my own university. Many of the fruits of that research I would describe as an uncontrolled growth of theory, an excessive emphasis on what is called the context in which teaching takes place, which is code for class, gender and ethnic issues, and an extreme paucity of testable hypotheses about what works and does not work.

Earlier in the same speech he said:

> Pedagogy is not analogous to medicine, law or accountancy. There is no theoretically based good practice which defines professional teaching. There are a number of arguments and approaches and they are in contention. … I can think of few things more destructive of effective teaching than a full understanding of educational theory. Educational theory is not in that state of development. We can still read with great profit Rousseau's *Emile,* written in the 18th century. We cannot read with great profit a medical text written in the 18th century. That is the difference. Education is an immature discipline and, because of the very strong element of politics, ideology and connection with wider social aims that are always part of the theory of how to teach, that will remain the case and educational theory will always be highly disputable. (Hansard, 7 December 1993, col, 882–883)

I wrote a fairly vitriolic article in the *Times Educational Supplement* on this (21 January 1994). I said:

> I have to challenge Lord Skidelsky since he claims authority by saying that he has 'had occasion to study professionally much of the research that has taken place.' Since there are over 200 journals currently reporting on different aspects of educational research, and at least 50 books a year published on research findings, he has been busy. It is regrettable that his comment on these writings is not marked with the scholarship for which he is respected in his own field. Let me illustrate this by responding to a few points made in his speech.
>   First let us examine his assertion that 'there is no theoretically based good practice which defines professional teaching.' Much of the good professional practice of teachers, as of doctors and lawyers, is embedded in their experience, and its quality depends upon factors such as their commitment, their enthusiasm, their memory of previous cases and their reflective intelligence. If Lord Skidelsky had

read Schön's 'The Reflective Practitioner' he would know this. But underpinning this good professional practice are theoretical ideas. As an example take the following summary account of the constructivist theory of learning:

> Learning has here been defined as the extension, elaboration or modification of children's schemata. Children achieve this by making sense of new knowledge in the light of their existing knowledge. The construction of this sense making is a continual intellectual process, an essential input to which is social interaction. Talk aids the organisation of experience into thought, and is thus central to learning.

This was written by Neville Bennett, Professor of Primary Education at the University of Exeter in a booklet called 'Managing Learning in the Primary Classroom' (1992). I fail to understand how Lord Skidelsky could think, for example, that a full understanding of constructivist theory would be destructive of effective teaching.

Secondly consider his assertion about ancient texts. I agree that the writings of Rousseau are of profit to teachers, but only in the same way that the writings of Hippocrates are of profit to doctors and of Locke to lawyers. They stimulate thought on philosophical issues, not on effective ways of tackling practical problems.

Thirdly he refers to 'an excessive emphasis on what is called the context in which teaching takes place' coupled with 'an extreme paucity of testable hypotheses about what works and does not work'. Here he shows a glimmer of understanding of one of the great achievements of educational research in recent years, but makes nonsense of it by failing to grasp its significance. The outcomes of teaching depend upon so many variables (in other words contexts are so complicated) that attempts to formulate testable hypotheses about effective teaching are rarely worthwhile. This is why qualitative work within an interpretive paradigm is favoured by many educational researchers in their attempts to advance knowledge and wisdom about classroom practice and management procedure. By contract, when the concern is to provide knowledge for policy makers, it is quantitative work in a positivist paradigm that is often appropriate.

Finally it seems from his speech that in order to prevent what he sees as 'an uncontrolled growth of theory' he would like to see a quango of eight – whose main concern would be the funding of teacher training – having responsibility for ensuring that better research is carried out. Help!

The academic research community is not complacent. There is much critical debate about the quality, credibility and impact of educational research. There is great awareness of past short-comings and of future potential. There is much concern about how researchers are trained – and how they can construct careers in research. There is disquiet that policy issues such as class size have not been adequately addressed.

But deeper than these there is grave concern about the future of our society. Any society only remains democratic while there is a free flow of information. Research provides one form of information and should entail trained intelligence focusing in depth on significant issues. Now, a society where quangos of government-appointees determine what significant issues are to be researched will soon decline. The uncomfortable issues, the ones that challenge orthodoxy, the ones that question fundamentals, will not gain funding and so this stimulus to the redevelopment of society will be lost. Decline will be inevitable. Please think again, Lord Skidelsky.

Lord Skidelsky replied a week later and while not accepting much of my argument, agreed that educational research should stay with the universities.

The importance of his speech is that it is not just the opinion of one outspoken peer, but is more or less typical of the view of a substantial number of his fellow academics and senior politicians. They fail to see that the reason why there is 'an extreme paucity of testable hypotheses about what works and does not work' is a natural consequence of educational research being predominantly a science of the singular. (Helen Simons used this phrase in a book title in 1980). They judge educational research as though it were a science of the general. [...]

This exchange of views serves to open the question, 'What kinds of research are there in educational settings?' In my view it is essential to recognise the plurality of this question. Most writers on educational research seem not to recognise this plurality and so, in espousing their own view as the unique one, endanger it from attacks by those who hold alternative views.

In 1968 Butcher introduced the series of books entitled *Educational Research in Britain,* of which he was editor, by stating that

> 'educational research' covers a multitude of activities. It is interpreted here as empirical research, based on experiment, on social surveys and on the clinical study of individuals. (p. 13)

This definition identifies the field of enquiry as empirical, but gives the enquiry no intention or purpose. It is noteworthy for its reference, at that time, to the study of individuals.

In a reaction against the assumption 'that educational research is a branch of psychology or social science', Peters and White (1969) suggested that

> educational research is sustained systematic enquiry designed to provide us with new knowledge which is relevant to initiating people into desirable states of mind involving depth and breadth of understanding

This broadens Butcher's definition to include philosophical and historical study, and gives the purpose of 'initiating people into desirable states of mind'.

Williams (1969), writing in Blond's *Encyclopaedia of Education*, gave a definition of educational research as:

> the process whereby information relevant to the decisions involved in the improvement of educational practices is obtained. (p. 235)

In 1973 Nisbet and Entwistle (who three years earlier had published *Educational Research Methods,* which became a standard textbook for students of educational research) gave a definition which included the concept of efficiency, viz:

> Educational research consists in careful, systematic attempts to understand the educational process and, through understanding, to improve its efficiency.

Simon (1978), in his presidential address to the British Educational Research Association in 1977, expressed the view that:

> the focus of educational research must be education, and that its overall function is to assist teachers, administrators, indeed all concerned in the field, to improve the quality of the educational process – and, in so doing, enhance the quality of life. (p. 5)

These quotations might give the impression that educational research had become free standing and quite distinctive from psychological, sociological, philosophical and historical research, but this was not so. When the Economic and Social Research Council produced its *Postgraduate Training Guidelines* (1991), the chosen description of educational research was a compromise between research on educational processes and research in educational settings.

> Educational research may include any disciplined enquiry which serves educational judgements and decisions or which is conducted in educational settings such as nursery, primary, secondary, further, higher, continuing and adult education; industrial, commercial and professional training; and local and national systems of education. This disciplined enquiry may draw on the methodologies of other social science disciplines, such as sociology, psychology, philosophy, or economics; or its methods and techniques may originate from an eclectic view of how knowledge is best generated and utilised by educational policy makers, educational managers and classroom practitioners. *ESRC Postgraduate Training Guidelines* (1991) (p. 23)

There is something paternalistic about the phrase 'may draw on the methodologies of other social science disciplines'. However my antagonism to this definition is more fundamental. In my view research in educational settings is only educational research if it is concerned with attempts to improve educational judgements and decisions. Research in educational settings which aims to develop sociological theory, psychological theory, philosophical constructs or historical ideas is not educational research, but sociological, psychological, philosophical or historical research in educational settings.

It is time for educational research to assert that it has come of age. It is time to leave the parental home (if sociology and psychology were the parents) and stand firmly on our own ground. That ground is the educational process of the making of decisions and judgements by practitioners and policy-makers, from the standpoint of trying to improve them.

This argument is not new. In 1977 Brian Simon, in the presidential address to BERA cited above, went onto say:

> Brief raids into educational territory are considered to be a good means of training the specialist sociologist, or psychologist, even if schools used for data collection are left in disarray. Research of this kind is not, in my book, *educational* research. It is psychological or sociological research conducted with educational materials which may, or may not, constitute a significant contribution to education. (Simon, 1978, p. 4)

A definition of educational research

In 1975, in *An Introduction to Curriculum Research and Development*, Stenhouse wrote:

> A research tradition which is accessible to teachers and which feeds teaching must be created if education is to be significantly improved. (p. 165)

This often repeated quotation, the ideas associated with it, and the endeavours of the many people which they have inspired, have helped change the climate of teacher opinion about educational research. Once denigrated by teachers as either stating the obvious or incomprehensible, it is now seen by many of them as potentially important for the advancement of educational practice. [It is still, regrettably, denigrated by some right-wing politicians, as discussed earlier].

Nearly 20 years later, David Tripp, in *Critical Incidents in Teaching* (1993) demonstrates through the medium of 62 researched 'critical incidents' the power of critical analysis of everyday occurrences in classrooms.

[…] Tripp is in no doubt that if educational research seeks to improve practice it needs to be grounded in educational events and not in academic theories. He says:

> It was only when I recognised the fact that I had been very successful in the classroom when I was very ignorant of what academics considered knowledge essential to teaching, that I became aware of the difference between the knowledge of academics and the knowledge of teachers. It has since become clear that most academic educational knowledge is of very little use to teachers and that teachers' knowledge and understanding of their practice is seriously under-represented and discounted in the university discipline of education. ...

> ... It appears to me that the most promising means of improving teaching is by grounding educational research (and thus theory) in the realities of teachers' everyday experience. Overall, I believe that an approach based on the interpretation of critical incidents has the potential to change the nature of the teaching profession by dealing with the fundamental practical, political and epistemological problems of education in teachers' terms (p. 152)

Trying to synthesise the above ideas in the form of a definition, leads to this. I believe that a definition like this needs to be nailed to the door and printed on the letterhead of everyone who claims to be an educational researcher!

> Educational research aims critically to inform educational judgements and decisions in order to improve educational action.

The reason for referring to 'judgements' and 'decisions' is this. Educational action depends upon judgements as to what is worthwhile and decisions as to what to do. As such it embraces both practice and policy. [...]

There are many ways of working towards the end of critically informing educational judgements and decisions in order to improve educational action. This definition embraces the realms of empirical, reflective and creative research; the categories of theoretical, evaluative and action research; the search for generalisations and the study of singularities; the audiences of researchers, practitioners and policy-makers; and the positivist and interpretive paradigms.

[...]

A definition of sociological research in education

Having staked out the ground for educational research, where does this leave the sociologists working in an educational setting? Their concerns are to construct new theoretical understandings, or to develop or to challenge existing ones, in relation to the expectations and existing theories of sociological knowledge. They are trying to make descriptions, analyses, interpretations and explanations in accord with the canons of their discipline. Those who call themselves 'educational sociologists' have chosen to work in an educational setting in order to achieve these ends, but if their work is effective it will rank with other sociological research conducted in other social settings. Thus a suitable definition for this kind of research is this:

> Sociological research in education aims critically to inform understandings of social phenomena in educational settings.

[...]

A definition of psychological research in education

Sociologists are not the only academics working in educational settings who are not engaging in the decisions-and-judgements-to-improve-educational-action type of research which I have defined as educational research. Some psychologists are also working in educational settings and striving to construct new, and challenge existing, theoretical understandings in relation to psychological knowledge. They are working in accord with the canons of their discipline. Those who see themselves as 'educational-psychological researchers' have chosen to work in an educational setting in order to achieve these ends. Thus a suitable definition for this kind of research is this:

> Psychological research in education aims critically to inform understandings of psychological phenomena in educational settings.

[...]

Other disciplinary researches in education

In addition to sociological and psychological enquiries in educational settings there are other disciplinary forms of enquiry, for example historical, philosophical and economic.

Educational action research

Educational action research is a subset of educational research as defined above. Certainly it 'aims critically to inform educational judgements and decisions in order to improve educational action', but it differs from other kinds of educational research in that it is research carried out by the actors themselves. It is what John Elliott has called 'insider' research. It is research carried out by practitioners to improve their own practice. Personal theory is created not as an end in itself, but in order to advance practice. The topics of enquiry, methods of data collection, analytical techniques, and styles of presenting findings (if communicated at all) reflect the pragmatic needs of teachers and educational managers. The intended audience may be no one other than the researcher, but may also be fellow teachers engaged in similar teaching, or fellow managers engaged in similar practice. The researcher in this kind of enquiry may find little in the education literature to guide the enquiries and may need to invent procedures grounded in practice in order to pursue the research.

Action research is often cyclical, because striving for improvement is seen by many practitioners (teachers, teacher-managers, administrators etc.) as an ongoing professional commitment.

Because action research entails an intention to change action involving people who are well known to the researcher, it is seen to demand not only a strong ethic of respect for persons, but also democratic involvement of those on whom it impinges. Thus openness, participation of others, and negotiation about the ownership of data and about the uses that the researcher may put it to, are deemed important.

Because they are 'insiders', action researchers are involved emotively as well as cognitively in their enquiries and so it is important to them that their research judgements and decisions are open to challenge. Thus criticism is important, for example as a means of testing whether findings represent what they purport to represent. To this end the action researchers have embraced the concept of the 'critical friend', meaning someone who responds to the invitation to invest some time and effort into critically examining a colleague's action research procedures and findings, and who agrees to work within the ethical framework of the enquiry – which defines matters such as the ownership of data.

[...]

Discussion

It is not always clear-cut as to which kind of research in education a particular study belongs. [...] Many research papers can be fitted into this typology, but there are likely to be problems arising from papers that 'don't fit', perhaps because they embrace more than one kind of research in education.

But I claim that the recognition of these different kinds of research in education effectively counters the criticism that Lord Skidelsky, at the beginning of this chapter, made when he said that 'education is an immature discipline' and 'there is no theoretically based good practice which defines professional teaching.'

Within the arena that I am describing as educational research, the concept of 'theory' is quite different from that of sociologists, psychologists, philosophers, historians, or economists. There are few general theories. Instead there are personal theories of practitioners and of policy-makers. Piaget, for example, is no longer significant. Gone are the days when the 'gurus' were Froebel, or Montessori, or Arnold, or Newman. Yet some of their ideas, merged with aspects of constructivist learning theory and theories of motivation and social dynamics, will be found in the personal theories of individuals. The competent teacher of today has a complex pattern of understandings that come partly from training and from reading, but largely from experience and from professional discourse with colleagues. Some are taking their understanding forward through personal action research, the development of which is probably the greatest achievement of all time of educational research. Educational research, seen as informing educational judgements and decisions in order to improve educational action, serves practitioners and policy-makers by contributing to the development of their personal theories, and in the process may serve other researchers by building frameworks for them to extend further.

I would add one further thought. I suspect that research into education is similar to research into management, health care, social work, criminology, and prison studies, in its paucity of general theory, but focus on personal theory that underpins practice and policy. I guess that, for example, there is a whole arena of management research which aims critically to inform management judgements and decisions in order to improve management action. And likewise there will be sociological research in management and psychological research in management which aim critically to inform understandings of social and psychological phenomena in management settings. Teasing these out for each of the professional studies listed above would help to clarify, across the social sciences, the legitimate roles of different kinds of researchers and, hopefully, clear the way for the development of parity of esteem between them.

References

Bassey, M. (1994) Why Lord Skidelsky is so wrong, *The Times Educational Supplement* (21 January).
Bennett, N. (1992) *Managing Learning in Classrooms*, Stoke-on-Trent, Trentham Books.
Butcher, H. J. (ed) (1968) *Educational Research in Britain* (vol 1) University of London Press.
Economic and Social Research Council (1991) *Postgraduate Training Guidelines*, Swindon, ESRC.
Entwistle, N. J. and Nisbet, J. D. (1972) *Educational Research in Action,* London, Hodder and Stoughton.
Nisbet, J. D. and Entwistle, N. J. (1970) *Educational Research Methods*, London, University of London Press.
Peters, R. S. and White, J. P. (1969) The philosopher's contribution to educational research, in: Taylor, W. (ed.) *Research Perspectives in Education*, London, Routledge and Kegan Paul.
Simon, B. (1978) Educational Research: Which Way? *British Educational Research Journal,* 4(1): 2–7.
Simons, H. (ed.) (1980) *Towards a Science of the Singular*, Norwich, CARE, University of East Anglia.
Skidelsky, Lord (1993) *Hansard*, 7 December col, 882–883
Stenhouse, L. (1975) *An Introduction to Curriculum Research and Development*, London, Heinemann.
Tripp, D., (1993) *Critical Incidents in Teaching*, London, Routledge.
Williams, J. D. (1969) Educational research, in *Blond's Encyclopaedia of Education*, London, Blond Educational.

Chapter 11

The paradigm wars and their aftermath

A 'historical' sketch of research on teaching since 1989

Nathaniel Gage

As I begin this history, we have arrived at the year 2009 – a decade after the turn of the millennium – and are looking back at what happened in research on teaching during the two decades since 1989. Why have I chosen 1989 as the year in which to begin this historical sketch and commentary? Because it was in 1989 that what came to be known as the 'Paradigm Wars' had come to a sanguinary climax.[1]

The situation in the 1980s

Although it is the ensuing years with which I shall be primarily concerned, we need first to look at the situation in the 1980s, because the events since 1989 grew out of that situation. As you will recall, research on teaching of the kind that had flourished in the 60s and 70s had come in for a severe beating during the 80s. Such research had been characterized as 'at best, inconclusive, at worst, barren' (Tom, 1984, p. 2) and 'inadequate to tell us anything secure and important about how teachers should proceed in the classroom' (Barrow, 1984, p. 213).

Taken from: *Educational Researcher,* Vol. 18, pp. 4–10.
© 1989 by the American Educational Research Association.
Reproduced with permission of the publisher.

The attempt to lay a scientific basis for the art of teaching had failed, said the critics. Beginning with Joseph Mayer Rice early in the 20th century, and continuing through the work of such men as E. L. Thorndike, A. S. Barr, and David G. Ryans, the effort to use scientific method to study and improve teaching had come a cropper. Even the correlational research of the 1960s and 1970s, using the relatively new idea of observing teaching in classrooms with fairly objective low-inference schemes, had not, according to the critics, paid off. Even the 12 successful field experiments with teaching practices derived from correlational findings – to assess the causal efficacy of those teaching practices in improving outcomes (Gage & Needels, 1989, pp. 268–287) – had not impressed the critics. The search for scientifically grounded ways to understand and improve teaching had led nowhere. Moreover, even if such 'positivistic social science' had succeeded, one writer said, it would have bred ideas that 'can only be implemented in an authoritarian, manipulative, bureaucratic system' (Cazden, 1983, p. 33).

The antinaturalist critique

The critics who asserted the failure of research on teaching also offered explanations of that failure. Perhaps the most fundamental explanation was the antinaturalist position that human affairs simply cannot be studied with the scientific methods used to study the natural world. Thus the term 'social science' is at its root an oxymoron. And why is the scientific study of human affairs impossible? First, because human affairs, including teaching and learning, are inextricably involved with the intentions, goals, and purposes that give them meaning. Second, a science is involved with direct, one-way causal links, but there are no such 'billiard-ball' causal connections between teacher behavior and student learning. Third, scientific methods can be applied only to natural phenomena that are stable and uniform across time, space, and context in a way obviously untrue of the human world of teaching and learning. So, the critics asserted, we should not search for the kind of prediction and control that scientific method might yield but rather for the kind of insight that historians, moral philosophers, novelists, artists, and literary critics can provide. The futility of scientific research on teacher planning, for example, was inherent in the futility of teacher planning itself, because

> the teacher may change objectives from month to month or from week to week; unforeseen events – a hot day or one student's open cruelty to another – may necessitate revising plans; the demands people place on the schools can change from year to year, from community to community … so that the teacher cannot necessarily construct his battle plan in 1984 for 1985, in September for May, on Monday for Friday, or during second hour for third hour. (Tom, 1984, p. 71)

So went the antinaturalist critique.

The interpretivist critique

A second barrage of criticism, often related to the criticisms I have just described, descended from the interpretivists.[2] These writers called for a focus on the 'immediate meanings of action from the actors' point of view' (Erickson, 1986, p. 120) – a focus that they found absent from the mainstream of research on teaching of the 60s and 70s. They saw sharp differences between their own theoretical presuppositions and those of the quantitative, objectivity-seeking researchers. They were 'pessimistic' (Erickson, p. 120) about the possibility of combining interpretive and objectivity-seeking approaches. Thus, in focusing on behavior rather than on behavior and its meaning (i.e., on 'actions'), the standard researchers had disregarded the interpretations of teachers and pupils. The interpretivists considered the focus on specifics of action and meaning-perspectives to be overlooked by the objectivists' research on teaching. Interpretive researchers differed from 'standard' researchers in their 'theoretical presuppositions about the nature of schools, teaching, children, and classroom life, and about the nature of cause in human life in general' (Erickson, p. 125). They rejected the conception of cause as mechanical or chemical or biological, a conception they said was used in the 'standard' approaches to research on teaching. They also rejected the assumption of uniformity in nature – the assumption that phenomena would occur in the same way in different places and times. They rejected the use of linear causal models applied to behavioral variables as a basis for inferring causal relations among the variables, because such models presupposed fixed and obvious meanings of certain types of actions by teachers.

Instead, the interpretive researchers emphasized the phenomenological perspective of the persons behaving. In this perspective, behavioral uniformities are seen 'not as evidence of underlying, essential uniformity among entities, but as an illusion – a social construction' (Erickson, 1986, p. 126). The effects on people's actions of their interpretations of their world create the possibility that people may differ in their responses to the same or similar situations.

Thus, interpretive researchers regard individuals as able to construct their own social reality, rather than having reality always be the determiner of the individual's perceptions. Thus they believe strongly in something akin to what political commentators during the 1988 U.S. presidential campaign called 'spin control.' As you will recall, spin control refers to the interpretation of an event to the advantage of a given party or candidate. Losing in a primary election could be interpreted as a victory if the spin controllers could point to very low expectations. The ordinary person's everyday construction of social reality is not done as consciously and manipulatively as that of the political operatives who used spin control. But it was such meaning-perspectives or interpretations of events that the interpretive researchers considered important. And, in their opinion, the 'standard' researchers had grievously neglected meaning-perspectives, because they tried to observe behavior (not action, defined as behavior plus meaning) objectively.

Because causation in human affairs is determined by interpreted symbols, the kinds of prediction and control that can be achieved in the natural sciences are not possible in human affairs. Because the positivistic and behavioral research on teaching of the 60s and 70s had typically been aimed at such prediction or control, it was clear that such positivistic and behavioral research was doomed to failure. So it ought to be supplanted by interpretive research on teaching, which would examine the conditions of meaning created by students and teachers as a basis for explaining differences among students in their achievement and morale. It was differences in organization and in the resulting meaning that, although they may be 'quite small indeed, and radically local,' might 'make a big difference for student learning' (Erickson, 1986, p. 129).

The critical theorists' critique

A third kind of attack on previous research on teaching came from the critical theorists. In their view, most educational research in general and research on teaching in particular had been governed by a merely 'technical' orientation aimed at efficiency, rationality, and objectivity. It exhibited a 'tendency to measure anything that moves,' a 'neglect of latent political commitments in research questions and designs,' an 'inclination to simply provide technical expertise for hire' (Apple, 1986, p. 15).[3]

Instead, the critical theorists implied, we should have been looking at the relationship of schools and teaching to society – the political and economic foundations of our constructions of knowledge, curriculum, and teaching. The critical theorists emphasized the importance of power in society and the function of schools in defining social reality. They stressed the ways in which education served the interests of the dominant social class, which in our society has consisted of the rich, the White, and the male, as against the poor, the non-White, and the female. These class interests had led educators to serve, however unwittingly, the functions of reproducing the inequitable social class structure and other arrangements that currently exist and to proceed as if the societal status quo should go unquestioned.

But, the critical theorists asserted, human beings can change the social structure, and they need not be dominated by it. Properly educated and motivated people can undertake to change our society into one in which the poor, the non-White, and the female will no longer be subordinate. Schools, like other social institutions, such as the media and the legislatures, must be the scenes of the necessary struggles for power. Educational research ought at least to be aware of the possibility of such struggles. Better, it ought to enter into them on the side of the oppressed so as to reconstruct education and the society at large for the achievement of greater social justice.

The implication of the critical theorists' position was that the kinds of research on teaching that had been done until 1989 by so-called positivists, attempting to use scientific methods, and even to some degree by interpretivists, exploring social constructions of reality, had been more or less trivial. This research has constituted a kind of technical attempt to improve the 'fine details' (Erickson, 1986, p. 120) of teaching – 'the little differences in everyday classroom life that [according to both the positivists and the interpretivists] make a big difference for student learning' (Erickson, p. 128). Instead, the critical theorists implied, what is needed is a reconsideration of the whole structure of society in which education, including teaching, goes on.

The effect of the criticisms

What happened as a result of this onslaught from the antinaturalists, the inter-pretivists, and the critical theorists? As you all know, the critics triumphed. During the 1990s and thereafter, the kind of objectivist-quantitative, or scientific, research on teaching that had been done up through the 1980s ground to a halt. The field saw almost no correlational or experimental studies of teaching using structured observation systems intended to enhance objectivity.

Faculty members, graduate students, and research workers were convinced of the futility of the old way of studying teaching. In schools of education, enrollment declined in courses in tests and measurements, statistics, experimental design, and survey research. Structured classroom observations, achievement tests, attitude inventories, and the use of statistics to estimate the reliability and the interrelationships of such measures virtually disappeared.

Research grants and contracts from foundations and governmental sources became virtually unobtainable for objective-quantitative researchers. The Division of Educational Psychology of the American Psychological Association saw its membership shrink to about a fourth of what it had been during the 1980s. AERA's Division on Teaching and Teacher Education saw its members become almost exclusively devoted to interpretive-qualitative studies and critical-theoretical analyses.

The journals that published research on teaching contained almost no articles reporting tests of statistical significance, correlations coefficients, effect sizes, or meta-analyses. Instead, they were filled with reports on ethnographic studies of classroom phenomena and by sociopolitical and economic analyses of the ways in which teachers, curricula, and schools perpetuated the unjust social order. The critical theorists also found ways to work toward the reconstruction of society along lines that would reduce the inequalities, the social-class cleavages, and the other injustices endemic in capitalist societies.

Research on teaching, having rid itself of the scientific methodology that had led it astray, became more a matter of observing teaching carefully and reflecting deeply on what was observed. Teachers became much more involved in research on teaching, but no longer as mere objects of study or recipients of the findings of technically oriented experts. Rather, doing action research, teachers became the generators of the findings, which they inferred from qualitative studies of their own teaching, from thinking about what worked well and what didn't, and from discussing their ideas with other teachers. Occasionally the teachers might collaborate with the professor brought in for a day or two to advise on ways to help teachers do better what teachers already had in mind.

These fundamental changes, which had been implicitly (and more and more often explicitly) demanded by the critics, did not merely change the mainstream of research on teaching. Rather, the changes had the effects on teaching that their proponents had implicitly promised. The ethnographers' findings made teachers aware of small changes in teaching that made a big difference in student achievement. Teachers realized that their ways of asking questions, giving children opportunities to recite, and conducting reading-group sessions, for example, had often been alien to their pupils' familial and community culture and their pupils' expectations and understandings of how to behave and think. So what went on in classrooms became much more culturally appropriate for the poor, the minorities, and the female students. In short, some of the fondest hopes of the interpretive students of classroom phenomena were realized.

Critical theorists also achieved the kinds of changes in teaching that their orientations and research had made them want. For example, in teaching history, teachers no longer relied on the standard history and civics textbooks that raised no questions about the status quo (Adler & Goodman, 1986). Instead, pupils were sensitized to the ways in which their previous history courses had neglected almost everything done by people who were not white men, political leaders, military heroes, or industrialists. Moreover, at least equal, if not greater, attention was given to what had been done in the course of history by white women, by men and women of color, by peace activists, and by labor leaders. The hard, cruel facts about what had been done to slaves, striking coal miners, union organizers, radical journalists, and left-wing political parties began to get equal time in the social studies classes of the nation.

Among academicians, many educational psychologists, for example, came to realize that they had gone into their field to realize their social values, their desire to contribute to the improvement of society and mankind's lot, while simultaneously adhering to the values of science and avoiding the passions and ambiguities of politics. They could thus improve education and society by cultivating and applying scientific methods and findings and yet steer clear of the political fray. What the critical theorist contributed to the educational psychologist was a realization of the futility of this strategy. Education is of necessity a political process, said the critical theorists, and even the act of refusing to get involved in politics – not necessarily the politics of political parties but nonetheless politics – is a political act.

An alternative effect of the criticisms

Now let me offer another look at what happened after 1989. In this second version of what happened, all but the first part is true. That is, the interpretivists did continue their work and did bring about the kinds of improvement in teaching that I have sketched. The critical theorists also continued their work and achieved the kinds of improvement in curriculum and teaching that their ideas implied, even if the peaceful social revolution to overthrow capitalism and install a democratic socialism has not yet occurred.

But what did not happen was the decline in so-called positivistic or mainstream research on teaching. This decline did not occur, because the field of research on teaching, and educational research at large, indeed the social sciences as a whole, recovered from their confusion and came to a great awakening.

The confusion was illustrated by one writer who, although denying that paradigms are 'competing,' considered them later in the same paragraph to be 'rival' (Erickson, 1986, p. 120); but the distinction between 'competing' and 'rival' is, of course, unrecognized in dictionaries. And some objective-quantitative researchers (e.g., Gage & Needels, 1989; Yates, Chandler, & Westwood, 1987) awakened from their torpor in responding to criticism and began to reply, point by point.

More important, all researchers realized that what might be called the 'oppositional component of the paradigm' was invalid. This component had stated that any paradigm inherently implied an opposition to alternative paradigms. Given their new understanding of the falsity of the oppositional component, researchers realized that there was no necessary antagonism between the objectivists, the interpretivists, and the critical theorists. Social researchers agreed with Howe (1988) that the 'incompatibilists' – those who said that the quantitative and qualitative perspectives must of necessity be mutually exclusive and antagonistic – were simply wrong. Philosophical analyses resulted in a triumph of pragmatic resolutions of paradigm differences over claims of exclusive possession of the one true paradigm. These resolutions did not result from merely glossing over basic philosophical differences. They came rather through new realizations among scholars that paradigm differences do not require paradigm conflict.

First, it became apparent that programs of research that had often been regarded as mutually antagonistic were simply concerned with different, but important, topics and problems. There was no essential incompatibility between, for example, process-product research on teaching (the search for relationships between classroom processes and students' subsequent achievements and attitudes) and research that focused on teachers' and students' thought processes and meaning-perspectives. The two kinds of researchers were simply studying different important topics. The implication of necessary antagonism or incompatibility was unjustified. A year after she characterized positivistic social science as necessarily authoritarian, manipulative, and bureaucratic, the same writer endorsed 'interdisciplinary collaboration' and acknowledged that she 'should not have exploited psychology/anthropology differences to make a point' (Cazden, 1984, p. 184).

Moreover, Shulman's pioneering attention to teachers' 'pedagogical content knowledge' (1987) – namely, the *content-specific* ways in which teachers understood, formulated, presented, explained, and discussed the content being taught – was recognized as long overdue and extremely valuable, but also as not at all antagonistic to process-product research. Although the latter kind of research had often been concerned primarily with *content-general* and managerial aspects of teaching – such as the ways in which teachers organized their classes, asked questions, or reacted to responses – nothing prevented process-product research from also being concerned with the teacher's pedagogical content knowledge.

Process-product research was also recognized to be compatible with interpretive, ethnographic studies of classroom phenomena. Thus, what Erickson (1986, p. 135) had endorsed as good examples of interpretive research (Au & Mason, 1981; Barnhardt, 1982) came to be recognized also as examples of process-product research, because they related ways of teaching to what students learned. Many process-product studies in the two decades since 1989 have employed both objective-quantitative and interpretive-qualitative methods.

In short, it was finally understood that nothing about objective-quantitative research precluded the description and analysis of classroom processes with interpretive-qualitative methods. Classroom processes need not be described solely in terms of behaviors or actions; they could also be described in terms of meaning-perspectives. No calamity whatever befell those who studied teaching in the same investigation with both objective-quantitative and interpretive-qualitative methods. Indeed, most of these investigations with both kinds of methods turned out to be more fruitful of insights, understandings, predictive power, and control resulting in improvements of teaching.

One persuasive harbinger of paradigmatic rapprochement came from Goldenberg and Gallimore (1989). They contrasted two hypotheses much used for the improvement of teaching: the 'universalistic' and the 'cultural compatibility' hypotheses, derived from the objectivist and the interpretive approaches, respectively. They laid out quite evenhandedly the strengths and inadequacies of the two approaches. They pointed to the omnipresent need for artistry in the implementation of scientific findings, as had also been done by Gage (1978, 1985). Finally, they noted the dependence of educational improvement on the political forces emphasized by critical theorists. All in all, their well-documented analysis demonstrated the value of a nondoctrinaire formulation.

The antinaturalists – those who believed that the methods of the natural sciences were inappropriate for the social sciences – also eventually became aware of the errors of their thinking. They realized that they had mistakenly loaded onto scientific method a lot of ontological baggage that was unnecessary in gaining the advantages of scientific method in objectivity and trustworthiness. They conceded that scientific method could be used for purposes other than building a science – a network of laws that would hold forever everywhere. Rather, scientific method could be used for 'piecemeal social engineering' as envisioned by Karl Popper, namely, for making 'small adjustments and readjustments which can be continually improved upon.' The piecemeal social engineer, Popper had said,

> knows that we can learn only from our mistakes … he will make his way, step by step, carefully comparing the results expected with the results achieved,

and always on the look-out for the unwanted consequences of any reform; and he will avoid undertaking reforms of a complexity and scope which make it impossible for him to disentangle causes and effects, and to know what he is really doing. (Popper [1944] 1985, p. 309).

Scientific method had reshaped our whole conception of the physical and bio-logical universe, including humankind itself – with enormous gains in human health and longevity, in freedom from hard physical labor, in mobility, in com-munication, and in the spread of culture. If science had also produced nuclear bombs and other technologies that threatened the very survival of our species and its environment, natural and social science also offered some of our major hopes of warding off those disasters. So research workers should hesitate a long time, perhaps forever, before tossing aside an intellectual tool as tremendously powerful as scientific method had proven itself to be. Scientific method need *not* be forgone in human affairs. Along with people all over the world, those who did research on teaching began to recognize, now that the second millennium was over, that the triumph of natural science and the advances of social science had been the greatest achievements of that millennium. It was Popper's piecemeal social technology rather than holistic social revolutions that came to be recognized as the proper orientation of the social sciences.

So the social sciences need not be based on any assumptions of uniformity in nature. Uniformity, it was recognized, is not an all-or-none matter. Although many human arrangements *may* change over time and place, it was not true that they *must* change. Many social arrangements, such as classroom teaching, had stayed put for many decades, even for centuries, and had been found occurring in the same form in many countries. While they lasted, they could be studied pro-ductively with scientific methods. When they changed, scientific method could track the change. Most teaching arrangements did not exhibit the random and rapid change over time and place that, the antinaturalists seemed to think, would make scientific method inapplicable. Whatever uniformity social phenomena might exhibit, as long as it was substantially greater than zero, would be good enough to make the methods of science usable.

So what happened in research on teaching in the decades after 1989? In partic-ular, what happened to process-product research on teaching, which especially had been belabored by the incompatibilists, the antinaturalists, the interpretivists, the cognitivists, and the critical theorists? As the years went by, the ineluctability of process-product research became ever more apparent. Educators simply wanted to know as much as possible about how different ways of teaching were related to different levels and kinds of student achievement and attitude.

The long and important agenda of process-product research continued to be acted upon. *Processes* in teaching were investigated in interpretive and cognitive terms as well as in terms of teachers' and students' actions. Through the use of multiple perspectives, the teachers' pedagogical content knowledge was described in ever more valid ways. *Products*, or the outcomes of teaching, were investigated in ever more authentic terms – with essay tests, real-life performances, group processes, and concrete products, as well as with the multiple-choice tests that had been prevalent through the 1980s. *Process-product relationships*, in all the various grade levels, subject matters, student cultures and economic levels, and combinations of these, were examined – sometimes through interpretive case studies, sometimes through correlational studies, sometimes through field experiments with random-assignment-to-treatment of real teachers and their classes, and sometimes through critical-theoretical analysis. The knowledge about process-product relationships began to become even more useful than it had been during the 1980s, when the first programs for incorporating such knowledge into teacher education programs and the practice of teaching had begun to blossom (e.g., American Federation of Teachers, 1983). The substantial value of even weak relationships in improving the probabilities of desirable effects of teaching practices became better understood (Gage, 1985, pp. 11–15), so that teacher educators no longer considered such a relationship to be useful only if the correlation coefficient equaled at least .39 (cf. Medley, 1977, pp. 7–8).

Another insight has made research on teaching more productive since 1989: the realization that the paradigm wars in educational and social research were in part wars between the disciplines. It was psychology, in large part, that bred the objective-quantitative approach to research on teaching. It was anthropology, in large part, that spawned the interpretive-qualitative approach. It was mainly the work of analysts from economics, political science, and sociology that produced critical theory.

Added to these disparate disciplinary origins of the approaches was the chronic scarcity of research funding and academic positions in these disciplines. The scarcity had led to competition between the disciplines – competition manifested in derogation of the concerns of the other disciplines and glorification of one's own. What had seemed to be merely intellectual disagreement also turned out, as experience accumulated, to be turf wars in the attempt to gain for one's own discipline a greater share of the research funds, the academic positions, and the other kinds of wherewithal needed for a discipline to flourish. Jobs and incomes had been at stake, as well as ideas about the best way to do research on teaching or educational-social research in general.

What ended the interdisciplinary war and brought about the present productive harmony among the paradigms? To some degree, it was the dawning of the realization that, if the social sciences did not get together, they would perish. The practical, everyday world of families, work, education, and government had looked upon the paradigm wars uncomprehendingly and, as time went on, with increasing impatience. The social scientists, including the educational researchers, had better put their house in order and agree upon a decent respect for one another, some standards of research conduct, some criteria of validity, some goals for their work, and some ways of achieving those goals. If they do not, we'll have to get along without them, said the citizens whose children and dollars were at stake.

Alarmed by this threat to the whole enterprise of social and educational research, the newer generations of research workers began to come to their senses. They understood well enough that scientists should learn from philosophers' analyses of their concepts and methods. But they also understood that the philosophers of science could accommodate their analyses to what scientists actually did. They began to be influenced more by old-fashioned pragmatism. They recognized that the moral and rational foundations of the three paradigms were virtually identical, dedicated to the same ideals of social justice and democracy and the goals of an education that would serve those ideals. So they paid more attention to effectiveness in achieving those ideals. If the research of the objectively and quantitatively oriented investigators led to improved student achievement and attitudes, the research community paid respectful attention. If such results were produced by interpretive-qualitative investigators, the arguments for their concepts and methods were considered to be strengthened. If the analyses of the critical theorists led to reforms that resulted in social and educational benefits, their ideas were also thus supported. As William James had put it:

> No particular results then, so far, but only an attitude of orientation, is what the pragmatic method means. *The attitude of looking away from first things, principles, 'categories,' supposed necessities; and of looking towards last things, fruits, consequences, facts.* (James, [1907] 1955, p. 47, italics in original)

Pragmatism also applies to ideas. Pragmatism means that 'ideas ... become true just in so far as they help us get into satisfactory relations with other parts of our experience' (James, p. 49).

Thus, as the years went by, the educational research community, including research on teaching, abandoned the debate on whether objectivistic-quantitative methods were compatible with interpretive-qualitative methods. Both kinds of methods were respected, sometimes used alone, and sometimes combined in the same study.

Similarly, the critical theorists came to appreciate the value to their own analyses of both kinds of methods. They discovered that structured and quantified observations in classrooms had already, in the three decades preceding the 1980s, compiled a strong record of effectiveness in revealing the unconscious biases of teachers along social-class lines, skin-color lines, and gender lines (Brophy & Good, 1974). Ethnographic studies in classrooms also revealed such biases. Both kinds of data entered into the arguments of the critical analysts, along with findings, from both kinds of sources, on matters of the hidden and the explicit curriculum, textbook production and consumption, school administration, school-community relations, and a host of other aspects of education in which the power relations of society manifested themselves. Today, not long after the start of the 21st century, critical theorists are embroiled in a debate about whether Popper's piecemeal social engineering or Marx's holistic social revolution holds the better promise of leading us to a more humane society.

These changes toward the recognition of paradigm compatibility undermined the hegemony of psychology in educational research – a hegemony that had existed throughout most of the 20th century because psychology had a half-century's head start in devoting itself wholeheartedly to the study of education. Thus, between 1964 and 1989, 19 of the first 26 recipients of the AERA Award for Distinguished Contributions to Educational Research had been psychologists. A large majority of the first 73 AERA presidents between 1915 and 1989 had come from educational psychology or from the testing and statistics allied to educational psychology; only a few represented such other fields as administration, philosophy, anthropology, curriculum, or sociology.

The realignment of the disciplines made sociology and anthropology recognize – much later than psychology – that education was properly their concern. So they began to have much more equal influence in educational research, including research on teaching. Thus, of the 20 AERA awards since 1989, only 5 went to psychologists; five went to sociologists, five to anthropologists, and five to various other fields.

Similarly, the lines between the disciplines were blurred as doctoral programs in education began to turn out people with broader training. The new training comprised courses in teaching and curriculum and also psychology, sociology, anthropology, relevant parts of economics and political science, and the philosophy of the social sciences. This ecumenical yet feasible training resulted in a generation of research workers equally adept in and loyal to the approaches of psychologists, anthropologists, sociologists, economists, and political scientists.

Thus, from the jungle wars of the 1980s, educational researchers, including those concerned with teaching, emerged onto a sunlit plain – a happy and productive arena in which the strengths of all three paradigms (objective-quantitative, interpretive-qualitative, and critical-theoretical) were abundantly realized, with a corresponding decrease in the harmful effects of their respective inadequacies. Educational researchers today look back with amused tolerance at the invidious recriminations that the paradigm-loyalists had hurled at other paradigms in the 1980s.

A third version of the effect of the criticisms

Now let me turn to a third version of the aftermath of the paradigm wars of the 80s. This version is epitomized by Alphonse Karr's apothegm: 'The more things change, the more they remain the same.' What happened after 1989 in research on teaching was pretty much the same as what happened before 1989. The invective and vituperation continued. The objective-quantitativists persisted, and the interpretive-qualitativists also carried on. The critical theorists continued to regard both groups as engaged in mere technical work, more or less, on the details of education and teaching while neglecting the social system that determined the basically exploitative and unjust nature of education in capitalist society.

Some psychologists suggested that the wars continued because they reflected deep-seated differences in human temperament and values – differences determined not genetically but by equally powerful features of early home and school experience. These temperamental differences inclined people toward basically different intellectual orientations that have been given such labels as tough-minded versus tender-minded, scientific versus humanistic, nomothetic versus idiographic, statistical versus clinical, and, of course, positivist (or postpositivist) versus hermeneutic.

Although differences among researchers in these orientations could be rationally resolved, it turned out that Thomas Kuhn had been right (Barnes, 1985). These were rational issues, but not purely rational issues. They were embedded in the ethos of *communities* of researchers, who huddled together in embattled camps and fought off the aggressions of their opponents.

Perhaps paradigm wars could eventually be resolved in the *natural* sciences, because the results of research in those sciences were unambiguous enough, consistent enough, and stable enough to compel the surrender of one paradigm community to another. But in the human sciences the results were not that unambiguous, consistent, and stable. What the results meant lay too much in the eye of the beholder. And the beholder's upbringing had made the beholder either tough-minded or tender-minded, scientific or humanistic, and so on.

At any rate, for whatever reason, we find ourselves in 2009 in very much the same condition of paradigmatic war that existed in the 1980s. How long the war will last, and whether it will lead to the demise of social and educational research, including research on teaching, are questions that cannot be answered in the year 2009.

Let me recapitulate this sketch of what has happened in research on teaching since 1989. I have given you three versions of those events. In the first, the so-called positivistic, establishmentarian, mainstream, standard, objectivity-seeking, and quantitative approach had died of the wounds inflicted by its critics. In the second version, peace had broken out, but it was not the peace of the grave. The three approaches were busily and harmoniously engaged in an earnest dialogue, lifting the discussion to a new level of insight, making progress toward workable solutions of educational problems, and generating theory that fit together, as seen from the perspective of each of the three approaches. In the third version, nothing that was true in 1989 had really changed, and the wars were still going on.

Which of these versions is the true one? To give you the answer, I shall have to return from 2009 to 1989, where we actually are, despite the rhetorical device in which I hope you have indulged me.

The answer to the future lies with us, with you. What you do in the years ahead will determine whether the wars continue, until one paradigm grinds the others into the dust. Or, on the other hand, whether pragmatic philosophical analysis shows us the foolishness of these paradigm wars and the way to an honest and productive rapprochement between the paradigms. Even as we hope that our political leaders will continue to avert the ultimate nuclear disaster, so we must hope that our intellectual leaders – the philosophers, scientists, scholars, research workers, in short, the members of AERA and their counterparts around the world – will keep us from getting bogged down in an intellectual no-man's-land.

I find myself better motivated to succeed at this difficult task whenever I remind myself of what we are all about. Educational research is no mere spectator sport, no mere intellectual game, no mere path to academic tenure and higher pay, not just a way to make a good living and even to become a big shot. It has moral obligations. The society that supports us cries out for better education for its children and youth – especially the poor ones, those at risk, those whose potential for a happy and productive life is all too often going desperately unrealized.

So even as we debate whether any objectivity at all is possible, whether 'technical' research is merely trivial, whether your paradigm or mine should get more money, I feel that I should remember that the payoff inheres in what happens to the children, the students. That is our end concern. It is up to us to decide which history of research on teaching since 1989 will be the true one.

Notes

I am extremely grateful for suggestions generously given by J. Myron Atkin, Clare Burstall, Christopher M. Clark, Margaret C. Needels, Denis C. Phillips, and Samuel S. Wineburg. My early work on this paper was done while I was a Spencer Fellow of the Center for Advanced Study in the Behavioral Sciences in 1987–1988, and I am greatly indebted to the Spencer Foundation and the Center for their support.

1 One set of battles took place at an 'International Conference on Alternative Paradigms for Inquiry,' sponsored by Indiana University and Phi Delta Kappa, directed by Egon Guba, and held on March 25–26, 1989, before the annual meeting of the American Educational Research Association in San Francisco. The conference announcement described the debate on paradigms as 'characterized by jockeying for position and the carving out of territory, sometimes resulting in *ad hominem* attacks and charges of lack of integrity … sometimes acrimonious but always lively.' In two days of lectures and discussions, more than 200 partisans struggled with paradigmatic issues. The conference ended with the expectation of more such strenuous engagements.

2 Space limitations preclude consideration of the differences between interpretivists, phenomenologists, constructivists, symbolic interactionists, hermeneuticists, and other protagonists of 'qualitative' approaches. For the present discussion, I consider only one spokesman (Erickson, 1986) for this broad category of thought; the resulting limitations of the discussion seem unavoidable in the present brief analysis. Similarly, for the sake of brevity, I shall consider the connoisseurship-and-criticism advocated by Eisner (1985) to belong in the general

category of 'qualitative' paradigms, although it is derived from aesthetics rather than anthropology.

3 Here, again, brevity precludes any attempt to represent critical theorists more than sketchily, and I can only hope that I have done justice to their general orientations and values.

References

Adler, S. and Goodman, J. (1986) Critical theory as a foundation for methods courses. *Journal of Teacher Education*, 37(4), 2–8.

American Federation of Teachers. (1983) *American Federation of Teachers Educational Research and Development Program: Executive summary (NIE-G–81–0021)*. Washington, DC: Author.

Apple, M. W. (1986) *Teachers and texts: A political economy of class and gender relations in education*, New York: Routledge and Kegan Paul.

Au, K. H. and Mason, J. (1981) Social organizational factors in learning to read: The balance of rights hypotheses. *Reading Research Quarterly*, 17(1), 115–152.

Barnes, B. (1985) Thomas Kuhn. In Q. Skinner (ed.), *The return of grand theory in the human sciences*, New York; Cambridge University Press.

Barnhardt, C. (1982) 'Tuning-in': Athabaskan teachers and Athabaskan students. In R. Barnhardt (ed.), *Cross-cultural issues in Alaskan education* (Vol. 2). Fairbanks: University of Alaska, Center for Cross-Cultural Studies.

Barrow, R. (1984) *Giving teaching back to teachers: A critical introduction to curriculum theory.* Totowa, NJ: Barnes and Noble.

Brophy, J. E. and Good, T. L. (1974) *Teacher-student relationships: Causes and consequences*, New York: Holt, Rinehart and Winston.

Cazden, C. B. (1983) Can ethnographic research go beyond the status quo? *Anthropology & Education Quarterly*, 14, 33–41.

Cazden, C. B. (1984) Response. *Anthropology and Education Quarterly*, 15, 184–185.

Eisner, E. W. (1985) *The art of educational evaluation: A personal view*, Philadelphia: Falmer.

Erickson, F. (1986) Qualitative methods in research on teaching. In M. C. Wittrock (ed.), *Handbook of research on teaching* (3rd ed., pp. 119–161). New York: Macmillan.

Gage, N. L., (1978) *The scientific basis of the art of teaching*, New York: Teachers College Press.

Gage, N. L. (1985) *Hard gains in the soft sciences: The case of pedagogy*. Bloomington, IN: CEDR, Phi Delta Kappa.

Gage, N. L. and Needels, M. C. (1989) Process-product research on teaching: A review of criticisms. *Elementary School Journal*, 89, 253–300.

Goldenberg, C. N., and Gallimore, R. (1989) Teaching California's diverse student population: The common ground between educational and cultural research. *California Public Schools Forum*, 3, 41–56.

Howe, K. R. (1988) Against the quantitative-qualitative incompatibility thesis, or dogmas die hard, *Educational Researcher*, 17(8), 10–16.

James, W. ([1907] 1955) *Pragmatism and four essays from* The Meaning of Truth, New York: Meridian.

Medley, D. M. (1977) *Teacher competence and teacher effectiveness: A review of process-product research*. Washington, DC: American Association of Colleges for Teacher Education.

Popper, K. ([1944] 1955) Piecemeal social engineering. In D. Miller (ed.), *Popper selections*. Princeton, NJ: Princeton University Press.

Shulman, L. S. (1987) Knowledge and teaching: Foundations of the new reform, *Harvard Educational Review*, 57(1), 1–22.

Tom, A. (1984) *Teaching as a moral craft*, New York: Longman.

Yales, G., Chandler, M. and Westwood, P. (1987) Teacher effectiveness and process-product research: Another look. *South Pacific Journal of Teacher Education*, 15(2), 18–24.

Chapter 12

Action research

Stephen Kemmis

Action research is a form of research carried out by practitioners into their own practices. In this article, the definition and character of action research is outlined with reference to its history. The resurgence of interest in educational action research is discussed. Action research is then distinguished from other forms of contemporary educational research through an examination of the 'objects' of action research: educational practices. These are not understood by action researchers as 'phenomena', 'treatments', or expressions of practitioners' perspectives, but rather as praxis. Examples of practices studied by action researchers are given. Research techniques employed by action researchers are noted; it is argued that action research is distinguished not by technique but in terms of method. Criteria for evaluation of action research are then outlined. The role of outside facilitators in educational action research is discussed, and different kinds of intervention by outsiders are shown to influence the form of action research studies. The article concludes with a discussion of the relationship between action research, policy research, and the control of education, suggesting that action research is a participatory democratic form of educational research for educational improvement.

Taken from: Keeves, J. P. (ed.) *Educational Research, Methodology, and Measurement: An international handbook,* (Oxford: Pergamon, 1988), pp. 177–90.
© S. Kemmis 1988
Reproduced by kind permission of Elsevier.

The definition and character of action research

Action research is a form of self-reflective enquiry undertaken by participants in social (including educational) situations in order to improve the rationality and justice of (a) their own social or educational practices, (b) their understanding of these practices, and (c) the situations in which the practices are carried out. It is most rationally empowering when undertaken by participants collaboratively, though it is often undertaken by individuals, and sometimes in cooperation with 'outsiders'. In education, action research has been employed in school-based curriculum development, professional development, school improvement programmes, and systems planning and policy development. Although these activities are frequently carried out using approaches, methods, and techniques unrelated to those of action research, participants in these development processes are increasingly choosing action research as a way of participating in decision making about development.

In terms of method, a self-reflective spiral of cycles of planning, acting, observing, and reflecting is central to the action research approach. Kurt Lewin, who coined the phrase 'action research' in about 1944, described the process in terms of planning, fact finding, and execution.

> Planning usually starts with something like a general idea. For one reason or another it seems desirable to reach a certain objective. Exactly how to circumscribe this objective and how to reach it is frequently not too clear. The first step, then, is to examine the idea carefully in the light of the means available. Frequently more fact-finding about the situation is required. If this first period of planning is successful, two items emerge: an 'over-all plan' of how to reach the objective and a decision in regard to the first step of action. Usually this planning has also somewhat modified the original idea.
>
> The next period is devoted to executing the first step of the overall plan. In highly developed fields of social management, such as modern factory management or the execution of a war, this second step is followed by certain fact-findings. For example, in the bombing of Germany a certain factory may have been chosen as the first target after careful consideration of various priorities and of the best means and ways of dealing with this target. The attack is pressed home and immediately a reconnaissance plane follows with the one objective of determining as accurately and objectively as possible the new situation.
>
> This reconnaissance or fact-finding has four functions: It should evaluate the action by showing whether what has been achieved is above or below expectation. It should serve as a basis for correctly planning the next step. It should serve as a basis for modifying the 'overall plan'. Finally, it gives the planners a chance to learn, that is, to gather new general insight, for instance regarding the strength and weakness of certain weapons or techniques of action.

The next step again is composed of a circle of planning, executing, and reconnaissance or fact-finding for the purpose of evaluating the results of the second step, for preparing the rational basis for planning the third step, and for perhaps modifying again the over-all plan. (Lewin 1952, p. 564)

Lewin documented the effects of group decision in facilitating and sustaining changes in social conduct, and emphasized the value of involving participants in every phase of the action research process (planning, acting, observing, and reflecting). He also saw action research as based on principles which could lead 'gradually to independence, equality, and cooperation' and effectively alter policies of 'permanent exploitation' which he saw as 'likely to endanger every aspect of democracy' (Lewin 1946, p. 46). Lewin saw action research as being essential for the progress of 'basic social research'. In order to 'develop deeper insights into the laws which govern social life', mathematical and conceptual problems of theoretical analysis would be required, as would 'descriptive fact-finding in regard to small and large social bodies'; 'above all', he argued, basic social research 'would have to include laboratory and field experiments in social change' (Lewin 1946, p. 35)

Lewin thus presaged three important characteristics of modern action research: its participatory character, its democratic impulse, and its simultaneous contribution to social science and social change. In each of these three areas, however, action researchers of the 1980s would take exception to Lewin's formulation of the significance of action research. First, they would regard group decision making as important as a matter of principle rather than as a matter of technique; that is, not merely as an effective means of facilitating and maintaining social change but also as essential for authentic commitment to social action. Second, though this is partly a matter of changing historical conditions, contemporary exponents of action research would object to the notion that participants should or could be 'led' to more democratic forms of life through action research. Action research should not be seen as a recipe or technique for bringing about democracy, but rather as an embodiment of democratic principles in research, allowing participants to influence, if not determine, the conditions of their own lives and work, and collaboratively to develop critiques of social conditions which sustain dependence, inequality, or exploitation in any research enterprise in particular, or in social life in general. Third, contemporary action researchers would object to the language in which Lewin describes the theoretical aims and methods of social science ('developing deeper insights into the laws that govern social life' through mathematical and conceptual analysis and laboratory and field experiments); this language would now be described as belonging to positivistic science (determinist, technicist) and incompatible with the aims and methods of an adequate and coherent view of social science, especially educational science.

Carr and Kemmis (1983, p. 158) argue that there are five formal requirements for any adequate and coherent educational science:

1. it must reject positivist notions of rationality, objectivity, and truth;
2. it must employ the interpretive categories of teachers (or the other participants directly concerned with the practices under inquiry);
3. it must provide ways of distinguishing ideas and interpretations which are systematically distorted by ideology from those which are not, and provide a view of how distorted self-understandings can be overcome;
4. it must be concerned to identify and expose those aspects of the existing social order which frustrate rational change, and must be able to offer theoretical accounts which enable teachers (and other participants) to become aware of how they may be overcome; and
5. it must be based on an explicit recognition that it is practical, in the sense that the question of its truth will be determined by the way it relates to practice.

Unlike a number of other forms of contemporary educational research, contemporary action research meets these requirements.

The resurgence of interest in action research

Lewin's early action research work was concerned with changes in attitudes and conduct in a number of areas of social concern (for example, in relation to food habits and factory production in the later years of the Second World War, and in relation to prejudice and intergroup relations immediately after the War). His ideas were quickly carried into education, when his co-workers and students (and often Lewin himself) began working with educationists on issues of curriculum construction and the professional development of teachers. Teachers College, Columbia University became a centre for action research in education. Stephen Corey, at one time Dean of Teachers College, became an influential advocate (Corey, 1953). Kenneth Benne, Hilda Taba, and Abraham Shumsky were other early exponents of educational action research.

After enjoying a decade of growth, educational action research went into decline in the late 1950s. Although some action research work in education has continued in the United States, Nevitt Sanford (1970) argued that the decline was attributable to a growing separation of research and action (or, as it might be put today, of theory from practice). As academic researchers in the social sciences began to enjoy unprecedented support from public funding bodies, they began to distinguish the work (and the status) of the theorist–researcher from that of the 'engineer' responsible for putting theoretical principles into practice. The rising tide of post-Sputnik curriculum development, based on a research–development–diffusion (R, D, and D) model of the relationship between research and practice, legitimated and sustained this separation. Large-scale curriculum development and evaluation activities, based on the cooperation of practitioners in development and evaluation tasks devised by theoreticians, diverted legitimacy and energy from the essentially small-scale, locally organized, self-reflective approach of action research. By the mid-1960s, the technical R, D, and D model had established itself as the pre-eminent model for change and practically inclined educationists were increasingly absorbed into R, D, and D activities.

Perhaps the greatest impetus to the resurgence of contemporary interest in educational action research came from the work of the 1973–1976 Ford Teaching Project in the United Kingdom, under the direction of John Elliott and Clem Adelman. This project, initially based at the Centre for Applied Research in Education, University of East Anglia, involved teachers in collaborative action research into their own practices, in particular in the area of inquiry/discovery approaches to learning and teaching (Elliott 1976–77). Its notion of the 'self-monitoring teacher' was based on Lawrence Stenhouse's (1975) views of the teacher as a researcher and as an 'extended professional'. It seems that Stenhouse had been influenced by certain action research work carried out at the Tavistock Institute of Human Relations. Lewin and his co-workers at the Research Center for Group Dynamics (established at the Massachusetts Institute of Technology and subsequently moved, after Lewin's death in 1947, to the University of Michigan) had collaborated with Tavistock social psychologists in founding the *Journal of Social Issues.*

Since his involvement in the Ford Teaching Project, John Elliott has continued to develop action research theory and practice, and has established the Classroom Action Research Network (publishing its own *Bulletin)* from the Cambridge Institute of Education.

Interest in action research is also growing in Australia and in continental Europe, and, once again, in the United States.

There are a number of reasons for this resurgence of interest. First, there is the demand from within an increasingly professionalized teacher force for a research role, based on the notion of the extended professional investigating her or his own practice. Second, there is the perceived irrelevance to the concerns of these practitioners of much contemporary educational research. Third, there has been the revival of interest in 'the practical' in curriculum, following the work of Schwab and others on 'practical deliberation' (Schwab, 1969). This work has revived interest in, and provided legitimacy for, practical reasoning (as against technical or instrumental reasoning) as the basis for decisions about educational practice. Fourth, action research has been assisted by the rise of the 'new wave' methods in educational research and evaluation (interpretive approaches, including illuminative evaluation, democratic evaluation, responsive evaluation, case study methods, field research, ethnography, and the like), with their emphasis on participants' perspectives and categories in shaping educational practices and situations. These methods place the practitioner at centre stage in the educational research process: actors' understandings are crucial in understanding educational action. From the role of critical informant to an external researcher, it is but a short step for the practitioner to become a self-critical researcher into her or his own practice. Fifth, the accountability movement has galvanized and politicized practitioners. In response to the accountability movement, practitioners have adopted the self-monitoring role as a proper means of justifying practice and generating sensitive critiques of the working conditions in which their practice is conducted (conditions often created by the policy makers who hold them accountable for their actions). Sixth, there is the growing solidarity of the teaching profession in response to the public criticism which has accompanied the post-expansion educational politics of the 1970s and 1980s; this, too, has fostered the organization of support networks of concerned professionals interested in the continuing development of education even though the expansionist tide has turned. And finally, there is the increased awareness of action research itself, which is perceived as providing an understandable and workable approach to the improvement of practice through critical self-reflection.

The objects of action research

The 'objects' of educational action research are educational practices. These are not construed by action researchers as 'phenomena' (by analogy with the objects of physical science, as if their existence was somehow independent of practitioners), nor as 'treatments' (by analogy with technical or agricultural research, as if they were mere techniques, valued only as alternative and more or less efficient means to a single set of known and universally desired ends), nor as expressions of practitioners' intentions and perspectives (by analogy with the objects of interpretive research, as if their significance could be understood solely by reference to the points of view of practitioners as these meanings emerged in response to historical circumstances).

Practice, as it is understood by action researchers, is informed, committed action: *praxis*. Praxis has its roots in the commitment of the practitioner to wise and prudent action in a practical (concrete historical) situation. It is action which is informed by a 'practical theory', and which may, in its turn, inform and transform the theory which informed it. Practice is not to be understood as mere behaviour, but as strategic action undertaken with commitment in response to a present, immediate, and problematic action context. Practical action is always risky; it requires wise judgment by the practitioner.

As one theorist of practical action remarks, 'practical problems are problems about what to do ... their solution is only found in doing something'. In this sense the significance of practices can only be established in context: only under the 'compulsion' to act in a real historical situation can a commitment have force for the practitioner, on the one hand, and definite historical consequences for actors and the situation, on the other. Action is thus both a 'test' of commitment and the means by which practitioners can determine the adequacy of their understandings and of the situations in which practice occurs.

Since only the practitioner has access to the commitments and practical theories which inform praxis, only the practitioner can study praxis. Action research, as the study of praxis, must thus be research into one's own practice. The action researcher will embark on a course of action strategically (deliberately experimenting with practice while aiming simultaneously for improvement in the practice, understanding of the practice and the situation in which the practice occurs); monitor the action, the circumstances under which it occurs, and its consequences; and then retrospectively reconstruct an interpretation of the action in context as a basis for future action. Knowledge achieved in this way informs and refines both specific planning in relation to the practice being considered and the practitioner's general practical theory. The interpretations of other participants in the situation will be relevant in the process of reconstruction; they may be treated as the perspectives of relevant 'others', in which case they inform the practitioner about the social consequences of the practice, or be regarded as the perspectives of coparticipants in the action, in which case they can inform collaborative reconstruction and contribute to the discourse of a community of practitioners researching their joint (collaborative) practices. The crucial point, however, is that only the practitioner can have access to the perspectives and commitments that inform a particular action as praxis, thus praxis can only be researched by the actor him/herself. The dialectic of action and understanding is a uniquely personal process of rational reconstruction and construction.

If it is only practitioners who can research their own practice, a problem seems to arise about whether the practitioner can understand his or her own praxis in an undistorted way – whether understandings reached will be biased, idiosyncratic (some would say 'subjective'), or systematically distorted by ideology. This problem is illusory. First, this way of construing the problem suggests that there is some medium in which praxis can be described and analysed in ways which are entirely unrelated to the values and interests of those doing the observing (for example, value-free, neutral, or 'objective' observation categories). This is an illusion created by the image of a value-free, 'objective' social science which cannot by definition be a science of human praxis which must always embody values and interests. Moreover, the study of praxis (informed action) is always through praxis (action with and for understanding) – it, too, is an embodiment of values and interests (in the improvement of praxis). Second, this way of construing the problem fails to acknowledge that the purpose of the critical self-reflection undertaken by the practitioner is to discover previously unrecognized distortions of interpretation and action (for example, the taken-for-granted assumptions of habit, custom, precedent, and coercive social structures and the limitations on action these assumptions produce). It is important to recognize that the medium in which these distortions are expressed (language) is itself social praxis and always subject to influence by values and interests. In short, the dialectic of reconstituting meanings from actions by interpretation is always a process of relative emancipation from the dictates of habit, custom, precedent, and bureaucratic systematization; it is never a complete emancipation from injustice and irrationality. Undistorted communication is purely ideal–typical: it is never achieved, though the practitioner seeking to understand her or his praxis is bound to pursue the ideal in order to discover concrete and particular distortions influencing his or her practice. This dialectical process of reconstruction is a key part of the critical self-reflection of the action researcher.

A range of practices have been studied by educational action researchers. Some examples may suffice to give a picture of how action research has helped practitioners to understand their own practices more deeply. In studies of inquiry/ discovery teaching, practitioners have come to understand how, even despite their aspirations, they have used questioning strategies which maintain student dependency on teacher authority rather than create the conditions for autonomy. In studies of the organization of remedial reading, practitioners have come to understand the contradictions of withdrawal practices that preserve rather than overcome the labelling of students as in need of 'remediation', which mystify the reading process rather than make it transparent to students, and which deskill students in terms of progress in other subjects by interrupting subject teaching to focus on reading skills out of context. In studies of teacher–student negotiation of curriculum, practitioners have come to understand that an overemphasis on student interest as the basis for curriculum formation may fragment the social relations of teaching and learning, and deny students access to the discourse of established fields of knowledge. Studies of assessment practices have helped practitioners to understand that notions of ability and achievement can confirm students in failure rather than create the conditions for further learning. Investigations of learning in the classroom, undertaken by students, have helped them to understand how their roles as learners may either imprison them in dependency on teachers or create the conditions for self-directed and collaborative learning. And studies of teaching and learning in higher education, undertaken collaboratively by students and teachers, have helped them to revise their working relationships so as to achieve their joint aspirations more completely.

Methods, techniques, and the evaluation of action research

Action research is not distinguished by the use of a particular set of research techniques. While it is common for educational action researchers to keep focused diaries about specific aspects of their practice, to make audiotape records of verbal interactions in classrooms or meetings, to carry out group interviews with students after particular lessons, and so forth, these techniques for recording are not particularly distinctive. Similarly, the techniques for analysis of data (such as content analysis of artefacts like audiotapes of interactions or portfolios of student work, analysis of the relative frequencies of different classroom events, or critical–historical analyses of classroom records to produce interpretations of the interdependence of circumstance, action, and consequence in the classroom) are not unique to action research. It is true, however, that in general the techniques for generating and accumulating evidence about practices, and the techniques for analysing and interpreting this evidence more closely resemble the techniques employed by interpretive researchers (ethnographers, case study researchers, historians, etc.) than empirical–analytic researchers (correlational analysis, comparative experiments etc.). This is so primarily because the 'objects' of research are actions (practices) and the viewpoints and historical circumstances that give these actions meaning and significance; the 'objects' of action research are not mere behaviours.

What distinguishes action research is its method, rather than particular techniques. The method is based on the notion of a spiral of self-reflection (a spiral of cycles of planning, acting, observing, and reflecting). It is essentially participatory in the sense that it involves participants in reflection on practices. It expresses a commitment to the improvement of practices, practitioners' understandings, and the settings of practice. And it is collaborative, wherever possible involving coparticipants in the organization of their own enlightenment in relation to social and political action in their own situations.

The rigour of action research does not derive from the use of particular techniques of observation or analysis (for example, measuring instruments or statistical analyses) or the use of particular metatechniques (for example, techniques for establishing the reliability or validity of measures, or for ascertaining the power of tests). Rigour derives from the logical, empirical, and political coherence of interpretations in the reconstructive moments of the self-reflective spiral (observing and reflecting) and the logical, empirical, and political coherence of justifications of proposed action in its constructive or prospective moments (planning and acting).

As in Habermas's (1974) critical social science, three separate functions in the mediation of theory and practice must be distinguished in action research. These supply criteria for the evaluation of action research studies. Separate criteria are relevant for evaluation in relation to each function, and each requires certain preconditions. First, at the level of scientific discourse, action researchers are engaged in the formation and extension of critical theorems about their practices and their situation, that is, in the formulation and articulation of their own practical theories. This can take place only under the precondition of freedom of discourse. Here the criterion is true statements; the truth of statements is evaluated through discourse which raises, recognizes, and redeems 'validity claims': claims that what is stated is comprehensible, true (accurate), truthfully or sincerely stated, and right or appropriate (in its normative context). Second, at the level of enlightenment of those engaged in the self-reflective process, action researchers are involved in applying and testing their practical theories in their own action in their own situations. This can take place only under the precondition that those involved commit themselves to proper precautions and assure scope for open communication aimed at mutual understanding. Here the criterion is authentic insights, grounded in participants' own circumstances and experience. Finally, at the level of the organization of action, action researchers are engaged in the selection of strategies, the resolution of tactical questions, and the conduct of 'political struggle' (that is, social and strategic action in a social and political context). This can only occur if decisions of consequence depend on the practical discourse of participants. Here the criterion is prudent decisions. Evaluating the quality of action research requires analysis at each of these 'levels' of discourse, the organization of enlightenment, and the organization of action.

These criteria provide the most stringent basis for the evaluation of action research. Typically, however, action research in progress tends not to be evaluated formally in this way. Variants of the questions 'Is it true?', 'Does it make sense in terms of our experience?', and 'Is it prudent?' are more likely to be asked by action researchers in the course of their work. This is an important observation since action research as it is actually practised by teachers and others is a part of their own social process. As such, it tends to be informal and convivial rather than formalistic and overtly 'theoretical'.

'Facilitating' action research

Since action research is research into one's own practice, it follows that only practitioners and groups of practitioners can carry out action research. It is common, however, for 'outsiders' to be involved in action research, providing material, organizational, emotional, and intellectual support to practitioners. The relationships established between outside 'facilitators' and action researchers can have profound effects on the character of the action research undertaken, however. To varying degrees, they influence the agenda of issues being addressed in the research and the 'ownership' (authenticity) of the questions asked, the data-gathering and analytic techniques employed, and the interpretations and findings of particular studies. The intervention of outsiders may introduce significant distortions in each of the three definitive characteristics of action research: the degree to which it is practical, collaborative, or self-reflective. Indeed, it can be argued that some of what passes for action research today is not action research at all but merely a species of field experimentation or 'applied' research carried out by academic or service researchers who coopt practitioners into gathering data *about* educational practices for them. This point needs to be emphasized since the rising popularity of action research in the 1980s (as in the late 1950s) has prompted many educational researchers aspiring to 'relevance' to go out into the field to work with practitioners in the investigation of contemporary educational practices. Forgetting the origins of action research, they have appropriated the term and carried out studies paradigmatically opposed to the nature and spirit of action research.

At worst, these facilitators have coopted practitioners to work on externally formulated questions and issues which are not based in the practical concerns of practitioners. To the extent that it can be described as action research at all, this form may be described as technical action research. It employs techniques (for example, techniques based on a technology of group dynamics) to create and sustain commitment to investigation of issues raised by the outsider, and it frequently concerns itself with the relative efficiency and effectiveness of practices (instrumental reasoning). It is sometimes carried out in order to test the applicability of findings from studies undertaken elsewhere. Such studies may contribute to the improvement of practices, of practitioners' understandings, and the situations of practice (both from an external point of view and from practitioners' own perspectives), but they run the risk of being inauthentic for the practitioners involved, and they may create conditions for the legitimation of practices by reference to outsiders' reputations or ascribed status as 'experts' or 'authorities' rather than being based in the practical discourse of practitioners themselves.

More often, outsiders form cooperative relationships with practitioners, helping them to articulate their own concerns, plan strategic action, monitor the action, and reflect on processes and consequences. This is sometimes described as a 'process consultancy' role. In such cases, outsiders may work with individual practitioners or with groups of practitioners interested in common practices. Where the aim is the improvement of individuals' own practices, however, the relationships between participants may still be mediated by the outsider. In these situations, the research may be described as practical action research (action research which sharpens individual practical reasoning). It can and typically does contribute to the improvement of practices, practitioners' understandings, and the situations in which practice occurs, but it need not develop collaborative responsibility for practices within participant groups.

Emancipatory action research, by contrast, shifts responsibility for practice and the action research process to the participant group. In this case, the group takes joint responsibility for action and reflection. The work of the group expresses a joint commitment to the development of common practical theories, authentic insights, and prudent decision making (based on mutual understanding and consensus). This kind of action research may be described as 'emancipatory' because the group itself takes responsibility for its own emancipation from the dictates of irrational or unjust habits, customs, precedents, coercion, or bureaucratic systematization. Here outsiders are unnecessary; where they do participate in the work of the group, they do so on the basis that they share responsibility equally with other members (not as legitimating authorities or merely as process facilitators).

Historically, it is possible to discern a shift from technical to practical to emancipatory action research from the late 1940s to the early 1980s, judging from reports of educational action research over the period. Arguably, the ideal of emancipatory action research has existed from the beginning; as the 'ownership' of the idea of action research has shifted from the academy to the profession itself, so the concrete relationship between outsiders and practitioners in particular action research projects has changed (from cooption to cooperation to collaboration). In some places in the world, the profession has sufficiently well-developed organizational structures to foster the development of emancipatory action research which can exist without conspicuous support from outsiders; in these areas, the profession is able to resist the legitimating role of the academy with respect to practice and to take a nondoctrinaire, critical and self-reflective stance on the bureaucratic control of curriculum and pedagogy (and, in particular, the nexus of policy making and policy research).

Action research, policy research, and the control of education

The choice of research methods depends on the presumed character of the object of the research (e.g. a 'natural' phenomenon, a product of 'subjective' views of participants, a product of historical and ideological process). Moreover, these presumptions will tend to be confirmed by the conduct of educational inquiries not because of any principled 'correctness' of the presumptions, but because the presumptions will appear to be vindicated merely by the practice of research. In this way, research practice alone (and ultimately research traditions) conventionalizes and legitimates the paradigmatic presumptions of researchers.

Educational research is generally justified by reference to its contribution to educational reform. In this sense, almost all educational research is policy research; that is, it has the aim of influencing educational practices through influencing local or systemwide policies about curriculum and pedagogy. Three points need to be made about this nexus of research and reform: (a) it assumes that researchers understand the nature of education as an object of research (including its nature as a social enterprise); (b) it assumes that researchers understand the social nature and consequences of educational reform; and (c) it assumes that researchers understand the research enterprise itself as inherently social and political, that is, as an ideological activity.

Different approaches to educational research have different perspectives on how reform relates to research. Put at its simplest, different approaches to educational research have different theories of educational change which underpin them. These theories of educational change embody different assumptions about the control of education.

Empirical–analytic research views educational events and practices as 'phenomena' susceptible to 'objective' treatment. It views schooling as a delivery system whose effectiveness and efficiency can be improved by improvements in the technology of the system. Its form of reasoning is technical, instrumental (means–ends) reasoning. Its interest is in the technical control of education systems, and this technical rationality readily expresses itself in an interest in hierarchical bureaucratic control of the social relations between systems personnel and between teachers and students.

Interpretive research sees education as a historical process and as a lived experience for those involved in educational processes and institutions. Its form of reasoning is practical; it aims to transform the consciousness of practitioners and, by so doing, to give them grounds upon which to reform their own practices. Its interest is in transforming education by educating practitioners; it assumes a relationship between educational researchers and educational practitioners based on mutual trust which leaves practitioners free to decide how to change their practices in the light of their own informed practical deliberation.

Critical social scientific research, including emancipatory action research, views education as a historical and ideological process. Its form of reasoning is practical (like that of interpretive research) but also critical: it is shaped by the emancipatory intent to transform educational organizations and practices to achieve rationality and social justice. It is predisposed towards ideology–critique: the recognition and negation of educational ideologies which serve the interests of specific groups at the expense of others and which mask oppression and domination with the appearance of liberation.

Empirical–analytic and interpretive research preserve a 'gap' between theory and practice. They institutionalize the separation of theory and practice in the separate roles of the researcher–theorist and the practitioner. Critical social scientific research requires the development of self-reflective communities of practitioner–theorists committed to critically examining their own practices and improving them in the interests of rationality and social justice. While the first two forms of educational research employ theories of change which are concretely realized in political relationships which seek to bring practitioners' practices into line with theorists' theories (explicitly in the case of empirical–analytic research and implicitly in the case of interpretive research), critical educational research does not. In this latter case, the development of practical theories is carried out by practitioners as part of the process of change; indeed, all change in the latter case is transformation by practitioners of existing conditions, perspectives, and practices in the interests of rationality and social justice.

Educational action research is a form of educational research which places control over processes of educational reform in the hands of those involved in the action. In principle, this control can be shared collaboratively by communities of teachers, students, administrators, parents, and others. In practice, most action research projects have involved only one or two, and occasionally three, of these groups.

It would be an exaggeration to argue that emancipatory action research in education is the only defensible form of educational research or the only form of educational research capable of bringing about stable transformations of educational practice towards more rational and more just educational arrangements in contemporary society. An argument can be mounted, however, that educational action research is grossly underutilized as an approach to educational reform in a democratic society and that it is, or should be, a key part of the role of the professional educator. Participatory democracy involves substantial control by people over their own lives, and within that over their work. Emancipatory action research is one means by which this ideal can be approached.

Bibliography

Carr, W. and Kemmis, S. (1983) *Becoming Critical: Knowing through Action Research.* Deakin University Press, Geelong, Victoria.

Corey, S. M. (1953) *Action Research to Improve School Practices.* Teachers College, Columbia University, New York.

Elliott, J. (1976–77) Developing hypotheses about classrooms from teachers' practical constructs: an account of the work of the Ford Teaching Project. *Interchange*, 7(2): 2–22.

Habermas, J. (1974) *Theory and Practice.* Heinemann, London.

Lewin, K. (1946) Action research and minority problems. *J. Soc. Issues*, 2(4): 34–46.

Lewin, K. (1952) Group decision and social change. In: G. E. Swanson, T. M. Newcomb & E. L. Hartley (eds) *Readings in Social Psychology.* Holt, New York, pp. 459–73.

Sanford, N. (1970) Whatever happened to action research? *J. Soc. Issues*, 26(4): 3–23.

Schwab, J. J. (1969) The practical: a language for curriculum. *Sch. Rev.* 78: 1–23.

Stenhouse, L. (1975) *An Introduction to Curriculum Research and Development.* Heinemann, London.

Chapter 13

Increasing the generalizability of qualitative research

Janet W. Schofield

Traditional views of generalizability

Campbell and Stanley (1963) laid the groundwork for much current thinking on the issue of generalizability just over twenty-five years ago in a groundbreaking chapter in the *Handbook of Research on Teaching*. They wrote, '*External validity* asks the question of *generalizability*: To what populations, settings, treatment variables, and measurement variables can the effect be generalized?' (1963: 175). They then went on to list four specific threats to external validity: the interaction of testing and the experimental treatment, the interaction of selection and treatment, reactive arrangements, and the interference of multiple treatments with one another. Although Campbell and Stanley specifically included populations, settings, treatments, and measurement variables as dimensions relevant to the concept of external validity, the aspect of external validity that has typically received the lion's share of attention in textbook and other treatments of the concept is generalizing to and across populations. This may well be due to the fact that, because of advances in sampling theory in survey research, it is possible to draw samples from even a very large and heterogeneous population and then to generalize to that population using the logic of probability statistics.

Taken from: Elliot W. Eisner & Alan Peshkin (eds.), *Qualitative Inquiry in Education: The Continuing Debate*, (New York: Teachers College Press, 1989).

Campbell and Stanley (1963), as well as many others in the quantitative tradition, see the attempt to design research so that abstract generalizations can be drawn as a worthy effort, although issues connected with internal validity are typically given even higher priority. Thus researchers in the quantitative tradition have devoted considerable thought to the question of how the generalizability of experimental and quasi-experimental studies can be enhanced. Such efforts are consistent with the fact that many quantitatively oriented researchers would agree with Smith (1975: 88) that 'the goal of science is to be able to generalize findings to diverse populations and times'.

In contrast to the interest shown in external validity among quantitatively oriented researchers, the methodological literature on qualitative research has paid little attention to this issue, at least until quite recently. For example, Dobbert's (1982) text on qualitative research methods devotes an entire chapter to issues of validity and reliability but does no more than mention the issue of generalizability in passing on one or two pages. Two even more recent books, Kirk and Miller's *Reliability and Validity in Qualitative Research* (1986) and Berg's *Qualitative Research Methods for the Social Sciences* (1989), ignore the issue of external validity completely. The major factor contributing to the disregard of the issue of generalizability in the qualitative methodological literature appears to be a widely shared view that it is unimportant, unachievable, or both.

Many qualitative researchers actively reject generalizability as a goal. For example, Denzin writes:

> The interpretivist rejects generalization as a goal and never aims to draw randomly selected samples of human experience. For the interpretivist every instance of social interaction, if thickly described (Geertz, 1973), represents a slice from the life world that is the proper subject matter for interpretive inquiry ... Every topic ... must be seen as carrying its own logic, sense of order, structure, and meaning. (1983: 133–4)

Although not all researchers in the qualitative tradition reject generalization so strongly, many give it very low priority or see it as essentially irrelevant to their goals. One factor contributing to qualitative researchers' historical tendency to regard the issue of external validity as irrelevant and hence to disregard it is that this research tradition has been closely linked to cultural anthropology, with its emphasis on the study of exotic cultures. This work is often valued for its intrinsic interest, for showing the rich variety and possible range of human behavior, and for serving a historical function by describing traditional cultures before they change in an increasingly interconnected and homogeneous world. For researchers doing work of this sort, the goal is to describe a specific group in fine detail and to explain the patterns that exist, certainly not to discover general laws of human behavior.

Practically speaking, no matter what one's philosophical stance on the importance of generalizability, it is clear that numerous characteristics that typify the qualitative approach are not consistent with achieving external validity as it has generally been conceptualized. For example, the traditional focus on single-case studies in qualitative research is obviously inconsistent with the requirements of statistical sampling procedures, which are usually seen as fundamental to generalizing from the data gathered in a study to some larger population. This fact is often cited as a major weakness of the case study approach (Bolgar, 1965; Shaughnessy and Zechmeister, 1985).

However, the incompatibility between classical conceptions of external validity and fundamental aspects of the qualitative approach goes well beyond this. To give just one example, the experimental tradition emphasizes replicability of results, as is apparent in Krathwohl's statement: 'The heart of external validity is replicability. Would the results be reproducible in those target instances to which one intends to generalize – the population, situation, time, treatment form or format, measures, study designs and procedures?' (1985: 123). Yet at the heart of the qualitative approach is the assumption that a piece of qualitative research is very much influenced by the researcher's individual attributes and perspectives. The goal is *not* to produce a standardized set of results that any other careful researcher in the same situation or studying the same issues would have produced. Rather it is to produce a coherent and illuminating description of and perspective on a situation that is based on and consistent with detailed study of that situation. Qualitative researchers have to question seriously the *internal* validity of their work if other researchers reading their field notes feel the evidence does not support the way in which they have depicted the situation. However, they do not expect other researchers in a similar or even the same situation to replicate their findings in the sense of independently coming up with a precisely similar conceptualization. As long as the other researchers' conclusions are not inconsistent with the original account, differences in the reports would not generally raise serious questions related to validity or generalizability.

In fact, I would argue that, except perhaps in multisite qualitative studies, which will be discussed later in this paper, it is impractical to make precise replication a criterion of generalizability in qualitative work. Qualitative research is so arduous that it is unlikely that high-quality researchers could be located to engage in the relatively unexciting task of conducting a study designed specifically to replicate a previous one. Yet studies not designed specifically for replication are unlikely to be conducted in a way that allows good assessment of the replicability issue. Of course it is possible, even likely, that specific ideas or conclusions from a piece of qualitative work can stimulate further research of a qualitative or quantitative nature that provides information on the replicability of that one aspect of a study. However, any piece of qualitative research is likely to contain so many individual descriptive and conceptual components that replicating it on a piece-by-piece basis would be a major undertaking.

The increasing interest in generalizability in the qualitative tradition

In the past decade, interest in the issue of generalizability has increased markedly for qualitative researchers involved in the study of education. Books by Patton (1980), Guba and Lincoln (1981), and Noblit and Hare (1988), as well as papers by Stake (1978), Kennedy (1979), and others, have all dealt with this issue in more than a cursory fashion. Two factors seem to be important in accounting for this increase in attention to the issue of generalizability. First, the uses of qualitative research have shifted quite markedly in the past decade or two. In the area of education, qualitative research is not an approach used primarily to study exotic foreign or deviant local cultures. Rather it has become an approach used widely in both evaluation research and basic research on educational issues in our own society. The issue of generalizability assumes real importance in both kinds of work.

The shift in the uses of qualitative work that occurred during the 1970s was rapid and striking. The most obvious part of this shift was the inclusion of major qualitative components in large-scale evaluation research efforts, which had previously been almost exclusively quantitative in nature (Fetterman, 1982; Firestone and Harriott, 1984). The acceptance of qualitative research as a valid and potentially rich approach to evaluation progressed to the point that Wolcott wrote, with only some exaggeration, 'By the late 1970s the term "ethnography" … had become synonymous with "evaluation" in the minds of many educators' (1982: 82). Evaluations are expensive and time-consuming undertakings. Although formative evaluations are usually site-specific, the worth of a summative evaluation is greatly enhanced to the extent it can inform program and policy decisions relating to other sites. In fact, as Cronbach (1982) points out, when summative evaluations are reported, no more than a fraction of the audience is interested primarily in the specific program and setting that was the object of the study. Even at the study site itself, by the time the evaluation is completed, changes may well have occurred that have important consequences for program functioning and goal achievement. Thus the question of whether an evaluation's findings can usefully be generalized to a later point in time at the site at which the evaluation was conducted is an issue that, although often ignored, requires real consideration.

The issue of generalizability is also salient for more basic qualitative research on educational issues […]. Funding agencies providing resources for qualitative studies of educational issues are presumably interested in shedding light on these issues generally, not just as they are experienced at one site. For example, I am currently directing a qualitative study of computer usage in an urban high school. It is clear that the impetus for the funding of this study by the Office of Naval Research derived from concerns about the Navy's own computer-based education and training efforts, not from concerns about the public schools. Quite apart from the goals of funding agencies, many qualitative researchers themselves hope to accomplish more than describing the culture of the specific school or classroom that they have chosen to study. For example, Peshkin writes of his study of school and community in a small town in Illinois, 'I hoped ... to explicate some reality which was not merely confined to other places just like Mansfield' (1982: 63), a hope tellingly reflected in the title of his book, *Growing Up American* (1978), as opposed to 'Growing Up in Illinois' or 'Growing Up in Mansfield'. This desire to have one's work be broadly useful is no doubt often stimulated by concern over the state of education [...] today. It is also clearly reinforced by the fact that, unlike most readers of ethnographic reports of exotic cultures, most readers of qualitative reports on American education have had considerable exposure during their own school years to at least one version of the culture described. Thus, unless the researcher chooses a very atypical site or presents an unusually insightful analysis of what is happening, the purely descriptive value of the study may be undercut or discounted.

So far I have argued that qualitative research's shift in both purpose and locale in the last decade or two has contributed to an increased interest in generalizability among qualitative researchers. There is yet one other factor contributing to this trend – the striking rapprochement between qualitative and quantitative methodologies that has occurred in the last decade (Cronbach *et al.,* 1980; Filstead, 1979; Reichardt and Cook, 1979; Spindler, 1982). Exemplifying this trend is the shift in the position of Donald Campbell. Campbell and Stanley at one point contended that the 'one-shot case study', which is one way of describing much qualitative research, has 'such a total absence of control as to be of almost no scientific value' (1963: 176). However, more recently Campbell wrote a paper to 'correct some of [his] own prior excesses in describing the case study approach' (1979: 52) in which he takes the, for many, rather startling position that when qualitative and quantitative results conflict, 'the quantitative results should be regarded as suspect until the reasons for the discrepancy are well understood' (1979: 52).

One result of the rapprochement that has occurred is that qualitative and quantitative researchers are more in contact with each other's traditions than had typically been the case heretofore. As is often the case when a dominant tradition makes contact with a minority one, the culture and standards of the dominant group make a significant impact on the members of the minority group. This trend has most likely been reinforced by the fact that a great deal of the qualitative research on education conducted in the past fifteen years has been embedded within multimethod evaluation projects undertaken by private research firms that have traditionally specialized in quantitative research. Thus the concept of external validity and the associated issue of generalizability have been made salient for qualitative researchers, whose own tradition has not predisposed them to have given the issue a great deal of thought.

Reconceptualizing generalizability

Although many qualitative researchers have begun to recognize the importance of dealing with the issue of generalizability, it is clear that the classical view of external validity is of little help to qualitative researchers interested in finding ways of enhancing the likelihood that their work will speak to situations beyond the one immediately studied – that is, that it will be to some extent generalizable. The idea of sampling from a population of sites in order to generalize to the larger population is simply and obviously unworkable in all but the rarest situations for qualitative researchers, who often take several years to produce an intensive case study of one or a very small number of sites. Thus most of the work on generalizability by qualitative researchers in this decade has dealt with developing a *conception* of generalizability that is useful and appropriate for qualitative work.

A second approach to the issue of generalizability in qualitative research has been very different. A number of individuals have worked on ways of gaining generality through the synthesis of pre-existing qualitative studies. For example, Noblit and Hare (1988) have recently published a slim volume on meta-ethnography. Substantially earlier, Lucas (1974) and Yin and Heald (1975) had developed what they call the 'case survey method'. Ragin (1987) has presented yet another way of synthesizing qualitative studies, one that employs Boolean algebra. I will discuss these approaches to generalizing from qualitative case studies briefly at the end of this chapter. [Editor: This discussion is omitted here.] At the moment, I would like to focus on issues connected with the first approach – that is, with transforming and adapting the classical conception of external validity such that it is suitable for qualitative work.

Important and frequently cited discussions of conceptions of generalizability appropriate in qualitative work can be found in Guba and Lincoln (1981, 1982), Goetz and LeCompte (1984), and Stake (1978). Guba and Lincoln's stance on the issue of generalizability is aptly summarized in two excerpts of their own words. Guba and Lincoln write:

> It is virtually impossible to imagine any human behavior that is not heavily mediated by the context in which it occurs. One can easily conclude that generalizations that are intended to be context free will have little that is useful to say about human behavior. (1981: 62)

They go on to say:

> The aim of (naturalistic) inquiry is to develop an idiographic body of knowledge. This knowledge is best encapsulated in a series of 'working hypotheses' that describe the individual case. Generalizations are impossible since phenomena are neither time- nor context-free (although some transferability of these hypotheses may be possible from situation to situation, depending on the degree of temporal and contextual similarity). (1982: 238)

Given these views, Guba and Lincoln call for replacing the concept of generalizability with that of 'fittingness'. Specifically, they argue that the concept of 'fittingness', with its emphasis on analyzing the degree to which the situation studied matches other situations in which one is interested, provides a more realistic and workable way of thinking about the generalizability of research results than do more classical approaches. A logical consequence of this approach is an emphasis on supplying a substantial amount of information about the entity studied and the setting in which that entity was found. Without such information, it is impossible to make an informed judgment about whether the conclusions drawn from the study of any particular site are useful in understanding other sites.

Goetz and LeCompte (1984) place a similar emphasis on the importance of clear and detailed description as a means of allowing decisions about the extent to which findings from one study are applicable to other situations. Specifically, they argue that qualitative studies gain their potential for applicability to other situations by providing what they call 'comparability' and 'translatability'. The former term:

> refers to the degree to which components of a study – including the units of analysis, concepts generated, population characteristics, and settings – are sufficiently well described and defined that other researchers can use the results of the study as a basis for comparison. (1984: 228)

Translatability is similar but refers to a clear description of one's theoretical stance and research techniques.

Stake (1978) starts out by agreeing with many critics of qualitative methods that one cannot confidently generalize from a single case to a target population of which that case is a member, since single members often poorly represent whole populations. However, he then goes on to argue that it is possible to use a process he calls 'naturalistic generalization' to take the findings from one study and apply them to understanding another *similar* situation. He argues that through experience individuals come to be able to use both explicit comparisons between situations and tacit knowledge of those same situations to form useful naturalistic generalizations.

Several major themes can be found in the work of qualitative researchers who have written recently on the concept of generalizability. Whether it is Guba and Lincoln (1981, 1982) writing of fittingness, Goetz and LeCompte (1984) writing of translatability and comparability, or Stake (1978) discussing naturalistic generalizations, the emerging view shared by many qualitative researchers appears to involve several areas of consensus. First of all, there is broad agreement that generalizability in the sense of producing laws that apply universally is not a useful standard or goal for qualitative research. In fact, most qualitative researchers would join Cronbach (1982) in arguing that this is not a useful or obtainable goal for any kind of research in the social sciences. Second, most researchers writing on generalizability in the qualitative tradition agree that their rejection of generalizability as a search for broadly applicable laws is not a rejection of the idea that studies in one situation can be used to speak to or to help form a judgment about other situations. Third, as should be readily apparent from the preceding discussion, current thinking on generalizability argues that thick descriptions (Ryle, cited in Geertz, 1973) are vital. Such descriptions of both the site in which the studies are conducted and of the site to which one wishes to generalize are crucial in allowing one to search for the similarities and differences between the situations. As Kennedy (1979) points out, analysis of these similarities and differences then makes it possible to make a reasoned judgment about the extent to which we can use the findings from one study as a 'working hypothesis', to use Cronbach's (1982) term, about what might occur in the other situation. Of course, the generally unstated assumption underlying this view is that our knowledge of the phenomena under study is sufficient to direct attention to important rather than superficial similarities and differences. To the extent that our understanding is flawed, important similarities or differences may inadvertently be disregarded.

Three targets of generalization

Given the growing emphasis on generalizability in qualitative research and the emerging consensus about how the concept of generalizability might most usefully be viewed by qualitative researchers, two questions present themselves:

To what do we want to generalize?
How can we design qualitative studies in a way that maximizes their generalizability?

It is to these two questions that I will devote the majority of the rest of this chapter. Although I will use the term *generalize* here and elsewhere, it is important that the reader recognize that I am not talking about generalization in the classical sense. Rather, I use it to refer to the process as conceptualized by those qualitative researchers to whose work I have just referred.

I believe that it is useful for qualitative researchers interested in the study of educational processes and institutions to try to generalize to three domains: to *what is,* to *what may be,* and to *what could be.* I will deal with these possibilities one at a time, providing the rationale for striving to generalize to each of these kinds of situations and then suggesting some ideas on how studies can actually be designed to do this.

Studying what is

From one perspective the study of any ongoing social situation, no matter how idiosyncratic or bizarre, is studying *what is.* But when I use the phrase *studying what* is, I mean to refer to studying the typical, the common, or the ordinary. The goal of describing and understanding cultures or institutions as they typically are is an appropriate aim for much current qualitative research on educational institutions and processes. If policy-makers need to decide how to change a program or whether to continue it, one very obvious and useful kind of information is information on how the program usually functions, what is usually achieved, and the like. Thus the goal of studying *what is* is one important aim for many kinds of summative evaluations. It is also appropriate outside of the area of evaluation for researchers hoping to provide a picture of the current educational scene that can be used for understanding or reflecting on it and possibly improving it. Classic works of this type that focus primarily on *what is* are Wolcott's *The Man in the Principal's Office* (1973) and Jackson's *Life in Classrooms* (1968). If one accepts the goal of designing research to maximize the fit between the research site and *what is* more broadly in society, an obvious question that arises is how this can be accomplished within the context of the qualitative tradition.

Studying the typical

One approach sometimes used is to study the typical (Bogdan and Biklen, 1981; Goetz and LeCompte, 1984; Patton, 1980; Whyte, 1984). Specifically, I would argue that choosing sites on the basis of their fit with a typical situation is far preferable to choosing on the basis of convenience, a practice that is still quite common.

The suggestion that typicality be weighed heavily in site selection is an idea that needs to be taken both more and less seriously than it currently is. When I say that it needs to be taken more seriously than it currently is, I am suggesting that researchers contemplating selecting a site on the basis of convenience or ease of access need to think more carefully about that decision and to weigh very carefully the possibility of choosing on the basis of some other criterion, such as typicality. When I say that the strategy of selecting a typical site needs to be taken less seriously than it may sometimes be, I intend to point out that choosing a typical site is not a *'quick fix'* for the issue of generalizability, because what is typical on one dimension may not be typical on another. For example, Wolcott (1973) chose to focus his ethnographic study of a principal on an individual who was typical of other principals in gender, marital status, age, and so forth. This choice most likely substantially enhanced the range of applicability or generalizability of his study. Yet such a typical principal operating in an atypical school or an atypical system or even an atypical community might well behave very differently from a typical principal in a typical school in a typical system. The solution to this dilemma cannot be found in choosing typicality on every dimension. First of all, not too many typical principals operate in environments that are typical in every way. So this strategy gains less in the realm of generalizability or fittingness than it might appear to at first glance. More important, even if one could achieve typicality in all major dimensions that seem relevant, it is

nonetheless clearly true that there would be enough idiosyncrasy in any particular situation studied so that one could not transfer findings in an unthinking
way from one typical situation to another.

Carried to extremes or taken too seriously, the idea of choosing on the basis
of typicality becomes impossible, even absurd. However, as a guiding principle
designed to increase the potential applicability of research, it is, I believe, useful. This is especially true if the search for typicality is combined with, rather
than seen as a replacement for, a reliance on the kind of thick description emphasized by Guba and Lincoln (1981, 1982), Goetz and LeCompte (1984) and Stake
(1978). Selection on the basis of typicality provides the potential for a good 'fit'
with many other situations. Thick description provides the information necessary to make informed judgments about the degree and extent of that fit in particular cases of interest.

In arguing that qualitative researchers would do well to seek to study the typical,
I am not suggesting that we study the typical defined solely by national norms.
Research that followed this prescription would greatly increase our knowledge of
typical situations, but in a nation as diverse as the United States, it would provide
too restricted, pallid, and homogeneous a view of our educational system. My
emphasis on typicality implies that the researcher who has decided on the kind of
institution or situation he or she wants to study – an urban ghetto school, a rural
consolidated school, or a private Montessori school – should try to select an
instance of this kind of situation that is, to the extent possible, typical of its kind.
Such an approach suggests, for example, that a researcher interested in studying
mathematics teaching choose to observe classrooms that use a popular text and generally accepted modes of instruction, rather than falling for convenience's sake into
the study of classrooms that may well do neither of these. Furthermore, to the extent
preliminary investigation of possible sites suggests that some or all are atypical in
certain regards, careful thought about the possible implications of this atypicality
for the topic under study may help to aid in site selection.

In sum, the point of my argument here is that choosing a site for research on
the basis of typicality is far more likely to enhance the potential generalizability
of one's study than choosing on the basis of convenience or ease of access –
criteria that often weigh more heavily than they should. However, even if one
chooses on the basis of typicality, one is in no way relieved of the necessity for
thick description, for it is foolhardy to think that a typical example will be typical in all important regards. Thus thick description is necessary to allow individuals to ask about the degree of fit between the case studied and the case to
which they wish to generalize, even when the fit on some of the basic dimensions
looks fairly close.

Performing multisite studies

An alternate approach to increasing the generalizability of qualitative research
was evident in the sudden proliferation in the 1970s of multisite qualitative

studies. Such studies were almost always part of federally funded evaluation efforts focusing on the same issue in a number of settings, using similar data collection and analysis procedures in each place. Well-known examples of this approach include the Study of Dissemination Efforts Supporting School Improvement (Crandall *et al.,* 1983; Huberman and Miles, 1984) and the study of Parental Involvement in Federal Educational Programs (Smith and Robbins, 1984). One of the primary purposes of conducting such multisite studies is to escape what Firestone and Herriott (1984) have called the 'radical particularism' of many case studies and hence to provide a firmer basis for generalization.

The multisite studies conducted in the 1970s were extremely varied, although they were all quite expensive and tended to take several years to complete. At least two kinds of variation have special implications for the extent to which this approach actually seems likely to produce results that are a good basis for generalization to many other situations. The first of these is the number of sites studied. Firestone and Herriott's (1984) survey of twenty-five multisite case study efforts found major variation on this dimension, with one study including as few as three sites and another covering sixty. All other things being equal, a finding emerging repeatedly in the study of numerous sites would appear to be more likely to be a good working hypothesis about some as yet unstudied site than a finding emerging from just one or two sites.

A second dimension on which multisite studies vary, which is also likely to affect the degree of fit between these studies and situations to which one might want to generalize, concerns the heterogeneity of the sites chosen for study. Generally speaking, a finding emerging from the study of several very heterogeneous sites would be more robust and thus more likely to be useful in understanding various other sites than one emerging from the study of several very similar sites (Kennedy, 1979). Heterogeneity can be obtained by searching out sites that will provide maximal variation or by planned comparisons along certain potentially important dimensions. An example of the second strategy can be found in the parental-involvement study previously mentioned. The sites chosen for study were selected to allow comparison between urban and rural settings, between those with high and low reported degrees of involvement, and so forth (Smith and Robbins, 1984). This comparative strategy is potentially quite powerful, especially if there is heterogeneity among cases within each of the categories of interest. For example, if several rather different rural cases all share certain similarities that are not found in a heterogeneous group of urban cases, one has some reasonable basis for generalizing about likely differences between the two settings. Although the most obvious comparative strategy is to select cases that initially differ on some variable of interest as part of the research design, it is also possible to group cases in an *ex post facto* way on the basis of information gathered during the fieldwork. For example, if one were studying numerous very different classrooms and found that student achievement gains were quite high in some and quite low in others, one could compare these two sets of classrooms as a strategy for trying to suggest factors that contribute to high or low gains.

In sum, the possibility of studying numerous heterogeneous sites makes multisite studies one potentially useful approach to increasing the generalizability of qualitative work to *what is*. Yet I am very hesitant to see this approach as the only or even the best solution to the problem. First, such studies can be quite expensive, and the current lull in their funding highlights the extent to which such research is dependent on federal dollars that may or may not be forthcoming. Second, as Firestone and Herriott (1984) point out, budget constraints make it likely that studies including very large numbers of sites are less likely than studies of a relatively small number of sites to be able to devote intensive and prolonged care to studying the details of each site. Thus there is typically a trade-off to be made between the increased potential for generalizability flowing from studying a large number of sites and the increased depth and breadth of description and understanding made possible by a focus on a small number of sites. In suggesting that an increased number of sites leads to increased generalizability, I am assuming that enough attention is paid to each site to ensure that problems of internal validity do not arise. To the extent such problems do arise, generalizability is obviously threatened, since one cannot speak meaningfully of the generalizability of invalid data. The fact that roughly forty percent of the multisite studies surveyed by Firestone and Herriott (1984) involved just one or two short visits to the research site raises serious questions about whether such studies can appropriately be categorized as qualitative research in the usual sense of that term. The term *qualitative research*, and more especially the word *ethnography,* usually implies an intensive, ongoing involvement with individuals functioning in their everyday settings that is akin to, if not always identical with, the degree of immersion in a culture attained by anthropologists, who live in the society they study over a period of one or more years (Dobbert, 1982; Spindler, 1982; Wolcott, 1975). Thus it is conceivable, though not logically necessary, that attempts to gain generalizability through studying large numbers of sites undercut the depth of understanding of individual sites, which is the hallmark of the qualitative approach as it has come to be understood.

Studying what may be

The goal of portraying typical schools – or, for that matter, typical instances of federal educational programs as they now exist – is, I believe, worthwhile. Yet accepting this as our only or even primary goal implies too narrow and limited a vision of what qualitative research can do. I would like to suggest that we want to generalize not only to *what is* but also to *what may be*. Let me explain. Here I am proposing that we think about what current social and educational trends suggest about likely educational issues for the future and design our research to illuminate such issues to the extent possible. Let me use some of my own current research to illustrate this possibility, without implying that it is the best or only example of such an approach.

One very obvious and potentially important trend in education recently has been the increasing utilization of microcomputers in instruction. In fact, micro-computers are being adopted in schools at an almost frantic pace (Becker, 1986) in spite of tight educational budgets and a generally acknowledged tendency on the part of educational institutions to resist change. There is a clear division of opinion about the likely consequences of this trend. At one extreme are those who see computers as having the capability to revolutionize education in absolutely fundamental ways. Proponents of this school of thought make the rather startling claim that 'the potential of computers for improving education is greater than that of any prior invention, including books and writing' (Walker, 1984: 3). Others take quite a different stance, emphasizing the inherent conser-vativism of the teaching profession with regard to pedagogical change and the failure of other highly touted educational innovations to bring about far-reach-ing changes. Thus it seemed important to me to design a research project focused on understanding the impact of computer usage on students and classrooms (Schofield and Evans-Rhodes, 1989; Schofield and Verban, 1988). One could approach this issue with an emphasis on what is. For example, it would be pos-sible to choose a school that is presently typical in terms of the uses it makes of computers in instruction. But this strategy encounters an immediate problem if one's goal is to speak to what may be. Changes in both microcomputer technol-ogy and in individuals' level of experience with computers have been so rapid in the past decade that a study of what is today could arguably be a study of pri-marily historical interest by the time it gets conducted, written, and published. In hopes of not just documenting the present, which is rapidly becoming the past, but of speaking to the future, I have made a number of methodological decisions that, in their abstract form, may be of use to others interested in making their work applicable to what may be.

Studying the 'leading edge' of change

First, since it is hard to know what kinds of computer usage will become most typical or popular in the future, I have made a point of studying a broad array of uses rather than just one particular kind. More important, I have not looked only for heterogeneity of usage but for types of usage that are now in their infancy but that many informed observers see as likely to be common in the future. Thus I consciously chose to study a school that not only uses computers as they are currently employed around the country to teach computer programing and word processing in fairly typical ways but that also was the field test site for the kind of artificially intelligent computer-based tutor that researchers in a number of centers around the country are currently developing for classroom use (Feigenbaum and McCorduck, 1983; Lawler and Yazdani, 1987). I see this choice as a step in the direction of increasing the chances that this work will 'fit' or be generalizable to the education issues important at the time the work is published. But this is only a mere first step.

Probing factors likely to differentiate the present from the future

One of the big problems in trying to make one's work applicable to even the fairly near future is, as Cronbach (1975) has so eloquently argued, that people and institutions change. Thus it is logically impossible to see the future even when studying futuristic uses of artificial intelligence, because one is studying that future technology in the context of a present-day institution peopled with individuals who are shaped by the era in which they live.

There is no completely satisfactory solution to this situation, but a partial one emerged as I grappled with the issue. It is to think through how the present and the future are likely to differ. Then the research can be structured in a way that explicitly probes the impact of things that are likely to change over time. Of course, if the analysis of the likely differences between present and future is wrong, this approach will not be particularly useful. But if the analysis is accurate, this strategy has the potential to enhance greatly the usefulness of the study.

Let me illustrate in concrete terms how I have done this. Given the rapidity with which computers are being adopted for use in widely varying arenas of life, especially in schools, it seems a reasonable expectation that one major difference between now and five to ten years in the future is what might be called the 'novelty factor'. Specifically, many of today's high-school students are having their first real introduction to the computer, or at least to its use for educational purposes, in their high-school classrooms. However, in ten years it is rather unlikely that high-school students will be having their first exposure to educational computing in the tenth or eleventh grade. I have used this assumption, which is, I think, relatively uncontroversial, to influence the shape of my study in a way that will allow it to speak more adequately to the future. For example, in interviews students were specifically asked about the impact of novelty on their reactions to the computer and its importance in shaping their feelings about computer usage. Similarly, observers in the study carefully looked for reactions that appeared to be influenced by students' unfamiliarity with the computers. Moreover, I have been careful to find out which students have had prior computer experience and what kind of experience this has been in order to see as clearly as possible whether these students differ from those for whom computer use is a completely novel experience. The fact that students were observed during the full course of the school year allowed assessment of whether any initial differences in students' reactions due to prior experience were transitory or relatively long-lasting. To the extent that novelty is crucial in shaping students' reactions, I will be forced to conclude that my study may not help us understand the future as well as it might otherwise. To the extent that students' reactions appear to be more heavily influenced by things that are unlikely to change in the near future, such as adolescents' striving for independence from adult control, the likely applicability of the findings of the study to the near future is clearly increased.

Considering the life cycle of a phenomenon

The preceding discussion of the possible impact of novelty on students' reactions to educational computing brings up an important point regarding qualitative work and the issue of generalizability. The ethnographic habit of looking at a phenomenon over substantial time periods allows assessment of one aspect of generalizability that quantitative research usually does not – of where a particular phenomenon is in its life cycle and what the implications of this are for what is happening. Qualitative research, when studying a dynamic phenomenon, is like a movie. It starts with one image and then moves on to others that show how things evolve over time. Quantitative research, in contrast, is more typically like a snapshot, often taken and used without great regard for whether that photograph happened to catch one looking one's best or looking unusually disheveled. This point can be illustrated more substantively by briefly discussing a study that I carried out in a desegregated school during its first four years of existence (Schofield, 1989). The study tracked changes in the school by following two different groups of students from the first day they entered the school to graduation from that school three years later. Important changes occurred in race relations over the life of the institution and over the course of students' careers in the school. Such findings suggest that in asking about what happens in desegregated schools and what the impact of such schools is on students, it is important to know where both the students and the institution are in their experience with desegregation. Yet virtually all quantitative studies of desegregation, including, I must admit, some of my own, tend to ignore these issues completely. In fact, as I discovered in reviewing the desegregation literature (Schofield and Sagar, 1983), many do not even supply bare descriptive information on the life-cycle issue. Paying attention to where a phenomenon is in its life cycle does not guarantee that one can confidently predict how it will evolve. However, at a minimum, sensitivity to this issue makes it less likely that conclusions formed on the basis of a study conducted at one point in time will be unthinkingly and perhaps mistakenly generalized to other later points in time to which they may not apply.

Studying what could be

As mentioned previously, I would like to argue that qualitative research on education can be used not only to study *what is* and *what may be* but also to explore possible visions of *what could be*. By studying what could be, I mean locating situations that we know or expect to be ideal or exceptional on some *a priori* basis and then studying them to see what is actually going on there.

Selecting a site that sheds light on what could be

When studying what could be, site selection is not based on criteria such as typicality or heterogeneity. Rather it is based on information about either the *outcomes* achieved in the particular site studied or on the *conditions* obtaining there. Perhaps the best-known example of site selection based on outcomes is choosing to study classrooms or schools in which students show unusual intellectual gains, as has been done in the voluminous literature on effective schools (Bickel, 1983; Dwyer *et al.*, 1982; Phi Delta Kappan, 1980; Rutter *et al.*, 1979; Weber, 1971). For an example of site selection based on the conditions obtaining at the site, a less common approach, I will again make reference to my own work on school desegregation.

When thinking about where to locate the extended study of a desegregated school mentioned previously, I decided not to study a typical desegregated school. First, given the tremendous variation in situations characterized as desegregated, it is not clear that such an entity could be found. Second, there is a body of theory and research that gives us some basis for expecting different kinds of social processes and outcomes in different kinds of interracial schools. In fact, in the same year in which the *Brown v. Board of Education* decision laid the legal basis for desegregating educational institutions, Gordon Allport (1954) published a classic analysis of racial prejudice in which he argued that interracial contact can either increase or decrease hostility and stereotyping, depending on the kind of conditions under which it occurs. Specifically, he argued that in order to ameliorate relations between groups such as blacks and whites three conditions are especially important: equal status for members of both groups within the contact situation, a cooperative rather than a competitive goal structure, and support for positive relations from those in authority. A substantial amount of empirical and theoretical work stemming from Allport's basic insight has been carried out in the past three and a half decades, most of which supports his emphasis on the crucial importance of the specific conditions under which intergroup contact occurs (Amir, 1969; Aronson and Osherow, 1980; Cook, 1978; Pettigrew, 1967, 1969; Schofield, 1979; Schofield and Sagar, 1977; Slavin, 1980; Stephan, 1985).

It is clear that desegregating school systems often take little if any heed of the available theory and research on how to structure desegregated schools in a way likely to promote positive intergroup relations, perhaps at least partly because much of this work is laboratory based and hence may seem of questionable use in everyday situations. Thus selecting a site for study on the basis of typicality might be expected to yield a site potentially rich in sources of insight about the problems of desegregated education but weak in shedding light on what can be accomplished in a serious and sophisticated effort to structure an environment conducive to fostering positive relations between students. Since both scholars in the area of intergroup relations and the public are well aware of the potential for difficulties in desegregated schools, the task of seeing whether and how such difficulties can be overcome seems potentially more informative and useful than that of documenting the existence of such difficulties. Thus I chose to study a site that at least approximated a theoretical ideal. My goal was not to generalize to desegregated schools as a class. Rather it was to see what happens under conditions that might be expected to foster relatively positive outcomes. If serious problems were encountered at such a site, there would be reason to think that problems would be encountered in most places or, alternatively, to revise or reject the theory that led to the site selection. However, if things went well at such a site, the study would then provide an opportunity to gain some insight into how and why they go well and into what the still-intractable problems are.

Of course, the strategy of choosing a site based on some *a priori* theoretical viewpoint or, for that matter, any seriously held expectation about it raises a difficult problem. If one is unduly committed to that viewpoint, one's analysis of both what happens and why may be heavily influenced by it, and one may not ask whether other more fruitful perspectives might emerge from a more dispassionate approach to studying the situation. This is the very danger that has led to the development of such elaborate safeguards in the quantitative tradition as the double-blind experiment. Although such procedures are rarely used in the qualitative tradition, a substantial literature on the issue of internal validity in qualitative research offers assistance with this problem to the researcher who pays it close heed (Becker, 1958; Bogdan and Biklen, 1981; Glaser and Strauss, 1967; Goetz and LeCompte, 1984; Guba, 1981; Guba and Lincoln, 1981; Kirk and Miller, 1986; Miles and Huberman, 1984a, 1984b; Patton, 1980; Strauss, 1987). Furthermore, if one's purpose is not to support or reject a specific *a priori* theory but to discover, using an approach that is as open as possible, what is actually happening in a site that was chosen with the assistance of a particular theory, problems related to internal validity are somewhat mitigated. For example, the fact that I chose to study a school that theory suggested might be conducive to positive relations did not keep me from exploring in considerable depth problems that occurred there (Sagar and Schofield, 1980; Schofield, 1981, 1989).

One characteristic of the school chosen for the study was especially helpful in assessing the degree to which the theory on which the site was chosen was useful. Specifically, for various reasons, conditions in two of the three grades in this school came much closer than conditions in the remaining grade to meeting those that theory suggests are conducive to producing positive relations. Thus it was possible to assess intergroup relations as the children went from one kind of environment to another within the school (Schofield, 1979, 1989; Schofield and Sagar, 1977). This suggests one very useful strategy for studying what may be – selecting an 'ideal' case and a comparative case that contrasts sharply on the relevant dimensions.

Generalizing from an unusual site to more typical ones

Although I indicated above that my goal was to learn about the possibilities and problems associated with a *certain kind* of desegregated education, I would like to argue that studying a site chosen for its special characteristics does not necessarily restrict the application of the study's findings to other very similar sites. The degree to which this is the case depends on the degree to which the findings appear to be linked to the special characteristics of the situation. Some of the findings from the study I have been discussing were clearly linked to unusual aspects of the school and hence have very limited generalizability to other situations, although they may nonetheless be important in demonstrating what is possible, even if not what is generally likely. For example, I found very low levels of overt racial conflict in the school studied (Schofield and Francis, 1982). It would obviously be misguided to conclude on the basis of this study that intergroup conflict is unlikely in all desegregated schools, since the school's emphasis on cooperation, equal status, and the like did actually appear to play a marked role in reducing the likelihood of conflict.

However, other findings that emerged from the study and were also related to atypical aspects of the situation may have a greater degree of applicability or generalizability than the finding discussed above. For example, I found the development of a color-blind perspective and of an almost complete taboo against the mention of race in the school studied (Schofield, 1986, 1989). Since the emergence of the color-blind perspective and the accompanying taboo appeared to be linked to special characteristics of the school, I would not posit them as phenomena likely to occur in most desegregated schools. But I feel free to argue that *when* they do develop, certain consequences may well follow because these consequences are the logical outcomes of the phenomena. For example, with regard to the taboo against racial reference, if one cannot mention race, one cannot deal with resegregation in a strightforward way as a policy issue. Similarly, if one cannot mention race, there is likely to be little or no effort to create or utilize multicultural curricular materials. Thus, although the taboo against racial reference may not occur in a high proportion of desegregated schools, when it does occur the study I carried out gives a potentially useful indication of problems that are likely to develop.

I would now like to turn to a third finding of the study, one so unrelated to the atypical aspects of the situation studied that it is a reasonable working hypothesis that this phenomenon is widespread. After I observed extensively in varied areas of the school and interviewed a large number of students, it became apparent that the white children perceived blacks as something of a threat to their physical selves. Specifically, they complained about what they perceived as black roughness or aggressiveness (Schofield, 1981, 1989). In contrast, the black students perceived whites as a threat to their social selves. They complained about being ignored, avoided, and being treated as inferior by whites, whom they perceived to be stuck-up and prejudiced (Schofield, 1989). Such findings appear to be linked to the black and white students' situation in the larger society and to powerful historical and economic forces, not to special aspects of the school. The consequences of these rather asymmetrical concerns may well play themselves out differently in different kinds of schools, but the existence of these rather different but deeply held concerns may well be widespread.

I have gone into some detail with these examples because I think they raise a crucial point for judging the applicability or generalizability of qualitative work. One cannot just look at a study and say that it is similar or dissimilar to another situation of concern. A much finer-grained analysis is necessary. One must ask what aspects of the situation are similar or different and to what aspects of the findings these are connected.

[...]

Summary and conclusions

Although qualitative researchers have traditionally paid scant attention to the issue of attaining generalizability in research, sometimes even disdaining such a goal, this situation has changed noticeably in the past ten to fifteen years. Several trends, including the growing use of qualitative studies in evaluation and policy-oriented research, have led to an increased awareness of the importance of structuring qualitative studies in a way that enhances their implications for the understanding of other situations.

Much of the attention given to the issue of generalizability in recent years on the part of qualitative researchers has focused on redefining the concept in a way that is useful and meaningful for those engaged in qualitative work. A consensus appears to be emerging that for qualitative researchers generalizability is best thought of as a matter of the 'fit' between the situation studied and others to which one might be interested in applying the concepts and conclusions of that study. This conceptualization makes thick descriptions crucial, since without them one does not have the information necessary for an informed judgment about the issue of fit.

This paper argues that three useful targets for generalization are *what is, what may be,* and *what could be* and provides some examples of how qualitative research can be designed in a way that increases its ability to fit with each of these situations. Studying *what is* refers to studying the typical, the common, and the ordinary. Techniques suggested for studying *what is* include choosing study sites on the basis of typicality and conducting multisite studies. Studying *what may be* refers to designing studies so that their fit with future trends and issues is maximized. Techniques suggested for studying *what may be* include seeking out sites in which one can study situations likely to become more common with the passage of time and paying close attention to how such present instances of future practices are likely to differ from their future realizations. Studying *what could be* refers to locating situations that we know or expect to be ideal or exceptional on some *a priori* basis and studying them to see what is actually going on there. Crucial here is an openness to having one's expectations about the phenomena disconfirmed. [...]

Note

Much of the research on which this paper is based was funded by the Office of Naval Research, Contract Number NOO 14-85-K-0664. Other research utilized in this paper was funded by Grant Number NIE-G-78-0126 from the National Institute of Education. However, all opinions expressed herein are solely those of the author, and no endorsement by ONR or NIE is implied or intended. My sincere thanks go to Bill Firestone and Matthew Miles for their constructive comments on an earlier draft of this paper.

References

Allport, G. W. (1954) *The Nature of Prejudice,* Cambridge: Cambridge University Press.

Amir, Y. (1969) 'Contact hypothesis in ethnic relations', *Psychological Bulletin*, 71: 319–42.

Aronson, E. and Osherow, N. (1980) 'Cooperation, prosocial behavior, and academic performance: experiments in the desegregated classroom', in L. Bickman (ed.), *Applied Social Psychology Annual*, Vol 1. Beverly Hills, CA: Sage, pp. 163–96.

Becker, H. J. (1986) 'Instructional uses of school computers', *Reports from the 1985 National Survey.* 1: 1–9. Baltimore, MD: Center for Social Organization of Schools, Johns Hopkins University, pp. 1–9.

Becker, H. S. (1958) 'Problems of inference and proof in participant observation', *American Sociological Review*, 23: 652–59.

Berg, B. L. (1989) *Qualitative Research Methods for the Social Sciences.* Boston: Allyn & Bacon.

Bickel, W. E. (1983) 'Effective schools: knowledge, dissemination, inquiry', *Educational Researcher*, 12(4): 3–5.

Bogdan, R. C. and Biklen, S. K. (1981) *Qualitative Research for Education: An Introduction to Theory and Methods.* Boston: Allyn & Bacon.

Bolgar, H. (1965) 'The case study method', in B. B. Wolman (ed.), *Handbook of Clinical Psychology*, New York: McGraw-Hill, pp. 28–39.

Brown v. Board of Education (1954) 347 US 483.

Campbell, D. T. (1979) 'Degrees of freedom and the case study', in T. D. Cook and C. S. Reichardt (eds), *Qualitative and Quantitative Methods in Evaluation Research.* Beverly Hills, CA: Sage, pp. 49–67.

Campbell, D. and Stanley, J. (1963) 'Experimental and quasi-experimental designs for research on teaching', in N. Gage (ed.), *Handbook of Research on Teaching.* Chicago: Rand McNally, pp. 171–246.

Collins, T. and Noblit, G. (1978) *Stratification and Resegregation: The Case of Crossover High School.* Final report of NIE contract 400–76–009.

Cook, S. W. (1978) 'Interpersonal and attitudinal outcomes in cooperating interracial groups', *Journal of Research and Development in Education*, 12: 97–113.

Crandall, D. P. *et al.* (1983) *People, Policies and Practices: Examining the Chain of School Improvement*, Vols 1–10. Andover, MA: Network.

Cronbach, L. J. (1975) 'Beyond the two disciplines of scientific psychology', *American Psychologist*, 30: 116–27.

Cronbach, L. J. (1982) *Designing Evaluations of Educational and Social Programs.* San Francisco: Jossey-Bass.

Cronbach, L. J., Ambron, S. R., Dornbusch, S. M., Hess, R. D., Hornik, R. C., Phillips, D. C., Walker, D. F., and Weiner, S. S. (1980) *Toward Reform of Program Evaluation.* San Francisco: Jossey-Bass.

Denzin, N. K. (1983) 'Interpretive interactionism', in G. Morgan (ed.), *Beyond Method: Strategies for Social Research.* Beverly Hills, CA: Sage, pp. 129–146.

Dobbert, M. L. (1982) *Ethnographic Research: Theory and Application for Modern Schools and Societies*, New York: Praeger.

Dwyer, D. C., Lee, G. V., Rowan, B., and Bossert, S. T. (1982) 'The principal's role in instructional management: five participant observation studies of principals in action'. Unpublished manuscript, Far West Laboratory for Educational Research and Development, San Francisco.

Feigenbaum, E. A. and McCorduck, P. (1983) *The Fifth Generation: Artificial Intelligence and Japan's Computer Challenge to the World.* Reading, MA: Addison-Wesley.

Fetterman, D. M. (1982) 'Ethnography in educational research: the dynamics of diffusion', In D. M. Fetterman (ed.), *Ethnography in Educational Evaluation.* Beverly Hills, CA: Sage, pp. 21–35.

Filstead, W. J. (1979) 'Qualitative methods: a needed perspective in evaluation research', in T. D. Cook and C. S. Reichardt (eds), *Qualitative and Quantitative Methods in Evaluation Research.* Beverly Hills, CA: Sage, pp. 33–48.

Firestone, W. A. and Herriott, R. E. (1984) 'Multisite qualitative policy research: some design and implementation issues', in D. M. Fetterman (ed.), *Ethnography in Educational Evaluation.* Beverly Hills, CA: Sage, pp. 63–88.

Geertz, C. (1973) 'Thick description: toward an interpretive theory of culture', in C. Geertz (ed.), *The Interpretation of Cultures.* New York: Basic Books, pp. 3–30.

Glaser, B. and Strauss, A. (1967) *The Discovery of Grounded Theory.* Chicago: Aldine Publishing.

Goetz, J. P. and LeCompte, M. D. (1984) *Ethnography and Qualitative Design in Education Research.* Orlando, FL: Academic Press.

Guba, E. (1981) 'Criteria for assessing the trustworthiness of naturalistic inquiry', *Educational Communication and Technology Journal*, 29: 79–92.

Guba, E. G. and Lincoln, Y. S. (1981) *Effective Evaluation: Improving the Usefulness of Evaluation Results through Responsive and Naturalistic Approaches.* San Francisco: Jossey-Bass.

Guba, E. G. and Lincoln Y. S. (1982) 'Epistemological and methodological bases of naturalistic inquiry', *Educational Communication and Technology Journal*, 30: 233–52.

Huberman, A. M. and Miles, M. B. (1984) *Innovation up Close: How School Improvement Works.* New York: Plenum Press.

Jackson, P. W. (1968) *Life in Classrooms.* New York: Holt, Rinehart & Winston.

Kennedy, M. M. (1979) 'Generalizing from single case studies', *Evaluation Quarterly*, 3(4): 661–78.

Kirk, J. and Miller, M. L. (1986) *Reliability and Validity in Qualitative Research.* Beverly Hills, CA: Sage.

Krathwohl, D. R. (1985) *Social and Behavioral Science Research: New Framework for Conceptualizing, Implementing, and Evaluating Research Studies.* San Fransisco: Jossey-Bass.

Lawler, R. W. and Yazdani, M. (eds) (1987) *Artificial Intelligence and Education: Learning Environments and Tutoring Systems*, Vol 1. Norwood, NJ: Ablex Publishing.

Lucas, W. (1974) *The Case Survey Method: Aggregating Case Experience.* Santa Monica, CA: Rand.

Miles, M. and Huberman, A. (1984a) 'Drawing valid meaning from qualitative data: toward a shared craft', *Educational Researcher*, 13: 20–30.

Miles, M. and Huberman, A. (1984b) *Qualitative Data Analysis: Sourcebook of New Methods.* Newbury Park, CA: Sage.

Noblit, G. W. and Hare, R. D. (1988) *Meta-Ethnography: Synthesizing Qualitative Studies.* Beverly Hills, CA: Sage.

Patton, M. Q. (1980) *Qualitative Evaluation Methods.* Beverly Hills, CA: Sage.

Peshkin, A. (1978) *Growing up American: Schooling and the Survival of Community.* Chicago: University of Chicago Press.

Peshkin, A. (1982) 'The researcher and subjectivity: reflections on an ethnography of school and community', in G. Spindler (ed.) *Doing the Ethnography of Schooling: Educational Anthropology in Action.* New York: Holt, Rinehart & Winston, pp. 48–67.

Pettigrew, T. (1967) 'Social evaluation theory: convergences and applications', in D. Levine, (ed.), *Nebraska Symposium on Motivation*, Vol 5. Lincoln, NE: University of Nebraska Press.

Pettigrew, T. (1969) 'Racially separate or together', *Journal of Social Issues*, 25: 43–69.

Phi Delta Kappan (1980) *Why Do Some Urban Schools Succeed? The Phi Delta Kappan Study of Exceptional Urban Elementary Schools.* Bloomington, IN: Phi Delta Kappan and Indiana University.

Ragin, C. C. (1987) *The Comparative Method: Moving beyond Qualitative and Quantitative Strategies.* Berkeley, CA: University of California Press.

Reichardt, C. S. and Cook, T. D. (1979) 'Beyond qualitative *versus* quantitative methods', in T. D. Cook and C. S. Reichardt (eds), *Qualitative and Quantitative Methods in Evaluation Research*. Beverly Hills, CA: Sage, pp. 1–33.

Rutter, M., Maughan, B., Mortimore, P., Ouston, J. and Smith, A. (1979) *Fifteen Thousand Hours: Secondary Schools and their Effects on Children*. Cambridge, MA: Harvard University Press.

Sagar, H. A. and Schofield, J. W. (1980) 'Racial and behavioral cues in black and white children's perceptions of ambiguously aggressive acts', *Journal of Personality and Social Psychology*, 39: 590–98.

Schofield, J. W. (1979) 'The impact of positively structured contact on intergroup behavior: does it last under adverse conditions?' *Social Psychology Quarterly*, 42: 280–84.

Schofield, J. W. (1981) 'Competitive and complementary identities: images and interaction in an interracial school', in S. Asher and J. Gottman (eds), *The Development of Children's Friendship*. New York: Cambridge University Press.

Schofield, J. W. (1986) 'Causes and consequences of the colorblind perspective', in S. Gaertner and J. Dovidio (eds), *Prejudice Discrimination and Racism: Theory and Practice*. New York: Academic Press, pp. 231–53.

Schofield, J. W. (1989) *Black and White in School: Trust, Tension, or Tolerance?* New York: Teachers College Press. (Original work published 1982.)

Schofield, J. W. and Evans-Rhodes, D. (1989) 'Artificial intelligence in the classroom: the impact of a computer-based tutor on teachers and students', paper presented at the 4th International Conference on Artificial Intelligence in Education, Amsterdam, The Netherlands, May.

Schofield, J. W. and Francis, W. D. (1982) 'An observational study of peer interaction in racially mixed "accelerated" classrooms', *Journal of Educational Psychology*, 74: 722–32.

Schofield, J. W. and Sagar, H. A. (1977) 'Peer interaction patterns in an integrated middle school', *Sociometry*, 40: 130–38.

Schofield, J. W. and Sagar, H. A. (1983) 'Desegregation, school practices and student race relations', in C. Rossell and W. Hawley (eds), *The Consequences of School Desegregation*. Philadelphia, PA: Temple University Press, pp. 58–102.

Schofield, J. W. and Verban, D. (1988) 'Computer usage in the teaching of mathematics: issues which need answers', in D. Grouws and T. Cooney (eds), *Effective Mathematics Teaching*. Hillsdale, NJ: Erlbaum, pp. 169–93.

Shaughnessy, J. J. and Zechmeister, E. B. (1985) *Research Methods in Psychology*. New York: Knopf.

Slavin, R. E. (1980) 'Cooperative learning', *Review of Educational Research*, 50: 315–42.

Smith, A. G. and Robbins, A. E. (1984) 'Multimethod policy research: a case study of structure and flexibility', in D. M. Fetterman (ed.), *Ethnography in Educational Evaluation*. Beverly Hills, CA: Sage, pp. 115–32.

Smith H. W. (1975) *Strategies of Social Research: The Methodological Imagination*. Englewood Cliffs, NJ: Prentice-Hall.

Spindler, G. (1982) 'General introduction', in G. Spindler (ed.), *Doing the Ethnogra Schooling: Educational Anthropology in Action*. New York: Holt, Rinehart & Winston, pp

Stake, R. E. (1978) 'The case-study method in social inquiry', *Educational Researcher*, 7: 5–8.

Stephan, W. J. (1985) 'Intergroup relations', in G. Lindzey and F. Aronson (eds), *The Handbook of Social Psychology*, Vol 2. New York: Random House, pp. 599–658.

Strauss, A. L. (1987) *Qualitative Analysis for Social Scientists*. Cambridge: Cambridge University Press.

Walker, D. F. (1984) 'Promise, potential, and pragmatism: computers in high school', *Institute for Research in Educational Finance and Governance Policy Notes*, 5: 3–4.

Weber, G. (1971) *Inner-City Children Can Be Taught to Read: Four Successful Schools*. Washington, DC: Council for Basic Education.

Whyte, W. F. (1984) *Learning from the Field: A Guide from Experience*. Beverly Hills, CA: Sage.

Wolcott, H. F. (1973) *The Man in the Principal's Office: An Ethnography*. New York: Holt, Rinehart & Winston.

Wolcott, H. F. (1975) 'Criteria for an ethnographic approach to research in schools', *Human Organization*, 34: 111–27.

Wolcott, H. F. (1982) 'Mirrors, models, and monitors: educator adaptations of the ethnographic innovation', in G. Spindler (ed.), *Doing the Ethnography of Schooling: Educational Anthropology in Action*, New York: Holt, Rinehart & Winston, pp. 68–95.

Yin, R. K. (1981) 'The case study crisis: some answers', *Administrative Science Quarterly*, 26: 58–64.

Yin, R. K. (1984) *Case Study Research: Design and Methods*. Beverly Hills, CA: Sage.

Yin, R. K. and Heald, K. A. (1975) 'Using the case survey method to analyze policy studies', *Administrative Science Quarterly*, 20: 371–81.

Yin, R. K. and Yates, D. (1975) *Street-Level Governments: Assessing Decentralization and Urban Services*. Lexington, MA: D. C. Heath.

Chapter 14

Critical incidents and learning about risks: the case of young people and their health

Martyn Denscombe

Peter Woods has demonstrated that the process of teaching and learning is significantly influenced by both 'critical *events*' and 'critical *incidents*' (Sikes, Measor and Woods, 1985; Woods, 1993). The distinction between the two is that critical events take the shape of planned occasions, such as the production of a drama or a school visit. These events are consciously orchestrated over a period of time; they are intentional and planned. Critical incidents, by contrast, are characteristically 'unplanned, unanticipated and uncontrolled. They are flash-points that illuminate in an electrifying instant' (Woods, 1993, p. 1).

Despite their differences, the two concepts share much in common in regard to the process of learning. First, they both focus on 'highly charged moments and episodes that have enormous consequences for personal change and development' (Sikes et al., 1985, p. 230). They place emphasis on the role of particular occasions in shaping the way people understand their world, rather than treating the learning process as a steady accumulation of knowledge or experience at an even pace. Attitudes and behaviours, from this perspective, are not shaped by a uniform process of socialization but by a sequence of 'high-spots'. Second, the two concepts share a focus on learning through personal experience and through real-world events. Critical incidents and critical events are based on

Taken from: Hammersley, M. (ed.), *Researching School Experience*, (London: Falmer, 1999), pp. 187–203.

things that actually happen, planned or otherwise. They are neither hypothetical nor abstract. In this sense, they tend to accord with a learning theory that stresses the importance of 'collecting first-hand evidence and material, on doing things oneself, on having a realistic aim. As in research, this heightens the validity of the output. Learning is integrated into the self' (Woods, 1993, p. 4).

Critical incidents, then, might be expected to promote learning in a rather special way, and the purpose of this chapter will be to explore this potential in relation to one specific area: young people's attitudes to taking risks with their health. The study of critical incidents might provide some insight into the way young people develop their attitudes to risk-taking and health. Equally, it might provide a valuable resource in health educators' efforts to make young people aware of the dangers associated with health-risk behaviours such as smoking tobacco, drinking alcohol and substance abuse. Either possibility, however, begs the question, 'Do critical incidents actually have an impact on young people's attitudes to taking risks with their health; and, if so, how do they do it?' The purpose of this chapter is to explore this issue.[1]

Health-risking behaviour and critical incidents

Young people seem to be prepared to take risks with their health in a way that defies the logic of health education messages. Though the messages are clear and plentiful, young people seem reluctant to 'learn the lesson'. By the age of 15–16 years, over a quarter of young people in Britain are regular smokers, a similar proportion drink regularly, and a sizeable minority use soft drugs like cannabis (Balding, 1993; Furlong and Cartmel, 1997; Measham, Newcombe and Parker, 1994; Plant and Plant, 1992). Despite health promotion campaigns, despite health education in schools, these young people persist in taking risks with their health.

This has proved to be an intractable problem from the point of view of teachers, health educators and the youth service. Time and again it has been shown that programmes designed to alert young people to the dangers of substance abuse have not been very effective (Lloyd and Lucas, 1998; Lynagh, Schofield and Sanson-Fisher, 1997; May, 1991; Tones, 1993; White and Pitts, 1997). It is not that young people are not exposed to the information. Nor is it that they do not understand the key points that are being put across. The problem is that, despite being aware of the dangers, they go ahead and do it anyway.

The apparent reluctance to learn the lesson of health education owes something to the fact that young people tend to operate with an exaggerated sense of immunity when it comes to risk-taking activity (Elkind, 1967; Jack, 1989). More than at other stages of life, there is a tendency for them to believe that 'it won't happen to me'. However, research on the perception of risk also points to the existence of certain factors that might be expected to weigh against the feeling of 'invulnerability' by *heightening* young people's sensitivity to risks (Denscombe, 1993; Douglas, 1986; Johnson and Covello, 1987). Experience of such events or situations serves to make the risk seem more likely to happen and/or to make people more conscious of the extent to which they personally might be vulnerable to the risk.

The kinds of things that heighten sensitivity to risk broadly comprise two categories – those that contribute to the '*dread factor*' and those that contribute to the '*vividness factor*', (Kahneman, Slovic and Tversky, 1982; Slovic, Fischoff and Lichtenstein, 1980, 1981). The dread factor concerns the depth of fear caused by a risk. It is influenced by a number of variables but, arguably, the primary one is the extent to which people feel *personally vulnerable* to the risk. Where they feel personally vulnerable to a risk it arouses passion, it causes worry, it increases their fear and sense of horror about the risk outcome. The *vividness* of the risk, on the other hand, has a bearing on people's perceptions of how likely it is that a risk outcome will actually happen. Vividness tends to heighten people's awareness of the risk and tends to make them more conscious of its consequences. A risk that is vivid tends to be more easily recalled, easily visualized and clearly imagined. The more people have the risk brought to their attention, for instance through media coverage, and the more dramatically the risk is presented, the easier it becomes to think of the consequences and regard them as a likely possibility (Combs and Slovic, 1979; Thaler 1983).

On the basis of these two factors – dread and vividness – it is reasonable to suppose that where someone has a personal experience of the nasty outcome associated with a given risk, then there is likely to be a heightened sensitivity to that risk. If people know of the dangers at first hand – if they personally have suffered or have close knowledge of someone else who has suffered – the risk is likely to become more real and foreboding for them. The experience might also serve to confront the individual with his or her own mortality and thereby undermine any false sense of invulnerability. To have some loved one – close friend or close family – fall seriously ill or suffer a serious accident or die, whatever the cause, might be expected to bring home to a (young) person the fact that personal health is not something that should be taken for granted. Such an experience would have the constituent features of a *critical incident*,[2] affecting attitudes to personal health through:

- *vivid*, highly charged moments;
- based on specific *real-world* occurrences (rather than vague and general dispositions); and
- involving things with which those concerned have some *personal experience*.

A study of critical incidents

The proposition that critical incidents in the lives of young people might shape their attitudes to health-risking behaviour has been investigated as part of ongoing research into young people's perceptions of risk. Between January and March 1997 a questionnaire survey of young people aged 15 to 16 years was undertaken in 12 schools in Leicestershire and Rutland – counties in the East Midlands of England. The schools were selected to be representative in terms of their catchment area (social class, ethnic composition, urban/suburban/rural). The questionnaire was distributed to half of the cohort of the Year 11 pupils in the schools via mixed-ability tutor groups. From the 1679 young people who took part in the survey, 1648 usable questionnaires were returned. The questionnaire included items on young people's alcohol and tobacco consumption, attitudes to their own bodies, and perceptions of risks related to health. The survey was followed up with focus groups conducted with a sub-sample of the 15–16-year olds (n = 123). Two groups, each comprising five or six young people, were used from 11 of the schools (one of the original schools did not take part in this phase of the investigation). Finally, a series of in-depth interviews was conducted with young people from five of the schools in the research (n = 20). To explore the effect of critical incidents on their willingness to engage in health-risking behaviour, the young people taking part in the survey were asked about any:

- first-hand experience of a serious accident or injury, or
- personal experience of a serious illness or a medical condition affect-ing their well-being.

They were also asked about any experience they had involving:

- the death of a close friend or someone in the close family, or
- a serious accident or illness affecting someone close to them.

They were asked to recall only situations that had happened since they were aged 10. This restriction on the time period was designed to eliminate from the research those childhood illnesses such as chickenpox and measles which, in the context of contemporary Britain, tend to be rather routine and mundane. Restricting the period to the previous five or six years also placed a reasonable time frame on what it was possible to remember with any clarity, and limited incidents to those that were likely to have had any substantial influence on their developing attitudes to health risks.

Young people speak about critical incidents

The questionnaire survey suggested that most young people had some experi-ence of a serious health-related incident (to themselves, family or a close friend). Responses from the survey revealed that only 12 per cent of the young people had *not* had that experience. Just one in eight, that is, reported that they had suffered no accidents or illness since they were 10 years of age, or had not had someone close to them die or suffer a serious accident or illness. The vast majority, though, had confronted some incident since the age of 10 that had involved some kind of situation which, in principle, might be expected to have had a marked impact on their thinking in relation to health.

There was some evidence from the focus group discussions and interviews that the experience of such incidents could, indeed, have the expected powerful influence on the young people's attitudes to taking risks with their health. For example, one girl described how she had fallen off her pony and suffered considerable bruising as a result:

> *Sarah:*   When I got home I thought – what if I had never been able to walk again. And it really freaked me out. Now I don't like jumping. It scares me to think how easily it could happen – I could have been in a wheelchair. (Focus group of four boys and three girls, 15–16 years, white, school 09, 19.3.97)

Falling from ponies, it has to be acknowledged, has not featured prominently in the concerns of health education. But, when it came to the more conventional concerns – such as substance use – other examples illustrated the potential of vivid and horrible realities to act as critical incidents. Frequently, though, the incident revolved around something that had happened to another person. During a focus group an example of this arose in connection with a teacher at the young people's school:

> *Sajid:*   We saw this video at school.
> *Sameena:*   In tutorial wasn't it?
> *Sajid:*   This man lost all his limbs, his legs. He couldn't live without smoking, so they used to get this cigarette and put it through his neck.
> *Haroon:*   There's even this teacher in our school. She was a really hard smoker, and unfortunately she lost …
> *Reena:*   … first it was her toe she had to have amputated …
> *Haroon:*   … and now it's part of her leg.
> *Interviewer:* Here? In this school?
> *Haroon:*   Yes. She's still working.
> *Interviewer:* Does she ever talk to you about smoking?
> *Sameena:*   Yes, she came round once.
> *Haroon:*   I think it's good that someone in this school has actually been affected because at least we learn. (Focus group of two girls and four boys, 15–16 years, two Hindus and four Muslims, school 01, 18.11.97)

The young people, here, seemed to have been influenced by the vivid outcome of the risk, coupled with the fact that the risk was brought close to home through the presence of the teacher in the school who had suffered the amputations.

The impact of situations that affect those close to the individual was evident on many occasions when young people referred to things that had happened to members of their family. When someone in the family was affected as a result of smoking, it hit close to home with a message about the risks involved – and this could serve as an effective deterrent:

> *Emma:*   My step-granddad died of some illness that he got because he had smoked all his life. So I found that very upsetting, and it put me off smoking.
>
> *Laura:*   Same with me. My granddad died of lung cancer, and we all just had to watch him die and it was really awful. (Shudders) So I'm never going to smoke. (Focus group of three girls and two boys, 15–16 years, white, school 04, 5.2.98)

Or again,

> *Guy:*   Well one of my brother's best friends – his mum smoked a lot and she had a leg amputated.
>
> *Interviewer:*   And do you think that really affected you in terms of your decision (not to smoke)?
>
> *Guy:*   Yes, and also my mum. This is why I want her to give up. She sometimes will wake up in the middle of the night, she says, and she can't breathe. And she's had bronchitis, and she said 'I'm never going to smoke again.' And as soon as it went away, as soon as her bronchitis stopped, she went back on to cigarettes again – and every three months or so she'll get it back.
>
> *Debbie:*   My mum's sister died of cancer, actually. But I only ever met her once or twice or something. I think she smoked a lot. But I think it's common sense more than anything. When you see, like, your friends from primary school and, like, they smoke like a chimney, and the way they have changed, it's like … I don't want to be like that. My gran always used to say 'If God had wanted you to smoke, he would have given you a chimney in the back of your head.' I've always thought of that – and it's true isn't it? I think that may have influenced me. (Focus group of two girls and two boys, 15–16 years, white, school 05, 16.4.97)

It was not just the tragedy of elderly relatives and cancer that acted as salutary lessons for the young people. Witnessing at first hand the impact of substance use by siblings was also referred to on occasion. In the focus group discussion reported below, the sister's behaviour is treated as a graphic justification for not 'doing [hard] drugs':

Lucy:	It's like my sister. She went through the phase when she tried loads of drugs because she was on the dole and she didn't have anything else to do. She went round to somebody else's house and she continually took drugs. She didn't even know what she was taking half the time and she used to come back and she used to go up to my mum and say 'I really hate you. I don't want to know you, you're always in my private life.' She turned into a monster.
Jake:	She all right now?
Lucy:	She's all right now, but like she wouldn't do things – she'd hardly have a bath or anything.
Jake:	What was she on?
Lucy:	She don't know – she had cannabis, she had speed once, she had no end of things, she was like someone different. I used to hate it. She'd like come home and she wasn't like my sister anymore. She was someone else.
Interviewer:	So that's had quite an impact on you?
Lucy:	I'd never do that. Cannabis maybe, but nothing else I don't think.
Jake:	I'm going to stick to beer.
Lucy:	Beer and sex I think. (Focus group of three boys and three girls, 15–16 years, four whites and two Hindus, school 10, 27.10.97)

The flash-points that affected the young people's attitudes towards taking risks with their health were not restricted to incidents affecting themselves directly, close friends or close relatives. The focus group discussions and interviews also revealed the impact that certain films or videos could have, specifically in relation to drug use. Powerful imagery coupled with a sense of realism caused films like *Trainspotting* and *Pulp Fiction* to be cited at times as a critical incident influencing a willingness (or otherwise) to take drugs:

Meg:	You might think you're going to get such a wonderful hit from it, but I just wouldn't want the bother. There was a documentary about somebody getting addicted to heroin and they were spitting up black vomit and it was disgusting.
Sandra:	It's a bit like *Pulp Fiction*. And you see them all injecting themselves and O.D.ing [overdosing]. It puts you off so much.

[At this point, various horrible bits of the film are recalled by a number of the group.]

Denise:	And, like, if you've seen *Trainspotting,* one of the guys in it can't use his arms any more for injecting because he's used them too much and he's got gangrene in them. So he has to use his leg and there are really vivid descriptions.
Sandra:	I'd never, ever do it.

Caroline:	It's too messy.
Meg:	My brother's got a Sex Pistols video and its got Sid and Nancy sitting in their flat and they're just like ... in such a state.
Alison:	It's not worth messing up your life is it? You know you're going to get addicted to it, plus the fact you can get AIDS from needles.
Meg:	It's just too risky.
Caroline:	Too much pain. It's not worth it. (Focus group of six girls, 15–16 years, white, school 08, 23.4.97)

Or, in similar vein:

Brian:	Films, like *Trainspotting.* Yeah. That really put me off. That bit with the baby crawling along the ceiling. It was really scary.
Interviewer:	Have you ever seen the video about Leah Betts?
All:	They showed it to us last week.
Brian:	It was good. *Trainspotting* was better though. That would put more people off doing it. The Leah Betts one was a bit clinical.

[A number of the group murmur agreement with this point.]

Michael:	No. I thought it [the Leah Betts video] was better because it was based on a real story.
Brian:	*Trainspotting* is based on real people. (Focus group of two boys and three girls, 15–16 years, white, school 04, 5.2.98)

The key things that made the videos powerful in terms of their message were, again, the vividness of the images involved and the degree to which the young people could identify with the events as part of the 'real-world' to which they belonged.

To this point, then, there are some indications that young people are encouraged to avoid health-risking behaviour where they come into contact with vivid and horrible incidents that, through their realism or through their proximity, bring home the dangers inherent in the particular activity – whether this be smoking, drinking or using other drugs.

There were, however, plenty of times when the young people drew attention to the way the impact of such critical incidents tended to be short-term. This was particularly the case when it came to the impact of incidents involving alcohol, as the following extracts illustrate:

Jimmy:	I was coming down the street and my mate was coming out of a party and like, all you could see was his swaying, and he was steaming – it must have been about 15

[drinks]. All of a sudden, he swerved off a bit ... knocked his head on the concrete post. I saw the ambulance come and I said 'What's wrong with him' and he said 'Oh, he's in a state of coma.' And he was like that for 32 days nearly. And he had his stomach pumped and everything.

Interviewer: So what impact does that have?

Jimmy: I thought to myself at the time 'Forget it. I'm never going to drink in my life.' ...

Jake: But that was in Year 10. Everybody's got a bit calmed down – and a bit older. The drinking stopped for about four or five months, and then it started back up. (Focus group of three boys and three girls, 15–16 years, four whites and two Hindus, school 10, 27.10.97)

Jake's comment on Jimmy's story qualifies the extent to which the episode can be considered to have had an influence on any willingness to take risks with health. The comment was not contested by Jimmy. It was tacitly agreed that, though the horror and the closeness of the events really did have an effect, the impact faded after four or five months.

Greg's comments in the extract below indicate a similar recognition that the impact of a critical incident may not be permanent and can fade with time. A bit like driving past the scene of a serious accident on the motorway, a new cautious approach is adopted for a while, but we generally slip back into old habits before too long:

Greg: When we were on holiday in Tenerife we were drinking on the beach. My elder brother got really drunk. He set fire to this palm tree, and then he was so drunk he couldn't move to get out of the way. I had to give him a 'fireman's lift'. We took him to the patio. He said 'Leave me alone for an hour to sleep it off.' When we came back later he still couldn't move.

[Laughter from him and the others].

Interviewer: Now, everyone's laughing, but what was that like for you?

Greg: It was frightening really. I thought he was really in danger. You can look back and laugh about it, but it wasn't very nice really.

Interviewer: So do you think it's had any impact on you. Would you try to avoid getting that drunk?

Greg: It did for a while, but not now. I probably might get drunk now. (Focus group of five boys, 15–16 years, white, school 04, 6.2.98)

The implications of this for the use of critical incidents might be quite far-reaching. It would suggest that in certain instances the vivid experience of a hazard associated with a health-risking behaviour need *not* lead to any alteration of behaviour beyond the short term. And, certainly, there was evidence from the discussions and interviews with the young people in this research that indicated precisely this:

> *Joanne:*   You know Jade – I was there when she had her stomach pumped, and … Oh God, it was terrible.
>
> *Interviewer:* Did you go to hospital with her?
>
> *Joanne:*   No, but I was there when she was drinking. And like the next day she rang everybody up and said like 'Thanks for helping us out.' And then she said to me on the phone 'I'm never going to get drunk again.' And then last night she got steaming with Johnny. (Focus group of three boys and three girls, 15–16 years, four whites and two Hindus, school 10, 27.10.97).

As this extract indicates, direct exposure to the consequences of the health risk does not automatically act as a deterrent. Neither does witnessing such events at close hand, as the comments by Krishna and Meg below illustrate:

> *Krishna:* My grandpa's dying because he's been smoking all his life. He's just had a bypass operation. And my other granddad died of cancer. So I'm, like, 'What the hell am I doing, I'm stupid.' And my dad quit smoking. He used to be on like 40 a day and he quit. I'm stupid smoking – but at the end of the day, I just can't help it. (Focus group of three boys and three girls, 15–16 years, four whites and two Hindus, school 10, 27.10.97)
>
> *Meg:*   I smoke, and my granddad had eight heart attacks off smoking. And that should really teach me a lesson, but it's something that I enjoy – it's sociable, it goes well with a pint and I enjoy it. I like it. (Focus group of six girls, 15–16 years, white, school 08, 23.4.97)

So, the young people did not always 'learn' from the experience of what should be a critical incident in their lives – close contact with the nasty outcome of a health risk. Of this they were quite aware. Indeed, many were able and willing to reflect on the contradiction between their health-risking behaviour and the situations they had witnessed close to hand. They drew on a repertoire of motives and explanations familiar to adults, principal among which was the idea that, even while recognizing that things like smoking increased the likelihood of contracting cancer or heart disease, whether or not any individual was actually smitten by the nasty outcome (e.g. cancer) still depended to some degree on (bad) luck. The young people invoked a spirit of fatalism to justify the dissonance between what their critical incident experience ought to have taught them, and the behaviours they actually engaged in:

Joanne: You can say that like, but my grandma she'd been smoking all her life, from when she was about 15 and she's now 56 and she's been smoking all her life and she's all right. She walks to work and back, she walks everywhere.

Lucy: Another thing. You're going to die of something anyway ... so if you enjoy it ... I mean, yeah, it's not advisable.

Jake: You are putting your life at risk ... you are doing something. But, I mean, you could die any time. You could be run over by a car or something.

Lucy: You could be run over tonight. (Focus group of three boys and three girls, 15–16 years, four whites and two Hindus, school 10, 27.10.97)

Furthermore, even where there was a negative attitude towards taking health risks, it emerged that the critical incidents might not actually play a key role. The incidents, in this respect, could serve to reinforce opinions and behaviour rather than change them:

Sameena: My cousin's brother, he took a lot of drugs and all that. And he had an accident because he got into a fight and he got stabbed. And he went to the hospital but he couldn't be helped because of what the drugs had damaged in his body. Mostly it was his brain that was affected. And he was a really close cousin, and he died. Actually, the whole family got really upset by that. It's the sort of thing that makes you think before doing anything.

Interviewer: Has it made you particularly anti all sorts of drugs then?

Sameena: No, I was anti drugs before, but this has made me even stronger. So if anybody else was doing it, I could actually give them an example – 'Look what happened to him'. (Focus group of two girls and four boys, 15–16 years, two Hindus and four Muslims, school 01, 18.11.97)

The reaction to critical incidents, then, is not uniform. As the extracts above indicate, the response to them was not dictated by the nature of the event itself so much as the disposition that the young people brought to it, for instance their existing attitudes. One girl emphasized this point in her account of her reaction to a suicide attempt she had made. For her, the brush with death had not persuaded her of the virtues of safe living, but had caused her to take more risks and 'live life to the full':

Sandra: Well I respect your views but I'm just saying that, what with me being so near to death once in my life, it's made me think that you've got to get out there and have as good a time as you can. I'm enjoying myself now. Before I wasn't and now I'm having a wicked time.

Meg:	I mean, tomorrow you could get run over by a school bus.
Sandra:	I just think you should go out and do what you want, and get drunk if you want.
Interviewer:	Could you tell us a bit more about the incident you just mentioned to us?
Sandra:	Sure, yeah. Well, everybody knows about it. I took an overdose of 25 paracetamol just before Christmas. And I got to hospital and the doctor said that he couldn't pump my stomach because I was too far gone and if I'd got in there three quarters of an hour later I would have died. And they still weren't sure if they could save me or not – but they did. Yeah, it was pretty bad.
Interviewer:	Has being in such danger altered your perspective on life?
Sandra:	It has a lot.
Interviewer:	Could you describe that a bit?
Sandra:	It made me more easy going. Like, before I was like 'Oh no, I can't go into pubs.' And now I go out and have a laugh with my mates and stuff because I think you should enjoy life more if you have got it.
Meg:	Live for the day.
Sandra:	Yeah, I agree with you totally. Now I'm really easy going.
Alison:	Don't you think that living for the present is a bit dangerous – when you're going to be up half the night after the moment, as it were, throwing up all over the place?
Meg:	I've found out if I drink beer, I'm going to be sick.
Sandra:	Yeah. If I drink cider, if I drink spirits, I'm going to be sick.
Interviewer:	It's interesting the way your experience affected you, Sandra. For some people, you might expect it to make them more cautious – to avoid danger …
Sandra:	… yeah, it's weird, but I just think like that now I just want to go out and have fun whilst I can. (Focus group of six girls, 15–16 years, white, school 08, 23.4.97)

The social construction of critical incidents

The discussions and interviews serve as a warning against treating health-related critical incidents as having some direct, automatic deterrent effect in relation to risk-taking behaviour. As we have seen, the young people recognized the impact as:

- sometimes being small,
- sometimes being short-term,
- sometimes serving to reinforce attitudes already held,
- even possibly having the effect of encouraging increases in risk-taking behaviour.

From the questionnaire survey part of the research it was evident that the experience of what would appear, on the surface at least, to be a health-related critical incident did not always result in a perceived change of attitude towards taking risks with health. It was found that only 42 per cent of those who had been hospitalized at some point since the age of 10 due to some injury or illness felt that such an experience had affected their attitude to health risks. And, among those with a medical condition affecting their well-being, the proportion was even less (35.8 per cent). Of those reporting a serious accident to a member of the family, just under 50 per cent felt that such an event had influenced their attitudes. And, again, around half of those who reported a serious health-related incident involving a close friend felt that such an event had affected their willingness to take risks with their health.

Ostensibly similar incidents, then, could affect some young people but not others in terms of their attitudes to health and their willingness to take risks with their health. For one half the experience of such an incident was perceived as a flash-point leading to change; for the other half such an incident was not perceived as leading to change.

This carries four important implications for the use of critical incidents as an explanation of learning in relation to personal health, and in terms of its potential value as a vehicle for getting health education messages across to a teenage audience. First, it alerts us to the danger of identifying critical incidents on the basis of objective criteria, to the exclusion of the way the happenings are *interpreted* by those involved. If events that are objectively similar, such as 'the death of a close relative' or 'the personal experience of being hospitalized since the age of 10 because of a serious accident or illness', can have different repercussions for different young people it is because the events carry different meanings for them. So, the focus of attention when dealing with critical incidents needs to include not just the occurrence of specific events but the significance that those happenings have *from the point of view of the young people themselves.*[3]

The second implication, following from this, is that critical incidents in the lives of young people need to be understood in the context of their own health agenda. To focus on critical incidents simply as happenings whose objective features would appear to confront a person with the physical dangers connected with a particular behaviour is to restrict the vision to a medical agenda. A medical agenda would suggest that, having witnessed the horrific consequences of smoking, drinking and drug abuse, young persons should react 'rationally' by doing all they can to protect their health and preserve their lives as long as possible. But this places the protection of health and the pursuit of longevity as top priorities. Now, while this might be true for some of the young people some of the time it is only one part of the whole picture, and needs to be taken in conjunction with other priorities in their lives. Emerging evidence, indeed, points quite strongly to the fact that young people are capable and willing, on occasion, of placing physical appearance above physical health in their sense of priorities. The desire to stay thin can lead young women to smoke even though they acknowledge the likely longer-term risk they are taking with their health. Likewise, the social spin-offs from alcohol, smoking and soft drug use are frequently seen as justifying the longer-term risks to health. It is not the purpose of the current discussion to examine these views in detail; the point is to note the need to include them in any use of critical incidents in relation to health-related behaviour.

The third implication is that the 'critical' nature of the incident for learning is not so much a product of what actually happened as a product of what was *perceived* to have happened and the *meaning* that is attributed in retrospect to such perceived events. As Tripp has noted:

> Critical incidents are not 'things' which exist independently of an observer and are awaiting discovery like gold nuggets or desert islands, but like all data critical incidents are created. Incidents happen, but critical incidents are produced by the way we look at a situation: a critical incident is an interpretation of the significance of an event.
>
> (Tripp, 1993, p. 8)

Finally, if we concede that critical incidents only become critical to the extent that they are perceived as such in retrospect by those involved in the event, we also need to acknowledge that the identification of those features of an incident that mark it out as something special and as 'critical' becomes the province of the respondent in the research rather than of the researcher. The respondent's perspective becomes the crucial factor in deciding what facets of the incident are important and why, not the expert's.[4]

Conclusion

The original conception of critical incidents employed in this research was one deduced from theory and based on previously published research. It seemed reasonable on the basis of the available expert knowledge in the area to regard personal experiences of vivid and severe threats to health as likely flash-points in the learning process concerned with risk-taking behaviour. And there was, indeed, some evidence from the research to support the proposition that health-related critical incidents in the lives of young people could serve to change attitudes towards taking risks with health. As the comments of the young people suggested, the impact of critical incidents reflected the way the incidents were (a) real-world happenings, (b) vivid and memorable and (c) based on personal experience.

However, the evidence coming from the young people equally draws our attention to the limitations inherent in relying exclusively on expert opinion and in treating such incidents as objectively defined moments in the lives of young people. The voices of the young people – those who take the risks or avoid the risks – remind us of the research approach influenced so strongly by Peter Woods during the 1970s, 1980s and 1990s: the need to respect the views of those being studied, to take them seriously and to recognize that their priorities may not accord with official theories.

At a substantial level, the research suggests that the limited success of health education in persuading young people to avoid risk-taking activities might be explained, in part at least, by the degree to which young people do not share the medical agenda that lies behind most health education. Progress in this field, therefore, demands that research focuses on the way young people themselves perceive their lives and the role of their health within it. It is vital that the focus of research turns away from the expert's view, from the medical view, to focus as well on the perspective of the young people themselves. Critical incidents, if their full value is to be realized within health education, need to be placed within the context of the lives of young people, their personal biographies, and the social circumstances influencing their lives.

Notes

1 The research reported here is drawn from the ESRC-funded research project Critical Incidents and Risk-Taking Behaviour Among Schoolchildren (R000 22 1802). Nicky Drucquer was the research officer on this project.

2 The notion of 'critical incidents' and its application to training and learning can be traced back to its use by people like Flanagan (1954) and Herzberg, Mausner and Snyderman (1959). A fuller account of the origins of the critical incident technique and the assumptions underlying its use can be found in Denscombe (1998).

3 This contrasts with some early uses of critical incidents, which preferred to treat critical incidents as objectively verifiable occurrences. Underlying the work of Flanagan and his colleagues, for instance, was a fundamental belief that critical incidents were 'objectively knowable': 'To be critical, an incident must occur in a situation where the purpose or intent of the act seems fairly clear to the observer and where its consequences are sufficiently definite to leave little doubt concerning its effect' (Flanagan, 1954, p. 327). Confusion, disagreement, uncertainty and differing interpretations of occurrences do not sit comfortably with such an approach.

4 Here, again, there is a contrast with some classic uses of critical incidents, which were essentially 'expert orientated'. As Flanagan (1954, p. 355), for example, asserts, 'Reporting should be limited to those behaviors which, according to competent observers, make a significant contribution to the activity.' In this approach, the identification of episodes that could be identified as 'critical' incidents, their significance for the task at hand, and the nature of what was revealed by the incident were all drawn from 'those in the best positions to make the necessary observations and evaluations' – which meant in effect the professionals, the researchers, the experts.

References

Balding, J. (1993) *Young People in 1992*, Schools Health Education Unit, Exeter: University of Exeter.

Combs, B. and Slovic, P. (1979) 'Causes of death: biased newspaper coverage and biased judgments', *Journalism Quarterly*, 56, pp. 837–43.

Denscombe, M. (1993) 'Personal health and the social psychology of risk taking', *Health Education Research*, 8, 4, pp. 505–17.

Denscombe, M. (1998) 'Risk-taking and personal health: the role of critical incidents', Paper given to the Association for Public Health: 6th Annual Forum, 'Working Together For Public Health', University of Lancaster, March.

Douglas, M. (1986) *Risk Acceptability According to the Social Sciences*, London: Routledge.

Elkind, D. (1967) 'Egocentrism in adolescence', *Child Development*, 30, pp. 1025–34.

Flanagan, J. (1954) 'The critical incident technique', *Psychological Bulletin*, 51, 4, pp. 327–58.

Furlong, A. and Cartmel, F. (1997) *Young People and Social Change: Individualization and Risk in Late Modernity*, Buckingham: Open University Press.

Herzberg, R, Mausner, B. and Snyderman, B. (1959) *The Motivation to Work*, New York: Wiley.

Jack, M. S. (1989) 'Personal fable: a potential explanation for risk-taking behavior in adolescents', *Journal of Paediatric Nursing*, 4, 5, pp. 334–8.

Johnson, B. and Covello, V. (eds) (1987) *The Social and Cultural Construction of Risk*, Dordrecht: Reidel.

Kahneman, D., Slovic, P. and Tversky, A. (eds) (1982) *Judgment Under Uncertainty: Heuristics and Biases*, New York: Cambridge University Press.

Lloyd, B. and Lucas, K. (1998) *Smoking in Adolescence*, London: Routledge.

Lynagh, M., Schofield, M. J. and Sanson-Fisher, R. W. (1997) 'School health promotion programs over the past decade: a review of the smoking, alcohol and solar protection literature', *Health Promotion International*, 12, 1, pp. 43–60.

May, C. (1991) 'Research on alcohol education for young people: a critical review of the literature', *Health Education Journal*, 50, 4, pp. 195–9.

Measham, F., Newcombe, R. and Parker, H. (1994) 'The normalisation of recreational drug use amongst young people in north-west England', *British Journal of Sociology*, 45, pp. 287–312.

Plant, M. A. and Plant, M. (1992) *Risk Takers. Alcohol, Drugs, Sex and Youth*, London: Routledge.

Sikes, P., Measor, L. and Woods, P. (1985) *Teacher Careers: Crises and Continuities*, Lewes: Falmer Press.

Slovic, P., Fischoff, B. and Lichtenstein, S. (1980) 'Facts and fears: understanding perceived risk', in Schwing, R. and Albers, W. (eds) *Societal Risk Assessment*, New York: Plenum Press, pp. 187–215.

Slovic. P., Fischoff, B. and Lichtenstein, S. (1981) 'Perceived risk: psychological factors and social implications', *Proceedings of the Royal Society of London*, A376, pp. 17–34.

Thaler, R. H. (1983) 'Illusions and mirages in public policy', *Public Interest*, 73, pp. 60–74.

Tones, K. (1993) 'Changing theory and practice: trends in methods, strategies and settings in health education', *Health Education Journal*, 52, 3 (Autumn), pp. 125–39.

Tripp, D. (1993) *Critical Incidents in Teaching*, London: Routledge.

White, D. and Pitts, M. (1997) *Health Promotion with Young People for the Prevention of Substance Misuse*, London: Health Education Authority.

Woods, P. (1993) *Critical Events in Teaching and Learning*, London: Falmer Press.

Chapter 15

Interrogating the discourse of home–school relations: the case of 'parents' evenings'

Maggie MacLure, with Barbara Walker

Preamble

Parents' evenings are familiar events in the secondary school calendar. On their allotted evening, the parents of students in a particular year-group are invited to school for a series of brief consultations with their children's teachers. This chapter takes a look at parents' evenings and, in particular, at the parent–teacher consultations themselves. It draws on a study of five schools jointly carried out with Barbara Walker.[1]

As well as being worthy of study in their own right, parent–teacher consultations are also of interest as concrete manifestations of 'home–school relations' – that 'important and pervasive abstraction', as Baker and Keogh (1995: 265) call it. As these authors point out, the notion of home–school relations is invested with enormous educational significance and political aspiration, but very little attention has been paid to how these relations actually play out in practice. Towards the end of the chapter, I consider how an understanding of parent–teacher

Taken from: MacLure, M., *Discourse in Educational and Social Research*, (Buckingham: Open University Press, 2003), pp. 48–69.

consultations might connect with the 'bigger' policy and public discourses that surround the notion of home–school relations.

The main focus in this chapter is on *spoken* discourse. The orientation is strongly influenced by the approach known as conversation analysis, itself an off-shoot of ethnomethodology. Conversation analysis, notable for its extremely fine-grained analysis of transcriptions of speech, is concerned with the ways in which speakers produce order, meaning and coherence in and through their interactions. The chapter is especially influenced by the studies of 'institutional talk' that have emerged as a major strand of conversational analysts' work in recent years (e.g. Drew and Heritage, 1992). Through their close attention to the details of interaction in settings such as courtrooms, surgeries, boardrooms and newsrooms, conversation analysts have illuminated the ways in which participants 'talk an institution into being' (Heritage, 1984: 290).

Parent–teacher consultations are doubly interesting, perhaps because the participants are generally talking not one but *two* institutions into being. Or trying to. These are 'threshold' events – encounters that construct a brief 'opening' between those two institutions that loom large in children's lives: the family and the school. As we will see below, this partly accounts for the tensions that people often report, since the two institutions do not necessarily carry the same definitions of expertise, responsibility and moral conduct. For instance, parent and teacher may find themselves at odds over what is in the student's 'best interests', who has the right to decide on this, and who is to blame if those interests are seen not to be served.

Parents' evenings are very much concerned with identity, with the making of *subjects*. As Jayne Keogh (1992) found in her study, the participants in these brief encounters are intensely preoccupied with establishing and defending their identities as 'good' parents, teachers and students. Definitions of what it means to be a teacher, a parent, a learner, an adolescent, a son, a daughter, an expert, are tacitly invoked in these consultations. As we shall see below, the participants hold one another accountable for conducting themselves 'properly' in these various personae.

Parents' evenings are suffused with *power,* therefore, in Foucault's sense of a mechanism that works in and through institutions to produce particular kinds of subjects, knowledge and truth (e.g. Foucault, 1979, 1980). For Foucault, power is not a force wielded by one group or sovereign figure against others, but a more sinuous and insinuating mechanism that works its way in a 'capillary' fashion into the 'very grain' of individuals, inhabiting their bodies, their beliefs and their self-hood, and binding them together as institutional subjects (Foucault, 1980: 39). Power, in this sense, is both coercive and enabling. It is not imposed from 'outside' or 'above', but circulates within institutions and social bodies, producing subjects who exert a 'mutual "hold"' on one another. Foucault called it, memorably, 'a mutual and indefinite "blackmail"', which binds superiors and subordinates in 'a relationship of mutual support and conditioning' (p. 159). The consultations described below offer telling examples of this kind of power at work in the interactions of parents and teachers.

The overall organization of parents' evenings

Parents' evenings are typically rather fraught and noisy affairs. Teachers sit at small tables set out around the school hall or other spaces, seeing a long succession of parents for pre-arranged, five-minute consultations. Queues form as appointments back up. Parents mill around looking for their next teacher. Students are not always expected or invited to attend; and those who do turn up may find there is no seat at the table for them (see Walker 1998). One commentator described these events as 'a cross between a social security office, a doctor's surgery and King's Cross station' (Nias 1981). Another ranked them 'close to a visit to the dentist in terms of discomfiture' (B. Limerick, quoted in Baker and Keogh, 1995: 264).

The comparison with consultations in other professions such as medicine, dentistry and social services is apt, since there are contextual similarities. The 'professionals' (here, the teachers) control the location, scheduling, duration and general agenda of each encounter; and they have access to specialist knowledge or resources that are not available to 'the clients'.[2] The talk tends to be 'asymmetrical' in terms of its organization and structure; that is, the 'expert' participant exerts more control over the direction and content of the talk than the other(s) (see, for example, ten Have, 1991; Drew and Heritage, 1992).[3] Institutional talk exhibits such 'standard patterns', according to Drew and Heritage, partly because of the inevitable routinization involved in repeated professional encounters. However, they also note that this is perhaps one of the most poignant sources of interactional 'asymmetry', since what is routine for the professional is emphatically not so for the 'client' (Drew and Heritage, 1992: 50–1).

The absent student

But parents' evenings also have features that make them rather different from other professional–client encounters. For a start, they are *three-cornered* interactions involving parent(s), teacher and student. This is no less the case in those consultations where the student is absent (about half in the study we conducted). Indeed, there is a powerful paradox concerning the presence or absence of students, which produces byzantine complexities of power, blame and accountability in these encounters. Common sense might predict that students would have more of a 'voice' in discussions of their schooling if they were allowed to attend the consultations. But our study found that this made very little difference to their power to intervene. In terms of active participation, students were effectively absent even when they were physically present. On the other hand, the (absent) student is the person around whom the whole dynamic of the consultation revolves. It is not just that the discussion is 'about' the student, but also that he or she is the figure that sets justification, gratification, blame and self-regard in motion. The reputations of teacher and parent are intimately tied to that of the student as this is elaborated during the consultation itself, and they fluctuate according to whose 'version' of the student prevails, as we shall see below. You could say that the figure of the student haunts the consultation, to a point where even those students who are physically present are rather ghostly apparitions – animating the interaction between parent and teacher, yet unable to make a direct impact upon it, and obliged to wait and see what the others 'make' of them.

Parent–teacher consultations are always 'triangular' therefore, even when only two people face one another across the table in the school hall, and this distinguishes them in some respects from professional–client encounters in other settings.[4] Another critical difference relates to the contested status of *expertise* in these educational consultations. Because the main concern is with the student's behaviour and disposition – including, crucially, what he or she does *at home* – the teacher's status as the 'expert' in these encounters is always potentially challengeable by counter-claims from parents to the effect that they know their child better. So the maintenance and management of expertise is an ever-present issue for the participants.

The organization of parent–teacher consultations

Let us now turn to some of the details of the consultations, as found in the study conducted with Barbara Walker. The consultations were strikingly similar across different schools and participants, in terms of their turn-taking patterns and episodic structure. Most of them began, after brief greetings and preambles, with an unbroken stretch of talk from the teacher, which we termed the *diagnosis,* during which the teacher would report on the student's current state of academic 'health' – her achievements, difficulties or progress – and often on her personal qualities and behaviour (enthusiastic, chatty, lively, quiet, etc.). The diagnosis was usually followed by a *dialogic* episode involving alternating turns by teacher and parent(s), devoted to the pursuit of issues arising from the diagnosis or from additional concerns raised by parents. The consultation ended with a *closing* episode. Students, if present, usually said very little, beyond responding when addressed directly.[5]

In terms of turn-taking patterns, the dominant form of the consultations can be thought of as a tadpole: the (largely uninterrupted) teacher diagnosis forming the head and the string of alternating turns of the dialogue and closing sequence as the tail. The length of the 'tail' varied considerably, from a few desultory turns followed by thanks and farewells, as in the example below, to extended and occasionally heated interchanges lasting up to ten minutes. The dominant episodic structure looked like this:

1 **PREAMBLE**   [greetings; orientations: finding coursework, etc.]
2 **DIAGNOSIS**   [teacher talking; parent(s) acknowledging]
3 **DIALOGUE**   [alternating turns]
4 **CLOSING**   [thanks; farewells, etc.]

The following is an example ['T' = Teacher, 'M' = Mother, 'S' = Student; '__' (underlining) = overlapping turns]

Example 1

T   Right, very good. Annabel, you are doing well. You're working hard and I'm thrilled to bits with your work, your notebook's good, and erm you ask good questions, you try to answer the questions, you've passed both tests. You got 66% for the first test, which was to do with the plant nutrition, you know, with all the ecology, all of that early work, yeah? And the respiration test you got 56%, you went down a bit, but it's a harder test, you know, the marks generally are harder on that, are lower on that one, because it's a harder test. Erm, I think that you're learning a lot of science. I'm happy with the way you're working. I think your notebook is good, and you do seem to understand what's going on, most of the time. I can only say you could improve on one thing and that is don't get sucked into the other group of too much gossip. Yeah? And I think I've done something about that, 'cause I've done some splitting up [M laughs] – all to help

M   Good

DIAGNOSIS
[*T addresses diagnosis to S*]

T   But you're a great girl and I'm very impressed

[*Summarizing: bringing diagnosis episode to a close*]

M   – Oh that's good, I'm really pleased, well, erm … the GCSEs with science [T: Yes], they obviously have to take science?

[*M acknowledging 'juncture'*]

DIALOGUE

[*M 'opens up' the dialogue*]

T   Yeah

S   – <u>double science</u>

M   double science

S   Is there double science?

T   Double science, yes, that's what we would … you would do, double GCSE science. So you get ten hours a fortnight next year, OK? That will be covering elements of physics, chemistry and biology, so you'd do double science, it would count as double. Two out of ten. <u>Is that all right?</u>

M   <u>That's fine</u>, I'm very pleased

[*signalling closure*]

CLOSINGS

T   Is there anything else you wanted to ask?

M   No, not really, I'm quite happy

T   Well you could double her pocket money on the basis of science

M   [laughs] Well I won't tell her dad then! Well that's lovely, yes, thank you very much. I'm very pleased

T   OK, we are, I am as well

M   Oh good

T   Mr Cheshire as well [other science teacher]

M   Lovely

T   Keep it up

M   Thanks very much

T   OK?

M   Thank you

T   Bye now, nice to meet you as well

S   Thank you

T   Bye Annabel

S   Bye

This is one of the briefer consultations, but it is characteristic in its outline structure. It exemplifies the 'tadpole' shape, with a monologue from the teacher, followed by a 'tail' of alternating turns initiated by the teacher, who 'hands over the floor' to the parent with a summary comment. The student, Annabel, takes very little part in the proceedings. Note that, even though the teacher addresses his remarks to her (which happened relatively rarely), it is her *mother* who responds.

'Membership categorization': sketches of identity

The opening diagnosis sets some crucial parameters for the rest of the consultation. Most importantly, it starts to elaborate who the participants 'are', and what sort of behaviour and responsibilities are expected of them. Carolyn Baker, who found virtually identical monologues in her study in Queensland, Australia, describes their 'categorization work' in these terms:

> [The teacher's opening statement] can be treated as an initial sketch, a proposal, for who the participants relevantly are in this interactional event [...] what they do and should do [...] and how these categories and activities (should) connect. It is an initial map of the social and moral terrain in which a representative of the school meets representatives of the home as idealised courses of action.
>
> (Baker 2000: 107–8)

The teacher's diagnosis in our example above assembles the three participants in their capacities as teacher, parent and student, and offers proposals as to what sorts of things people belonging to those identity categories (should) do. This particular account proposes that teachers know their subject, teach lessons according to a structured syllabus ('all the ecology, all that early work'), set coursework, administer tests, know the nature of the demands these make on students, and monitor students' learning using such sources of information. They know each individual student; they can tell whether or not he or she is understanding the lessons; and they are alert to the dynamics of their peer groups. They expect students to work hard, try to answer teachers' questions, present their work clearly, get good test scores, follow 'what's going on', and listen to the teacher rather than talking to classmates. They experience pleasure when students meet those expectations. They have a sense of humour. Parents, in so far as they assent to these proposals (which this parent implicitly, and at times explicitly, does), are the sort of people who share the teacher's goals and aspirations for the student, and who recognize their daughter or son in the teacher's description. And so on.

This list probably seems both banal, as a description of a teacher's activities (nothing new there) and inflated, as an interpretation of the identity work initiated by the teacher's diagnosis (all that from so few words?). But ethnomethodologists, on whose work Baker draws, suggest that this kind of 'membership categorization analysis' is routinely done by people in order to assign one another to relevant identity categories (mother, wife, teacher, daughter, etc.), and to hold one another accountable for 'proper', moral conduct within those categories (see Jayyusi 1984). People do not simply 'belong' to these various categories; rather, belonging is 'made to happen' in and through the talk. And it is done anew each time people speak or write. It is not the case that you simply 'are' a teacher, a mother or a student. You have to 'bring off' each particular identity as a practical accomplishment, repeatedly, every time afresh.

As already noted, this identity work always has a *moral* dimension. Claiming a particular identity brings obligations to (be seen to) act in consensually 'appropriate' ways. Part of the accomplishment of 'being' a teacher (however minor a part) is precisely the ability to carry off a parent–teacher consultation. Suppose that, instead of using test scores or coursework to represent a student's attainments, you reported intimations gleaned during a seance, or brought along a picture you had painted? You could have trouble being accepted as a bona fide teacher. Questions might be raised about your sanity, or at least your qualifications. There are numerous other, more subtle ways in which participants can court failure 'as' parents or teachers in these consultations, and these are explored below. For the moment, note that the opening episodes are highly significant as markers of what will count as relevant information and activities for the participants. It scarcely needs pointing out that the agenda is emphatically that of the school rather than the home at this point in the proceedings.

'Asymmetries' of power and status

Parents' silence during the opening episode mirrors the 'remarkable passivity' noted by Heath (1992) in patients' responses to diagnoses in general practice consultations. Heath noted that patients did not respond to doctors' diagnoses as 'newsworthy' – that is, with 'news receipts' of the kind identified by conversation analysts, such as 'Oh' or 'Really', or follow-up assessments. He argued that minimal responses are characteristic of responses to 'expert' talk. So the expert status of one of the participants is *jointly* established through the interactional contributions of both or all parties.[6]

Parents' passivity may seem surprising, given that the consultations concern a person whom parents might claim to know better than the teacher. Indeed, parents often did challenge teachers on the implicit grounds of 'privileged' knowledge of the student, but not usually until later in the interaction. This is perhaps because these opening sequences firmly locate the teacher's knowledge of the student in domains to which the parent does not have direct access – test scores, reading ages, exam predictions. Parents are encouraged to defer to teachers' superior knowledge of their own child in matters of schooling, and to wait until they are invited (at the closing of the diagnosis episode) to take a more active part in the interaction.

These features might seem to confirm a view of parents' evenings as events over which, 'like a server in tennis, the teacher still has the advantage' (Macbeth 1989). Teachers claim, and are granted, the right to speak first, and at some length, to control the topic and the release of specialist information and to sum up what the diagnosis 'means'. Parents and students are positioned as passive recipients of expert information and advice (which, moreover, may be 'pre-packaged' to an extent).[7] These are typical features of 'institutional talk'. This is not to say that parents were powerless in these interactions. Parents could, and did, challenge teachers' judgements or practice. However, it could be argued that even their resistance is constrained by the terms of engagement offered and accepted in the consultations and, more generally, by normative assumptions about the nature of institutional talk. It is important to recognize, all the same, that the 'asymmetries' in these interactions, as in institutional talk in general, are *collaboratively produced.* Parents cooperate, by and large, in assuming the conversational role of 'client' or layperson offered by teachers.

Opening up a space for dialogue: the entry of the parental 'voice'

Teachers usually brought their opening statements to an end with some kind of summary statement which marked a conversational 'juncture' – that is, a point at which topic shifts and even possible 'closings' were up for negotiation. Closing junctures are places where speakers indicate to one another that the topic in hand is 'understood to be either exhausted, concluded or suspended' (Button 1991: 260). Speakers do this in several ways; for instance, by providing a summary of the 'gist' of the talk or by doing a series of mutual agreements about what has been discussed. You can see a summary statement in the example above ('But you're a great girl and I'm very impressed').

Parents almost always took the option of continuing the dialogue at this point rather than allowing it to close down completely, no matter how positive the teacher's diagnosis. Annabel's mother, for instance, in the example above, asked a question about double science. The following examples show similar 'junctures' where a teacher's summary statement is first endorsed by the parent(s) and then followed by a question which inaugurates a new topic:

Example 2

T   – and I'm quite pleased with the way that Martin is working
M   Oh that's good
T   I really can't say much more than that

M→   I was a bit worried, although I wanted him in the middle group, I
       was a bit worried that he might have trouble keeping up

Example 3

T   But on the whole he's working, you know, pretty well –
M   – good
T   – coping very well with all the work
M→   How do you find his spelling, 'cause that's quite a weak point
       with him?

Example 4

T   So you know, it's all good news
M→   Great, he doesn't find it hard-going or anything?

Since conversational junctures can be heard as offers to bring the conversation to a close, the onus is on the parents to keep them 'open' past this first juncture.[8] As noted, most parents in our study took this option, however positive the report. Indeed, there seemed to be a certain resistance to unmitigated 'good news' diagnoses. Most parents want to hear nice things about their child; but good news stories can be problematic. They may insinuate that the teacher has not given her full attention to the student, especially if they lack detail. This possibility seems to be tacitly acknowledged by this teacher, who jokingly offers to 'make up' some problems [see also example (2) above]:

Example 5

T   … I mean, really, on the whole, erm, I think she's doing well, no
       problems at all
M   None at all?
T   No
M   Keeping up with her work?
T→   I mean I could find some if you want me to try, I'll make some up
M   No, no, no, no, if –
T   – honestly, she's really, you know, I'm quite happy with the work
       she's doing
M   Brilliant!
T   Good

Teachers may find themselves in something of a 'double bind', therefore, in trying to meet parents' expectations – obliged *both* to deliver good news *and* to display a 'proper' degree of engagement with the specific needs and abilities of this particular student. A further problem with good news stories is that they deny parents the chance to fulfil one of the main symbolic purposes of these encounters – namely, offering 'moral versions of themselves' as concerned parents (Baker and Keogh 1995: 263). They also offer little in the way of specific, practical things for parents to *do* by way of further supporting their child. In short, parents may need to *open up a space* within the consultation process, in which they are able to demonstrate their knowledge of such matters as their child's previous attainments, home-working habits, subject preferences, and so on, and thus display their active support for the school's work.[9] Issues of identity and accountability are thus intimately bound up in the fine details of the structure of these interactions.

Resisting and securing closure

There is a kind of *inertia* in these consultations, therefore – a tendency towards closure from the point where the teacher indicates that she has finished her diagnosis. From that point onwards, the possibility of closure hovers over the talk, and the onus of deferring it generally rests with the parent(s). It was clear that keeping the dialogic space open was often something of a struggle for parents, not just at the first juncture, but also at later points, when teachers again offered to bring the consultation to a close via summary statements and other 'pre-closing' turns. It was not uncommon to find a series of junctures in a consultation at which a parent deflected offers of closure by asking another question or pursuing the existing topic. Equally, it was not uncommon to find some *resistance* by teachers to these attempts to keep the dialogue open. A closer look at an example may help to explain why negotiations over closure can be tricky for teachers as well as parents (beyond the obvious reason that teachers must keep a tight rein on the length of consultations if they are to keep on schedule). Let us look, for instance, at how the dialogue that was initiated in example (2) above continued.

Example 6

[Student present, but silent throughout]

T	(concluding his diagnosis) … and I'm quite pleased with the way Martin is working	**Proposed closing #1** [*closing summary*]
M	Oh that's good	
T	I really can't say much more than that	[*overt closure*]
M	I was a bit worried, although I wanted him in the middle group, I was a bit worried that he might have trouble keeping up	**Reopening #1**
T	Well, I mean [inaudible] … fairly good effort. Mrs X, who is Head of English, has looked at the files recently – [M: Yes] – and really he's,	

he is a little bit quiet in class and
maybe he doesn't fully sometimes –
sort of things like he's not sure
what he's doing, but he really is
getting in there with the work and
<u>getting it done</u> –

Proposed closing #2
[*Closing Summary*]
Reopening #2

M   – <u>does he</u> ask if he's not sure?
T   (hesitantly) Not as much as he
ought to, I'm sort of aware that he
doesn't, so I tend to check that he –
[M: – yeah] – he hasn't shown
any problems, everything has been
done, he's coped with everything –
M   – yes
T   – so, I mean he's doing well

Proposed closing #3
[*reiterated summary*]
Reopening #3

M   He takes so long, I'm not just saying
English, but he takes a long time
over his homework, so I didn't know
whether he was sort of keeping up
the pace in class, he sits there, but
then there's five children at home –
T   – oh right
M   – and whether he's distracted or not
T   No, he does well, he really is doing a
good job, he's working . . . he's not a
fast worker –
M   – <u>no</u>
T   <u>but</u> he's working and I mean the
thing is, he's working along, he's
trying, he's getting neat working, it's
completed correctly, and the time
he's spending on it has proved he's
actually looking at the errors and
making sure he's not making them

[*T and M beginning
to negotiate closing
via agreements and
overlapping speech
from about here on*]

M   Yes
T   So, in fact, it's working to his benefit,
instead of rushing it – [M: Yes] –
which a lot, some, <u>lots of children</u> –
M   <u>want to get it over with</u>
T   <u>– get it</u> over and done with, he's
consistently trying to make sure it
looks good
M   Yeah
T   And I'm pleased with the way he's
working

Proposed closing #4

M   Oh that's good

T   Yeah, no, he's doing a good job
M   Oh that's good
T   Don't forget if you're not sure of
    something ask me [to S]. That's
    important [M laughs], I won't bite
    your head off [laughs] OK?   [*finalizing closure*]
M   It's just, it's confidence, I think with   **Reopening #4**
    youngsters anyway, especially with
    special needs, there's so many
    different teachers aren't there?
T   mmm [inaudible]. But no, he's doing   **Proposed closing #5**
    nice – doing well
M   Oh that's good   [*accepted*]
T   I'm pleased
M   Very good then
T   Right?
M   Yes?
T   Good lad! Keep it up
M   All right, thank you for seeing us
T   That's all right. Ni ... b'bye
M   B'bye

The teacher proposes closure five times in this example, each time via a summary of his opening diagnosis, the 'gist' of which is that Martin is doing well. His mother averts the closure four times. Her re-openings represent a challenge to the teacher's version of Martin's progress, setting in motion a series of justifications by the teacher, and something of a tussle over whether Martin is or is not 'keeping up'.

Refusals of closure always carry the potential to be heard as challenges, however courteously and tentatively framed, because they indicate, at the very least, that the teacher's account up to that point is *not* complete and self-sufficient. They also signal a subtle shift in the interactional dynamics, since it is the parent who is now taking the initiative in prolonging the talk. Moreover, they usually take this initiative in order to raise some concern about their child, and there is always the risk that concern about the child will trigger concern about the *teacher* and his or her competence. The teacher, in the example above, appears to be alert to this possibility. When Martin's mother expresses her worry about whether her son has been 'keeping up', the teacher's response is justificatory. He cites the agreement of his head of department. He also partially acknowledges Martin's mother's concerns by describing some aspects of Martin's demeanour in class that *could* lead one to conclude that he was not keeping up ('a little bit quiet in class ... not sure what he's doing') but dismisses these as not significantly changing the overall positive message. Note that this partial acknowledgement of the mother's point also allows the teacher to demonstrate further his knowledge of Martin.

Martin's mother picks up on an aspect of the teacher's justification in order to reopen a second time: 'Does he ask if he's not sure?' At this point the spectre of blame, which hovers over *any* mention of students' difficulties in these consultations, becomes more overt. For if Martin is 'not sure', or if he does not ask for help, whose 'fault' is it? The teacher locates the fault with Martin ('Not as much as he ought to') and describes the steps he takes to compensate for this, testifying once more to his alertness to Martin's needs in the classroom ('I'm sort of aware that he doesn't, so I tend to check ...'). Martin's mother is still not ready to accept the teacher's 'good news' summary and move towards closure, and reopens on another tack, with new 'evidence' of Martin not keeping up ('He takes so long ... over his homework'), which is grounded in her *personal* knowledge of her child in his home circumstances. This does not shift the teacher's positive summary; on the contrary, he incorporates the point about Martin's not being 'a fast worker' as further evidence for his *own* view – that unlike 'lots of children', Martin does not rush his work.

At this point in the consultation, the teacher and parent begin to converge. Martin's mother actively endorses the teacher's position by reformulating his point about children who rush it ('want to get it over with'), which he, in turn, mirrors ('get it over and done with') and both start to move towards closure. There is one further reopening, around the teacher's instruction to Martin (the first time he has been addressed directly during the consultation) to ask 'if you're not sure of something', an injunction which, though humorously phrased, decisively confirms the location of the fault with Martin. His mother attempts to develop this topic by introducing the issue of students' confidence to ask for help, when they have 'so many different teachers', especially in the case of those who, like Martin, are in special-needs classes. The teacher only minimally acknowledges this contribution and restates his summary closing proposal. On this fifth occasion, he secures the mother's acceptance of his offer and the consultation moves through mutual agreements to a speedy conclusion.

A sense of muted struggle runs through this consultation. Martin's mother has to struggle to keep the consultation open in the face of the teacher's repeated offers of closure. And although she achieves some success in this through her persistence, she is less successful in her struggle to modify the teacher's opinion of Martin's progress. Although she is able to avert the teacher's proposals for closure, she is not very successful in securing any *extended* discussion of the points she raises. The teacher is, of course, engaged in a complementary struggle to maintain his version of Martin's progress in the face of his mother's counter-ascriptions.

Identity

Most of all, perhaps, the consultation enacts a struggle over *identity*. There are at least two Martins produced in this interaction – the careful non-rusher who is coping well under the teacher's careful eye, and the silent child who is failing to thrive in his school work.[10] Intricately woven into this struggle over Martin's identity is another over the identity of the teacher: as careful monitor and astute judge of his students' needs, versus one who is not alert to the problems of a child in difficulty.

Is there a *third* 'Martin' – that is, the student who was actually 'there', sitting at the table beside his mother? It is interesting – although not in any way unusual during such consultations – that this person was not consulted about the competing versions of Martin's progress and welfare that were being negotiated. The adult participants might have asked Martin whether or not he felt able to ask for help; whether or not he was 'keeping up'; whether he was 'distracted' by his siblings, and so on. But this Martin was not consulted and was not addressed in any way until the end of the consultation when he was 'brought in' in order to be encouraged to ask for help. In this sense, there were indeed only two Martins produced in the interaction itself. The living, breathing embodied boy was, in the sense foreshadowed above, a kind of spectre at the table. This is not to conclude that those other two Martins, the ones produced in and through the consultation, had no link to, or effect upon, the third Martin. It is quite possible that descriptions such as these offer possible versions of himself for Martin's contemplation.

Blame and responsibility

Struggles over identity are intimately linked to issues of competence and are, therefore, a fertile site for accusation, blaming and justification. Negotiations over where the blame should 'settle' were sometimes more protracted than those in the above example. An extended 'blaming' sequence can be found in Appendix 3, where the blame for the student's reported difficulties in understanding his homework assignment is 'shifted' around several possible locations, as it were (i.e. parent, student, teacher, external circumstances), before finally being allowed to 'settle' with mother and student.

Negotiating expertise: the 'management' of Personal talk

Martin's mother, in the example above, referred at one point to his home circumstances as a 'warrant' for her anxiety as to whether he was doing as well as his teacher stated. The teacher made very little acknowledgement of this personal information. This disregard of personal matters by teachers was widespread across the consultations. Overwhelmingly, teachers paid scant attention to personal information relating to students' home circumstances, emotional well-being, and so on, *where this was volunteered by parents*. Teachers often elicited this kind of information themselves (for example, about students' work habits, social pursuits, emotional well-being, friendship choices, etc.). But they tended to give it minimal acknowledgement when parents introduced it without being asked. This was the case even when such information appeared to be potentially relevant. For example:

Example 7

T   [advising M to test her (year 10) daughter's German vocabulary] … 'cause again, I've a really strong suspicion that Mary doesn't learn because –

M→   – My cousin speaks about seven languages and teaches five here in Norwich, so she's always said that she'll give her all the extra tuition that she needs

T→   Mmm. This is the classic Mary [referring to mark sheet] – a test we did … [continues]

This tendency to pass over personal information ('girlfriend problems', family troubles, unhappiness, anxiety, withdrawal, 'acting up', etc.) is all the more surprising given the rhetoric of home–school communication that under-pins parents' evenings. The teachers interviewed in this and an earlier study (see Walker, 1998) stated that parents' evenings were of value precisely because of the insights they could give into personal circumstances that might be influenc-ing students' achievement or behaviour. However, the tendency to 'downgrade' unsolicited personal information is characteristic of 'asymmetrical' talk in pro-fessional situations (cf. ten Have, 1991). Teachers, like doctors, may feel a need to 'manage' the emergence and deployment of personal information, not least because unsolicited information introduces an element of unpredictability into encounters that need to be kept to strict time limits. The management of the per-sonal dimension of the talk also allows teachers to define what will count as *edu-cationally relevant* personal information, and thus to maintain their 'expert' status in the face of rival claims from parents to speak as experts on matters con-cerning their child. There are other possible reasons. Teachers may be reluctant to enter into discussion of students' personal lives because they feel that this could compromise their relationship with students. Or they may want to avoid complicity with parents over the disciplining of students (see below).

Parents sometimes attempted to engage in 'expertise trading', by displaying the kind of specialist knowledge or registers deployed by the teachers – for example, when they showed their familiarity with the National Curriculum or their awareness of controversies over testing. Displays of 'insider' knowledge could be brief and allusive, as when a father asked a craft, design and technol-ogy teacher, 'Is this all resistant materials?', or when the mother of a dyslexic student said, 'She's had no multi-sensory teaching'. These parental claims to expertise did not, on the whole, seem to be any more successful in opening up the dialogue than their attempts to claim expert status on personal grounds.

Teachers seldom attempted to trade expertise in the 'other' direction – that is, by referring to their own experiences as parents and, therefore, their personal, as opposed to their professional, understanding of young people. Overall, the teachers in the consultations attempted to manage the interaction so as to maintain the boundaries around their expertise as the 'professionals'. This boundary maintenance is rather significant, given the universal rationale for these events as occasions for home–school 'partnership' and mutual endeavour in the interests of the student.

'Double binds'

Demonstrating competence, avoiding blame and maintaining a 'virtuous' identity are not simple matters. The complexities of managing these difficult, often contradictory goals gave rise to a number of interactional 'double binds', similar to those identified by David Silverman (1987) in his study of paediatric consultations involving diabetic teenagers. To demonstrate their competence, parents in Silverman's study were obliged *both* to demonstrate that they were acting 'responsibly', by monitoring their child's behaviour, *and* that they were helping their child to take control of their own health. Parents resorted to a variety of 'rebuttal strategies' to try to demonstrate competence on one of these counts, without incurring blame on the other.

The parents in these consultations courted similar risks. Showing an interest in students' homework and classwork could be seen as exhibiting responsible concern; but it could also be construed as being over-protective, or even interfering. And, as we have already seen, it was possible for parents to know 'too much' as well as too little about educational matters. One teacher summed up this 'no-win' situation for parents in his (only half-joking) categorization of them as 'over-protective, deferential or middle class'. This points to a general dilemma about the notion of parental 'support' for schools and teachers. As Gill Crozier (1998) notes, while parental support is universally desired, it can also present a threat. Parents who take an active interest may be seen as 'watchful'. Support can transmute into perceived counter-surveillance.

A further dilemma facing parents when demonstrating support relates to the *triangular* nature of the consultation, which, as noted above, always involves three parties, even when one is not physically present. Parental support for one party (student or teacher) could tacitly be taken as 'betrayal' (though this is too strong a word) of the other. For instance, a parent who defended the student in response to the teachers' criticism could easily be seen as biased or bothersome. Yet, on the other hand, attempting to support the *teacher,* by endorsing his or her criticisms of the student, could also be read in negative ways by teachers – as 'ganging up' on the student, or even as recruiting teachers against their will to do parents' disciplinary work. One teacher was critical of parents who allegedly came to the consultation 'to tell the child off', and who were 'out to just doubly prove what's gone on at home'. Another teacher was uncomfortable about endorsing parents' criticisms of sixth-formers, on the grounds that these were responsible young adults and that his relationship with them might be threatened if he was seen to be aligning himself with their parents. Allegiances between the three parties to the consultation triangle are not, therefore, clear-cut or pre-dictable in advance of each particular consultation.

Teachers were also subject to double binds. For instance, they could fall prey to the double imperative of making their subject enjoyable, and thus motivating the student, yet also being expected to 'push' or challenge them. A teacher who claimed to make maths fun, for instance, might be interpreted as making it too easy. Teachers could be held responsible either for overestimating or for under-estimating a student's abilities. This double bind was even more acute in the case of teachers of students with special needs, where there was an obligation to demonstrate that they were taking special care of special children *and* that they were not treating them differently, in terms of lowered expectations, from other children. A further double bind, already discussed above, concerned favourable reports of students. Teachers wishing to convey their genuine appreciation of good work might disappoint by failing to demonstrate 'engagement' with the student, or by telling parents 'what we already know'.

Questions of competence are never settled in advance of the consultation. There are no 'right answers', in the abstract, to such questions as: how rigor-ously one needs to monitor homework in order to be seen as a 'good' parent; what is the correct balance between fun and pain in the teaching of maths; how much consideration for special-needs children is too much; where are the lines between parental concern, interference and deference; who is at fault when a stu-dent does not understand. Although parents and teachers undoubtedly come to the encounter with their own apprehensions and expectations of each other (their own 'axe to grind', as one teacher said of the parents), praise, blame and esteem are traded in real time in the course of each individual consultation. It is during the talk itself that conduct comes to be construed as virtuous or blameworthy.

Conclusion

Parent–teacher consultations offer a paradoxical mixture of predictability and high uncertainty for those involved. On the one hand, they are routinized and formulaic. Participants all over the country repeat the same kinds of five-minute encounters, moving through the same series of episodes, making the same kinds of moves, out of which they fashion their oppositional identities 'as' parent or teacher. On the other hand, these are unpredictable encounters, fraught with jeopardy and risk of censure for all concerned. Issues of moral conduct, accountability, identity and responsibility are (un)settled on-the-spot. This helps to explain, perhaps, why people tend both to dismiss parents' evenings as empty routine *and* to experience them as traumatic (see Walker, 1998).

You begin to glimpse, in these consultations, how Foucault's notion of power as 'mutual and indefinite blackmail' actually works in practice. The adversarial structure which sets teacher and parent against one another unfolds inexorably as the consultation proceeds. This does not mean that it is impossible to 'subvert' the usual dynamics of these interactions. There were instances of parents who did not wait passively during the opening diagnosis, for example (see note 6). But there will always be interactional consequences when these (very subtle) conventions are breached, such as heightened defensiveness and hostility, or challenges to a speaker's credibility.

The consultations also show how subjects are produced in and through discourse. The identity of mother, father or teacher is not just something that a person 'has' or 'is': it has to be worked for, and worked up, during each interaction. But this process of self-elaboration is done according to criteria that are not freely chosen by the participants. It is also clear that these are *situational* identities. What will count as relevant to your conduct – and even your credibility – as a mother, or a teacher, will be only a very small sub-set of all the possible acts and experiences associated with mothering or teaching in other situations. You could say, in fact, that parent–teacher consultations offer rather stripped-down, minimalist identities for the participants.

This is not to suggest that all parents, or all teachers, are 'the same' in other contexts. Studies of parental involvement have emphasized the considerable diversity that exists across families, in terms of gender, class, family practices, attitudes towards education and benefits from it (cf. David, 1993). And teachers are no less diverse in their interests and personal lives (e.g. Sikes *et al.*, 1985). But it appears that such differences are generally displaced onto a more crude, binary distinction in the context of a consultation, where parent and teacher confront one another in a rather stark opposition between 'us' and 'them'. The identities of parent and teacher in these settings are *structurally oppositional:* it is impossible to be in both (interactional) places at once. And because of this fundamentally oppositional relation, it may be especially difficult for each participant to envisage the world from the position of the 'Other'. Teachers who are themselves parents, for instance, do not seem to show greater empathy with their parental 'clients' than teachers who do not have children – *within the consultation itself.* It may well be the case that teacher-parents are more sympathetic to the experiences of parents in other circumstances (see Sikes, 1997). But within the confines of the consultation, teachers are obliged, it seems, to engage with parents very much 'as' teachers, leaving their parental identity at home. This non-reversibility of identities also helps to explain why teachers who are attending parents' evenings 'as' *parents* do not seem to feel any more powerful than any other parent (e.g. Walker, 1998: 170). The consultations demonstrate in a particularly crystalline form, therefore, how subjects are constituted in and through discourse.

This 'up-close' look at parent–teacher consultations problematizes the ideals of 'partnership', 'parental involvement' and 'support' that underpin public aspirations for successful home–school relations. All of these aspirations depend on some kind of breaching, or dissolution, of the boundaries that insulate schools and homes. The evidence from this study suggests that the *proximity* that would ensue is something to be both feared and desired. Teachers and policy makers may want to breach those boundaries to recruit parents to do educational 'outreach' work, or even to smuggle school culture into homes (Baker and Keogh 1995). They may, in other words, want parents to act (be) more 'like' teachers. But perhaps not *too* like them. We saw above how parents could be deemed to know too much about curriculum or assessment; or how their indications of support could be construed as surveillance or interference. We saw too how personal, home-centric information is carefully (although not necessarily deliberately) managed and contained. The evidence from parents' evenings shows that the boundaries between home and school cannot simply be dissolved by good intentions or state interventions (such as home–school agreements).

Retrospect

I hope that this chapter has demonstrated something of the way in which selves and social lives are constructed through *talk.* Conversation analysis, which I have unfaithfully drawn on here, engages with discourse on what often seems like a very 'technical' level – the fine grain of turn-taking and sequential structure.[11] But I hope to have shown how these technical features 'carry' subtle meanings and effect significant social acts. Who you 'are', how you are treated, the constraints and possibilities that are open to you as a social actor, all of these are intimately tied up with interactional issues, such as who speaks when, how topics are developed and closed off, and so on. This kind of close focus on the details of mundane interaction has the potential to provide the missing link that some discourse analysts find in Foucauldian approaches, where the focus tends to be on the production of subjectivities at the level of institutions and social formations. As Poynton and Lee (2000) point out, Foucauldian discourse analysis has lacked a 'textual analytics' that is capable of tracing the effects of power in the 'specificity of what actual people actually say and do' (p. 6). A focus such as the one offered here has the potential to elaborate *how* subjects are 'constituted' in discourse, while still exercising agency and energy in their encounters with one another.

More generally, I hope you [...] have been able to glimpse the ways in which a discourse orientation can open up well-worn educational topics to new questions and directions. I hope this chapter has been useful in helping to see those routine and somewhat tiresome events known as parents' evenings in new ways,

and to re-mobilize some rather stale concepts (such as partnership and involvement) that easily become either empty of meaning or overstuffed with discursive
and ideological investments.

Notes

1 The research was supported by the Economic and Social Research Council, ref.
R000222287. See the End of Award Report (MacLure and Walker 1999) for an account of
the methodology and research design.

2 It depends, of course, how you construe 'control'. It is doubtful whether main grade
teachers (perhaps even headteachers) feel that they have a great deal of say in how parents'
evenings are organized (see Walker 1998). And although we did find many of the features of
interactional dominance characteristic of professional talk, I suggest in this chapter that teachers are no more free than parents to step 'outside' the institutional identities and responsibilities that are elaborated within the consultations.

3 Classroom talk between teachers and pupils has also been shown to be 'asymmetrical' in
terms of the unequal distribution (in favour of the teacher) of speaking turns, topic control and
evaluative comments (see, among many others, Sinclair and Coulthard 1975; Edwards and
Furlong 1978; Torrance and Pryor 1998).

4 Similar 'three-cornered' interactions do occur in other settings, however. Silverman
(1987) has analysed interactions between doctors, parents and adolescent children in paediatric medical consultations concerning the management of diabetes. I am indebted to
Silverman for unravelling the complexity of these interactions, in particular to his identification of the 'double binds' that they create for the participants.

5 Of 184 consultations, 126 exhibited this episodic structure. Most of the remainder took
the form that we called 'socratic dialogue', where the teacher took the student through a series
of 'leading questions designed to establish key points concerning behaviour or progress.
Despite their dialogic structure, these consultations were strongly teacher-controlled (see
MacLure and Walker 1999).

6 There were a few interesting departures from this pattern of minimal responses in opening episodes. One occurred in a consultation where it emerged later that the student's mother
had a very clear agenda, which brought her into conflict with the teacher's assessment of her
son. She responded immediately to the teacher's opening statement with a 'news receipt'
rather than a minimal response:

T   ... well, Jake's, he's doing very well.
M → Is he?
T   He got 63% in a recent test, which compares, you know, it's on the same
       standard as his test marks for last year, erm ... and ... I think he should
       aim to go for a grade A because he's capable of getting it.
M   What that's a B is it?

It is possible that this marked response is an early indication of 'trouble to come' in the consultation and, therefore, a potential challenge to the teacher's expert status. Note that it
prompts a justification from the teacher.'

7 The teachers in our study appeared to have an agenda of issues that provided the basic
structure for their diagnoses, which they 'ran through' with each parent. So, for example, a

year 7 special needs teacher tended to include in her diagnoses: a report on the child's reading age as measured on reading tests; a description of the group in which the child had been placed (lower/middle/upper; a 'nice' group); a description of the student's behaviour in the group or in class; and a general statement (usually positive) about how well the child was 'coping'. Other teachers had their own agendas, partly linked to the year group in question. Thus teachers of year 10 students generally included a prediction of the GCSE examination grade that the student might attain.

8 Teachers sometimes handed 'the floor' over to parents explicitly; with invitations such as 'Do you have any questions?', 'Was there anything you wanted to talk about', etc.

9 Parents who took part in the follow-up interviews confirmed their resistance to 'good news' stories. One father, for example, approved the fact that 'a couple of alarm bells' had been rung at the recent parents' evening: 'To be honest, up to the last one I've tended to find them, a waste of time. 'Cause they'd all say he was doing very well. "Just keep it up. Lovely boy"'. This accords with other work on parent–teacher consultations, which has reported that parents find little value in 'progress satisfactory' messages (Clark and Power 1998: 45).

10 My commentary here is directly influenced by Carolyn Baker's (2000) description of the 'two Donnas' in her analysis of a parent–teacher consultation.

11 Conversation analysts would consider this to be a very unfaithful appropriation indeed, since it rides roughshod over some fundamental tenets, such as the proscription on using social and sociological categories (such as 'power' or 'identity'), unless there is evidence in the data that the *participants* are orienting to such abstractions. See Hutchby and Wooffitt (1998) for an introduction to conversation analysis.

Appendix

Anatomy of a blaming sequence

[T = teacher; M = mother; underlining = overlapping speech]

T ... I'm, personally I think Josh is doing well and seems quite happy. Have you any problem, any questions you want to ask? ... You look like you have a question, yeah g –   *[concluding his 'diagnosis]*

M [Hesitantly mutters] He's ... he has not understood on a couple of occasions the actual homework that he has been set to do, He hasn't understood.   **problem statement/ accusation**

T Right, so he's been, what? In English, in particular?

M Yeah, in particular about the Diary of the erm, the Witches' Diary thing. He, he was kind of quite upset that he didn't really understand what it was he was being asked to do –

T – oh r –, he misinterpreted, oh that's a sh –   **blameshift → student**

M   – no. he just didn't really understand –   **blameshift → teacher**
T   – follow it:
M   – what he was being asked to do,   [*personal information*]
yeah, and he got a little bit upset about
it, getting quite stressed in actual fact,
that he wasn't, he couldn't understand,
well not he didn't understand, he just
didn't understand what he was being
asked to do, you know?

T   Right, er, it's a shame in a way if he   **blameshift → student/**
hadn't, [stutters] you could have easily   **parent**
phoned up, or asked him to ask me.
I mean what they were doing was
we'd read the play, the book sorry,
'cause it was The Witches, wasn't it?
[M: Yes] And we'd actually read the   **blameshift →**
book, The Witches, and what I'd said   **justification**
for them to do, I said, 'Right, imagine
you are the main character   [*pedagogical explanation*]
– [M: mm] – the lad that's in the story
and choose the bits you enjoy, and
imagine you just write a little diary
of some of the *main* events in the
story to show' –

M   – yeah, well he –
T   [*loudly*] and that's what they were,
and it was like a, a   [*talking simultaneously*]
M   well he kind of
T   very easy way of
M   he kind of interpreted that to mean,   **reassertion of**
erm, that he was expected to write   **problem/accusation**
a diary of every single event that
happened in the book.

T   I did quite, and it was actually   **denial**
written on the book, quite clearly,
it wasn't – one of the things I
actually said [M: Yeah] was at
the time, 'you are *not* expected
to write the book'.
M   Yeah I know.
T   'cause if that was the case
M   yeah, no, that's what –
T   – I'd have got, you'd have written
the book –
M   that's what, he, he seemed to, he   **reassertion of problem/**
seemed to think that's what he   **accusation**
was meant

T	oh. it was a misunderstanding	**blameshift →** **nominalization** **('no fault' version)**
M	– to be doing	
T	But no, that was, that's unfortunate.	
M	Yeah.	
T	In the case of that, if he misinterprets something, or he's unsure, by all means, contact me or tell him to come up and ask, you know.	**blameshift → student/ parent'**
M	Yeah.	
T	'Cause quite often, I tell the whole class, there's thirty of them, you know,	**blameshift → 'neutral object'**
M	well, I –	
T	you assume that they've actually –	
M	[*tries to interrupt*] yes, so –	
T	– it's on the board and written, it doesn't always follow –	
M	– yes I know the problem [laughs].	**agreement**
T	So, I mean if that's the case, then by all means make sure that you –	
M	–Yeah.	
T	The next day he comes up, or if either one of you contact me and say he's not sure, I'm quite happy to re-explain it to him.	
M	Okay.	**acceptence of T's version**

References

Baker, C. (2000) Locating culture in action: membership categorisation in texts and talk, in A. Lee and C. Poynton (eds) *Culture and Text: Discourse and Methodology in Social Research and Cultural Studies.* Lanham, MD: Rowman & Littlefield.

Baker, C. and Keogh, J. (1995) Accounting for achievement in parent–teacher interviews, *Human Studies*, 18(2/3): 263–300.

Button, G. (1991) Conversation in a series, in D. Boden and D. W. Zimmerman (eds) *Talk and Social Structure: Studies in Ethnomethodology and Conversation Analysis.* Cambridge: Polity Press.

Crozier, G. (1998) Parents and schools: partnership or surveillance?, *Journal of Education Policy*, 13(1): 125–36.

David, M. (1993) *Parents, Gender and Education Reform.* Cambridge: Polity Press.

Drew, P. and Heritage, J. (eds) (1992) *Talk at Work: Interaction in Institutional Settings.* Cambridge: Cambridge University Press.

Foucault, M. (1979) *Discipline and Punish: The Birth of the Prison* (translated by A. Sheridan). Harmondsworth: Penguin.

Foucault, M. (1980) *Power/Knowledge: Selected Interviews and Other Writings 1972–77 by Michel Foucault* (edited by C. Gordon). London: Harvester Wheatsheaf.

Heath, C. (1992) The delivery and reception of diagnosis in the general-practice consultation, in P. Drew and J. Heritage (eds) *Talk at Work: Interaction in Institutional Settings*. Cambridge: Cambridge University Press.

Heritage, J. (1984) *Garfinkel and Ethnomethodology*. Cambridge: Polity Press.

Jayyusi, L. (1984) *Categorisation and the Moral Order*. London: Routledge.

Keogh, J. (1992) Identity, ideology and power: a study of parent–teacher interviews, unpublished M.Ed. dissertation. Victoria: University of Wellington.

Macbeth. A. (1989) *Involving Parents*. Oxford: Heinemann.

Nias, J. (1981) Highstones: mirror images and reflections, in *Case Studies in School Accountability*, Vol. II. Cambridge: Cambridge Accountability Project, mimeo.

Poynton, C. and Lee, A. (2000) Culture and text: an introduction, in A. Lee and C. Poynton (eds) *Culture and Text: Discourse and Methodology in Social Research and Cultural Studies*. Lanham, MD: Rowman & Littlefield.

Sikes, P. (1997) *Parents Who Teach: Stories from Home and from School*. London: Cassells.

Sikes, P., Measor, L. and Woods, P. (1985) *Teacher Careers: Crises and Continuities*. Lewes: Falmer Press.

Silverman, D. (1987) *Communication and Medical Practice*. London: Sage.

ten Have, P. (1991) Talk and institution: a reconsideration of the 'asymmetry' of doctor–patient interaction, in D. Boden and D. Zimmerman (eds) *Talk and Social Structure: Studies in Ethnomethodology and Conversation Analysis*. Cambridge: Cambridge University Press.

Walker, B. (1998) Meetings without communication: a study of parents' evenings in secondary schools, *British Educational Research Journal*, 24(2): 163–78.

Chapter 16

Labouring to learn? Industrial training for slow learners

Paul Atkinson, David Shone and Teresa Rees

Introduction

The growth in youth unemployment has been matched by an increase in state intervention to manage the 'social problems' thought to be an inevitable and direct consequence. One aspect of this has been intervention in the process of work socialization of young people now no longer necessarily experiencing work itself straight after leaving school. This chapter examines one such intervention measure which has as its client group slow learners. The project is overtly attempting to increase the students' life-chances by preparing them for working life: this involves not only the inculcation of certain industrial skills designed to make them more marketable, but also the instilling of a range of social skills seen to be appropriate in a 'good worker'. [...]

[This] of this chapter is based on an ethnographic study of one institution designed to ease the transition from school to working life for adolescents who are 'educationally subnormal' or 'slow learners'. (We shall not enter into

Taken from: Barton, L. & Tomlinson, S. (eds), *Special Education: Policy and Practices and Social Issues* (London: Paul Chapman Publishing, 1982).

any discussion at this stage as to the precise definition of the young people involved, since in practice there is no single educational, psychological or social characteristic which delimits the client group.) We shall describe some features of the working of an industrial training unit in industrial South Wales. We shall make no claims as to the 'typicality' of this one institution: indeed, we have reason to believe that in some respects it is rather unusual. On the other hand, we do wish to claim that the issues *raised* by this 'case study' are of more general relevance. In particular, we wish to highlight some aspects of the training and socialization for work that goes on in the training unit, and some of the ways in which the young people there are evaluated and assessed.

The industrial training unit: an introduction

The unit is part of a college of further education, but is physically distinct and self-contained. It is located on an industrial site, rather than the college campus. The unit consists of a workshop, with woodwork and metalwork machines, an industrial sewing room, a canteen and staff facilities. It can accommodate up to twenty-one students at a time. It is staffed by a manager, whose background is woodwork craft teaching, one other lecturer specializing in woodwork, two lecturers in metalwork (all male), one sewing teacher, one part-time machinist/ nurse, and one part-time tutor in literacy and numeracy (all female).

Broadly speaking, three components can be identified in the training provided: specific 'industrial' tasks and skills, 'social and life skills', and remedial numeracy and literacy. We shall not comment on this last aspect in this chapter. In practice the former two aspects are not sharply differentiated. At the time of our observations, the unit's day-to-day work was not organized in accordance with a preset curriculum in the normal sense of the term. Rather, the pace and content of the work was framed by *production* processes. The philosophy of the unit reflected a belief that students should engage in and be responsible for 'real' work, and most of the tasks they perform are aimed at the completion of contracts placed with the unit by local firms. The range of tasks performed by the students is also determined largely by the sort of machinery available, which in turn constrains the range of contracts that can be attracted by the manager and his staff. The 'curriculum' of the unit, then, is embodied in its physical plant, the contracts which are placed, and the production processes which these imply.

Most of the machine tasks performed by students are simple and repetitive. They require students to conduct a simple set of sequenced activities which form a complete cycle which is then repeated. A typical task of this sort on the metalwork side would include drilling components – placing them in a vice or jig, lowering the drill and raising it again, by simply pulling a lever. While it is more difficult to preset the woodworking machinery, similarly repetitive tasks, such as sawing or planing lengths of timber, are undertaken. The sewing tasks involve the operation of industrial sewing machines, a button machine and a hand-operated press.

The unit takes male and female students. There is a degree of gender differentiation in the allocation of tasks in the unit. Most of the girls are allocated work in the sewing room, except those whose ability is regarded as too low to cope with industrial sewing machines. When the sewing room is not in operation, the girls are usually provided with the more simple tasks in the workshop.

Over and above the routines of productive work, the students also receive more general instruction, through talks and lectures. These arise out of particular incidents that crop up in the course of the day's work.

Lectures on workshop practice

Certain general principles of workshop practice are communicated to the students as a group, through a lecture. For example, breaches of the safety procedures have been occasions for a lecture on the potential danger of machinery. Such lectures are used to emphasize the necessity of safety procedures and they underline the precept that the students must 'do exactly as you're told', in order to avoid danger.

Other problems which occur, such as continual faulty workmanship, may form the basis of a lecture of this sort. These lectures reinforce the procedures and safety rules of the workshop by demonstrating the potentially dangerous, and sometimes expensive, consequences of failure to obey them. Thus students are enjoined 'always stack materials tidily and correctly'; 'no smoking in the workshop'; 'always switch off machines when leaving them'; 'do as you're told'; 'inform staff if you see something going wrong'.

It is a common ploy of the lectures to include dramatic and vivid demonstrations of matters of danger and safety precautions. For instance, on one occasion the observer noticed the manager hurrying over to where one boy, Dennis, was using a circular saw.

> He switched off the main power and called everybody to 'gather round'. He said something to Dennis which I couldn't hear[1] and then he asked if anyone would put their hand on the bench while he picked up a piece of wood and waved it up and down aggressively.
>
> Someone replied 'No', then the manager said 'Why not?' I was at the rear of the assembled group and as I shuffled forward I saw that it was Tina who was replying to the questions. 'Well this saw blade is travelling at 120 mph and it cuts this wood. What do you think it could do to your fingers?' (Rhetorically). The telephone rang and then the manager asked another lecturer to take over and to 'show them the other display'.

He moved over to the edge planer machine and selected a long length of wood about 6 feet and said something to the effect that 'imagine this was a finger'. He then pushed it against the rotating cylindrical blade of the planer, and in a matter of a few seconds it was reduced to about 18 inches in length. Stuart said, 'You've proved your point' (sarcastically).

The lecturer then said that the saw travels at 120 mph which is 'the same speed as the high speed train ...'

The lecturer then pointed out that putting their hands near the unguarded saw was as dangerous as standing in front of the high speed train. Then the students were directed back to work. The impression here is of a well-established 'routine' to make the safety point: and the point was certainly well made. Our field notes contain numerous examples of such teaching episodes.

Given the nature of the workshop, the machinery in it, and the nature of the youngsters who work there, safety must be a major preoccupation for the staff. The following extract from our notes may convey something of the urgency with which staff members attempt to instil safe workshop practice in the students. The workshop is noisy, and staff have to gain students' attention above the roar of the machinery.

The manager then entered the workshop just after a lecturer had called lunch. Then he shouted everyone to gather round. But some had already left for the canteen. The manager said 'C'mon will you all gather round.' Just a few students who had been in the immediate vicinity remained. Someone asked if they should fetch the others. The manager said, 'If you could, if it's not too late.' Then he said 'I'm bringing in this machine. It's a very dangerous machine. It may not look it but that blade can cut your fingers off. If I ask a lecturer which is the most dangerous machine in the workshop he'll say "this one,"' as the lecturer pointed to the cutter. 'You only have to have the handle slip down and it can take four fingers off. We've got machines working fast in this workshop but they're not nearly so dangerous as this because you can see how dangerous they are. I was once working with this and the handle slipped, and the blades are very, very sharp and it took the skin off the top of all my fingers.' The girls went 'eugh'. 'They were only little cuts though but it was painful. Now I'm going to put one of you on this machine this afternoon and whoever it is I don't want you to put your fingers through there. Keep well clear of it. And the others, I don't want you to go anywhere near the one who's using it. Do you hear me, you've got to keep well away from whoever it is 'n I don't want to see anybody near it.'

Understandably, such warnings are not sufficient to eliminate dangerous practices altogether. Like many factory workers, the young people in the unit take dangerous short cuts when dealing with the machinery, or they are simply forgetful or careless. Staff supervising the workshop must therefore be on the lookout for this, and as we have already indicated, may treat any such incident as the occasion for a general lecture in an attempt to reinforce the basic safety message. The lectures and demonstrations about workshop practice are often concerned with more mundane aspects of work, such as tidiness. Such lectures deal not only with the particular event or action which sparks them off, but many also include more general advice on good workmanship and relations with future employers. For instance, in the following example, the operation of a simple task like sweeping the floor can become the occasion for general advice on employers:

> The cleaning up operation began and one of the charge-hands, Rhian, went around collecting the ear protectors. Apart from that particular piece of work the two charge-hands were doing nothing different from the others. Most were busily brushing down benches, stacking timber and two were sweeping the floor. The manager then stopped the cleaning up operation and asked every-body to gather round Colin who was sweeping the floor. He stated to every-one: 'I have shown you how to sweep up haven't I? Look what I just saw this boy, Colin, doing.'
>
> He proceeded to sweep in a straight line from one point to another, he then went back and swept in a straight line adjacent to the one he had just swept. He then finally demonstrated the correct way of sweeping, i.e. all around a particular spot. The manager concluded by pointing out that 'An employer wants to see results. He wants to get value for money. Employers don't like people who insist on time wasting. They're not worth paying', or words to that effect. I happened to be standing next to one of the other lecturers at this point who stated to me, 'I don't know what's the matter with that boy. He always works untidily and I can't get him to work any better.'

This last example from the field notes illustrates how a topic of workshop practice can be expanded into a talk on 'good workers', and how students should behave in order to impress or please their future or potential employers. This is a central theme to a good deal of the more formal teaching which goes on in the unit. There is a good deal of instruction which is concerned with general matters of social and personal behav-iour, and much of this is directed at how students can 'make the most of themselves', and hence make the most of their employment opportunities. We describe this com-ponent of the training as 'social and life skills'.

This aspect of the unit's work is not designated 'social and life skills training' as such by the staff, but it seems useful to describe some of the teaching that goes on under this heading. The description is that given to a major component of a great deal of comparable work training and experience for young people. As with most of the teaching, this is not necessarily a prescheduled part of the work but staff members normally capitalize on particular occurrences to make some gen-eral point to the students as a group. All the workshop staff contribute to teach-ing of this sort. The teaching normally takes the form of lectures to the students; the topics covered include issues relevant to students' work and employment prospects and to general social and personal behaviour.

Training for working life

The sort of topics that have been taken up include: 'motivation', 'attention span', 'confidence', 'appearance', and 'smoking'. By and large the staff identify personal attributes or habits among the students which they regard as undesirable for working life.

Often a particular student is singled out to exemplify the undesirable trait, and his or her 'shortcomings' are generalized upon. A common strategy is for the lecturer to suggest that some supposedly undesirable characteristic is liable to give employers, or potential employers, a poor or false impression of the student. They therefore attempt to point out the undesirability of such behaviour and exhort the students to adopt more acceptable characteristics. In tone, then, these lectures are partly punitive, in drawing attention to a particular student and 'showing up' him or her. They also have the air of moral homilies and exhortations to self-improvement.

The following extract from the field notes exemplifies a lecture of this sort:

> The machines had been switched off four times that morning for the manager to cite an incident that he had noticed, and to indicate the things that had been going wrong. Once more the manager walked over to the main power switch. 'Will you gather round,' he called. Students wandered halfheartedly from their respective positions in the workshop towards the place where the manager was now standing. The manager turned to Clive and said: 'Will you Clive walk over to the door and then walk back.' Puzzled looks appeared on students' faces and one or two voiced the complaint: 'What for?' The manager said: 'You'll see in a moment.' Clive looked up at the manager and then walked over to the door and back. The manager then asked Stuart to walk over to the door and back. Stuart arrived back and was asked to repeat the procedure. One further student was asked to complete this procedure.

The manager made a joke about the slovenly way in which the students walked about.

> Several students laughed at this remark. The manager continued: 'I particularly noticed you, Stuart, walking earlier, you were straight. You looked as if you were going somewhere, as if you knew what you were doing, but you didn't do it then. Most of you slouch around, all down and out as if you couldn't care a damn. When I saw Stuart walking straight I thought to myself, he's got a purpose; he knows what he's doing. Most of you look as if you don't know what you're doing. An employer would think that you were a good worker if you were walking straight. Yes, you may know this, people can only judge us on appearances and the way we walk is very important. Don't you agree?' At this point Geraint entered into an argument with the manager:

> Geraint: 'People don't just think of the way we walk.'
> Manager: 'Well how else can an employer tell what we're like?'
> Geraint: 'Not just by the way we walk though' (laughing as he said it).

Manager:	'People do make these impressions on the way we walk and our general attitude when we first meet.'
Geraint:	'But that's not right.'
Manager:	'You're deliberately misunderstanding me you are. Does anybody think that I'm talking through the back of my head?'
Geraint:	'Yes.'
Manager:	'What about the rest of you? Do you think that I'm talking through the back of my head?'
Stuart:	'No.'

This question was then posed to most of the students in turn. Only three students actually disagreed with him.

This particular lecture is a typical instance of how the staff members take a particular youngster's personal characteristics as the starting point for more general homilies and maxims. It is also characteristic of this teaching approach that the students are allowed, even encouraged, to 'answer back' and agree or disagree with the points that have been made. These lectures are a particularly characteristic feature of the teaching strategy and training content of the unit.

In such ways the students were exhorted to mind their demeanour and appearance so as to create the most favourable impression with employers. In various ways, images of the 'good worker' are presented to the students, who are exhorted to behave in a manner which conforms to such a view. This is amply illustrated in the following extract from our notes:

> The manager then went over to the main power switch and asked everyone to 'gather round'. He stood at the top of the workshop by the barrier which separated most of the metal working jobs from the woodworking machinery. He asked: 'What do we need to get by in life, what are the basic necessities?' One boy, Dennis, said 'food'. Another one, Stuart, said 'shelter'. A further one said 'money'. The manager then said: 'What about sex, do we need that?' Someone shouted that 'it makes you feel tired'. The manager said, 'It doesn't do that for me', at which there were a few approving giggles from the kids. He then said: 'What about this one, not many people realize this but we all like to be important: you may not have thought of it before but it's true. Everyone needs to feel important in some ways. The point is there are all sorts of ways of being important.'

The manager then mentioned people wearing 'punk' clothing such as chains, earrings and rubbish bags to make themselves feel important. He went on:

> 'What they don't realize is that the only people they impress are children and others who do the same. Most people just laugh at them. An employer wouldn't give them a job if they came to an interview like that, he'd think they were loonies.
>
> 'Well what I'm saying is that we all like to feel important but there are some ways of feeling important or trying to be important that are better than others. The outrageous ways, such as wearing black rubbish bags, are not going to get you a job nor help you keep that job. But you can be important by being a good worker, and that is better because you're then important to the man who pays your wages.

'Anyway that's all I wanted to say. Jeremy when are you going to get your hair cut?'

Jeremy: 'I don't know' (laughing as he said it).

Manager: 'You need to buck up a bit my lad.'

On such occasions, some students' personal habits will be commented on adversely, and general maxims on their 'self-presentation' offered. In the following example, the stress on 'importance' seems to be carried through in the lecturer's choice of 'role models' for the students to emulate:

At this point Geraint noticed the manager writing on the board. He indicated that I should look. I laughed with him. He then shouted across to Daniel, 'look what he's writing'. On the board the manager had written:

How do you know if someone is an idiot?
Harold Wilson
Raquel Welch
_____

Esther Rantzen

The manager gathered all the students together again and said something to the effect that: 'C'mon this is a serious question. How do you know if someone is an idiot? Well, from the way they behave. Are Harold Wilson, Raquel Welch or Esther Rantzen idiots?' Someone answered 'No'. 'We tell that by the way they behave, by what they do. I bet you've never seen any of these on the television biting their nails or leaving their mouths hanging open. That's one way that people will definitely know you're an idiot. We only know people are idiots if we see them acting like idiots.' (Geraint gave a glance across to Deirdre, accusing her of being the nail-biting culprit.) 'These people don't bite their nails on the television.' Geraint commented, 'They could do', but the manager ignored the remark and concluded. He said, 'I bite my nails sometimes but I don't do it where anybody can see me. I make sure nobody's watching and I do it in the car. So if you have to bite your nails make sure you do it when nobody can see you and then they won't think you're an idiot. Go on have your lunch.'

As they all filed past to go to lunch the manager said to Tina, 'Did you know who I was talking about then?' (jokingly). Tina said, 'Me.'

It is noticeable in this example how the lecturers use colloquial speech forms to produce an informal, relaxed atmosphere. These lectures to the students exhorting them to self-improvement also include injunctions to improve their general attitude, their concentration and motivation.

Social training

Again, these lectures arise as specific responses to particular incidents in the workshop. In such cases the students concerned are particularly likely to be singled out and named in the course of the lecture to the whole group. The lecturer will often attempt to demonstrate the negative consequences of the behaviour in question and provide advice on how to avoid such behaviour in the future. These lectures are particularly concerned with the students' social relationships and their general behaviour. As the manager has put it, it is a matter of 'teaching them how to get on with each other'. Clearly there can be no hard and fast distinction between such general 'social' skills, and the work-related concerns mentioned above. It is not a distinction made by the staff themselves and the two are necessarily closely related. Both kinds of lecture have to be delivered amid the machinery for lack of a class-room. The following report provides a representative example of this sort of inter-vention by a member of staff and of the sort of lecture it can give rise to.

> The manager had observed Geraint and Frank arguing as they were returning to the workshop after loading a van. The manager asked everybody to assem-ble together at the front of the workshop in readiness for a lecture. The man-ager began: 'Before I start I want you two to shake hands and make friends. Will you do that now?' Frank moved forward to shake hands with Geraint who was sitting on a milk crate opposite to him. Geraint's head was held low and he looked up at Frank approaching and immediately looked down again. The manager continued: 'Did you notice that gesture? He's adult enough to say, "let's forget it". There's nothing worse than walking around with poison in your stomach which is what you two had. And he's not adult enough to shake hands. If you have a bit of difficulty with somebody, if they're getting on your nerves, you just go up and tell him. It's terrible if you can't get on with the people you work with. So if you have to have a row you'll have to remember to make it up. You two, each of you had poison in your stomach. When you get older you just can't do that, because what happens, you talk to somebody and then you call them names, and then you go and talk about how horrible he is to somebody else. Then that person thinks you're a great bloke and then you get on his nerves ...'

The moral here was that quarrelling led to loss of friends and hence loneliness.

The following incident is very similar, in that an event relating to work-shop practice and discipline is turned towards a concern with interpersonal relationships:

> Geraint had been instructed to plane down some wood on the planer. He began to run the machine and Tony noticed that some dust was blowing out of the air bags of the waste collector. From where he was working on the rear circular saw he shouted to a lecturer who was standing just in front of the bench saw, and indicated the blowing dust. The lecturer ran and switched off the planer and shook hands with Tony for the deed he had performed. The lecturer then instructed Dennis and Geraint to repair the canvas bag. The air had been seep-ing from the seal between the bag and the machine. Presumably the metal band which was fitted to the bag like a belt with saw teeth fastenings had worked loose, allowing the bag to ride up. The lecturer instructed them how to unleash the band ... The two boys then replaced the band and went over to switch

on the machine again. However, the bag began to leak again and Geraint turned the planer off, and he and Dennis raced over to the bag. As they began to ply the metal band and pull at the canvas in order to replace the broken seal, the lecturer approached them. He said to Geraint, 'Oh you've put it back on wrong haven't you?' Dennis then answered 'No, it was me.'

The lecturer then shouted everybody to gather round and began to relate what Dennis had just done. He said: 'Y' know what he just did? I accused Geraint of making a mistake and Dennis said to me, "No, it was my fault". It takes a brave man to admit when he's in the wrong.' At which point the lecturer beckoned Dennis nearer and held his hand out for him to shake it. As they shook hands he said 'congratulations'.

Sometimes these incidents are basically matters of 'telling off' students who are misbehaving in some way. One day the lecturer called everybody together and said:

'I've just overheard Stuart telling Rhian to shut up. That's not the way to get on with each other, it's a childish way to talk. What happened?' he said to Rhian. She said, 'He was throwing things at me.' The lecturer's eyes returned to Stuart who said with his head held down, 'She started it.' The lecturer said 'There's no need for you to sulk, stop sulking and tell me what happened.' He said, 'I'm not sulking, she started it.' The lecturer went on, 'I was praising you for being so grown up this morning and now look how childish and stupid you are. This calling each other names and saying "she started it" and telling people to shut up is not the way to get on with each other. Honestly it's just so stupid and childish. Get back to work, and you two stop fighting.'

In addition to the lectures we have just described where working relations are stressed, general topics of demeanour and self-presentation are sometimes emphasized:

Immediately on returning to the workshop the lecturer began with a lecture on swearing. He proceeded to say something to the effect that you've got to be careful when you're swearing. 'I don't mind swearing at all. But don't do it in public where other people can hear you because they might not like it. You might get done for obscene behaviour. The other thing is, don't swear in front of girls because they may not like it either. Don't swear on buses and other public places.'

Training for adult life

This training is less concerned with changing students' immediate behaviour, and is more informative in character. Lectures are aimed at providing students with knowledge which the staff regards as potentially important for adult life in general. These lectures, unlike the first two types, are not necessarily triggered by particular incidents of poor behaviour or workmanship. In fact, unlike the other training, they are routinely provided at fixed points during the day – before students begin work in the morning, or immediately after the lunch break.

It did appear, however, that as with other components of 'social' training, the content of these talks was rather *ad hoc*. There was little evidence of any pre-planning or sequencing of topics and so on. The result was a somewhat disparate series of topics. Over the fieldwork period, the topics covered were: 'capitalism'; 'democracy'; 'advertising'; 'literature'; 'classical music'; and 'mortgages'. In style and tone these sessions differed little from those we have already described. They tended to take the form of 'improving' lectures from members of staff. The students had little or no active part to play, and the presentation of the topics was not always grounded in the students' own immediate experiences. The students were not involved in any practical activities, and no attempt was made to make use of such techniques as role playing and so on.

We reproduce here the notes on just one session of this sort. The first example shows how the students were introduced to topics 'out of the blue'. It is also revealing about some of the distinctive social and political views of the staff members themselves. The emphasis on self-help and the moral virtue of work is a theme which runs through a good deal of the unit's work. It is a recurrent theme in what we can only describe, metaphorically, as 'homilies'.

The capitalism lecture

Everybody had just started back to work and Jeremy was leaning on the bench with eyes half closed. The manager had looked over towards him, and that seemed to spark off the lecture he gave. He switched off the machinery and invited everybody to stand over by the blackboard. He began by saying something like, 'Did you know that we live in a capitalist society?' (as he wrote the word *capitalist* on the blackboard). 'What that means is that machinery and factories are owned by capitalists. This is not just one person, it's a lot of people, and they run factories to make a profit. Most people are workers and the trouble is we depend on each other for a living. The worker gets his pay at the end of the week and the capitalist gets his profit. But when workers are lazy or continually make high pay demands a lot of employers go broke and then the workers lose their jobs. Like British Leyland. So employers can't afford to carry lazy workers as passengers. Now, you're all passengers now, and you've depended on your parents for most of your lives. People on the dole, they are passengers, they take their living from people who are working. If you're very lucky you may go to college and become a passenger for a lot longer. But you'll all hopefully get a job and you won't lose it for laziness, with one or two exceptions.' The telephone rang and he instructed another lecturer to continue.

The lecturer began by saying, 'What he was saying about passengers is that when you leave here and get a job you won't be a passenger any longer. There are too many people today who think they're owed a living. So you've got to try to be independent, to look after yourselves and stop being passengers.'

Staff evaluations of student ability

In organizing the day-to-day activities of the unit, and in assessing the suitability of students for particular tasks, the staff members base their decisions on evaluations of students' ability and motivation: these are based on their observation of the students rather than the use of standardized tests. It seems that the staff feel themselves qualified to make such assessments of students' skill, character and personality.

During the early period of fieldwork it became apparent that the students were being evaluated according to two basic dimensions. The first of these reflected the assessment of a given student's relative intelligence; it boiled down to whether they were seen as 'bright' or 'dull'. The second evaluative dimension reflected their ability and orientation with respect to work; that is, whether they were 'good' or 'bad' workers. In addition to these two basic categorizations, students were characterized in terms of their personal characteristics – sometimes their personal or social shortcomings, sometimes their more 'endearing' qualities. Examples from the field notes include:

> She's ever so dull but she's a very nice kid though.
> He's a nice kid but he's so shy.
> He's a good lad this one only he lets himself go.

The informal assessment of students' abilities is of considerable importance for the running of the unit, and it seems to be the case that the identification of students as 'bright' or 'dull' (able or unable) is reflected in the tasks they are given and in the way they are treated. As we have just suggested, some jobs – such as the use of the woodwork lathe – were reserved for students who were regarded as 'good workers'. The evaluation of a student as a 'good worker' does not rest on *ability* alone. In practice, a major criterion of 'good work' is a student's willingness to conduct tasks for relatively long periods of time, on his or her own, without disruptive contact with other students. A good worker, then, can be left to get on with his or her work, without needing constant supervision, and without upsetting the work of other students.

Since 'good' workers are given 'good' jobs, and may be left to get on with it, there is an inbuilt bias against any systematic attempts to introduce students to progressively more demanding tasks, or to rotate students through a large range of available jobs. Rather, there is a tendency for students to be allocated to their perceived level of competence, and then for them to stop there. Of course, we do not wish to suggest that there is absolutely no fluidity and movement between jobs. Nevertheless, there is a tendency for students to spend long periods of time at the same task, and hence to work constantly at the same level, in terms of the demands made on them, intellectually and manually.

The staff's impressions of students not only have some bearing on the training they receive, but also on the types of employment they are considered suitable for. In general they are considered to be destined for manual and semiskilled work.

Occasionally, when a student shows 'promise' he or she may be steered towards a particular skill in the hope that employment in that line of work may become available. It does appear that the students so assessed and selected have a passive role, although they occasionally object to the work they are steered towards. Such objections may be that they 'want to work with their friends' or that they have unrealistic expectations of wages elsewhere. It was also suggested to us that students might object to particular sorts of employment by virtue of inaccurate assessment of their own abilities (as lower than the staff's evaluations of them).

There were, for instance, two boys who were regarded as exceptionally 'bright'. They were routinely given relatively skilled carpentry jobs to perform, and were eventually channelled into relatively skilled employment of this sort. After 'proving' their ability in routine work they were rarely allocated to repetitive tasks. In contrast, two of the girls were assessed by the staff as particularly 'dull', and as likely candidates for the adult training centre. They were provided with what the staff themselves regarded as simple, routine, uninteresting work. The manager has pointed out to us that he regards such work as necessary, in that it closely approximates the kind of work the least able students would be likely to find in open employment.

As we have already remarked, the most obvious categorization of students is on gender lines, and this overlaps with the assessment of student ability. Most of the girls are allocated work in the sewing room, except those whose ability is regarded as too low to cope with the sewing machines. When the sewing room is not in operation (approximately eight hours a week, because of timetabling problems), the girls are allocated to the more simple tasks in the workshop. Only rarely do they operate woodworking or metalworking machinery, although in theory they may do so if they wish. The manager attributes the gender differentiation to the girls' preference for the more 'congenial' atmosphere of the sewing room. There is a consensus among the staff that certain of the metalworking jobs – simple drilling and tapping operations – are safe and simple, and therefore particularly suitable for the less able student. When the girls have to leave the sewing room for varying periods of time they are given such metalworking jobs, along with the least able boys. One of the boys who was regarded as one of the 'least able' and was also seen as 'troublesome' spent most of his time conducting simple metalwork operations. He frequently complained that he would be 'dreaming of these brackets' in his sleep.

The criteria on which staff opinions are based appeared to include: attendance, timekeeping, and evidence of working ability (e.g., judged by the number of components made). But these aspects are mediated by a global impression of less tangible matters, such as aspects of students' personality. Guidelines for student assessment are explicitly included in a *Readiness for Work Chart,* which forms part of the student's record. But staff rarely articulate their assessments in terms of these explicit criteria, but rather in terms of students' personal idiosyncracies and characteristics. Thus those students who seem unable to conform to the standards expected, or who appear to possess less favourable or likeable attributes are often those who benefit least from their stay at the unit, in that they will not be considered for placement if a work vacancy arises.

Although many of the students may have extremely low IQs they may not be regarded as exceptionally dull or relatively bright unless their performance at the unit confirms or disconfirms such an impression. Thus, attempts at training on tasks and at inculcating work speeds may prove to be difficult, and may thus reinforce prior categorizations. In other words, IQ is not considered to be particularly important in itself. Appearance, demeanour and a willingness to accept subordinate roles and discipline have a far greater influence on staff impressions, and may be influential in obtaining jobs for these students.

More important, however, is the implicit notion of 'work readiness' which the staff adopt. Unless jobs are actually sought after for particular students, who are thought to have 'shown improvement', it seems to be the case that most of the student body are regarded as 'not ready' for such work. Of course the seeking out and finding of jobs does not necessarily depend on their being 'work ready', but more importantly on other factors such as the availability of work, the geographical location of students' homes, their length of stay at the unit, and the point at which their course terminates. In other words, there are various contingencies involved in finding jobs for students, the most pressing of which is the need to find work at the end of a course or before long college holidays.

However, categorization of students as outlined above is rarely articulated fully. The staff seem to glean their impressions of who are the better students from conversations between each other. Thus, one student was regarded as particularly annoying and the following was heard during a break-time conversation in the staffroom:

'Oh she gets on my nerves she does. She's always wanting to organize everything.'

It would appear that others concur in this particular evaluation of the student: we have learned that the employers who subsequently took on this girl have found her unsatisfactory, not least because of her 'attention seeking'.

Perhaps the most illuminating area in which these non-articulated categorizations are elicited is in connection with job opportunities that arise. In such instances the staff would suggest particular students as suitable for that employment. Thus, the following exchanges occurred:

A: 'I've got these two apprenticeships at ——— joinery.'
B: 'But what are we going to do about the interview?'
A: 'Oh I'd forgotten about that, we could put somebody else in.'
B: 'What about Stuart?'
A: 'Oh that would be an improvement.'

and also:

A: 'They've got a vacancy up there for a good lad, one like they had before. But I told them I don't think we've got anybody ready.'
B: 'What about———?'

A: 'He's not been here long enough.'
B: 'His attitude's not right.'

One student was found a job and the staff kept him back because they were afraid that he might 'mess up another student's chances'. Thus, when the decisions finally had to be made two members of the staff consulted:

A: 'What are we going to do about Geraint?'
B: 'He'll only mess up James's chances.'

In this case the staff members felt that while one of the boys would work well, together they could be 'troublesome'.

Another example relating to the problem that students present is as follows:

Staff: 'What would you do with somebody like that?'
Researcher: 'Well he works alright doesn't he?'
Staff: 'But there's a communication problem somewhere. You can't just get through to him.'

In other words, the students are categorized as having particular problems which mitigate against their consideration as 'work ready'. It seems to be the case that the problems which the students present during early training are either reinforced or not according to the problems they present on a daily basis. Although the staff may operate an implicit conception of work readiness this is subject to shifting criteria in response to day-to-day contingencies. Thus, the age of students, the imminence of their course termination, their length of stay at the unit, are all aspects that may be taken into account when decisions as to finding employment are made.

Some of the features of the staff evaluation of student ability can be illustrated by the following case study of one student, Tina. Tina was regarded as particularly dull and immature. She was normally allocated to the most simple and undemanding of tasks: drilling and tapping, and sorting springs. (This last job involved unwinding tangled springs – something which was also being done by adult workers in a nearby factory.) She was often referred to as being suitable for the adult training centre (ATC), and was given tasks which did not involve her in any potential danger. Unlike most of the other girls she was not allowed to use the sewing machines, except on rare occasions under close supervision.

Of course Tina was assigned to other tasks during her long period at the unit, but during the fieldwork period she was only provided with the opportunity of attending for one interview. This was for sheltered employment at Remploy, and she expressed considerable antagonism at this chance of employment.

Although Tina did not seem to present the staff with any particular problems that were required to be discussed among them, she was consistently allocated to the most simple tasks and was sometimes reprimanded for particular misdemeanours. The most common of these misdemeanours was that if she was assigned sitting next to Kevin, they would spend considerable periods of time telling jokes and hence Tina would end up in prolonged spasms of laughter. This laughter led on several occasions to a lecture by the manager on 'not speaking up above the machines since that may indicate that an accident has occurred'. It also led to members of staff having to instruct her to 'get on with her work'. (It seemed to be the case that often most of the misdemeanours Tina committed could be regarded as petty and in no way antagonistic.)

It would appear that the manager's view of Tina's abilities was not whole-heartedly shared by other members of staff who claimed that despite 'immature' behaviour, she had 'work rhythm', which might enable her to survive in selected open employment. The manager regards admittance to the ATC as a 'backward step to be avoided if at all possible'. During one incident during the early field-work, Tina was heading for lunch; she jumped down the last four stairs to the locker room and shouted 'Geronimo'. The manager turned to the fieldworker and remarked that she was likely to wind up in the ATC. It seemed to be the case that most of the tasks that she was assigned to reflected this estimation of her. That is to say, there was no conception of her progressing or improving and she was destined for sheltered employment.

There may be something of a paradox in the way in which most of the students are found jobs. That is, jobs are often found by the manager of the unit, using the network of informal relationships he has built up in local firms. As we have sug-gested, students are selected for vacancies which arise in line with the staff's eval-uations as to their 'readiness' and suitability. Hence there is a built-in bias against the students looking for jobs themselves. It is also apparent that they are not usu-ally aware of the nature of the staff assessments of them (although they may be made aware of particular areas of perceived 'weakness'). The resulting overall impression is that jobs are 'rewards', allocated by the manager, on the basis of compliance, good behaviour and hard work. This is not necessarily a matter for criticism in itself. The process may well be a reasonable approximation of how such youngsters might find work anyway: through the intervention of a parent, rel-ative or elder brother or sister, rather than through formal agencies. Nevertheless there does seem to be a tension between the way jobs are found and allocated, and the professed aim of the unit's training, in fostering a degree of self-reliance and competence in the students when it comes to the world of work. Our strong impression as a result of the fieldwork so far is that the students are very *passive* in the process whereby they are channelled towards jobs. They rarely object to jobs which are found for them and are generally acquiescent.

Conclusion

In this chapter we have been able to touch on just some aspects of the organization and working of an industrial training unit. As we remarked at the outset, we advance no claims as to the 'typicality' of the unit we describe. It does, however, exemplify a number of themes which are generic to contemporary programmes to ease the transition from education to working life.

The work of the unit interweaves 'formal' and 'informal' components. At the level of its overt, official aims and objectives, the unit is intended to provide the young people with specific skills and competencies which will enhance their chances of finding and keeping a job in a shrinking labour market. At a more informal level, the day-to-day training is couched in terms of the model 'good worker' and the values of 'good work'. The unit's activities are pervaded by a distinctive work 'ethos' or 'ideology'.

As we have described, the industrial training unit is not run in accordance with a set 'timetable' or 'curriculum', in the sense usually used in educational settings. The work is organized primarily in terms of the production process of the unit's contract work. Many of the instructional episodes we have exemplified stem directly from threats to production, or 'failures' of workshop practice. Other types of instruction stem from staff members' perception of students' failure to live up to the model worker, in terms of deference and demeanour.

For the most part, it is not at all clear that the students' skills are significantly changed, in terms of their competence with industrial machinery. There is little or no sense of their progressing through graded tasks, and of measurable improvement in performance. Rather, the students find a level at which they work satisfactorily, and stick to it. There is also little to suggest that the actual skills and tasks mastered in the workshop correspond to those most appropriate for the available sectors of the labour market. Training in carpentry may be unlikely to produce directly marketable skills.

As high levels of youth unemployment persist, the number of projects of the kind described here appear to be increasing sharply. Those directed purely at the needs of the slow learner are in the minority, but share with other innovations a concern with work preparation in the broadest sense. Evaluations of such projects abound. [...] What such studies appear to lack, however, is a questioning of the aims and objectives of the schemes themselves. In this chapter we have attempted to draw out into the open some of the implicit assumptions that projects set up to ease the transition process for slow learners appear to make.

Acknowledgements

[...] The Industrial Training Unit described in this paper, which was set up to prepare slow learners for working life, is an associated project of the European Community Action Programme on the Transition from School to Work set up in 1977. It is one of many such innovative projects throughout the Community being evaluated for the Commission. We are grateful to IFAPLAN, the social research institute in Cologne coordinating the evaluation of the Community

Action Programme, for funding the work reported here through Professor Alan Little of Goldsmiths College, London, the UK evaluator.

We are also indebted to numerous organizations and individuals in Wales for their support and cooperation, in particular the manager, staff and students of the unit. Finally our thanks are due to Dr Sara Delamont of the Department of Sociology, University College, Cardiff, for her comments upon an earlier draft.

Note

1 The observer was later told that the manager was seeking the boy's permission to use the incident as a teaching example.

References

Department of Employment (1977) 'Attitude and personality lose young people jobs', *DE Gazette*, October, p. 1127.

Gregory, D. (1980) 'Current trends in the local labour market of Mid Glamorgan', Report No. 6 of Evaluation of Industrial Training Units, Sociological Research Unit, Department of Sociology, University College, Cardiff.

Gregory, D. and Markall, G. (1982) 'State intervention – assumptions and programmes', in P. Atkinson and T. L. Rees (eds) *Youth Unemployment and State Intervention,* Routledge & Kegan Paul.

Hudson, B. (1977) 'Time to rethink policy for forgotten jobless', *Health and Social Services Journal*, pp. 1702–04.

Manpower Services Commission (1980) 'The Sheffield and Rotherham Labour Market Survey', MSC.

Chapter 17

An appraisal of 'Labouring to learn'

Martyn Hammersley

This article provides a methodological assessment of a study of an industrial training unit for 'slow learners' in South Wales, the research for which was carried out in the late 1970s (Atkinson, Shone and Rees, 1981 [Chapter 16 in this volume]).[1] [...] The appraisal was written as one of several attempts to explore what is involved in assessing the validity of qualitative research (see Hammersley, 1991). Out of this work came a framework around which the description of studies can be organized as a basis for methodological assessment. This specifies the need for information about the focus of the research and its rationale, the case(s) studied, the methods of data collection and analysis employed, the main claims made and the evidence offered for them, and the conclusions drawn. The discussion that follows is structured along these lines.

The focus

The main focus of this study is government-sponsored projects designed to facilitate the transition of 'slow learners' from school to work; though the results

Taken from: Gomm, R. & Woods, P. (eds), *Educational Research in Action,* (London, Paul Chapman Publishing, 1993), pp. 171–183.

may also be intended to be applicable to similar projects not restricted to slow learners. The goal of the account is presented as descriptive, being concerned to identify some of the assumptions implicit in the socialization of young people for work by such units. However, the origins of the research lie in a programme of work concerned with the *evaluation* of projects tackling the transition from school to work [p. 262].[2] The character of the account is somewhat ambiguous, then, between description and evaluation.

The rationale presented for the focus is that, at the time, training units of this kind were on the increase as part of State intervention designed to deal with the social problems resulting from growing unemployment. [...]

If we examine this rationale, it appears to be entirely factual. That there has been an increase in the number of industrial units for slow learners (and for young people in general) designed to prepare them for work, and that slow learners experience special difficulties in obtaining jobs, are taken to imply that this research focus is important. There is no reason to doubt the validity of these factual claims, even though the authors provide no evidence for them. We can take their truth to be common knowledge, I think. However, the rationale for a focus can never be solely factual. We must ask: in terms of what values is a study of this phenomenon justified? While the authors do not make the values involved explicit, it is not difficult to identify them. They relate to a common theme in discussions about education and training in modern industrial societies: how far should education/training be geared simply to prepare young people for work, in the sense of fitting them to the requirements of employers, as opposed to being designed to prepare them for work in a more general sense (for example, by informing them of their rights, maximizing their career prospects, etc.) and/or to enhance their personal development? Some of the values implicated in this theme are: ensuring that the economy has a labour force with the right skills and attitudes for smooth, effective and efficient operation; ensuring that young people (and especially those who are disadvantaged in some way) can compete as successfully as possible in the labour market; and ensuring that young adults experience the maximum personal development possible.[3] It seems to me that few people would question any of these values in principle. What *is* a source of discord is their priority in particular cases. But this is not an issue that arises when judging the validity of the rationale for a descriptive study like this one. For this purpose it is enough that these values are legitimate, and are widely regarded as legitimate, for the focus to be established as relevant. So, [...] the rationale for the focus is valid, if partly inexplicit.

The case studied

The research consisted of an in-depth study of a single case, over a limited (though unspecified) time period. The authors provide some background information about this case. It was a training unit in industrial South Wales that formed part of a college of further education (though it was located in a manufacturing industrial site not on campus). It consisted of a woodwork/metalwork workshop, and an industrial sewing room. It catered for 21 male and female students, and was staffed by four male woodwork/metalwork lecturers, one of whom was the manager, plus a sewing teacher, a part-time machinist/nurse and a part-time literacy/numeracy tutor (all of whom were women).

There is no reason to doubt that this background information is accurate, since it is of a kind where serious error is unlikely. Whether this background information is sufficient is an issue that can only be decided in the light of what would be required for conclusions about the focus to be drawn on the basis of information derived from this case, an issue I consider later.

Methods of data collection and analysis

The authors tell us very little about the methods used to collect data about this case. We can glean from what they write that some form of participant observation was used, both in the workshop and in staff meetings, plus some interviews with the staff. However, when and over what period the data collection took place, how intensive it was, how many observers were involved and what roles they adopted, how many of the staff were interviewed and in what way, etc., we do not know. This makes it difficult to judge the appropriateness of the methods adopted in relation to the focus of the research and the nature of the case, and therefore difficult to judge what threats to validity might be involved. There is also no information about the methods of analysis employed, though these seem to have been of a conventional ethnographic kind.

Main claims

As indicated earlier, the explicit goal of the research was descriptive, and in this section I shall begin by discussing the authors' account of the main features of the unit and its operation.

The descriptive claims

Two aspects of the operation of the unit are highlighted by the authors:

1 The staff's attempts to socialize students for work.
2 Their assessments of students and the consequences of these assessments.

The unit's day-to-day work was organized around production in the workshop and sewing room which was directed towards meeting outside contracts. Most of the machine tasks were simple and repetitive, but some made more demands on the students than others. The fact that production work was central to the unit reflected the staff's commitment to work preparation:

> The project is overtly attempting to increase the students' life-chances by preparing them for working life: this involves not only the inculcation of certain industrial skills designed to make them more marketable, but also the instilling of a range of social skills seen to be appropriate in a 'good worker'. [p. 245]

However, they argue that 'There is also little to suggest that the actual skills and tasks mastered in the workshop correspond to those most appropriate for the available sectors of the labour market. Training in carpentry may be unlikely to produce directly marketable skills'. [p. 261].

Over and above participation in work tasks, the students were given lectures, both scheduled and impromptu, designed to achieve the same goal of work preparation. The authors identify four broad types of lecture, varying according to topic. These were concerned with

1 workshop practice, dealing with safety;
2 training for working life, aimed at inculcating the attitudes and habits of the 'good worker';
3 training for adult life, concerned with interpersonal relationships; and
4 social training, pertaining to more general and diverse issues such as democracy, advertising and classical music.

However, despite this variety of topic, the authors argue that the primary emphasis in the lectures was on inculcating attitudes and motivations in the students that employers were believed to require:

> A common strategy is for the lecturer to suggest that some supposedly und
> sirable characteristic is liable to give employers, or potential employers, a pc
> or false impression of the student. They therefore attempt to point out the
> undesirablility of such behaviour and exhort the students to adopt more
> acceptable characteristics. [p. 250]

This extract relates to lectures classified as concerned with 'training for working life'; but the authors also quote what they call 'the capitalism lecture', dealing with training for adult life, which praised self-help and the virtue of work, themes which the authors claim were central to the staff's attempts to socialize students.

Subsidiary to this description of the *content* of the lectures, Atkinson, Shone and Rees also give some attention to the pedagogical strategies that the staff employed. They report that the use of 'dramatic and vivid demonstrations of matters of danger and safety precautions' was a common ploy in the lectures [p. 247]. More generally, they note that students are 'allowed, even encouraged, to "answer back", and agree or disagree with the points being made' [p. 251]; and that the staff use colloquial speech to produce 'an informal, relaxed atmosphere' [p. 252].

As regards assessment, the authors claim that this takes place informally on the basis of the staff's judgements of the ability and 'attitude' of students, mediated by global appraisals of their personalities. The authors report that these assessments were 'based on (the staff's) observation of the students rather than the use of standardized tests', and they comment that 'it seems that the staff feel themselves qualified to make such assessments of students' skill, character and personality' [p. 256].

As might be expected the main basis on which the staff assess students is the extent to which they match the image of the 'good worker', and this was by no means solely a matter of ability. The authors report that 'appearance, demeanour and a willingness to accept subordinate roles and discipline have a far greater influence on staff impressions ...' [p. 258]. And they elaborate this theme as follows [p. 256]:

> In practice, a major criterion of 'good work' is a student's willingness to conduct tasks for relatively long periods of time, on his or her own, without disruptive contact with other students. A good worker, then, can be left to get on with his or her work, without needing constant supervision, and without upsetting the work of other students.

These staff assessments of students were not merely independent judgements on the part of particular staff members, staff discussed students among themselves and reached more or less consensual views about the capabilities and characters of particular students. However, the authors also argue that staff assessments of students have a contingent character: 'Although the staff may operate an implicit conception of work readiness this is subject to shifting criteria in response to day-to-day contingencies. Thus, the age of students, the imminence of their course termination, their length of stay at the unit, are all aspects that may be taken into account ...' [p. 259].

Staff assessments had two related types of consequence; it is claimed:

1 they were the basis for the allocation of students to tasks within the unit.
2 they also determined the staff's recommendations of students to employers for jobs. The students tended to get jobs through the unit manager's

contacts with local employers, and the authors suggest that there was a 'bias' against students looking for jobs themselves.

The process of assessment and allocation of students to tasks within the unit cannot be entirely separated from socialization. Atkinson, Shone and Rees suggest that:

> Since 'good-workers' are given 'good' jobs, and may be left to get on with it, there is an inbuilt bias against any systematic attempts to introduce students to progressively more demanding tasks, or to rotate students through a large range of available jobs. Rather, there is a tendency for students to be allocated to their perceived level of competence, and then to stop there[;] . . . and hence to work constantly at the same level, in terms of the demands made on them, intellectually and manually. [p. 256]

And they claim that this has serious consequences for student learning: 'For the most part, it is not at all clear that the students' skills are significantly changed, in terms of their competence with industrial machinery. There is little or no sense of their progressing through graded tasks, and of measurable improvement in performance' [p. 261].

The authors also note the sexual division of labour operating in the unit. Girls are allocated to sewing machines (whereas boys are presumably not), except for those judged to be unsuited on the basis of ability and/or attitude. The latter are allocated to the simple and boring tasks in the workshop; and all girls are given these tasks when the sewing room is not operating.

The authors are claiming, then, that the way in which the allocation of tasks took place minimized the extent to which students learned new skills, and was based on assumptions about gender-specific abilities. They also argue that students are given a passive role by the unit, both in relation to their assessment and allocation to tasks within it and in terms of obtaining jobs outside. It is suggested that they are expected to be (and perhaps encouraged to be?) dependent on the staff [p. 260]:

> There may be something of a paradox in the way in which most of the students are found jobs. That is, jobs are often found by the manager of the unit, using the network of informal relationships he has built up in local firms. As we have suggested, students are selected for vacancies which arise in line with the staff's evaluations as to their 'readiness' and suitability . . . The resulting overall impression is that jobs are 'rewards', allocated by the manager, on the basis of compliance, good behaviour and hard work. This is not necessarily a matter for criticism in itself. The process may well be a reasonable approximation of how such youngsters might find work anyway: through the intervention of a parent, relative or elder brother or sister, rather than through formal agencies. Nevertheless, there does seem to be a tension between the way jobs are found and allocated, and the professed aim of the unit's training, in fostering a degree of self-reliance and

competence in the students when it comes to the world of work. Our strong impression as a result of the fieldwork so far is that the students are very *passive* in the process whereby they are channelled towards jobs. They rarely object to jobs which are found for them and are generally acquiescent.

Assessing the descriptive claims

Here we need to consider both the relevance of the claims made and their validity.

Assessing the *relevance* of the claims is not straightforward since, because the values providing the rationale for the study were not explicit, all we have is the reconstruction of them provided above. We can assess the consistency of the descriptions with those reconstructed relevances, but any incoherence is as likely to reflect the inadequacies of the reconstruction as inconsistency on the part of the authors.

Given my reconstruction of the rationale for the study, we would expect the unit's operation to be described in terms of a framework of concepts that map the various features we would expect to find in the unit if each of the values identified had been pursued exclusively and effectively as a goal. So, we might expect information about such things as:

- whether there are attempts to socialize students into the sorts of skills and attitudes required by employers (this would be relevant both where the unit is geared to smooth integration of students into industry and/or to maximizing students' chances of getting and retaining jobs);
- whether students are introduced to new skills and in a way that allows them to acquire these effectively (this might be expected if the unit were geared to maximizing students' career prospects and/or their personal development); and
- whether students are encouraged to play an active role in the organization of the unit and in decisions about their future (this might be expected if the unit were committed to some notion of industrial democracy and/or to the personal development of the students).[4]

If we look at Atkinson, Shone and Rees's account of the staff's attempts to socialize students, it does seem that much of it conforms to these relevances. The organization of the work in the unit and the content of the lectures are described in terms that suggest their closeness to the goals of integrating the students into the workplace and/or maximizing their chances of getting a job (and their distance from forms of socialization designed to facilitate industrial democracy or personal development).

The relevance of the descriptions of pedagogical strategies is not so obvious. In the case of the use of 'dramatic and vivid demonstrations', this can only be relevant background information, since we might expect to find it whichever of the goals was being pursued. The same may be true of the other two descriptions of pedagogical strategies, encouraging students to 'answer back' and the use of colloquial speech; though these could be relevant to the values of industrial democracy and personal development.

The relevance of the descriptions of assessment also seems assured; and once again the import is that the predominant concern of the staff is with economic integration and with the students getting jobs. By contrast, the authors indicate that there is a relative neglect of improving students' skills and of developing their capacity for autonomous decision-making. There are, however, one or two aspects of the description of assessment procedures whose relevance is not immediately obvious. Notable here are the report that assessments are based on observations by staff rather than on standardized tests, and the description of the assessment process as affected by contingencies of various kinds. The relevant value here is perhaps the rationality of the assessment process, but it is difficult to unpack the interpretations of this value assumed here and such claims do not seem to be central to the article.

The argument that the students are allotted a passive role within the unit is obviously relevant to the value of personal development, conceived in terms of taking control of one's own circumstances, or at least participating in decisions about one's life and future. The authors are also pointing here to a discrepancy between the 'professed aim' of the unit and its practice. Of course, apparent discrepancies between aims and actions are not automatically relevant and worthy of discussion, but this one is clearly central to the relevances that seem to underly the account.

Besides assessing whether all of what is presented is relevant, we must also consider whether there is anything that would have been relevant that is omitted. There are two areas that might be mentioned here. First, there is the nature of the contacts between the staff and individual students in the workshops. Did these have the same character as the public lectures? And what about *informal* contacts between staff and students, for instance in the canteen? Was there much of this, and how did it relate to the relevances identified? Second, the account focuses primarily on the socialization *attempts* of staff, rather than on socialization *effects*. But, of course, effects are at least as important from the point of view of the rationale for the study, and the authors do make claims about effects in at least one place (as regards students' skills not improving). Relevant here would be students' perspectives towards the unit, and accounts of changes in attitude over time.

Turning to the *validity* of the descriptive claims made, the account of the industrial tasks on which students were employed and of the lectures designed to socialize students in preparation for work seem convincing at face value. It does seem clear that the staff were very much concerned with work preparation, conceived in terms of a fairly traditional and employer-centred conception of work. Even their more general concerns with safety and preparation for adult life are apparently framed within a political philosophy that accords a central place to the notion that students must be trained to be 'good workers' who conform to work requirements.

Many of the claims about the lectures are supported by evidence, usually in the form of quotations from the researchers' observations (including transcriptions of what the staff said in key incidents). The four types of lecture are illustrated with examples. However, we are not told how frequent the impromptu lectures were, or how frequent examples of each type of lecture were. This would have been useful information, particularly in allowing us to judge the degree to which the 'good worker' formed the core theme of the socialization. It would also have been useful to know whether the lectures were the same irrespective of which staff members gave them, and whether there was any change in their content over time. (Here, of course, we are concerned with the accuracy of the authors' generalizations within the case they studied.)

The account of the pedagogy is also supported by evidence. However, in the case of one claim, the evidence seems less than conclusive. The authors argue that the students are encouraged to answer back, but in the example cited the lecturer's response to a student's refusal to accept what he says does not seem calculated to encourage this (it seems concerned above all with getting the students to accept his point of view – see p. 250).

There is generally rather less documentation about assessment, its basis and its consequences. Thus, there is little information about the process by which students are allocated and reallocated to tasks. The authors imply that this was based on judgements of students in terms of the criteria of the 'good worker'. This is plausible given the previously described content of the socialization, and a case study of one student (Tina) is provided. But more detail about the formation and use of the staff's assessments would have strengthened the basis for judging the validity of this aspect of the account.

There is little evidence about the extent to which assessments of students were a matter of staff consensus (indeed, at one point some dissensus is noted, see pp. 259–60). Nor are we given information about the relative power of the manager in relation to other staff in making assessments. Furthermore, the contingent character of the assessment process is not explored or documented. There is an implied contrast here, perhaps with a more universallistic allocation procedure, but certainly with one that is geared to the development of student attitudes and skills rather than simply matching tasks to existing capacities. Clearly this focus would have been illuminated considerably by information about particular allocation decisions.

Similarly, the argument about the relative immobility of students between tasks and its effects is not established, though there seems no reason to doubt the authors' claims about the sexual division of labour among students in the unit. No support is offered for the claim that students' competence in dealing with industrial machinery is not significantly changed by the work of the unit, and this is a claim whose significance and character requires considerable evidence for it to be accepted, it seems to me. Nor are the claims about the passivity of students in relation to their assessment and their recruitment to jobs supported with evidence; and once again this is necessary, in my judgement, especially given the claim that this passivity is discrepant with the expressed aim of the unit.

Information about the recommendation of particular students, or the failure to recommend students, for jobs would also have enabled us to get a clearer idea of the criteria underlying assessment. The authors do use the case of Tina to illustrate this, but more detailed information about more students might have helped to clarify the criteria and the contingencies involved.

Evaluative claims

I noted earlier that while presented as a descriptive account, the research on which this article is based had its origins in an evaluation. Not surprisingly then, there are places in the account where explicit evaluations occur, and others where evaluations seem strongly to be implied. For example, at a mundane level, Atkinson, Shone and Rees commend the staff's concern with safety precautions. They note that 'given the nature of the workshop, the machinery in it and the nature of the youngsters who work there, safety must be a major preoccupation for the staff' [p. 248]. Similarly, they comment that 'staff supervising the workshop must … be on the lookout for [students taking dangerous short cuts]' [p. 248]. However, evaluations are not restricted to positive evaluations of the staff's concern with safety. Here is another evaluation [p. 257]:

> Guidelines for student assessment are explicitly included in a *Readiness for Work Chart,* which forms part of the student's record, but staff rarely articulate their assessments in terms of these explicit criteria, but rather in terms of students' personal idiosyncracies and characteristics. Thus those students who seem unable to conform to the standards expected, or who appear to possess less favourable or likeable attributes are often those who benefit least from their stay at the unit, in that they will not be considered for placement if a work vacancy arises.

Here we have an explicit evaluation of which students benefit most from the unit, though it should be noted that there is no explicit evaluation of the fact that some benefit more than others, or of which ones benefit.

In addition, implicit evaluation seems to be contained in the use of qualifiers, and of scare quotes, which are presumably intended to distance the authors from what they are describing. For example:

> A common strategy is for the lecturer to suggest that some *supposedly* undesirable characteristic is liable to give employers, or potential employers, a poor or false impression of the student.
>
> ([p. 250], my emphasis)

There were, for instance, two boys who were regarded as exceptionally *'bright'*. They were routinely given relatively skilled carpentry jobs to perform, and were eventually channelled into relatively skilled employment of this sort. After *'proving'* their ability in routine work they were rarely allocated to repetitive tasks.

([p. 257], my emphasis)

It is also possible that some of what I have treated as descriptions were intended to be read as evaluations in the sense that the authors assume a particular evaluation of what they describe to be automatic on the part of their audience.

In the case of evaluations about safety, the value involved and its justification is obvious, and in no need of explicit treatment. However, the other evaluations are more questionable, and therefore suffer from the fact that the basis on which they were made is not explicit or provided with justification. It also seems to be necessary to consider how far the staff would have been able to rectify the defects the authors claim to identify, given the circumstances in which they had to work. Little attention is given in the account to the constraints under which the staff worked, and yet these must be of considerable relevance to any assessment of the unit's operation.

Conclusions drawn

While the authors investigate a single case, their focus seems to be the wider population of industrial training units. However, they appear ambivalent about the generalizability of their findings. They state that they '. . . make no claims as to the "typicality" of this one institution: indeed, we have reason to believe that in some respects it is rather unusual. On the other hand, we do wish to claim that the issues *raised* by this "case study" are of more general relevance' [p. 246]. The same point is repeated towards the end of the article: '... we advance no claims as to the "typicality" of the unit we describe. It does, however, exemplify a number of themes which are generic to contemporary programmes to ease the transition from education to working life' [p. 261]. The authors seem to believe that the findings of their study have general relevance even though the unit may not be typical.

Given this argument, we must ask about the grounds for the authors' claim that the issues/themes that they discuss are of general relevance. It is true that the issue that underlies the authors' account (concerning the balance between work preparation – narrowly defined – and personal development) is undoubtedly of general relevance. But, presumably, the information that this study is intended to provide does not consist of this issue itself, but rather of information about industrial training units relevant to it. If this is so, and given that events in this unit at the time it was studied have little intrinsic relevance for a wide audience, we must conclude that the value of the information will depend not only on whether it is true for the unit studied but also on whether it is generalizable to other units. Indeed, the authors make this quite explicit at the end of their article in claiming that they have 'attempted to draw out into the open some of the implicit assumptions that *projects set up to ease the transitional process for slow learners* appear to make' [p. 261], my emphasis). Here it is quite clear that what is being claimed is that some of the features of the unit studied, namely some of the assumptions made by the staff, are typical of many such units.

The information about the wider population of units necessary to make an assessment of the generalizability of the findings of this study is not provided, however.[5] Given this, I think we must reserve judgement on this issue.

Concluding comments

In this discussion of Atkinson, Shone and Rees's article I have outlined the focus of the research, the case studied, the methods used, the main findings reported and the conclusions drawn. I have also assessed the rationale for the focus, as well as the relevance and validity of the findings and conclusions. It is worth emphasizing that this is not intended as an assessment of the competence of these researchers. I have given no attention to the constraints under which the research was carried out or to those on the length and character of the article that have been involved in its publication. The aim, rather, has been to assess the value of the knowledge that the study provides. However, there are features of the account which make it difficult to judge the relevance and validity of the claims. Notable here is the absence of information about the methods of inquiry used and the lack of explicitness about the relevances and values that structured the account. The former is important because it makes it more difficult to assess the threats to validity that may have distorted the account. The latter is an important weakness in a descriptive study because it makes the assessment of the relevance of the findings problematic; and it is even more serious to the extent that what is intended is an evaluation.

In general, the article seems to offer valid and useful information about the unit studied, though some parts of the account are questionable. Whether the authors' claims are generalizable to other similar units is much more doubtful in the absence of more information about the target population. In these terms the value of the account is limited, but could be increased substantially if it were possible to derive such information from other sources.[6]

Notes

1 The appraisal relies solely on the cited account of the research.

2 Page references are to this volume.

3 See Bowles and Gintis's (1976) discussion of the conflict within Dewey's writings (and in US culture generally) between economic integration and other values like personal development. Much the same conflict is to be found in Britain. Wringe (1991) provides a useful general discussion of the values involved.

4 It is impossible to specify all the relevances that might be applicable. Relevances are not derived in strict logical fashion from values: they depend on what are and are not accepted as constraints and on how values are interpreted in particular situations.

5 For discussions of the problem of generalizability in relation to case studies, see Schofield (1990: [see Chapter 13 in this volume]) and Hammersley (1992, Chs. 5 and 11).

6 Since the publication of this study at least one other study of a unit concerned with the preparation of unemployed youth for work has been carried out (see Corbett, 1990). The staff of this unit had a rather different ideological orientation, though Corbett's conclusions about the staff's treatment of students and its effects are consistent with those of Atkinson, Shone and Rees.

References

Atkinson, P., Shone, D. and Rees, T. (1981) Labouring to learn: industrial training for slow learners, in L. Barton and S. Tomlinson (eds.) *Special Education: Policy, Practices and Social Issues*, Harper & Row, London. [Also see Chapter 16 in this volume].

Bowles, S. and Gintis, H. (1976) *Schooling in Capitalist America*, Routledge & Kegan Paul, London,

Corbett, J. (1990) It's almost like work: a study of a YTS workshop, in J. Corbett (ed.) *Uneasy Transitions: Disaffection in Post-Compulsory Education and Training*, Falmer Press, Lewes.

Hammersley, M. (1991) *Reading Ethnographic Research: A Critical Guide*, Longman, London.

Hammersley, M. (1992) *What's Wrong with Ethnography?*, Routledge, London.

Schofield, J. W. (1990) Increasing the generalizability of qualitative research, in E. Eisner and A. Peshkin (eds.) *Qualitative Inquiry in Education: The Continuing Debate*, Teachers College Press, New York, NY. [Chapter 13 in this volume].

Wringe, C. (1991) Education, schooling and the world of work, in D. Corson (ed.) *Education for Work*, Multilingual Matters, Clevedon.

Chapter 18

The obviousness of social and educational research results

Nathaniel Gage

Is what we find out in social and educational research old hat, stale, platitudinous? Are the results of such research mere truisms that any intelligent person might know without going to the trouble of doing social or educational research?

The importance of the obviousness question

The obviousness question has important ramifications. It can influence the motivation of any person who is thinking about doing social or educational research. Why do research if you are not going to find anything new, anything not already known? Obviousness also relates to the justification of social science departments and schools of education in expecting or requiring their faculties and graduate students to do social and educational research. It also concerns government funding policies, such as those of the National Science Foundation and the National Institute of Mental Health that support social research, and those of the U.S. Department of Education, particularly the Office of Educational Research and Improvement, that support educational research. Foundations, school boards, state legislatures, and Congressional committees need to be convinced, before they

Taken from: *Educational Researcher*, Vol. 20, no. 1, pp. 10–16.
© 1991 by the American Educational Research Association.
Reproduced with permission of the publisher.

put up the money, that social and educational research will produce something that any intelligent adult might not already know.

So, the issue of obviousness, apart from piquing our intellectual curiosity, has tremendous practical importance. Unless social and educational researchers face that issue, they may lack motivation to do research and lose societal support expressed in dollars.

The charge of obviousness

Does anyone really hold that social and educational research yields only the obvious? I begin with an old joke attributed to James T. Farrell, the novelist who became famous in the 1930s for *Studs Lonigan*. Farrell was quoted in those days as having defined a sociologist as someone who will spend $10,000 to discover the location of the nearest house of ill fame. He actually used a less polite term, and nowadays he would have said a quarter of a million dollars. I also remember a fellow graduate student who could always get a laugh by referring to the content of some of his textbooks as 'unctuous elaborations of the obvious.'

Schlesinger's critique

The first serious piece of writing that I know of that made the same charge appeared in 1949 in *The Partisan Review*. It was in a review by Arthur Schlesinger, Jr., of the two volumes of *The American Soldier*, which had just been published. *The American Soldier* was written by a group led by Samuel A. Stouffer, who later became a professor of sociology at Harvard. It reported on the work done by sociologists and other social scientists in surveying, with questionnaires and interviews, the attitudes of American soldiers during World War II. The first volume, subtitled 'Adjustment During Army Life,' dealt with soldiers' attitudes during training, and the second, subtitled 'Combat and Its Aftermath,' dealt with soldiers' attitudes while they were engaged with the enemy and risking their lives. As a young assistant professor, I found the two books impressive for their methodological thoroughness, sophisticated interpretation, and theoretical formulations of such concepts as 'relative deprivation.'

So I was taken aback after some months when I discovered a review of those two volumes by Arthur Schlesinger, Jr., the distinguished historian. Then a young professor at Harvard University, Schlesinger had just won a Pulitzer Prize for his *Age of Jackson*. Witty and vituperative, Schlesinger's review also denounced what he considered the pretensions of social scientists. Schlesinger wrote:

> Does this kind of research yield anything new? … [T]he answer … is easy. Most of the *American Soldier* is a ponderous demonstration in Newspeak of

such facts as these: New recruits do not like noncoms; front-line troops resent rear-echelon troops; combat men manifest a high level of anxiety as compared to other soldiers; married privates are more likely than single privates to worry about their families back home. Indeed, one can find little in the 1,200 pages of text and the innumerable surveys which is not described more vividly and compactly and with far greater psychological insight, in a small book entitled *Up Front* by Bill Mauldin. What Mauldin may have missed will turn up in the pages of Ernie Pyle. (p. 854)

Lazarsfeld's examples

At about the same time as Schlesinger, Paul Lazarsfeld, a professor of sociology at Columbia University, also reviewed *The American Soldier*. Lazarsfeld (1949) was clearly aware of the same problem of obviousness. He wrote:

[I]t is hard to find a form of human behavior that has not already been observed somewhere. Consequently, if a study reports a prevailing regularity, many readers respond to it by thinking 'of course, that is the way things are.' Thus, from time to time, the argument is advanced that surveys only put into complicated form observations which are already obvious to everyone.

Understanding the origin of this point of view is of importance far beyond the limits of the present discussion. The reader may be helped in recognizing this attitude if he looks over a few statements which are typical of many survey findings and carefully observes his own reaction. A short list of these, with brief interpretive comments, will be given here in order to bring into sharper focus probable reactions of many readers.

1 Better educated men showed more psychoneurotic symptoms than those with less education. (The mental instability of the intellectual as compared to the more impassive psychology of the man-in-the-street has often been commented on.)
2 Men from rural backgrounds were usually in better spirits during their Army life than soldiers from city backgrounds. (After all, they are more accustomed to hardships.)
3 Southern soldiers were better able to stand the climate in the hot South Sea Islands than Northern soldiers. (Of course. Southerners are more accustomed to hot weather.)
4 White privates were more eager to become noncoms than Negroes. ([Because of their having been deprived of opportunity for so many years], the lack of ambition among Negroes was [quite understandable].)
5 Southern Negroes preferred Southern to Northern white officers [because Southerners were much more experienced in having interpersonal interactions with Negroes than Northern officers were].
6 As long as the fighting continued, men were more eager to be returned to the States than they were after the Germans surrendered [because during the fighting, soldiers were in danger of getting killed, but after the surrender there was no such danger]. (pp. 379–380)

Keppel's position

For a later sample of the worry about obviousness, we can turn to an essay by Frank Keppel, titled 'The Education of Teachers,' which appeared in 1962 in a volume of talks on American education by American scholars that had been broadcast by radio to foreign audiences. Keppel had left the deanship of the Harvard Graduate School of Education to serve as U.S. Commissioner of Education under President Kennedy. As Commissioner he led the movement that resulted in the Elementary and Secondary Education Act of 1965, the first major effort in the U.S. to improve the education of children from low-income families. In his article, Keppel (1962) indicated that some people question the principles that have emerged from psychological studies of teaching and learning. Without committing himself as to whether he agreed, he summed up the critics' arguments this way:

> The efforts to use scientific methods to study human behavior seem to them [the critics] ridiculous if not impious. The result is a ponderous, pseudo-scientific language which takes ten pages to explain the obvious or to dilute the wisdom long ago learned in humanistic studies. ... To build an art of teaching on the basis of the 'behavioral sciences,' they suggest, is to build on sand. (p. 91)

Conant's position

The very next year, obviousness was mentioned again, by another prestigious educator, namely, James Bryant Conant, who had been president of Harvard University for 20 years, and then the U.S. High Commissioner (and eventually the U.S. ambassador) in West Germany. During World War II, he had been a member of the highest scientific advisory committees, including the one that led to the production of the atom bomb. When he returned from Germany, he devoted himself almost exclusively to educational problems. In 1963, he published a book titled *The Education of American Teachers*, in which he reported on his studies of teacher education programs and schools – studies made through much interviewing, reading, and visiting. His book gained extremely wide and respectful attention. Yet, when I looked into it, as an educational psychologist, I couldn't help being dismayed by Conant's assertion that educational psychology largely gives us merely common-sense generalizations about human nature – generalizations that are 'for the most part highly limited and unsystematized generalizations, which are the stock in trade of every day life for all sane people' (p. 133).

Phillips's critique

These references to obviousness take us only into the 1960s. Did the attacks disappear after that? Or are there more recent statements on the obviousness of educational and social research results? In 1985, a volume of papers appeared on the subject of instructional time, which had been central in a variety of formulations, such as John B. Carroll's model of school learning, Benjamin Bloom's mastery approach to teaching, and the concept of academic engaged time developed by Charles Fisher and David Berliner. All of these writers seemed to agree that the more time students spend in studying, practicing, and being engaged with the content or skills to be learned, the greater the related learning they achieved. The correlations between academic engaged time and achievement were not perfect, of course, because outside of the laboratory, correlations are never perfect, even in the natural sciences and certainly not in the social and behavioral sciences.

The subject of instructional time thus received a lot of attention in many articles and several books, including the edited volume, *Perspectives on Instructional Time*, to which the philosopher of the social sciences, Denis Phillips (1985), contributed a chapter entitled 'The Uses and Abuses of Truisms.' Here Phillips first cited Hamlyn, also a philosopher, who had criticized the work of Piaget. Hamlyn had asked his readers to try to imagine a world in which Piaget's main ideas were untrue:

> a world where children mastered abstract and complex tasks before concrete and simple ones, for example. Such a world would differ crazily from our own, and one gets the sense that many of Piaget's views are unsurprising and necessarily (if not trivially) true. (p. 311)

Phillips then raised the same kind of question about the research on instructional time: 'What sort of world would it be if children learned more the *less* time they spent on a subject? If achievement were not related to the time spent engaged on a topic?' (p. 311). So, just as with Piaget's major findings, 'one gets the sense that these findings [about instructional time] are almost necessarily (and perhaps even trivially) true' (p. 311). 'Indeed, it suddenly seems strange to dress up these truisms as "findings"' (p. 312).

Phillips then went on to make a distinction between truisms and statements that are trivially true. '[T]he latter are, in effect, a subgroup of the former. A truism is a statement the truth of which is self-evident or obvious … whereas a trivially true statement is one that is true by virtue of the meaning of the terms involved (e.g., 'All colored objects are colored,' or 'All bachelors are unmarried')' (p. 312). He went on to say that 'It is easier to keep a small group of children working on a task than it is a large group' is a truism, for it is obviously true, but it is not true by virtue of the meanings of the terms involved' (p. 312). Phillips also pointed out that:

> truisms and statements that are trivially true are not thereby *trivial*. The terms *truism* and *trivially true* refer to the patentness of the truth of statements, whereas *trivial* refers to their degree of value or usefulness. The two do not automatically go together; many a statement the truth of which is far from obvious is of no practical use … and many truisms are vitally important and even theoretically significant ('The sky is dark at night' [this truism bears on the theory of the expanding universe]). (p. 313)

Furthermore,

> truisms uncovered by researchers, then, are not necessarily trivial. But on the other hand *truisms do not require research in order to be uncovered.* Agencies would be wasting money if they awarded grants to researchers who wanted to determine if all bachelors in the United States were unmarried, or if the sky is dark at night, or if small groups are easier to control than large groups. (p. 313, emphasis added)

In short

Let me summarize the argument so far. I have presented a series of opinions quite damaging to the notion that social and educational research yields results that would not already be known to any intelligent and thoughtful citizen. These opinions are hard to ignore. Extremely estimable people – Farrell, Schlesinger, Keppel, Conant, Lazarsfeld, and Phillips – all have made statements that might well give pause to any sensible person considering the pursuit of social and educational research or any organization being asked to part with money to support such research. I have presented these statements in chronological order extending from novelist James T. Farrell in the mid-1930s to philosopher Denis Phillips in the mid-1980s.

Empirical examination of obviousness

One noteworthy characteristic of all of these criticisms is that they were what might be called nonempirical or, at least, not systematically and formally empirical. Informal and personal, the appraisals were not made with any great specificity, detail, explicitness, or exactitude. Presumably, Schlesinger had not actually compared the statements of results reported in *The American Soldier* with statements made by Bill Mauldin or Ernie Pyle. He did not perform a content analysis of the two kinds of reports about soldiers to show in any literal way that the sociologists' statements of results had been anticipated by the insights of the cartoonist and the journalist. The same point can be made about what was said by Keppel and Conant: They did not go into any detail, or become at all specific, to support their allegations. However, the sociologist Lazarsfeld did go into detail and referred to specific results, namely, soldiers' attitudes of various kinds. Phillips referred to specific findings about instructional time, or time on task, and also findings about size of group or class size.

Rice's studies

Now I should like to go back and look at some empirical efforts that seem to me to bear upon the whole issue of obviousness. I begin with what may be the first process-outcome study in the history of research on teaching. The results of this investigation were published by Joseph Mayer Rice (1897/1913) under the title 'The Futility of the Spelling Grind.' Rice reported, after studying tests on 33,000 school children, that there was no correlation worth noticing between amount of time devoted to spelling homework and classwork and competence in spelling.

Rice's evidence is still being cited in support of the argument that spelling competence results from 'incidental' learning, rather than from any 'systematic' teaching; that is, spelling is 'caught' rather than 'taught.' So far as instructional time or 'academic engaged time' is concerned, the issue does not appear to be the open-and-shut case implied by Phillips (1985) when he asked, 'What kind of world would it be if achievement were not related to the time spent engaged on a topic?' (p. 311). As Rice (1897/1913) put it, 'concerning the amount of time devoted to spelling … an increase of time … is not rewarded by better results. … The results obtained by forty or fifty minutes' daily instruction were not better than those obtained where not more than ten or fifteen minutes had been devoted to the subject' (pp. 86–87).

Apparently, showing a relationship between time on task and achievement was not as easy as falling off a log, as it should have been if the relationship between time-on-task and achievement were necessarily true, that is, a truism. At least in one subject matter, namely, spelling, the relationship between time-on-task and achievement was fragile, perhaps even nonexistent. So perhaps the relationship depended on the subject matter. Perhaps other factors also made a difference. Things may be more complicated than we should expect if the relationship were a truism.

Similarly, if smaller groups were always easier to control, a relationship that Phillips assumed to be a truism, then they should show higher time-on-task and thus higher achievement. However, the trickiness of the relationship between class size and achievement is by now well established. Reducing class size from 40 to 20 does not improve achievement with any consistency at all. Glass (1987) reported that it required an 'exhaustive and quantitative integration of the research' to refute well-nigh unanimous older assessments (e.g., Goodlad, 1960) that class size made no difference in achievement, student attention, and discipline. Even then Glass found that the relationship of class size to achievement appeared only probabilistically (in 111 of 160 instances, or 69%) when classes of approximately 18 and 28 pupils were compared. Moreover, the duration of the instruction made a big difference: the relationship was stronger in studies of pupils taught for more than 100 hours. In addition, the class size had to be reduced dramatically to make a major improvement: 'Bringing about even a 10 percentile rank improvement in the average pupil's achievement … may entail cutting class size (and, hence, increasing schooling costs) by a third to a half' (p. 544).

Alleging that a relationship (e.g., the size-of-group relationship to the ease of control) is a truism implies that it should always be found and that no exceptions should occur. Thus, all bachelors without exception are unmarried, all colored objects without exception are colored. By the same reasoning, if the group size-controllability relationship were a truism, all smaller groups should be easier to control than all larger groups. If the age-reasoning ability relationship were a truism, all older children should be capable of more abstract and valid reasoning than all younger children. But, of course, the last two examples are untrue. If a truism is 'an undoubted or self-evident truth, especially one too obvious or unimportant for mention' (*Webster's New Collegiate Dictionary*, 1979), then these relationships are not truisms because they are not always 'undoubted' or 'self-evident.'

Suppose we change the 'truism' to a probabilistic statement (e.g., children *tend* to learn more, the more time they spend on a subject; time on task is positively but *imperfectly* correlated with achievement). Now the research aims to determine the strength of the tendency, or the magnitude of the positive correlation. Does the [probability] equal .05, .25, .45, .65, or .85? It seems to be a truism that the size of the time on task versus achievement correlation depends on many factors: the reliability of the achievement measure, the variabilities of the two variables, perhaps the subject matter, and so on. Is the research to answer these important and specific practical questions still unnecessary?

Here may lie one key to the problem: To enhance the truism with the specifics that make it have value for theory and practice, the research does become necessary. Even if the broad generalization is a truism, the specifics of its actualization in human affairs – to determine the magnitude of the probability and the factors that affect that magnitude – require research. Even if 'smaller groups tend to be more easily controlled' were a truism, we would ask, how much difference in group size is needed to produce a given difference in controllability? How do other factors – age and gender of group members, task difficulty, and the like – affect the difference in controllability resulting from changes in group size? Similar questions would apply to all the other seemingly truistic findings. Even if intelligent people could always (without any research) predict the direction (positive or negative) of a relationship between two variables, they could not predict its size and its contingencies without research-based knowledge.

Lazarsfeld's examples

Let us go back now to Lazarsfeld's examples of obvious results from the World War II studies of *The American Soldier*. Recall his examples of the 'obvious' conclusions from that study: better educated men showed more psychoneurotic symptoms; men from rural backgrounds were usually in better spirits than those from cities; Southern soldiers were better able than Northerners to stand the climate in the South Sea Islands; White privates were more eager to become noncoms than Black privates were; Southern Negroes preferred Southern to Northern White officers; and men were more eager to be returned to the States during the fighting than they were after the Germans surrendered.

Lazarsfeld (1949) asked, 'Why, since they are so obvious, is so much money given to establish such findings?' However, he then revealed that

> *Everyone of these statements is the direct opposite of what was actually found.*
> Poorly educated soldiers were more neurotic than those with high educations;
> Southerners showed no greater ability than Northerners to adjust to a tropical cli-
> mate; Negroes were more eager for promotion than whites, and so on. ... If we
> had mentioned the actual results of the investigation first, the reader would have
> labelled these 'obvious' also. Obviously something is wrong with the entire
> argument of obviousness. It should really be turned on its head. Since every kind
> of human reaction is conceivable, it is of great importance to know which reac-
> tions actually occur most frequently and under what conditions ... (p. 380)

Lazarsfeld's rhetorical ploy has always impressed me as fairly unsettling for
those who make the allegations of obviousness, but its force depends on whether
we are willing to grant him his assumption that we accepted the first version of
the research results as valid, so that he could then startle us with his second presentation, which gave the true findings: the results that were actually obtained. It
might be argued that Lazarsfeld's assumption was unwarranted and that most of
us would not have believed that the first set of statements that he later revealed
were spurious.

The Mischels' study

So I took notice when I heard about investigations that made no assumptions of
the kind that Lazarsfeld's exercise required. The first of these (Mischel, 1981;
Mischel & Mischel, 1979) consisted of giving fourth- and sixth-grade children
(Ns = 38 and 49, respectively) items presenting psychological principles stated
in both their actual form and the opposite of the actual forms. For example, the
first item dealt with the finding by Solomon Asch that college students would
respond contrarily to the evidence of their senses about which of three lines had
the same length as a comparison line when the students first heard four other
students (confederates of the investigator) misidentify the same-length line. The
second item concerned Harry Helson's finding that the same water temperature
feels cooler on a hot day than on a cool day. In all, there were 17 such items,
some of which were presented to only one of the two grade-level groups. The
children circled the one of the two to four choices that they thought described
what would happen in each situation.

   Of the 29 opportunities for either the fourth graders or the sixth graders to
select the actual research result to a statistically significant degree, the groups
did so on 19, or 66%. One group or the other was wrong to a statistically significant degree on five opportunities, and there was no statistically significant
correctness or incorrectness on five opportunities. Clearly, the children had substantial success, but far from the perfect record that would support the allegation
of almost universal obviousness.

   But these were only children. What about college students and adults? And
what happens when the research results are presented as flat statements rather

than as multiple-choice items requiring the selection of the actual result from two or more alternatives?

Baratz's study

Baratz (1983) selected 16 social research findings from various studies, and then did an experiment. She manipulated, for each of the findings, whether the statement concerning that finding was the true finding or the opposite of the true finding. She also presented each finding, either the true one or the opposite one, with or without an explanation of the finding. That second manipulation was intended to 'explore the possibility that adding explanations to the findings may render the findings more obvious' (p. 20). Thus, each of her subjects – 85 male and female undergraduates enrolled in introductory psychology at Stanford University – evaluated 16 findings: four statements with a true finding plus explanation, four statements with the opposite finding plus explanation, four statements with a true finding without explanation, and four statements of an opposite finding without an explanation. Each finding was presented in the same format: first, the question addressed by the study, such as 'a study sought to determine whether people spend a larger proportion of their income during *prosperous* times or during a *recession.*' And for this study the reported finding was 'In prosperous times people spend a larger proportion of their income than during a recession.' The statement of the opposite finding differed from that of the true finding only in the order of the critical terms, and half of the findings were followed at the time by a short explanation, which was presented as the 'explanation given by our subject.'

Here are two sample pairs of the true and opposite findings used by Baratz in her experiment: 'People who go to church regularly tend to have more children than people who go to church infrequently' versus 'People who go to church infrequently tend to have more children than people who go to church regularly' and 'Single women express more distress over their unmarried status than single men do' versus 'Single men express more distress over their unmarried status than single women do.'

For each of the 16 findings presented to each student, the students were asked how readily predictable or obvious the finding was and were instructed to choose one of the responses on the following four-point scale:

1 I am *certain* that I would have predicted the result obtained rather than the opposite result.
2 I *think* that I would have predicted the result obtained rather than the opposite result, but I am *not certain*.
3 I *think* that I would have predicted the opposite to the obtained result, but I am *not certain*.
4 I am *certain* that I would have predicted the opposite to the obtained result.

The subjects were asked to express their 'initial impressions of the relevant findings, i.e., the kind of impression that you might form if you read a brief article about the research in your daily newspaper' (p. 25).

In a summary table, Baratz presented the mean percentage of subjects who marked either 'I am *certain* that I would have predicted the reported outcome' or 'I *think* I would have predicted the reported outcome' for pairs of opposite findings. When the reported outcome was 'A,' 80% of her students claimed they would have predicted that outcome. When the reported outcome was 'B,' 66% of her subjects claimed they would have predicted that outcome. Thus, as Baratz put it, 'It is clear that findings that contradict each other were both retrospectively judged 'obvious'. ... These results show clearly that reading a result made that result appear obvious. No matter which result was presented, the majority of the subjects thought that they would have predicted it' (p. 26).

I considered Baratz's experiment and her findings to be persuasive. They seemed to provide evidence against the argument that social research yields only obvious findings. Her results indicated that intelligent people, namely, Stanford undergraduates, tend to regard any result they read, whether it is the true one or the opposite of the true one, as obvious. This tendency to say results are obvious was, of course, only a tendency; not all of her subjects followed that tendency, but it was a majority tendency.

Wong's study

Baratz's research on obviousness dealt with results from a fairly wide range of the social sciences, but I had been focusing on research on teaching and particularly on one area within that field: process-outcome research. That kind of research seeks relationships between classroom processes (what teachers and students do or what goes on in the classroom) and outcomes (what students acquire by way of knowledge, understanding, attitude, appreciation, skill, etc.). Would such research results elicit obvious reactions similar to those obtained by Baratz?

A few years ago, Lily Wong, a Stanford graduate student from Singapore, replicated and extended Baratz's experiments, but with findings from process-outcome research on teaching. Wong chose her respondents from four different categories of persons who differed on the dimension of how much they might be expected to know about classroom teaching. At the low end of that dimension were undergraduates in engineering; next, undergraduates majoring in psychology; next, teacher trainees; and at the high end, experienced teachers. Each of these four groups of respondents was sampled both from Singaporeans and from Americans residing either at Stanford University or in the neighboring area. In total, Wong used 862 Singaporeans and 353 Americans. For the research findings, she used 12 statements based on results of process-outcome research carried out in the elementary grades, results that had been cited in the third edition of the *Handbook of Research on Teaching* (Wittrock, 1986) and in textbooks of educational psychology. Her items came from the results of research by Anderson, Evertson, and Brophy; Brophy and Evertson; Good and Grouws; Soar and Soar; and Stallings and Kaskowitz. Here is the first of her 12 items: 'When first-grade teachers work on reading with a small group of children, some attend closely to just the children in the small group, whereas others monitor children's activities throughout the classroom. The class's reading achievement is higher *when teachers monitor the entire classroom*' versus '*… when teachers attend to just the children in the small group.*' Here is the second item: 'When first-grade teachers work on reading with a small group of children, some call on the children in a fixed order, whereas others call on children in a random order. Reading achievement is higher *when children are called on in a fixed order*' versus '*… when children are called on in a random order.*'

Wong had five forms of questionnaires: Form A, Forms B_1 and B_2, and Forms C_1 and C_2. Subjects completing Form A had to select in each item the true finding between two options – one stating an actual finding of research on teaching at the primary-grade level and the other stating the opposite of the actual finding. The subject then rated the chosen statement on a four-point scale from 1, 'extremely obvious' to 4, 'extremely unobvious.'

Subjects completing Forms B_1 or B_2 were required to rate the obviousness of each of 12 single statements presented as actual research findings. In fact, 6 were true findings and 6 were the opposite of true findings. Each of the 24 statements from Form A thus appeared in either Form B_1 or B_2.

Form C subjects were given the same purported findings as Form B subjects, but in Form C, each statement was accompanied by a possible explanation. Subjects in Form C had to rate not only the obviousness of the findings but also the clarity of the explanations.

Wong's results on Form A showed that her respondents chose both actual findings and opposite findings. On 4 of the 12 items, her subjects chose the actual finding more often (see p. 37), but on the other 8, they chose the false finding more often. The [correlation] between percentage choosing a finding and the mean obviousness rating of the finding was .66. The respondents to Forms B and C rated about half of the opposite findings as obvious. Wong concluded that

> Judging by the smaller proportions of respondents choosing the actual findings as the real findings, and the mean rating of obviousness on the presented (both actual and opposite) finding statements, we can say reasonably that people can not distinguish true findings from their opposites. (p. 86)

The Singaporeans rated most of the items as more obvious than the American subjects did in all conditions. There were few gender differences in the average responses to the various forms. Teachers were no more accurate, on the average, than the other groups in the selection of true findings: 'In the rating of obviousness of items, knowledge and experience [in teaching] were found to have some significant effect on several items. This does not mean that teachers and trainees rated true findings more obvious or opposite findings less obvious than the psychology undergraduates and the engineering undergraduates' (Wong, 1987, p. 87).

Wong concluded that her results 'clearly confirmed the idea that knowledge of outcome increases the feeling of obviousness. Thus, when people claim to have known it all along when an event is reported to them, their claim is often not warranted' (p. 88).

Where the issue stands

From the work of Baratz and Wong we can conclude that the feeling that a research result is obvious is untrustworthy. People tend to regard as obvious almost any reasonable statement made about human behavior. A recent example comes from the *Arizona Daily Star* of March 8, 1988, in an article about the booklet entitled *What Works*, compiled by the U.S. Department of Education. The booklet contains brief discussions, with references to the research, of 41 research findings considered potentially helpful to schools and teachers. The headline read, 'Restating the Obvious.'

My most recent example comes from the June 1990 issue of *The Atlantic* (Murphy, 1990): 'A recent survey (by me) of recent social-science findings ... turned up no ideas or conclusions that can't be found in Bartlett's or any other encyclopedia of quotations' (p. 22).

As suggested by an anonymous referee for this article, the results of Baratz and Wong are consistent with the conclusions of Nisbett and Wilson (1977): '[T]here may be little or no direct introspective access to higher order cognitive processes' (p. 231). Thus the cognitive processes that lead one to regard a research result as obvious are probably non-veridical unless, as Ericsson and Simon (1980) argued, the response is based on (a) short-term memory leading to verbalization of information that (b) would have been attended to even without the instructions given. It is questionable whether judging the obviousness of research results always meets these requirements.

The same reviewer also suggested that these results do not belie the fact that most adults' generalizations about human interactions are at least functional. I agree; otherwise human society would be impossible. [...]

The issue joined by Schlesinger when he attacked students of human affairs who use scientific methods has its roots in the old controversy that C. P. Snow (1964) examined later in *The Two Cultures: And a Second Look*. Snow was concerned with the mutual disregard and disrespect of natural scientists and scholars in the humanities. Snow regretted this condition, but it still exists. Schlesinger's denunciation of social research reflected what Karl Popper called the antinaturalist position: the position that the scientific method useful for studying the natural world is inappropriate for the study of human affairs. The response of Paul Lazarsfeld reflects the position, held by Karl Popper and many others, that scientific method *is* appropriate for the study of human affairs.

Scientific method need not be used, in my opinion, only for the construction of a social science – where such a science is defined as a network of laws that will hold over whole eras and in many different cultural contexts, just as the laws of mechanics hold in different historical periods and in contexts as different as planetary motion and the motion of a pendulum. Rather, scientific method can be used for what Popper called 'piecemeal social engineering,' a more modest enterprise aimed at improving human affairs by applying scientific methods to the development and evaluation of new 'treatments' – in education, in social welfare projects, or in fighting against drugs.

I have speculated (Gage, 1989) that people gravitate toward one or the other of Snow's two cultures – toward science (natural or social) or toward humanistic insight and sensibility – because their upbringing and intellectual experience have inclined them toward one or the other. The wars between the several paradigms in social and educational research may result from temperamentally different (i.e., not entirely rational) intellectual predilections, often developed during the secondary school years. If so, improved education may someday produce scholars and educational researchers who experience no conflict between their scientific and humanistic orientations.

In any case, the allegation of obviousness may now be countered with the research result that people tend to regard even contradictory research results as obvious. Perhaps even that result will henceforth be regarded as obvious.

Note

This article is based in part on the Maycie K. Southall lecture at George Peabody College, Vanderbilt University, on February 27, 1990.

I am grateful to my daughter, Sarah Gage, for calling the Murphy (1990) article to my attention.

References

Baratz, D. (1983) How justified is the 'obvious' reaction. *Dissertation Abstracts International, 44/02B*, 644B. (University Microfilms No. DA 8314435.)

Conant, J. B. (1963) *The education of American teachers*. New York: McGraw-Hill.

Ericsson, K. A. and Simon, H. A. (1980) Verbal reports as data. *Psychological Review*, 87, 215–251.

Gage, N. L. (1989) The paradigm wars and their aftermath: A 'historical' sketch of research on teaching since 1989. *Teachers College Record*, 91, 135–150.

Glass, G. V. (1987) Class size. In M. J. Dunkin (ed.), *The international encyclopedia of teaching and teacher education* (pp. 540–545). Oxford: Pergamon.

Goodlad, J. I. (1960) Classroom organization. In C. W. Harris (ed.), *Encyclopedia of educational research* (3rd ed., p. 224). New York: Macmillan.

Keppel, F. (1962) The education of teachers. In H. Chauncey (ed.), *Talks on American education: A series of broadcasts to foreign audiences by American scholars* (pp. 83–94). New York: Bureau of Publications, Teachers College, Columbia University.

Lazarsfeld, P. F. (1949) *The American soldier* – an expository review. *Public Opinion Quarterly*, 13, 377–404.

Mischel, W. (1981) Metacognition and the rules of delay. In J. H. Flavell and L. Ross (eds.), *Social cognitive development: Frontiers and possible futures*. New York: Cambridge University Press.

Mischel, W. and Mischel, H. (1979) *Children's knowledge of psychological principles*. Unpublished manuscript.

Murphy, C. (1990) New findings: Hold on to your hat. *The Atlantic*, 265(6), 22–23.

Nisbett, R. E. and Wilson, T. D. (1977) Telling more than we can know: Verbal reports on mental processes. *Psychological Review*, 84, 231–259.

Phillips, D. C. (1985) The uses and abuses of truisms. In C. W. Fisher and D. C. Berliner (eds.), *Perspectives on instructional time* (pp. 309–316). New York: Longman.

Rice, J. M. (1913) *Scientific management in education*. New York: Hinds, Noble & Eldredge. (Original work published 1897)

Schlesinger, Jr., A. (1949) The statistical soldier. *Partisan Review*, 16, 852–856.

Snow, C. P. (1964) *The two cultures: And a second look*. New York: Cambridge University Press.

Walberg, H. J. (1986) Syntheses of research on teaching. In M. C. Wittrock (ed.), *Handbook of research on teaching* (3rd ed., pp. 214–229). New York: Macmillan.

Wittrock, M. C. (ed.) (1986) *Handbook of research on teaching* (3rd ed.). New York: Macmillan.

Wong, L. (1987) Reaction to research findings: Is the feeling of obviousness warranted? *Dissertation Abstracts International*, 48/12, 3709B. (University Microfilms No. DA 8801059.)

Index

academic disciplines, divisions between, 100
accountability, 33, 36, 54, 75, 172
action research, x, xiv, 18, 35, 51–2, 82–3,
    128, 148–9, 155, 167–80
  definition and character of, 168–70
  educational, 179
  emancipatory, 177–80
  evaluation of, 175–6
  facilitation of, 176–8
  methodology of, 174–5
  objects of, 172–4
  practical, 177–8
  resurgence of interest in, 170–2
  technical, 177–8
actionable knowledge, xi, 52, 67–71, 82–5
Adelman, Clem, 171
aims of education, 73–7, 85–7
Alex Moore, iiii; *author of Chapter 9*
Alexander, Robin, 51
Allport, Gordon, 196
Althusser, L., 118
Altman, D.G., 29
American Psychological Association, 155
Angus, Laurie, 112
anthropology, 160, 162, 192
  cultural, 182
anti-naturalism, xiv, 152, 155, 158–9, 288
Apple, Michael, 154
applied research, 5, 8, 24
Aristotle, 72
Asch, Solomon, 284
assessment of students, 256–60
Atkins, Sir Hedley, 46
Atkinson, Paul, xv, 30, 46, 267–9, 272, 274;
    co-author of Chapter 16
autonomy
  of learners, 174
  professional, 13, 37, 54, 56, 70, 72, 109

Baker, Carolyn, 220, 226–9
Ball, Stephen, xiii–xiv; *author of Chapter 8*
Baratz, D., 285–9
Barr, A.S., 152
Barrow, R., 151
basic research, 5, 8, 11, 24, 49, 169, 184

Bassey, Michael, xii–xiii, 11; *author of*
    Chapter 10
Becker, Howard, 29, 46
behavioral research, 153–4
Benne, Kenneth, 170
Bennett, Neville, 51, 53, 143
Bentham, Jeremy, 111
Berg, B.L., 182
Berlin, Isaiah, 48–9
Berliner, David, 279–80
Bernstein, Basil, xi, 67, 107, 125–7
Beyer, L.E., 134
bias, 90, 100, 161, 173
Bloom, Benjamin, 69, 279–80
Blunkett, David, 93–4
Boruch, Bob, 100
Bourdieu, Pierre, 131
British Educational Research Association, 55
Broadfoot, P., 27
Butcher, H.J., 144
Button, G., 228

Campbell, Donald (and Campbell
    Collaboration), 95, 181–2, 185
Carr, W., 169–70
Carroll, John B., 279
case study research, xii, 77, 85, 90, 160, 183–6
causal relationships, 23, 26, 34, 58, 67, 152
Cazden, C.B., 152, 157
'charismatic subjects', 124, 129
childcare, 94–5
Chomsky, Noam, 125
class size, 282
Cochrane, A.L., 32
Cochrane Collaboration, 95, 102
cognitive science, 57
Cole, A.L., 130–1
Collins, Randall, 116
commodification of education, 111
'competence-based' model of teacher education,
    xiii, 122–3, 127–35
computers, use of, 193–4
Comte, Auguste, 92–3
Conant, James Bryant, 279, 281
consciousness-raising, 114

control groups, 100
control of education, 178–9
conversation analysis, 221
Corey, Stephen, 170
cost-effectiveness, 27, 32
Council for the Accreditation of Teacher
    Education (CATE), 123–6
Cox, Caroline, 12, 30
'critical friends', 149
critical incidents, xv, 146, 204–15
    as distinct from critical events, 204–5
    social construction of, 215–17
critical reflexivity, 112–13
critical social science, xiv, 113–15, 118, 179
critical theory, 154–63
Cronbach, Lee J., 184, 187–8, 194
Crozier, Gill, 236
'cultural compatibility' hypothesis, 158
Cummins, J., 121
cumulative knowledge, xi, 5, 19–23, 28, 33–4,
    51, 68, 94
curriculum development, 73, 79, 86, 170–1

Dale, Roger, 118
Denscombe, Martyn, xv; author of Chapter 14
Denzin, N.K., 182
Department of Education and Science, 94
'dilettante' tradition, 11
discourse analysis, xv, 239
discovery learning, 81, 171, 174
dissemination of research findings, 9–10, 19, 33
Dobbert, M.L., 182
Donzelot, J., 110
double-blind experiments, 197
Downie, R.S., 47
Drew, P., 222
Dunn, G., 53

Eco, U., 117
Economic and Social Research Council (ESRC),
    10–11, 24, 145
education reforms, viii, 18, 109, 159, 178
educational psychologists, 156
educational research
    academic bias in, 6
    changing agenda for, 10
    in a comparative professional framework, 4–8
    definitions of, 144–7
    forms of, xiii
    impact of, 8–9, 20, 26–7, 43
    links with policy, 70–3, 108
    national strategy for, 10–11, 19, 35, 56
    nature of, 5–7, 11–13, 19–21, 24
    plurality in, 144
    role of, 36, 55, 69–71, 77, 82–4, 87, 154, 164
    user involvement in, 9–10, 14, 56, 77,
        90, 169

educational researchers, 5–6, 29, 52, 55–7, 71,
    89, 94, 108–9, 143, 161–2
educational studies, xiii, 107–9, 113, 116–18
Eliot, George, 57
Elliott, John, xi–xiv, 89–90, 122, 148, 171;
    author of Chapter 5
emancipatory action research, xiv, 177–80
empirical-analytic research, 179
engineering model of research, x–xi, 25, 27,
    67–8, 71–2, 89, 170
enlightenment model of research, x–xi, 26–7,
    55–6, 67, 72, 83
Entwistle, N.J., 145
EPPI-Centre, 102
Erickson, F., 153–5, 158
Ericsson, K.A., 288
ethical issues, 73–7, 82–5
ethnography and ethnographic research, xv, 52,
    128, 135, 155–8, 161, 184, 192, 195
ethnomethodology, 221, 226–7
evaluation, formative and summative, 184, 189
Everitt, B., 53
evidence-based practice in education viii–xii, 7,
    11–13, 36–7, 47, 51–2, 55, 66–9, 73–4, 83
evidence-informed practice in education,
    67, 86, 89
experimental research, ix, xii, 23, 52–4, 67,
    82–5, 90, 93, 95, 99, 182–3
expert opinion, 53, 90

Farrell, James T., 277, 281
Fay, Brian, 109–10, 113–14
feminist theory, 118
Firestone, W.A., 191–2
Fisher, Charles, 280
'fittingness' concept, 187
Ford Teaching Project, 171
Foucault, Michel, xiii, 106–7, 110–13, 117–18,
    221, 238–9
Fowler, P.B.S., 31
Freidson, Eliot, 46
Freud, Sigmund, 135
funding bodies for research, 9–11, 19, 24, 55–6,
    142–4, 170, 184, 276–7

Gage, Nathaniel, xiv–xvi, 158; author of
    Chapters 11 and 18
Gallimore, R., 158
Galton, Maurice, 51
generalizability of research, xii–xv, 68–70, 86,
    90, 94, 181–99, 273–4
    increasing interest in, 184–5
    reconceptualization of, 186–8
    traditional views of, 181–4
    see also probabilistic generalizations
Giddens, Anthony, 130
Giroux, H.A., 128, 134

Glass, G., 101–3, 282
Goetz, J.P., 187
Goldenberg, C.N., 158
Goodson, I.F., 129
Gorz, André, 118
Guba, E.G., 186–7

Habermas, Jürgen, 51, 175
Hammersley, Martyn, xi–xv, 43–8, 51–7, 68;
    editor and author of Chapters 2, 4 and 17
Hare, R.D., 186
Hargreaves, Andy, 130
Hargreaves, David, x–xiv, 19–30, 33–7, 66–74,
    77, 82–7, 89, 94; author of Chapters
    1 and 3
Harlen, Wynn, 53
Hawthorne effects, 53
health risks and health promotion, xv, 96–7,
    101–2, 205–18
Heath, C., 227
hegemony, 134–5, 162
Helson, Harry, 284
Heritage, J., 221–2
Herriott, R.E., 191–2
'hidden curriculum', 79
Hippocrates, 143
history teaching, 156
Holmes, Oliver Wendell, 46–7
Howe, K.R., 157
Huberman, M., 50
Humanities Project, 73, 78, 84
hypothesis-testing, 142–4

induction into knowledge, 79–82
Institute of Employment Studies, 94
instrumentalism, 75–7, 83–5, 109–10
intellectuals, role of, xiii, 118
interactionism, 55
interpretivism, xiv, 113, 143, 153–62, 179, 182
intrinsically worthwhile educational
    activities, 74–5, 79
'iron law of evaluation studies', 100

Jadad, A.R., 31
James, William, 161
Johnson, B., 129

Karr, Alphonse, 162
Kemmis, Stephen, xiv, 169–70; author of
    Chapter 12
Kennedy, M.M., 188
Keogh, Jayne, 220–1, 229
Keppel, Frank, 279, 281
King, L.S., 57
Kirk, J., 182
knowledge, nature of, 80–1
knowledge-base for teachers, 49–51, 57

Knowles, J.G., 130–1
Krathwohl, D.R., 183
Kuhn, Thomas, 163

Labour Party, 108
'Labouring to learn' project, 245–61, 263–89
The Lancet, 54
Lauretis, Teresa de, 118–19
Lazarsfeld, Paul, 278, 281–4, 289
learning, concept of, 23
LeCompte, M.D., 187
Lee, A., 239
Lewin, Kurt, xiv, 34, 51, 168–71
Limerick, B., 222
Lincoln, Y.S., 186–7
literacy, 49
literature-based knowledge, 31–2
literature reviews, 96
Locke, John, 143
London School of Economics, 108

Macbeth, A., 228
Machiavelli, Niccolo, 68
MacIntyre, Alasdair, xii, 68–73, 77, 89
McLaren, P.L., 128, 134
MacLure, Maggie, xv; author of Chapter 15
management research, 150
management theory, 110–11
managerialism, 72
Manpower Services Commission, (MSC) 261
Marxism, 24
Mauldin, Bill, 278, 281
measurement of social phenomena, 23, 26, 34
medical research, x–xi, 4–9, 13, 19, 22, 28–34,
    44–53, 93–5
mental health research, 98–9
meta-analysis, 101–2
Mill, John Stuart, 93
Miller, M.L., 182
Mischel, W. and H., 284
Moore, Alex, xiii
Mortimore, Peter, 51
multisite studies, 190–2

National Curriculum, viii, 69, 79
natural science model for research, ix, xiv, 4–5,
    22, 48, 68, 158–9, 163
naturalistic generalizations, 187
neo-liberalism, xiii
Nisbet, J., 27, 145
Nisbett, R.E., 288
Noblit, G.W., 186

Oakeshott, M., 56
Oakley, Anne, xii–xiv; author of
    Chapters 6 and 7
objectives model of curriculum design, 78–80

objectivist research on teaching, 153–62
obviousness of research findings, xv–xvi, 118, 276–89
Office for Standards in Education (OFSTED), 12–13, 19, 34
ORACLE project, 51
outcome-based research, 89
outcome measures, 26
outcomes-based education (OBE), 69–71, 78, 87

paradigm shifts and paradigm wars, xiv, 5, 151, 157, 160–4, 289
parents' evenings, xv, 220–40
peer review, 9–10
performativity of teachers, 69, 72
Peshkin, A., 185
Peters, Richard, xi, 73–9, 82–3, 86–7, 89, 144
Phillips, Denis, 279–81
philosophy of education, 73, 129
Piaget, Jean, xi, 67, 149, 280
Platt, Lord, 46
Polanyi, Michael, 35
policy entrepreneurship, 114–17
policy research, 18–19, 178
policy scholarship, xiii, 109
policy science, xiii, 109–10, 113, 117
Popper, Karl, 158–61, 288–9
populism, 54
positivism and positivistic research, ix–x, xiv, 22, 24, 47–8, 51, 66–9, 89–90, 102, 143, 152–7, 169
post-modernism, 5, 129–30
post-structuralism, xiii, 115–18
Poynton, C., 239
practical aspects of teaching, 4, 20, 24, 26, 45–6, 171–2
practical wisdom, 48–9
praxis, 167, 172–4
probabilistic generalizations, 68, 84–6
procedural values and principles in education, 75–81, 84
process consultancy, 177
process model of curriculum design, 78, 80, 83, 87
process-product research, 157–60
professional practice in education, 8–9, 18, 43–5, 49, 67, 83, 94, 142–3
professionalism, 28, 33, 37, 47, 54–5
psychological research, 85, 160, 162
    definition of, 147–8
psychotherapy, 101
Pyle, Ernie, 281

qualifications for teachers, 8
qualitative research, xii–xv, 22, 85, 94, 98–9, 135, 143, 155–8, 161–2, 182–99
quality assurance, 71–2

quantitative research, xii, xiv, 99, 143, 155–7, 160–2, 182, 185, 195
Quételet, A., 92

racism and anti-racism, 84–5
Ragin, C.C., 186
randomised controlled trials, xi–xii, 32, 53–4, 67, 77, 89–90, 95, 98, 100
rationalism, 109–10, 117, 134
Ravitch, Diane, 92
RDD model, 170–1
Rees, Teresa, xv, 267–9, 272, 274; *co-author of Chapter 16*
reflective practice, xiii, 51, 86, 122–3, 127–32, 135
reflexivity, xiii, 112–13, 132–5
replication of research, 5, 20–3, 183
Research Center for Group Dynamics, 171
research-based teaching, 73, 77–87
Rice, Joseph Mayer, 152, 281–3
risk perceptions, 205–10
risk-taking, 212–18
Rorty, Richard, 117–18
Rothschild, Lord, 35
Rousseau, Jean-Jacques, 142–3
rule-following in education and in medicine, 45–6
Ryans, David G., 152

sampling, 186
Sanford, Nevitt, 170
Saussure, F. de, 125
Schlesinger, Arthur, 277–8, 281, 288
Schofield, Janet W., xiv–xv; *author of Chapter 13*
Schön, Donald, 45–6, 51, 122, 142–3
school effectiveness research, xiii, 26, 109–12
Schütz, Alfred, 45
Schwab, J.J., 171
scientific approach to research, 21–5, 35, 92–3, 152, 155, 158–9, 163, 288–9; *see also natural science* model and positivism
Sheridan, Alan, 117
Shilling, Chris, 116
Shone, David, xv, 267–9, 272, 274; *co-author of Chapter 16*
short-termism, 13
Shulman, Lee S., 157
Shumsky, Abraham, 170
Sikes, Pat, 204
Silverman, David, 236
Simon, Brian, 145–6
Simon, Herbert A., 288
Simons, Helen, 144
site selection for research studies, 195–7
situational analysis, 85–6
Skidelsky, Lord, 142–4, 149

Skinner, B.F., xi, 67
slow learners, 263–4
Smith, Adrian, 94
Smith, H.W., 182
Smith, Mary Lee, 101–2
Snow, C.P., 288–9
social class differences, 108
social engineering, 70, 158–61, 289
Social Science Research Unit 96, 102
social theory, 113
sociological research, 29, 147
sociology of education, xiii, 21, 107–9, 116, 162
Socrates, 56
SPECTR database, 95
'spin' control, 153
Stake, R.E., 187
standards for teaching and learning, 11–12,
    70, 72, 75, 78
Stanley, J., 181–2, 185
Stenhouse, Lawrence, xi–xii, 51, 73–4, 77–87,
    89, 146, 171
Stouffer, Samuel A., 275
systematic reviews of research, xii, 90,
    96–7, 101–3

Taba, Hilda, 170
target-setting, 72
Tavistock Institute, 171
Taylor, Williams, 27
teacher education and training, 4, 45, 115,
    122–3, 130, 135
Teacher Training Agency (TTA), 11–13, 19,
    51–2, 124–7, 141–2
teachers-as-experts 80
teachers-as-researchers, 51, 86, 171
technical discourse, 239
'technical rationality' (Schön), 45
'technicians' in education, xiii, 101, 109, 128,
    154, 163
theory, role of, 4, 20, 24, 51, 87, 115–19, 142
thick description, 188, 190, 199

Thomas, D., 131
Thorndike, E.L., 152
Times Educational Supplement, 6
Tom, A., 151–2
trainability, concept of, 126
training
    for adult life, xv, 74–5, 79, 254–5
    industrial, 245–52, 261–74
    social, 252–4
    of university teachers, 57
    see also teacher education and training
'trial and error' learning, 50
Tripp, David, 146, 217
truisms, 280–3
typical situations for study, 188–93, 196

UK Evaluation Society, 115–16
'universalistic' hypothesis, 158

validity of research
    external, 181–6
    internal, 182–3, 197
value added, xiii
Verstehen concept, ix

Walker, D.F., 193
Walker, Rob, 129
Walkerdine, Valerie, 135
Webb, Beatrice and Sidney, 93, 95
'what works', evidence on, 49–51, 54,
    67–72, 144
White, J.P., 144
Williams, George C., 50
Williams, J.D., 144–5
Wilson, T.D., 288
Wolcott, Harry F., 184, 189
Wong, Lily, 286–8
Woods, Peter, 121, 128, 131, 134, 204–5, 217
Wright Mills, C., 115

Zeichner, K., 134